D1393653

OSS in China

OSS IN CHINA

Prelude to Cold War

Maochun Yu

Yale University Press

New Haven and London

Designed by James J. Johnson and set in
Stemple Garamond types by Rainsford
Type, Danbury, Connecticut.
Printed in the United States of America by
BookCrafters, Inc., Chelsea, Michigan.

A catalogue record for this book is
available from the British Library.

The paper in this book meets the guidelines
for permanence and durability of the
Committee on Production Guidelines for
Book Longevity of the Council on Library
Resources.

*Library of Congress Cataloging-in-
Publication Data*

Yu, Maochun, 1962–
    OSS in China : prelude to Cold War /
Maochun Yu.
        p.   cm.
    Includes bibliographical references and
index.
    ISBN 0-300-06698-8

    1. United States. Office of Strategic
Services—History. 2. World War, 1939–
1945—Secret Service—United States. 3.
World War, 1939–1945—Secret
Service—China. 4. World War, 1939–
1945—China. 5. World War, 1939–
1945—Military intelligence—United
States.   I. Title.
D810.S7Y82   1996   96–22593
940.54'8673—dc20

1001380878

10 9 8 7 6 5 4 3 2 1

In a global and totalitarian war, intelligence must be global and totalitarian.

—WILLIAM JOSEPH DONOVAN

Contents

Illustrations

Preface

In the summer of 1944, General William Donovan, director of the Office of Strategic Services, decided to compile a general history of the agency. He appointed one of his agents, the Harvard historian Conyers Read, to head a history office under the direct supervision of OSS deputy director Otto Doering. But Donovan never anticipated the controversy from all sides that would be associated with the history of OSS in the years to come. The Conyers Read project was dropped near its completion "for grim economic" reasons before the war ended, at a point when virtually every other war agency of the U.S. government had composed a history.[1] Long after the abrupt termination of OSS by President Truman, an official history project was undertaken by the Strategic Service Unit (SSU) under the Central Intelligence Group (CIG). Yet when the draft was finished in early 1948, General Donovan was so enraged by the account and by the response of CIA to his criticism that he refused to comment further and threatened to repudiate everything in the history.[2] In frustration, Rear Admiral R. H. Hillenkoetter, the director of CIA and then in charge of the OSS history project, was forced to take the bickering directly to the Joint Chiefs of Staff.[3]

If writing a general history of OSS was difficult, writing the China story of OSS was almost impossible. In 1944, as part of the Read project, OSS headquarters in Washington appointed the University of Michigan scholar Mischa Titiev to chronicle OSS accomplishments in the China-Burma-India (CBI) theater under General Joseph Stilwell. Stilwell adamantly opposed this appointment, insisting that if the history should ever be written, it should not be done by OSS. Stilwell blocked the Titiev appointment and abruptly assigned Colonel M. Wright from his own army headquarters to produce a history of OSS in the CBI theater under Stilwell's command—a history that was, as Colonel Wright told Donovan's people, "secret and not for publication but was to be considered only as a matter of record because of the high-powered nature of the material."[4] Stilwell's action antagonized OSS, and its Washington headquarters immediately instructed the field station chiefs that "it is necessary for the history of OSS, China, to be finished at the earliest possible date."[5] But when this CBI history finally arrived in Washington, it was considered so "high-powered" and startling that the first 164 pages of the 278-page manuscript—the only copy OSS had received—were "loaned" to Colonel Doering. Doering never returned the material, and no one ever saw it again.[6]

Why was all of this shrouded in such mystery and secrecy? The history of OSS in China brought to light several major points of contention. During the Cold War, any examination of U.S. policy toward China during World War II became a smoke-ridden political battleground. The debate over "who lost China" was partisan and bitter. Pit-bull politicians, notably Senator Joseph McCarthy of Wisconsin, were obsessed with finding villains in order to display their political prowess and fortify their partisan agendas. McCarthyism was the single most important condition corrupting the nature of postwar discourse on U.S. wartime policy toward China. Objective discussion has been rare ever since. Policy reevaluation invited political persecution. Even worse, to counter McCarthy's accusations and crusade, many talented historians spent considerable energy reinterpreting the same facts that he used in his attacks, thus reinventing new villains and heroes, all in an intellectual framework that is equally teleological and polemical. In 1969 John Paton Davies reevaluated his own deeds during World War II and admitted that "my mistake in 1944 was in saying that the Chinese Communists were democratic. . . . I confused the popularity of the Communists with democracy. . . . They had a democratic façade."[7] But even that lukewarm concession could not be delivered in the United States; Davies spoke from Peru, where he was in virtual exile, far away from U.S. party politics.

The OSS story in China has not escaped this skewed intellectual environment because OSS was so closely tied to the issue of communism there. OSS was by turns an enthusiastic advocate for intelligence cooperation with the Chinese Communists and their ultimate enemy. The murder of OSS agent John Birch by the Chinese Communists and the systematic purging by Mao Zedong after 1949 of all those who had any association with OSS, are just two cases to ponder.

An objective history of OSS was also made difficult if not impossible by contentious debate in the late 1940s within the U.S. government over the necessity of establishing a centralized intelligence organization. Proponents wanted to preserve and continue the legacy of OSS, while opponents vehemently supported a departmentalized intelligence system, as had existed in the armed forces during the war. When the rivals were unable to come to terms, the wartime experience of OSS became a victim of polemics and policy arguments. Each side used OSS history to support its own case.

Moreover, federal agencies closed many of the essential archives and personal papers on OSS, often not for national security reasons but to protect individuals from accusations and attacks. By the same token, many archives have been only partially opened to the public and have been excessively sanitized. Even the presidential libraries have not been exempt. The finding guide to the President's Safe Files at the Roosevelt Library in Hyde Park states, "Materials that might be used to harass, embarrass or injure living persons have been closed." In the case of OSS/China, many essential files remain unavailable.

Fortunately, the 1980s marked a real thaw in this state of secrecy and closure. First, the concerned agencies of the U.S. government opened the operations files of OSS, now known as Record Group 226 at the National Archives in Washington. This has been a windfall for researchers. As the project archivist of the National Archives, Larry McDonald, notes, RG226 "draw[s] heavy reference because this vast assortment of files reveals information never before available about one of the great defining moments in modern history. . . . [It] offer[s] the researcher a kind of precis of that war, providing a wealth of research material on every theater of the war in the form of intelligence files or of records on all aspects of covert operations in combat and behind enemy lines."[8] Bradley Smith, a prominent authority on the history of OSS, adds, "Never before have scholars been able to see, study, and ponder the raw record of what an intelligence/covert operations organization did and how it did it. . . . This collection is most important to historians because it provides organizational context and will make possible more complete, complex, and 'normal' historical examinations of OSS than have previously been possible for any intelligence organization."[9]

The past ten years also have proved an auspicious period for historians in China to study World War II because of the increased availability of Chinese documents.[10] An outpouring of articles and books in Communist China dealing with World War II intelligence will undoubtedly enrich our understanding both of Communist intelligence and of OSS operations in China.

This sudden Chinese interest in World War II intelligence is the direct result of a political thaw in the 1980s under Deng Xiaoping's reign. The most important mark of this relaxation was the large number of "political rehabilitations" granted to those World War II Communist intelligence veterans, dead and alive, who had been systematically purged by Mao Zedong for almost three decades. Broadly speaking, these purges had had two motives. The first was to suppress any mention of the spectacular contribution of the "Underground Work" *(Dixia Gongzuo)*—intelligence and political penetration, in Chinese Communist Party (CCP) jargon—leading to the triumph of the Chinese Communists over the Kuomintang regime (KMT, or the Nationalists), in order to emphasize the virtuosity and ideological correctness of Mao's military philosophy of "people's war." Second, Mao wanted to get rid of the heavily pro-Moscow intelligence establishment of the CCP that by and large did not, due to their fieldwork, go through Mao's power-consolidating, faction-eliminating campaigns of the famous thought reform and rectification movements in Yenan in the late 1930s and early 1940s.

The newly published materials bear two prominent themes: they display the intelligence achievements of the CCP during World War II, and they restore the Moscow tie. Hundreds of articles, for example, have commemorated the brilliant leadership and achievements of CCP's spymaster, Pan Hannian, since Pan was "rehabilitated" by the Central Committee of the CCP on 23 August 1982—five years after his death in a labor camp in Hunan Province.[11] The recently published memoirs by many Moscow-connected Chinese Communist spies of extraordinary savvy and experience, all Mao era survivors, such as Shi Zhe and Chen Hansheng, reveal information that no historian, either in China or the West, has ever had access to.[12] These revelations have created a pressing need for reinterpretation of many major events in wartime China. In 1981 a biography of Kang Sheng, Mao's espionage and internal security chief, was published and quickly banned inside China. This work inspired some major studies in the West that are reshaping our views on the inner workings of the Chinese Communists.[13] Books and articles by or about such CCP intelligence operatives as Xiong Xianghui, Yan Baohang, Zhang Luping, and Wang Zhengyuan have demonstrated in minute detail the stunning Communist intelligence penetration into the Kuomintang—particularly Chiang Kai-shek's command headquarters and Tai Li's Bureau of Investigation and Statistics—as well as into the U.S. armed forces in China, including OSS, during World War II.[14] Even the chief agent for the U.S. Treasury Department in wartime China, Solomon Adler, has resurfaced in China in open publication, now identified as a bona fide Communist intelligence official.[15] These post-"rehabilitation" materials cover a wide range of issues related to Communist intelligence activities during the Anti-Japanese War and provide a wealth of revelations.[16] This book is thus overwhelmingly based upon the above two types of primary sources: RG 226 and the newly published Chinese materials.

The existing historical writing on OSS in China has been inadequate both in volume and in completeness of scholarship. Nearly fifty years after the demise of OSS, not a single manuscript length OSS/China history has been written based on original archives. Of the authors who have tried to provide a sense of what the wartime experience of OSS in China was actually like, some have merely provided a chapter on China in an OSS history, as in *The OSS War Report* and books by Bradley Smith, who has written an excellent, albeit scanty, chapter on OSS/China, and R. Harris Smith, whose chapter on OSS/China is mainly based upon pre–RG 226 materials, particularly extensive interviews. Others, like Michael Schaller and Thomas Troy, have written a few pages on OSS/China in histories of other "bigger" issues. Some authors have abandoned all attempts to deal with the China theater in their historical analyses of OSS history—Barry Katz, for example, in *Foreign Intelligence.* Neither General Stilwell's biographies nor General Wedemeyer's memoir, *Wedemeyer Reports!,* provides any meaningful mention of OSS. On the Chinese side, the situation has not been any better. The non-Communist historiography in Taiwan and Hong Kong rarely mentioned OSS and its important role in wartime China. Except for a series of propaganda publications in the *People's Daily* during the Korean War, the Chinese Communists remained mostly quiet about OSS for decades. In fact, the term OSS is almost unheard of in China amid voluminous studies on Sino-American relationships during World War II. This is peculiar because OSS played a crucial role in most cases related to wartime intelligence, strategy and diplomacy in the China theater.

For this reason, I have decided to adopt the form of narrative, intertwined with brief analyses, so that a basic sense of what was going on can first be presented.

I have employed the pinyin spelling system for most names of people and places. But to preserve the sense of the historical era under discussion, and to conform to the style with which Western audiences are most familiar, the traditional Wade-Giles system is retained for some important names, including Tai Li (not Dai Li, as in pinyin), Chiang Kai-shek (Jiang Jieshi), T.V. Soong (Song Ziwen), Chungking (Chongqing), Mukden (Shenyang), Peiping (Beijing), and Yenan (Yanan).

Acknowledgments

I would like to thank the following people, whose help and encouragement have proved invaluable. Three scholars at the University of California, Berkeley, Diane Clemens, Frederic Wakeman Jr., and Tom Leonard, have given me timely and precious help. Particularly to Fred Wakeman goes my deep appreciation for the many hours during which we swapped cloak-and-dagger stories with utter enjoyment. Diane Clemens's consistent encouragement proved equally essential for this project. I am most grateful to Larry McDonald, the OSS Project Archivist at the National Archives in Washington, D.C., whose enormous knowledge of OSS records and generous guidance for countless hours during my research trips to the National Archives have been truly indispensable; John Taylor, also at the National Archives, has provided me with his saintly wisdom on military records and other skills necessary to navigate the archival maze. Of course, I also appreciate the assistance of John Sweeney at the Center for Chinese Studies Library in Berkeley, who has tirelessly helped me track down the large amount of Chinese materials I requested.

My sincere thanks go also to the following veterans of OSS and those most closely associated with OSS/China, who generously confided insights to me during my interviews with them that have provided me with a deeper understanding of the complicated inside story of OSS/China: Elizabeth McIntosh (formerly Elizabeth MacDonald, and once the wife of Colonel Richard Heppner, chief of OSS/China), Carl Eifler, Edwin Putzell, Wilma "Billy" Miles, Peter Karlow, Lawrence Houston, Mike McHugh (son of

James McHugh), Malcolm Magruder, John Service, Eddie Liu (Tai Li's interpreter), Oscar Fitzgerald, Ray Cline, and Thomas Troy.

Throughout the research and writing process, many friends and colleagues have provided me with much-needed emotional support as well as professional encouragement. I owe special debt to Therese Lawless, E. Bruce Reynolds, Christof Mauch, Chen Jian, Betty Dessants, Zhai Qiang, Janet Theiss, Brett Sheehan, Susan Barnes, Marcia Ristaino, Barbara Rogers, and J. C. Williams

Yale University Press has been helpful throughout. I have been deeply impressed by the efficiency and professionalism of my editor, Chuck Grench, and his able assistant Otto Bohlmann. I am most grateful to them for their faith in me and in this project. I owe an especially deep debt to my manuscript editor, Dan Heaton, whose thoroughness and superb editing skill have not only made this a better book but also inspired me to be a more careful writer in the future. Of course, any mistakes in this book are completely my own.

I reworked the manuscript during my transition from Berkeley to Annapolis, which was by no means an easy one. My colleagues in the history department of the U.S. Naval Academy have been most gracious in tolerating my initial West Coast cultural residue. I am particularly thankful for this and for their generous advice on the manuscript. I should also mention Matt Brook of the Naval Institute Press, whose professional editing skill has made this manuscript more readable.

Some of this material appeared in "OSS in China: New Information About an Old Role," *International Journal of Intelligence and Counterintelligence* 7(1994), and is used by permission of that publication.

I am most grateful to Christine Kelley for her help in checking my English grammar and spelling.

Abbreviations

A-2   Air Force intelligence service [American]

AGAS   Air Ground Aid Service [American]

AGFRTS   Air and Ground Forces Resources Technical Staff, an
                OSS offspring in China under the 14th Air Force
                [American]

APPLE   Chinese Communists–proposed intelligence plan with
                OSS

AVG   American Volunteers' Group, the Flying Tigers under
                Claire Lee Chennault [Chinese, American]

BAAG   British Air Aid Group, London's secret intelligence
                organization in wartime China under the protection
                of the U.S. AGAS

BEW   Board of Economic Warfare under Henry Wallace
                [American]

BIS   Bureau of Investigation and Statistics under the
                National Military Council [Chinese]

CBI	China-Burma-India theater
CCP	Chinese Communist Party
CCS	Combined Chiefs of Staff [Anglo-American]
CIC	Counter Intelligence Corps of the U.S. Army
CIG	Central Intelligence Group [American]
CNAC	China National Aviation Corporation
COI	Coordinator of Information [American]
COMMO	Communications, OSS
CT	China theater
FEA	Foreign Economic Administration [American]
FEB	Far Eastern Bureau of the Ministry of Information [British]
FP	field photographic branch of OSS
G-2	Army intelligence [American]
GBT	Gordon-Bernard-Tam intelligence network in Japanese-occupied French Indochina
GRU	Soviet military intelligence agency
IDC	Interdepartmental Committee for the Acquisition of Foreign Periodicals [American]
JCS	Joint Chiefs of Staff [American]
JICA	Joint Intelligence Collection Agency [American]
JPWC	Joint Psychological Warfare Committee [American]
Jun Tong	same as BIS [Chinese]
KMT	Kuomintang, the Chinese Nationalist Party

MA	military attaché
MAGIC	American code name for decoded Japanese diplomatic messages
MID	Military Intelligence Division, or G-2 [American]
MO	morale operations branch of OSS
MOI	Ministry of Information [British]
NA	naval attaché [American]
NKVD	predecessor of the KGB [Soviet]
OG	operations group of OSS
OMS	Department of Overseas Relations, the Communist International (Comintern)
ONI	Office of Naval Intelligence [American]
OPD	operations division, War Department [American]
OSS	Office of Strategic Services
OWI	Office of War Information [American]
P Division	intelligence umbrella agency under Mountbatten in SEAC [British]
R&A	research and analysis branch of OSS
S&T	school and training branch of OSS
SACO	Sino-American Special Technical Cooperative Organization [Sino-American]
SAD	Social Affairs Department [Chinese Communist]
SEAC	Southeast Asia Command under Mountbatten
SEPM	*Shanghai Evening Post and Mercury*

SI   secret intelligence branch of OSS

SO   special operations branch of OSS

SOE   Special Operations Executive [British]

SSU   Strategic Services Unit [American]

X-2   counterespionage branch of OSS

YENSIG   OSS signal intelligence project with the Chinese
                      Communists

Zhong Tong   Bureau of Investigation and Statistics under the
                      Organization Department of the Chinese
                      Nationalist Party (KMT)

OSS in China

Introduction

Throughout his presidency, Franklin Roosevelt liked dispatching personal representatives to foreign countries to accomplish important tasks. The sensation created by these "special envoys" enhanced the reputation of several figures in U.S. public life who were regarded as mysteriously clever and intriguingly powerful.

This dramatic public diplomacy reached its high point at the end of 1940 and beginning of 1941, when Roosevelt simultaneously dispatched three such emissaries to the most troubled spots of the globe. To England went FDR's gray eminence, Harry Hopkins. To China went FDR's Canadian-born, pedigreed Lauchlin Currie, described by the press as "a shy little man with a professorial air . . . and a passion for anonymity."[1] Lastly, to the war-torn Mediterranean area went a man of great consequence in the realm of U.S. clandestine operations overseas, William Joseph Donovan. The press added extra color to Donovan's mission. The *New York Times* termed it "mysterious." Another newspaper depicted Donovan as "suave," called him by his nickname, "Wild Bill," and added that he had "commanded the old 69th Infantry during the World War—knows his military tactics and also a lot about persuasion learned during a successful legal career, part of the time as assistant to the U.S. Attorney General."[2]

The inclusion of William Donovan among FDR's special emissaries seemed to affirm the already publicized friendship between the two men. The president announced in July 1941 that Donovan would be christened the Coordinator of Information (COI), a title also used to designate Donovan's organization, the precursor to the Office of Strategic Services—the first national intelligence apparatus in U.S. history with an overarching mandate to coordinate *all* branches of intelligence gathering overseas. FDR's trust in the "suave" yet simultaneously "wild" Bill Donovan seemed evident.

But this was a grand façade. Roosevelt was never a close friend of Donovan's.[3] William Donovan's fame from his highly publicized globe-trotting of 1941 was misleading. Among the three envoys, Donovan was the only one without official status.[4] Unlike Hopkins and Currie, his entire trip was paid for not by the U.S. government but by a seemingly unlikely source, British intelligence.[5] Moreover, behind the presidential cover, Donovan's real sponsor was not FDR at all but Frank Knox, his old Republican friend and Roosevelt's newly appointed secretary of the navy. Most important, the appointment of Donovan as America's spymaster occurred almost by accident.

The genesis of the Coordinator of Information unequivocally illustrates some innate problems with the way Roosevelt handled his foreign policy— problems that would have a much more profound impact on Sino-American relations than on the United States' relations with any other major powers in the world.

After World War II broke out in Europe in September 1939, FDR developed the idea of forming a coalition cabinet of Democrats and Republicans to combat the still rampant isolationism in the United States. On the suggestion of his interior secretary, Harold Ickes, Roosevelt decided to approach Knox, the publisher of the *Chicago Daily News* and the Republican vice presidential candidate in 1936. On 10 December, Roosevelt summoned Knox to the White House for a discussion and then asked him to be his secretary of the navy.[6] Surprised by FDR's unorthodox move, Knox did not want to be the only Republican in Roosevelt's cabinet and risk being scorned as a traitor to the GOP. Knox indicated that he would accept the post on the condition that Donovan be made secretary of war.

"I know Bill Donovan very well and he is a very dear friend," Knox wrote to Roosevelt. "He not only made a magnificent record in the world war, but he has every decoration which the American government can bestow for bravery under fire. Frankly if your proposal contemplated Donovan for the War Department and myself for the Navy, I think the appointments could be put solely on the basis of a non-partisan, non-political measure of putting our national defense departments in such a state of preparedness as to protect the U.S. against any danger to our security that might come from the war in Europe or in Asia."[7]

"Bill Donovan is also an old friend of mine," Roosevelt wrote in reply.

Fig. 1. Major General William Joseph Donovan, director of OSS (National Archives)

"We were in the Columbia Law School together. . . . Here again the question of motive must be considered and I fear that to put two Republicans in charge of the armed forces might be misunderstood in both parties."[8] But Roosevelt's claim was disingenuous. Six months later, he *did* make two Republicans, Frank Knox and Henry Stimson, his secretaries of navy and war, respectively.

Immediately upon joining Roosevelt's cabinet, the guilt-ridden Knox asked Donovan to serve as undersecretary of the navy.[9] Donovan refused, but he agreed to his old friend's next request, going to England on Knox's behalf to conduct a survey on the question of whether or not England could withstand a fierce German assault. This was in July 1940, one year before his British-sponsored trip to the Mediterranean.[10] In London, Donovan was lavishly and anxiously entertained by the king and queen, Winston Churchill, and all the high-ranked officials the British could produce. It is significant that Donovan was kept in daily contact with a "Mr. C," code name for the MI-6 chief, Stewart Menzies, and the director of British naval intelligence, John Godfrey, who gave Donovan a list of things the British wanted him to lobby for in Washington.[11]

Two weeks later, Donovan came back to the United States and was immediately approached by William Stephenson, British intelligence chief for the Western Hemisphere, who was working as security officer in the British Purchasing Commission, Britain's version of Chiang Kai-shek's China Defense Supplies, one of the many war materiel lobbying groups operating in Washington. Donovan and Stephenson immediately became "collaborators and friends." Donovan reported to FDR and Knox that Britain could survive but needed materiel, particularly battleships. On 8 August, Stephenson cabled London that Donovan was striving to sell the White House on the idea of the British exchange of bases for destroyers. Two weeks later, the British got fifty U.S. destroyers for military bases in the Western Hemisphere.[12]

This vital lobbying effort for the British in Washington by Knox's friend prompted enthusiastic hobnobbing between Stephenson and Donovan. In early December 1940, Donovan proposed to Knox that he would like to make another trip, this time to the Mediterranean area, accompanied by Stephenson. Knox at once made Donovan his official representative, unofficially representing the president. The trip would be paid for by the British government.

Donovan's Mediterranean journey lasted from 8 December 1940 to 8 March 1941. At a dizzying pace, he went to Bermuda, Portugal, and Britain, then to Gibraltar, Malta, Egypt, and Libya, then back to Egypt, to Greece, Bulgaria, Yugoslavia, Turkey, Cyprus, Palestine, and so forth. According to Thomas Troy, that trip inspired Donovan's ambition for a national intelligence agency: "The idea of COI was fairly well formulated in his mind, the idea of centralizing intelligence, coordinating intelligence."[13]

Now Donovan needed the help of his old friend Knox to realize his ambition of becoming the U.S. intelligence chief. On 26 April 1941, Donovan sent a long letter to Knox in which he described to the secretary the instrumentality through which the British government gathered its information in foreign countries. "Intelligence operations," he wrote, "should not be controlled by party exigencies. It is one of the most vital means of national defense. As such it should be headed by someone appointed by the President and directly responsible to him, and to no one else. It should have a fund solely for the purpose of foreign investigation and the expenditures under this fund should be secret and made solely at the discretion of the President." Donovan continued, "On all of these various factors I have obtained firsthand information which I think better not to set down here. I refer to it now only because I feel all of these activities should be considered in relation to the necessity of setting up a Coordinator." Donovan ends his letter with, "If you wish me to talk with you more in detail, let me know."[14]

Knox must have responded to Donovan's suggestion enthusiastically, for by the end of May, Donovan had drafted his first formal recommendation for a new U.S. intelligence organization.[15] On 10 June a formal memorandum from Donovan to the president was sent to the White House.[16] A week later Knox himself took Donovan directly to Roosevelt for a meeting of extreme importance about the plan. Only four people were present: Knox, FDR, Donovan, and a member of the White House legal staff named Ben Cohen. When the meeting adjourned, Donovan walked out of the White House a jubilant man. Immediately, he told Stephenson that he had been appointed by the president as the chief of U.S. intelligence. Donovan would be the coordinator of all forms of intelligence, including offensive operations, and most importantly, would be responsible only to the president.[17]

FDR's response to the Knox-Donovan plan was more than curious, for it displays a striking degree of informality in a matter as important as this. The next day, on 18 June 1941, Roosevelt wrote on the cover sheet of Donovan's memorandum of 10 June a cursory message to the acting director of the budget bureau, John B. Blandford Jr.: "Please set this up *confidentially* with Ben Cohen—military, not OEM. FDR."[18]

The meaning of the word *confidentially* is enigmatic here. Some historians believe it referred to the use of secret funds.[19] *Military* meant that Donovan would be a major general, an idea fiercely opposed by the War Department; *not OEM* referred to the Office of Emergency Management, which meant that Donovan would not be subject to all kinds of war agencies under the OEM umbrella and would directly report to FDR.

This vague little note, an incomplete sentence, is one of the most important documents of the twentieth century, for it authorized the establishment of the first centralized and interdepartmental foreign intelligence service of the United States since the time of George Washington. It formally authorized the usage of unorthodox warfare. But equally telling and even more remarkable was the way in which Roosevelt made such a decision, without consulting any of the existing intelligence and information agencies of the government. "There is also no doubt," writes Troy, "that Colonel Donovan proceeded to operate like a man fully authorized not only to coordinate intelligence, but also to conduct a whole range of operations—psychological, political, or unconventional warfare. The president and the colonel had thus taken a giant step in the establishment of the country's pioneer organization for central intelligence and special operations." On 11 July 1941, Roosevelt picked up the final draft of the order that he had ignored for a week in his in box and signed it.[20]

CHAPTER ONE

Building an Empire

Roosevelt's decision to create Donovan's new empire for foreign intelligence sent an instant shock wave through Washington. On Capitol Hill, FDR's opponents found a new target. One senator immediately labeled COI an OGPU (predecessor to the KGB) and a Gestapo organization.[1] In the U.S. intelligence community, the creation of Donovan's new agency crystallized and intensified a three-way struggle between the army, the navy, and COI (OSS). The very first battleground was over control of intelligence gathering in China.

The Magruder Mission and Donovan's China Team in Washington

The army felt it had to take swift action against Donovan. On 11 July 1941, the same day Roosevelt signed and issued the order to create COI, General George Marshall's Military Intelligence Division (MID) made a preemptive strike to control the China theater. Hours after the presidential order became official, Brigadier General Sherman Miles, acting assistant chief of staff and number one man of MID (G-2), ordered "the immediate establishment of an American military mission in China."[2]

Sherman Miles had been Donovan's most vigilant enemy in Washington. With great anxiety, he had been closely watching the growth of Donovan's ambition for controlling American intelligence. In April he had warned General Marshall: "There is considerable reason to believe that there is a movement on foot, fostered by Colonel Donovan, to establish a super agency controlling *all* intelligence. This would mean that such an agency, no doubt under Colonel Donovan, would collect, collate and possibly even evaluate all military intelligence which we now gather from foreign countries. From the point of view of the War Department, such a move would appear to be very disadvantageous, if not calamitous."[3]

Sherman Miles's military mission to China had long been requested by Lauchlin Currie, who had come back to the United States from Chungking in early March.[4] The Army had three names to consider for heading this China mission: Joseph Stilwell, A. J. Bowley, and John Magruder.[5] With Donovan's new organization in mind, Miles resolutely picked Brigadier General John Magruder, who was a straightforward intelligence officer then stationed in Fort Devens, Massachusetts. In his hurriedly dictated message to Magruder, Miles urged his colleague to realize that although the purpose of this mission would be to "advise the Chinese Government in all military matters, particularly in the use of Lease Lend credits or Lease Lend material which they may receive from us," an additional task would be to "keep the Chinese Government informed as to such military plans or progress made here as we may want them to have" so that "when we get into this war actively, the mission will be *the* liaison for strategic planning and cooperation with our ally, China." The MID chief asked Magruder to understand that the Army's China mission was going to be "very important and will increase in importance as time goes on." Finally, Magruder was told of the urgency for such a mission at a time when Donovan was starting to build a foreign intelligence organization of his own. "As a matter of time," Miles instructed Magruder, "as you can readily see, we would want to establish this mission as early as possible. *It should have been done some time since.*"[6]

Magruder was considered a China expert in the U.S. Army. He had served in China from 1920 through 1924 as assistant military attaché at the American Legation, then became military attaché in Berne, Switzerland, and later went back to China as military attaché from 1926 to 1930.[7] During those years, Magruder learned the Chinese language and became intimately acquainted with many Chinese people.[8] Sherman Miles's preemptive strike against COI was being carried out effectively by Magruder. Named the Magruder mission, it was designed by Marshall and Miles as strictly the army's show. Rear Admiral Willis Lee of the Navy's Interior Control Board requested that a navy observer named Milton Miles be attached to the Magruder mission, but this idea was rejected by the army.[9] When Donovan heard of the formation of this China mission, he immediately began to negotiate for a COI representative to be attached to the mission. The army flatly refused to accept this proposal from the newly christened intelligence chief of the United States. Donovan resented Magruder and later took the matter directly to the White House, complaining to Roosevelt: "Before General Magruder left for China, I suggested that we should give him an officer who could be attached to the mission for the activities connected with our agency. . . . I thought that we might be able to help him, not only in the gathering of information, but also on broadcasting. He said it was unnecessary."[10] The Magruder mission arrived in China in early October 1941, and as predicted the army was in complete control. Starting on 13 December 1941, with the United States at war in the Pacific, a daily intelligence summary was initiated and most of the intelligence Magruder got was from Chinese sources.[11]

After COI's first attempt to penetrate into China through the Magruder mission failed, Donovan was clear about one thing: he was a chief of intelligence without spies. Not only was he unable to take over the existing intelligence apparatus, he could not even get willing cooperation from them. But Donovan was willing to accept the challenge and start establishing his own force. The first such step he took frightened Sherman Miles and other competing figures in the U.S. intelligence community. Donovan decided to establish a "brain bureau," the most crucial part of the intelligence process: evaluation and analysis.

Charm and charisma gave Donovan tremendous advantage in recruiting people of high analytical ability from academia, law firms, and business offices. William Langer of Harvard's history department wrote in his autobiography that Donovan "had an exceptional gift for arousing the interest and enthusiasm of others and of enlisting their loyalty and devotion."[12] Research and analysis, or R&A, would become Donovan's greatest asset in his OSS empire and the heaviest bargaining chip he had in dealing with other intelligence branches.

Donovan's choice to head R&A was James Penney Baxter, the president of Williams College, who immediately recruited Langer and two other scholars from the history department of Harvard University: Don McKay and a young, ambitious junior instructor named John King Fairbank.[13] They arrived in Washington in mid-August 1941 and occupied a space at the Library of Congress, where Donovan had already worked out a deal with the head librarian, Archibald MacLeish.[14] Baxter soon resigned for personal reasons. Langer succeeded him as the chief of R&A and remained at that post throughout the war. Langer divided his people into eight geographic sections, "set up to deal with strategic information concerning the British Empire, Western Europe, Central Europe, Russia and the Balkans, the Near East, the Mediterranean and Africa, the Far East, and Latin America."[15]

The process of recruiting scholars into R&A heavily relied upon departmental association. Langer would have made his Harvard colleague Fairbank chief for the Far East, but the latter was far too junior and little known at the time.[16] Consequently, Joseph Ralston Hayden, chairman of the political science department at the University of Michigan, was recruited to head the Far East Division of Research and Analysis.

Upon Hayden's arrival in Washington, Donovan immediately showed great interest in this portly yet strong professor from the Midwest, for Hayden seemed to represent the ideal type of scholar–intelligence officer Donovan desired. Donovan, who was a World War I hero and proud of his war memories, discovered with much delight that Hayden, too, was an accomplished figure of the world war. While a professor at the University of Michigan at the outbreak of the war in Europe in 1914, Hayden was commissioned an officer in the U.S. Naval Reserve. Reaching the rank of lieutenant, Hayden won a silver star after the gun crew he commanded fired the last shot from an artillery piece in the war.[17]

Donovan and Hayden shared connections in the Pacific islands, as well. Hayden, who had specialized on the Philippines as an academic, was nominated by Roosevelt in 1933 to serve as the vice governor of the archipelago. Similarly, Donovan had been asked by Herbert Hoover to be the governor of the Philippines in 1929. He refused to serve in that post because he wanted to be attorney general or secretary of war. Although the Hoover request represented "the greatest disappointment in his life," Donovan acquired a strong sensitivity and curiosity toward the Philippines.[18]

As a result of this personal tie, Hayden rose rapidly within Donovan's establishment and was entrusted with a great deal of responsibility. Hayden soon left the Far East Division of R&A and was elevated to the highest level in COI, the Board of Analysts.[19] On 3 January 1942, Donovan issued a directive to Hayden "to undertake the establishment within this organization of a Training School for instruction of individuals in the principles and practices of special intelligence."[20] Thus, the scholar from Michigan began a most unlikely task, the training of spies for the first national intelligence agency of America. Within several months Hayden would find himself transplanted to Chungking, trying to peddle his fabulous plan of clandestine operations for OSS.

After the departure of Hayden, the Far East Division recruited a new chief, Charles Remer, also of the University of Michigan. The fifty-two-year-old professor of economics was a senior China hand in the United States and had taught economics from 1913 to 1925 at St. John's College in Shanghai. At the same time, Charles Burton Fahs, a Japan expert, was called in by Langer from Pomona College in California. In September 1941, Donovan employed another person with great China connections, Esson M. Gale of the University of California at Berkeley, in the capacity of consultant.[21]

Donovan's amassing of scholars as intelligence officers presented a challenge and profound dilemma to the American intellectual community. University campuses and classrooms were a symbol for free thinking, intellectual innovation, and human creativity—the antithesis of bureaucracy. By contrast, government service was routinized and rigid. There was, however, a trade-off here. Although noble and lofty, academia seemed ethereal and tranquil, and was regarded by many as of little consequence; officialdom might be smug and boring, but it offered power and influence. This contradiction was particularly felt by self-assured scholars who were solemnly summoned by the mighty U.S. government to be the ears and eyes of the powerful. To many of Donovan's recruits, this conflict between intellect and intelligence posed a painful ambivalence that was properly characterized by Langer as "a dual existence."[22]

By the end of October 1941, the Far East Division of the R&A was moving ahead. Remer, Fairbank, Fahs, and Gale constituted the core of this division and were primarily engaged in surveying the existing materials available at the Library of Congress. Three months after the inception of COI, Donovan singled out the achievements of the Far East Division, R&A, in his report to Roosevelt. This division, Donovan proudly proclaimed, was at work on really "strategic questions," specifically "(1) regionalism as a solution of Japan's economic problem, (2) a preliminary review of American aid to China, (3) the relation of nationalist movements to Japanese penetration into other Far Eastern countries, and (4) the sufficiency of Japanese resources for waging war against possible new opponents."[23]

However, the mustering of scholars in Washington was not enough for Donovan. His 1941 trip to the Mediterranean area had brought him a thorough admiration for British commando units. This was based upon his conviction that "there was a place for aggressive, small mobile forces which might greatly increase the enemy's misery and weaken his will to resist."[24] With this thought in mind, Donovan started to organize an essential part of his empire, the special operations, or in OSS parlance, the SO.

Special Operations in the Far East

From the very beginning Donovan's SO effort met strong skepticism in high military quarters.[25] But right away, George Marshall and Sherman Miles were outwitted by their foe. In fact, during the contentious period of drafting and rewording the presidential order creating the Co-ordinator of Information, the army had managed to strike out all the sentences that would make Donovan's organization part of the regular military. But a brilliant lawyer and a former assistant attorney general, Donovan kept one crucial sentence in the final order of 11 July 1941. COI was authorized to carry out *"supplementary activities* as may facilitate the securing of information important for national security not now available to the Government."[26] This provided a statutory basis for his SO efforts. Later in 1946, Donovan proudly told an internal historian of OSS, "This [the keeping of the phrase 'supplementary activities'] was done by me to cover situations that might arise."[27]

In fact, such a situation arose very quickly and had a direct bearing to Donovan's ambitions in the Far East. In August 1941, Sherman Miles sent Colonel M. Preston Goodfellow to Donovan as a liaison officer "with authorization from G-2 to serve COI." This provided Donovan with an excellent opportunity to organize his SO activities because Goodfellow had begun a training program in the military even before COI's establishment and had already been working training G-2 army officers to do special operations.[28] Goodfellow was won over by Donovan's plan and provided many of his trainees for Donovan's use, among them Robert A. Solborg and Warren J. Clear. Donovan immediately appointed Solborg his first chief of special operations and sent him to England to learn from the British. Moreover, at the time Goodfellow became liaison for G-2 in COI in August, he had already sent off Warren Clear on a special mission to the Far East for Sherman Miles; now he let Donovan take over Clear's mission.[29]

The Clear mission became Donovan's first field intelligence gathering effort in the Far East. It was designed to determine "the advisability and practicability of setting up an intelligence system" in the Far East and the Philippines. Clear departed in July 1941 and spent two months with British Air Marshall Brooke-Popham in Singapore. After that, Clear went on to Thailand, French Indochina, the Dutch East Indies, Timor, and the Moluccas, before landing in the wrong territory at the wrong time. That territory was the Philippines, General Douglas MacArthur's sphere of influence; the time was around the Japanese blitzkrieg at the end of 1941. MacArthur, his air and ground forces completely uncoordinated, had been unceremoniously defeated by the Japanese. He had earlier ridiculed the Chinese for a lack of "air-mindedness" and had strongly urged General Magruder in China to use the "maximum number of foreign pilots" to "control" the Chinese air force.[30] Yet MacArthur's own failure to coordinate his forces resulted in the destruction of his entire air force on the ground by Japanese bombers on 8 December 1941.[31]

The infamy of defeat and the failures of MacArthur's defense strategy were dutifully recorded by Clear, whom MacArthur understood to have direct communication with Washington. "Their coordination of air and land forces is superb," recorded Clear of the Japanese, "and they are thinking way ahead of their enemies in this respect." Clear ended one report with an account of "a captured Japanese aviator [who] emphasized the contrast when he said that his experience bombing the American fields had been 'delightful.' If he missed the field he was certain to hit a hanger or a repair shop."[32]

Clear's intelligence-gathering activities and his direct communication line with Washington infuriated MacArthur, who kicked Clear out of Bataan just a week before its fall to the Japanese. Clear escaped by submarine in February 1942. He reached Washington in mid-April and submitted a comprehensive report on MacArthur. Donovan was bitter about MacArthur's intransigence and hostility toward his COI agent and promptly sent Clear's report to the White House to prove MacArthur's "incompetence." That report by Clear came to be regarded by the OSS internal historian as having "general historical interest."[33]

Warren Clear's Far East mission did not cover China, but it did have enormous impact on Donovan's China plans. To MacArthur, Donovan's intelligence organization was an outrageous infringement upon his own territory. After the Clear mission, MacArthur declared that Donovan's agent had given COI a "bad name throughout the Far East."[34] For Donovan, this hostility coming from MacArthur in the Far East was an impetus to speed up his China project.

Donovan's First China Operation

COI's first idea for a China mission had been suggested in September 1941, to be carried out by Esson Gale. At that time, Donovan, anticipating the final Japanese takeover of Shanghai's International Settlement—the major supply source of China-related publications and raw intelligence for the newly formed Far East Division of R&A—ordered preparation for undercover intelligence activities in Shanghai. Meetings that month included Donovan, Hayden, Goodfellow, David Bruce (Donovan's deputy and a member of the Mellon family), Gale, and Wallace Phillips (COI's chief of the Secret Intelligence Service, or SI). The planning meetings lasted until the beginning of December, and it was finally decided that Gale would leave the United States for Shanghai on 10 December. But the Pearl Harbor attack forced Donovan to abandon the entire project.[35]

With a declaration of war between the United States and Japan, Donovan immediately formed a Far East Committee within COI. This committee was chaired by James Phinney Baxter and included Wallace Phillips, Joseph Hayden, Charles Remer, John K. Fairbank, Amry Vandonbosh, and Esson Gale. After Baxter's short tenure with COI ended, Remer took charge. His laissez-faire working style failed to hold his committee together. Fairbank was allowed to spend most of his time and energy "moonlighting" in Room 224 at Lauchlin Currie's office in the White House, occasionally coming back to the committee to report on his conferences with Currie.[36] The bitter and jealous Stanley Hornbeck, a chief policy adviser on China at the State Department, had been snooping for a while into Donovan's realm, trying to discern COI's real intentions, and finally succeeded in getting information from Gale, who was more than happy to be summoned in January 1942 by the famous "Political Adviser Hornbeck."[37]

In spite of all this, the Far East Committee did accomplish a major project. The desire to set up a COI network in China was quickly rekindled after the aborted Shanghai intelligence plan. With the return of Robert Solborg from the British training camp in early January 1942 and the appointment of Wallace Phillips as Donovan's first secret intelligence chief, a combined SO and SI China mission was soon started under the direction of the Far East Committee. Once again, Gale was chosen to go to China. After more than one month's meticulous planning and painstaking coordination with other U.S. agencies, the first China mission of COI began.

On 8 February 1942, Gale left LaGuardia Airport in New York on his way to China. He traveled through South America and Africa, where he was picked up by General Stilwell's plane in Cairo, then arrived in India in late February. Among the people Gale visited while in India was M. N. Roy, a Comintern presidium member and Stalin's powerful agent in China only a few years earlier.[38] R. C. Chen, a Chinese agent working for T. V. Soong, Chiang Kai-shek's brother-in-law and plenipotentiary in Washington, greeted Gale in Calcutta and moved his flight to China up six days to 8 March. This seemingly trivial rescheduling assumed huge proportions when the 14 March plane mysteriously crashed at the Kunming airport; among those killed was the British general L. E. Dennys.[39] Gale arrived in Chungking early in the morning of 8 March.

The Gale mission marks the beginning of Donovan's China saga. In a quite remarkable way, it highlights all the major aspects of COI's intrinsic problems with conducting clandestine operations in China. First and foremost, the mission thoroughly exposed a fundamental mistake made on the issue of operational strategy, the surrogate policy. Gale's ostensible task was to establish a counterpropaganda team for COI in Chungking. This had been desperately requested by Magruder in late December 1941.

("China is being deluged with all kinds of propaganda by the Japanese through the different radio stations that have been taken over," Magruder reported to the War Department.) After ridiculing Magruder's earlier refusal of any COI participation in the Magruder mission, a vindicated Donovan received a directive from the War Department that COI should employ somebody in Chungking to coordinate with Magruder on counterpropaganda aimed at the Japanese. In late December, Charles Remer, chief of R&A Far East Division in Washington suggested to Donovan that F. M. Fisher, of the United Press in Chungking, and David Rowe, a China scholar obsessed with "quantitative studies" of things Chinese, also in Chungking, be hired to collect and microfilm propaganda materials.[40] In the meantime, Donovan arranged with RCA for direct transmission of world news reports to Chungking from San Francisco on a daily basis between 5 and 6 P.M. and 1 and 2 A.M. EST.[41] Gale was supposed to go to Chungking to take charge of this two-man team.

But this was only a cover. Gale's real mission was to organize a secret intelligence and sabotage system by using Koreans in exile in Chungking. Donovan's secret memo to Roosevelt of 24 January 1942 stated the Gale mission's goal as "to negotiate for us the possibility of using the Koreans to operate against the Japanese in Japan proper and in Korea and certain occupied areas on the Continent, including Manchuria." But why Koreans? Donovan explained to Roosevelt in the same memo, "The distribution of the Koreans in important centers opens the way for their employment in intelligence and sabotage work against the Japanese. This is not the case with other nationals, particularly whites and Chinese, who are readily identified in the Japanese Domain."[42]

Using Koreans as a surrogate for American intelligence work in China was calamitous, and fault can be easily found. First, this surrogate plan was a direct, dogmatic, and most awkward adaptation of the British method. The British had been widely employing their surrogate policy in Asia. American enthusiasts for this method were plenty, not only in COI but also in the regular army. The U.S. military attaché in London once even suggested to the War Department, with absolute seriousness, that Africans be sent to Burma to conduct "jungle warfare" on behalf of the United States.[43]

To the Chinese, however, this strategy gave off a strong odor of British colonialism, manifested in Britain's use of other nationals to achieve its own ends. SOE's non-British Europeans were already resented by Tai Li, Chiang Kai-shek's powerful chief of secret police and guerrilla forces in China. But what was seen as even worse was the British employment of Chinese Canadians and even Chinese Americans trained in SOE camps in Ontario for

Fig. 2. Major General Tai Li (Dai Li) of the Chinese Army, director of SACO and head of BIS (courtesy of the family of Admiral Milton Miles)

the specific purpose of "joining forces" with the Chinese Communists in the defense of Hong Kong.[44] As a result, Donovan's Korean surrogate policy instantly ignited a fire of opposition from Tai Li.

Moreover, this plan was based on an excessive enthusiasm rather than a realistic and rational evaluation of the battlefield situations in China. The person in COI who most actively supported the idea of using surrogates was by no means a China expert. Robert Solborg, Donovan's first SO chief, had come back from London around New Year's Day 1942 after going through intensive training by the British in the most ruthless sabotage methods.[45] Totally taken in by the British method of clandestine warfare, Solborg's zealotry for SO led him to draft the first comprehensive blueprint of COI's Special Operations on 13 January 1942. He outlined the primary method of operation, stating that COI "should work in closest possible cooperation with emigré governments established in America and in Great Britain and with foreign groups in the United States."[46] Under Solborg's scheme, Donovan's people in Washington went out to contact the foreign groups. Without much difficulty, they found a Korean man named Syngman Rhee, the Washington representative of the provisional government of Korea based in Chungking.[47] Donovan immediately decided to use Koreans as surrogates in China.

But Donovan's choice of Syngman Rhee as COI's surrogate in China was another vital mistake, for it ignored the complexity of the Korean issue in Chinese politics. Korea had officially become Japan's colony in 1910. Overseas Koreans in exile had gained considerable strength after the March First Uprising of 1919. The provisional government of Korea was established that year in Shanghai with Syngman Rhee as its president. But a fierce internal struggle broke out among the Koreans in exile. Syngman Rhee fled Shanghai to the United States in disgrace in 1921, leaving the provisional government in disarray. Chiang Kai-shek realized the value of these Koreans in China and started to provide them with substantial support. Many young Koreans were admitted into his Whampoa Military Academy. In 1933, Chiang decided to give his full backing to Kim Ku as the leader of the strife-ridden Korean population in China. A Korean Restoration Army was formed under the auspices of the Nationalist government. Tai Li was ordered to train many Koreans as intelligence officers and sabotage experts. By September of 1940, the headquarters of the Korean Restoration Army had been set up in Chungking. Most important, these armed Koreans in China were organized by the Chinese in such a way that they were all under the control of Tai Li through the titular command of General He Yingqin.

Thus, when Donovan's Korean initiative came to China, it was a blunder on two fronts. One, Chiang Kai-shek and Tai Li were supporting one faction of the Korean provisional government while Donovan was touting another. This initial policy discord proved deadly later on.[48] Moreover, COI's fabulous Korean surrogate plan flew right in the face of Tai Li's virtual control over the core of Korean exiles in China.

The second profound problem with the Gale mission pertained to the "Old China Hands": to what degree should an intelligence organization engage scholars in strategic planning, and exactly what kind of scholars should be utilized for intelligence operations? Donovan's contingent of erudite academics congregating under Langer's R&A were scattered in eight regions. As Barry Katz pointed out in his pioneering work, the intellectual discourse within R&A was avid and intense among those scholars of Europe.[49] Their discourse was mostly one of different philosophical understandings of a well-defined, specific country.

In the case of China, however, there was no developed scholarship sophisticated enough to forge an integrated and holistic strategic evaluation for Donovan's agency. The official definition of R&A for every new recruit in OSS was "an organization of scholars and research specialists who possess unusual language qualifications and have expert knowledge on particular geographic areas."[50] But China was not just "a particular geographic area," it was a huge country that was endowed with highly volatile and often intriguing central-provincial relations. In much the same regard, China scholars in Donovan's organization were perceived as Old China Hands not because they had an overall knowledge of that vast country but because they had physically lived in one or two provinces or subregions in China, thus acquiring a particular affinity to a small area, be it Guangdong (Kwangtung), Yunnan, Shanghai, Manchuria, or Mongolia. The boundary of their knowledge was often much narrower than the boundary of China.

This problem would have a compounding effect later when the OSS agent Oliver Caldwell became obsessed with promoting his Sichuan Gelaohui (secret society in Sichuan Province). But the first problem Donovan had to deal with was his parochial scholar, Esson Gale, whose passion for the Chinese border state of Korea started a political whirl in that Far East peninsula, the impact of which can still be felt.

Gale had strong family connections in Korea. His uncle, James S. Gale, was among the first Americans to settle in Korea as missionaries after the 1882 Korean-U.S. treaty. Esson Gale had frequently visited Korea since 1909, and his wife was born of American parents in Seoul.[51] Throughout this initial stage of COI strategic planning for a U.S. clandestine empire, Gale promoted the Korean surrogate scheme with unusual tenacity and often passionate defense against opposition from all sides.[52] His arguments were so effective that within COI, and later OSS, this Korean-oriented strategy never lost its priority, particularly with Goodfellow's SO people. Eventually Goodfellow himself personally escorted Syngman Rhee back to Seoul after World War II to be the president of the U.S.-backed Republic of Korea.[53]

But this problem with regionalism among China scholars was not Gale's alone in COI. Besides Korea, another subregion of China that aroused excessive enthusiasm from Old China Hands in the United States was the Northeast or Manchuria. In late December of 1941, two Old China Hands named Larsen and Underwood presented Donovan with a special operations plan designed to "liberate 43 million Chinese people from Manchu-kuo," as well as people in Mongolia and Korea. The essence of this scheme was the proposal that "a commission of four men be sent to China for the purpose of preventing a decisive Japanese victory by the augmentation of effective guerrilla warfare."[54] Fortunately, after serious discussions with these two zealous gentlemen, more cautious people in COI argued persuasively that "the whole scheme is conceived on much too large a scale."[55] The plan was gracefully dropped in January 1942.

Within a month, however, Donovan received a document forwarded from Adlai Stevenson, then special assistant to the secretary of the navy. It was a detailed "Plan To Give Further Aid to China and Russia and to Establish Air Bases Behind the Japanese Lines" by Earnest B. Price, a noted Old China Hand.[56] Donovan took it seriously, for he asked his R&A chief, William Langer, to evaluate it. Langer replied on 3 March, "I am utterly unimpressed with this effusion and it seems to me that so long as the Russian Government cannot be brought to allow American Forces to use Russian air fields it is most unlikely that it would consider for a moment all the finagling that is suggested in this document. I am almost forced to conclude that my conception of Japanese control in Manchuria is sadly erroneous if it is possible to play around behind the lines as Mr. Price suggests."[57] Price's plan was thus killed. Five months later, in mid-August 1942, Price was appointed by Donovan as the chief for secret intelligence, Far East Division of OSS.[58]

The Gale mission reflected a third problem: COI's all too close ties with the British SOE. COI's symbiotic bond with the British was obvious from the very beginning. Donovan's agents were first trained in the SOE camps in Canada. Once COI started its own training facilities in Virginia and Maryland in early 1942, the British furnished the key instructors, including a former British police commissioner in Shanghai named William Fairbairn.[59] Donovan's people also shared intelligence facilities with the SOE. He organized a massive mail censorship station at the British SOE headquarters in Bermuda.

Roosevelt knew all this and was alarmed by Donovan's cozy relationship with the British. The president planted an agent of his own, William Phillips, as Donovan's chief representative in London in early July 1942. FDR asked Phillips, his family friend, to give him frequent direct reports without telling Donovan. Phillips, nervous about his "double-agent" status, once wrote from London to the suspicious president, "You asked me to write to you now and then, which of course I am delighted to do. On the other hand I don't want you to think of acknowledging such letters, otherwise I should feel that it was wrong for me to write to you."[60]

The Anglo tie in clandestine operations would plague OSS in China throughout World War II. The unequivocal British tinge on the Gale mission inevitably invited its demise since China had developed a passionate hatred and distrust of the British. Donovan's untimely comradeship with the SOE in China was both conspicuous and profound. Gale was ordered to directly go to the British Embassy—not the U.S. one—in Chungking, to organize the Koreans there in cooperation with British intelligence in China. Moreover, he was not to contact Tai Li for such activities. Donovan reported to Roosevelt on 24 January 1942, "We have made arrangements with the British for a tie-up with [Gale]."[61]

The "tie-up" Donovan mentioned to Roosevelt was with none other than John Keswick, the director of the SOE-run China Commando Group. Keswick had obtained cover as the first secretary in the British Embassy in Chungking. Valentine Killery, the SOE chief of the Oriental mission and Keswick's titular boss, was also staying at the embassy. Both men were already in serious trouble with Tai Li at the moment Gale arrived in China in early March 1942. Before his departure from Washington, Gale had been instructed by Donovan and Wallace Phillips to get "in contact with the intelligence personnel of the British Embassy." Specifically, Wallace had asked Gale to meet with Keswick and Killery, whom Gale claimed as personal acquaintances. Gale reported to Washington later on his encounter with Keswick and other British citizens in China, "It was fortunate that he had established close working relations with the British information service, the personnel of which cooperated splendidly with Dr. Gale. Even the officers whose work involved the most confidential matters . . . frequently shared with Dr. Gale information of vital importance to COI representative and his principals at Washington."[62]

Gale's elation over his intimacy with Keswick and Killery came at the expense of COI's reputation in China. Esson Gale should have realized what was at stake: the British had grown notorious in China at the same time American prestige was rapidly rising. But Gale wanted everyone to know about his profound friendship with the British. He even conjured for Keswick and Killery ways of lessening Chinese hostility toward the British. He expediently suggested to the two Old British China Hands that a concession to the Chinese was necessary to obliterate, in his words, "the so-called inequalities in order to placate Oriental self-esteem." Unfortunately, Gale's good-hearted suggestion was rejected by Keswick and Killery.[63]

Another problem for this mission was Gale himself. As an Old China Hand, Gale clearly reaffirmed Tai Li's suspicion of such a person's worth as an intelligence officer. The historian Bradley Smith sums it up: "Gale was a talker and socializer, a man who liked to make grandiose plans and show off his importance."[64] He went around Chungking showing off his prominence—passing out business cards with his name and title as an agent for the "American Intelligence Office" (Mei Guo Qing Bao Chu). Before long, cogent people all over Chungking paid extra attention to this—in Fairbank's words—"slightly rounded sinologue with a small British-type mustache."[65]

To make matters worse, Gale moved into Jialing Hotel (the so-called press hostel), where most of the foreign correspondents stayed. Immediately, Gale's approach was seen as evidence of an American "imperialist conspiracy to suppress the Chinese people." Anna Louise Strong, a writer with close ties to the Communists, was in Chungking and wrote for the International News Service. She dispatched "important news" all over the world that a Dr. Esson Gale had arrived in Chungking "as Far Eastern representative" of an American espionage organization called the Coordinator of Information.[66] Donovan and Wallace Phillips were furious over Strong's news story. A cable was immediately sent to Gale for explanation as to how his undercover identity had been discovered. Gale had no satisfactory response.[67]

More trouble for COI's Gale mission came from interagency rivalry, chiefly from the U.S. embassy in Chungking. The ambassador, Clarence Gauss, had several reasons to be obstructive. First, Donovan had instructed Gale to directly approach the British embassy, bypassing Gauss. This was obviously insulting to the highly territorial ambassador. Second, the political sensitivity of the Korean issue made Gauss very angry at Gale's open and vociferous lobbying for Washington's official recognition of the Syngman Rhee faction of the Korean provisional government. Once again, Donovan's man stumbled, rather mindlessly, into a minefield of Chinese internal politics. Gale was instructed to approach the pro-Soviet and pro-Communist faction of the KMT to promote the Korean contingents in Chungking who were under the firm control of Tai Li, a staunch anti-Communist. At a public rally for Koreans organized by Gale, Song Qingling (Soong Ching-ling) and Sun Ke (Sun Fo), Sun Yat-sen's widow and son, respectively, and Tai Li's political opponents, were invited to speak for the Korean cause, along with the left-leaning Christian general, Feng Yuxiang. Gale's simpleminded meddling angered Gauss. Since the powerful Stanley Hornbeck in Washington was now supporting Gale's plan as a means to further his own influence in Donovan's empire, Gauss could only remain defiantly silent toward Gale's Korean initiative.[68]

Moreover, Gauss was particularly sour about Gale's communications method. The COI agent insisted on using his own secret code that Wallace Phillips had given him instead of the State Department channel. The ambassador demanded that Gale give him, for approval, a paraphrase of every message that went to COI. Moreover, Gauss vetoed many of Gale's personnel proposals and openly stated, "I did not see that Dr. Gale could perform any useful services." Gale reported back to Washington that Gauss "proved particularly obdurate in any form of cooperation with COI as a government organ."[69] By April 1942, Gale had exhausted his usefulness for Donovan. The KMT hated him; Gauss hated him; even Stanley Hornbeck in the State Department finally acknowledged that Gale was "generally a minor disaster."[70]

But the worst news to Donovan by now was not Gale. It was the unceremonious flight of the British SOE from China; Chiang Kai-shek suddenly demanded withdrawal of Keswick's China Commando Group, the SOE enterprise in China. Keswick was no longer welcome in Chungking. This was a big blow to Donovan, for he had lost his prime partner in China for setting up an American clandestine network. This prompted Donovan's next strategic move to find another partner with whom to implement his overall scheme. Donovan had two choices now: Tai Li or Stilwell.

However, it was impossible for Donovan to directly approach Tai Li at this time, partly because of Gale's highly visible closeness with Keswick and Killery in Chungking, but for the most part because of a fierce harangue of British propaganda against the Chinese secret police chief. This propaganda campaign was of shrewd British design, tantamount to an Anglo conspiracy against American intelligence through ostensible friendship and cooperation. Its chief purpose was to discourage the establishment of a U.S. intelligence network in China independent of British influence. The major theme of this propaganda was that the Chinese had now suddenly turned extremely hostile to *all* foreigners, particularly British and American.

This turned into a very powerful weapon in preventing Americans from entering China alone. The British effort had grown out of desperation and fear over what the SOE people in London internally called the Chungking taint: "admiration of all things American and scorn for all things British."[71] SOE had to drive a wedge between rapidly rising American prestige in China and COI officials in Washington. The British had to convince Donovan that the Chinese were totally responsible for the failure of the China Commando Group and that the Chinese were not only anti-British, but also anti-American.

Erik Nyholm, the executive officer of the China Commando Group, promptly drafted a comprehensive report on the fiasco of the China Commando Group. Based on this report, on 13 April 1942, Keswick wrote a lengthy memo and immediately gave it to the U.S. naval attaché in Chungking, James McHugh, who was an enthusiastic collaborator with British intelligence. McHugh had from the beginning championed a dominant role for British intelligence in China. He had for a while virtually lived in the British Embassy. His secret cable of 27 January 1942 bluntly stated that "no separate American organization should be set up but we should co-ordinate closely with the British." McHugh in the same cable straightfor-wardly asked to be designated "as Liaison Officer for Colonel Donovan." But the Navy Department firmly rejected McHugh's request in February 1942.[72]

At once McHugh circulated Keswick's memo all over Washington, emphasizing the point that "China in her present mood will not allow foreigners to play with her guerrillas. . . . Until the Far Eastern situation changes we cannot expect anything better."[73] McHugh himself wrote abun-dantly during this propaganda tirade. He pointed out that any independent U.S. clandestine operation in China would be "wholly impracticable and should be abandoned forthwith for despite the particular anti-British angles involved, the basic implication affects *all foreigners*."[74]

But Donovan now understood the "Chungking taint." Whatever effect the British line had on COI is not exactly known; this British effort to sway Donovan was going to continue for a long while. Donovan's only remaining choice for a "partner" was General Stilwell, who arrived in China in early March 1942 to be Chiang Kai-shek's chief of staff. Stilwell was to be the most senior U.S. military official in China. Just two days after the with-drawal of the British China Commando Group from China, on 22 April 1942, the U.S. Coordinator of Information activated an American special operations group to China led by a captain named Carl Eifler, who was chosen by General Stilwell.[75]

COI/China and the Coming of Stilwell

Stilwell's appearance in the picture of American clandestine ac-tivities in China was an important event in the history of OSS. It reflected a fundamental ambivalence that would plague OSS throughout the war: who would command the field teams of OSS, a theater commander such as Stilwell, or Donovan in Washington? Stilwell's mentor was George Mar-shall, whose military philosophy was the "unity of command."[76] The over-whelming emphasis of this philosophy led Stilwell to centralize his command over all American personnel in China—an effort not much liked by all the U.S. agencies in Chungking. Resistance created considerable con-fusion. To Donovan, the opacity of command lines for the OSS field teams created a dual loyalty that constantly pestered him in Washington; Donovan was forced to spend most of his time traveling around the world consolidating his own authority.

Moreover, the conflict over command between theater commander and Donovan addressed an even more sensitive issue: the nature and role of OSS intelligence operations. There was no doubt in Donovan's mind about this question: his people should collect information that had *strategic* value to the U.S. government. But the military theater command overwhelmingly demanded the OSS field team perform only *tactical* tasks, such as determining the enemy's order of battle fifty miles ahead of the U.S. troops or interpreting photographs of enemy airdromes.

This struggle over strategic versus tactical intelligence was waged from day one of Donovan's tenure. His very first proposal for Roosevelt was entitled "Memorandum of Establishment of Service of Strategic Information." The original White House draft of Roosevelt's order (25 June 1941) had the title, "Military Order Designating a Coordinator of Strategic Information." However, the military, especially George Marshall, vehemently objected to such wording. As a result, the two most sensitive words, *military* and *strategic,* were struck out. *Strategic,* mentioned six times in the original order, was thrown out entirely, and the final order of 11 July 1941 simply reads "Order Designating a Coordinator of Information"—nonmilitary, nonstrategic.[77]

The conflict between Stilwell and Donovan over command began almost immediately after Stilwell's appointment to go to China in mid-January 1942. It started with a rather personal matter that shows once again the tenacity of the struggle for control and operational turf.

After Donovan reached Syngman Rhee in Washington and decided to operate a Korean contingent in China, he needed an officer to train a corps d'elite for the Koreans, and he needed this from the army, which was not normally cooperative. The suave colonel understood how to reach his goal in the most efficient way. He cautiously yet confidently approached the army chief of staff, George Marshall, for a person whom Donovan was sure he could get from the powerful yet difficult general. He asked Marshall for Lieutenant Colonel Morris B. DePass, Marshall's personal protégé in Fort Benning, Georgia, where Marshall had been a commander many years before. Donovan succeeded.[78]

In January 1942, DePass was sent to the SOE camp in Canada and started a training program for COI mostly oriented toward the use of Koreans in China. Before long, DePass submitted to Donovan a comprehensive, if not overly ambitious, secret intelligence and sabotage scheme called "Olivia." This proposal evidenced a strong British influence. It stipulated that a COI headquarters should be set up in the vicinity of Chungking and command intelligence and sabotage groups in Korea, Manchuria, North China, the Yangtze River, Formosa, Indochina, Thailand, the Philippine Islands, and the Dutch East Indies. It demanded that "key personnel . . . be given the full course of training at the British School in Toronto," and that each of the field groups "be headed by an English speaking foreign civilian."[79]

When Stilwell was appointed to go to China, Donovan wanted to know whether he could somehow send a combined SI/SO unit to Stilwell's new China-Burma-India Theater (CBI). Donovan asked Goodfellow to approach the temperamental general with the Olivia plan. Stilwell initially liked the plan.[80] This unexpected warmth from the general excited Donovan's top-level staff, since this meant COI would have begun to establish itself in the Far East, despite strong opposition from MacArthur and others. But the morning after, Stilwell suddenly changed his mind. A stunned Goodfellow went to see him and asked what was wrong with the plan. Stilwell told him that he had no criticism of the plan itself but did not approve of the officer Donovan nominated to head the project.[81] The officer Stilwell did not like was the author of the plan, Morris DePass—George Marshall's protégé at Fort Benning and an old rival of Stilwell's.[82] Goodfellow explained that he had submitted the name of this man following the suggestion of the adjutant general's office, which asked for someone with a knowledge of the Far East and an Asian language qualification. Goodfellow asked Stilwell whom *he* would like to see nominated.[83] Stilwell gave Goodfellow the names of two officers he felt were qualified for the job and stated that if either one was available he would approve the project. The senior officer died before his transfer could be effected.[84] The remaining officer was Captain Carl F. Eifler, an army reservist at the time in charge of a detention camp on Oahu.[85]

Eifler was Stilwell's protégé. Years earlier, Stilwell, then a lieutenant colonel, had been Eifler's instructor at an army training school in San Diego. At the time, Eifler had been an undercover agent at the Mexican border patrol narcotics section. A virile, flamboyant, ruthless, and enormous man, Eifler called himself the "deadliest colonel" in the U.S. Army.[86]

The effort to obtain Eifler's services for COI was a perfect example of the difficulty and obstructionism Donovan faced with the military at the time. After talking with Stilwell, Goodfellow immediately sent a message to Eifler's commanding officer in Hawaii asking for his transfer to COI. The request was denied. Desperate, Goodfellow sent another request. It was denied again. Furious, Goodfellow then sent a peremptory message ordering Eifler to report to "Colonel Goodfellow" and signed it "STIMSON," forging the secretary of war's signature.[87] Eifler hurriedly came to Washington and took over the affairs from DePass.[88]

Fig. 3. Colonel Carl Eifler, third from left, wearing tie, head of OSS Detachment 101, shown escorting a group of rescued Allied airmen who had been downed near the waters of Rangoon (courtesy of the family of Admiral Milton Miles)

Donovan would not easily bow to any manipulation of personnel control. The shrewd colonel adopted a countermeasure aimed at reducing COI's reliance on the personal relationship between Stilwell and Eifler. Donovan immediately dispatched several COI loyalists to Asia to serve under Eifler. Among them were Captain John S. Coughlin, head of "a rival company in Eifler's regiment on Oahu"; Coughlin's confidant, William

Peers; and "Montana Chan," a Korean from Montana.[89] Thus were sown the seeds of a major conflict in the near future between the Stilwell faction and the Donovan faction within OSS's much celebrated Detachment 101.

The Ousting of General Magruder

Perhaps the single most important result of the Marshall-Stilwell military philosophy of unifying the command in the China theater was the defection of General John Magruder from the army to Donovan. While the unity-of-command theory was undoubtedly brilliant and much needed in the wartime situation, the implementation of this theory unfortunately resulted in enormous personal bitterness and political manipulation in both the United States and China. The victim of all this maneuvering was the reticent General Magruder, who had been in China since October 1941.

Magruder had a dual task in China: to handle U.S. lend-lease materials for China and to be an intelligence officer for the U.S. government. Both tasks rendered him enormous power. The growth of hostility between the British and Chinese underscored the importance of lend-lease supplies. U.S. lend-lease materials that had been designated for China before the attack on Pearl Harbor had been intercepted by the British in Burma, for they desired the Chinese quota to defend their colonial empire in the Far East. The British now threw out a card to play in achieving their goal: the Burma Road, which they could threaten to close at any time. Both Chiang Kai-shek and Magruder were acrimonious toward the British over this.[90] U.S. ambassador Clarence Gauss was particularly unhappy about this British strategy and openly protested to the British ambassador over the Anglo desire, in Gauss's words, "to use the Burma link in lend lease aid as a club over the heads of the Chinese."[91]

Stilwell picked up on this British policy immediately after his appointment in Washington. Ironically, the person who handed him the club to dangle over "the heads of the Chinese" was T. V. Soong, Chiang Kai-shek's brother-in-law and plenipotentiary in Washington. Stilwell was originally appointed the chief of staff to the Chinese supreme military commander— "In carrying out Chiang Kai-shek's instructions," he said, "I carry out command". But Stilwell's ultimate goal was to control the entire Chinese army, and this appointment would not satisfy his ambition. Stilwell threatened, in his own words, "Either they refuse and I don't go, or they accept [his command over the entire Chinese army]."[92]

T. V. Soong instantly heard of this threat. Quickly a tacit understanding tantamount to a minor conspiracy was worked out between Soong and Stimson, under which Magruder would lose control over U.S. lend-lease materials to China. On 30 January, Soong stated to Stimson, "I wished to confirm our understanding that the functions of the U.S. Army Representative are to be generally as follows: To supervise and control all U.S. defense aid affairs for China; to command under the Generalissimo all U.S. Forces in China and such forces as may be assigned to him; to represent the U.S. Government on any international war council in China and act as Chief of Staff for the Generalissimo."[93] Nowhere in the agreement did Soong ever overtly promise Stilwell that he could command the Chinese army. But Stilwell certainly understood how easy it would be now to reach his goal with the control of the "U.S. defense aid affairs"—namely the lend-lease materials that Chiang Kai-shek most desperately needed. Satisfied, he left for China in mid-February 1942.

This was the death sentence for Magruder's position in China. Why did T. V. Soong do this to Magruder? The answer can be found in the second function of Magruder's dual task in China, intelligence reporting. Chiang Kai-shek's regime was in large part controlled by the powerful Soong dynasty—his own in-laws. The Soong family consisted of an alliance based upon money and corruption few people could penetrate. Even Chiang Kai-shek's awesomely powerful secret police chief, Tai Li, frequently got himself into trouble with the Soong family because he was appointed by Chiang as the director of the Wartime Antismuggling Bureau and the Soong clique was the major smuggler at the time.[94] Magruder reported dutifully to Washington on the power and corruption of the Soong dynasty, particularly H. H. Kung, Chiang's wife's brother-in-law and the finance minister of China. Moreover, Magruder expressed in his reports excessive pessimism about China's ability to resist Japanese military prowess.[95] Those reports went back to Washington, where the trouble for Magruder originated and led to his downfall.

Soong was then an influential figure in the highest echelons of the U.S. government and one of the best political lobbyists of the time. Without much difficulty, Soong convinced someone in the top ranks of the army to send him copies of Magruder's reports from China so that he, "through his intimate knowledge of his brother-in-law, Chiang Kai-shek, could smooth over and adjust any differences that might arise."[96] The result was obvious. Soong grew furious with Magruder for his damaging reporting. This tension was further intensified by Magruder's extremely complicated relationship with international espionage in China, and Soong began to contemplate a scheme to get rid of Magruder and his power in China.

Soong's desire to remove Magruder came to fruition in mid-January 1942 when Stilwell spelled out his terms for going to China. Stilwell's own anchor man in the Pentagon, Colonel T. S. Timberman, had been ordered to personally pass U.S. military reports from China to Soong. Timberman confessed that Magruder's reports were also given by the War Department to Soong and "that the Chinese had been instrumental in getting him replaced by Stilwell."[97]

The clumsy handling of this Magruder-Stilwell transition astonished many. Magruder was left entirely in the dark when the deal was being made in Washington in January. He was not consulted either by army headquarters back home or by the Chinese. The extreme impropriety of replacing a high military official at the highest level of the U.S. military aroused a bit of sympathy from a staff general in the War Department.[98] On 20 January, Dwight Eisenhower summoned Esson Gale, who was soon to depart for China, to his office. He asked Gale to perform a tough task upon arriving in Chungking: to convey to Magruder a personal message that his approaching replacement by General Stilwell was by no means to be considered as any reflection upon General Magruder's highly appreciated services. Gale later reported Magruder's evident unhappiness to Washington.[99]

To make matters worse, the supersedence of Magruder by Stilwell was not officially announced even after Stilwell's arrival in China in early March. Magruder, who was "snubbed outrageously by Stilwell," sent a cable back to Washington demanding an explanation as to the status of his mission.[100] On 15 March, two months after the Stimson-Soong agreement, George Marshall finally told Magruder about it. Marshall's telegram to Magruder reads, "Secretary of War-T. V. Soong Agreement that one of Stilwell's functions was to supervise and control all United States defense aid affairs for China was included in Stilwell's directive. This latter directive canceled Magruder's original directive. Due to the changed military situation since issue of Magruder directive, Stilwell is granted complete freedom of action to make use of the personnel of China mission as he may deem appropriate in the accomplishment of his mission."[101]

Without any further instructions, Magruder sank into oblivion in China. He fell ill and was bedridden in Chungking for two months. The depressed brigadier general of the U.S. Army was abandoned by his own command in Washington. In May, John Magruder left Chungking for the United States. When he arrived in Washington, the army denied him a job in the War Department unless he would agree to accept the humiliation of being demoted to colonel. Outraged, Magruder looked elsewhere. While conferring on a casual occasion in Washington with Donovan about his experience in China and his ideas on intelligence matters, Magruder expressed his strong belief in the need for joint intelligence operations among different services, as he had advocated and put into practice so successfully in his most recent tour of duty in China. Donovan enthusiastically agreed and "assured him that the Office of Strategic Services was designed for just that purpose, and invited him to join the organization as its Deputy Director for Intelligence."[102] Thus began a new career for General Magruder, and Donovan gained the most able deputy in his growing intelligence empire.

For Donovan, the net gain from this initial clash with Stilwell was abundant: he sacrificed a lieutenant colonel but got a general. DePass eventually was sent by Marshall to China as the American military attaché and would play an important role in the future OSS operations there. Eifler joined COI yet maintained his loyalty to Stilwell, but John Coughlin and his man William Peers would soon successfully manage to get Eifler replaced. The best windfall Donovan received was undoubtedly the disgruntled and brilliant brigadier general just back from China, for Magruder would become Donovan's stalwart throughout the war and a powerful deputy director of OSS, in charge of all OSS intelligence services, including secret intelligence and counterespionage worldwide.

On 28 May, Eifler and his small regiment of about twenty men took off for Asia, and the field operation of Donovan's China saga entered a new stage. But before any of Donovan's China plans became fully operational, a dramatic alliance was being formed that would fundamentally alter the entire strategic planning of OSS in China: the U.S. Navy was negotiating an overarching intelligence project with China's Military Bureau of Investigation and Statistics under Major General Tai Li. That project had the potential to immediately freeze out any other intelligence operations in China, including those from the army, the British, and Donovan's fledgling agency.

CHAPTER TWO

Chungking Fog
Intelligence Warfare in China and a
Lost Opportunity for OSS

Stanley Lovell, chief scientist of OSS, whom General Donovan regarded with endearment as "a villain, a scientific thug with a sense of humor," gives by far the best summary of the diametrically opposed ways in which Tai Li has been understood by Americans: "No figure in World War II is more black, seen from one side; more white viewed from the other."[1]

To virtually all of the U.S. government agencies—other than the navy— Tai Li was undoubtedly the most controversial figure in China during World War II. To most people, he was omnipotent: one whose power was terrifying and dreadful, whose spirit was byzantine and evil, and whose obsession was to hunt down the good and progressive in China. As Barbara Tuchman succinctly sums up, Tai Li was "China's combination of Himmler and J. Edgar Hoover."[2]

At the same time, Tai Li was not without his defenders. Admiral Ernest King of the U.S. Fleet wrote that Tai Li contributed to the war against Japan "with distinction."[3] Milton Miles of the U.S. Naval Group China and deputy director of the SACO noted: "General Tai's greatness rest [sic] in his indifference to worldly fame and in his fearless stand against malicious opposition. A sincere and loyal follower of his leader, he had never boasted of his achievements, whose value could not be ascertained, he impressed people as being mysterious. Because he was entrusted with the job of uprooting corruption, he faced opposition and attacks from influential quarters. Because he was faithful to his duty, he had to shoulder criticism."[4]

To counter the U.S. intelligence community's claim that "the great majority of American officials who know him have developed a deep dislike for Tai Li both personally and officially," Tai Li's fiercest defender, Jeff Metzel of the U.S. Navy, argued that "very few do know him, but most of those who do have become his firm friends and admirers." Metzel further compiled a detailed list of Tai Li's love-hate ratio—more than three to one—among "responsible American and Allied Officers who know General Tai Li."[5] Ironically, even now in Communist China "the withering away of the state" has for the first time allowed biographies of Tai Li to be published that contain kind words and praises for the otherwise utterly "counterrevolutionary" "running-dog" of Chiang Kai-shek—the number one "public enemy of the people."[6]

No overall attempt will be made here to judge a character as complicated and controversial as Tai Li. At least this much was certain to most American wartime intelligence agencies, including OSS: first, as the initial report to Donovan on Tai Li and his organization concludes, "Tai's organization is very efficient and we can use it to great advantage—it is also considered utterly ruthless, and the inner circle impresses me as a bunch of cutthroats."[7] Second, both the passionate hatred and respect with which Tai Li has been described derive from one single fact: Tai Li amassed awesome power through his vast empire of wartime intelligence.[8] However, as ruthless and powerful as he was, Tai Li was never free of challenges and vulnerabilities.

The Cryptography War and Yardley's Chinese Black Chamber

In Chungking, a city one of Donovan's agents correctly described as "a hotbed of political intrigue and jealousy," numerous factions within the Nationalist regime manipulated each other in order to gain favor from Chiang Kai-shek.[9] Here, Tai Li's fanatical loyalty and complete devotion to Chiang Kai-shek undoubtedly earned him heavyweight status in the power struggle. Yet precisely because of the intensity with which the battle for political power within the Nationalists unfolded, Tai Li's rising role as China's intelligence chief evoked much jealousy and brought forth deadly antagonism. In the face of all kinds of challenges, this aggressive, ambitious, highly efficient and ruthless military intelligence chief of China appeared determined and unyielding, thus getting himself into serious trouble over many years. His chief competitors were in the Nationalist Soong-Kung faction—Chiang Kai-shek's in-laws. The chief battleground of this strife for power and influence within the KMT was the control of cryptography, or radio-signals intelligence, which proved to be the most valuable bargaining chip in Chinese politics.

Signals intelligence has been the most important asset in modern intelligence gathering. From Herbert Yardley's American Black Chamber immediately after World War I to Ultra and MAGIC during World War II, the decisive role played by the interception and deciphering of enemies' intelligence communications cannot be overestimated. The morality expressed in Henry Stimson's famous dictum, "Gentlemen don't read each other's mail," is the first casualty of modern warfare. In the case of China, Chiang Kai-shek had an unmistakable edge in "reading others' mail" in his wars against those warlords dissenting against the Nationalist Central Government. From the late 1920s to 1933, the Nationalist regime was seriously challenged by at least three major separatist wars waged by warlords Li Zongren in Guangxi (1929), Yan Xishan/Feng Yuxiang in the North (1930), and Li Jisheng/Cheng Mingshu in the southeastern province of Fujian (1933). To a large degree Chiang Kai-shek was able to win all battles against his enemies in those years because he possessed a smart weapon: the tools for radio interception and decoding of enemy intelligence communications.[10] This was the contribution of T. V. Soong, who later at the White House in 1943 boasted to President Roosevelt, "I have won two civil wars for Chiang Kai-shek by setting up an efficient decoding service which kept him posted about movements of his enemies."[11]

Chiang Kai-shek's reliance on intercepting and decoding his enemy's radio intelligence created fierce competition among different factions in the Nationalist regime. The first competitor arose from the C.C. (Chen-Chen) faction of the KMT, led by Chen Lifu and Chen Guofu, through Chiang Kai-shek's initial national intelligence agency, the Zhong Tong, founded in March 1928, under the KMT Ministry of Organization.[12] The chief task of the agency was to root out Communist moles inside the KMT. The Zhong Tong, headed first by Chen Lifu and then by Xu Enzeng (U. T. Hsu), both radio experts with degrees from the United States, started immediately to set up a secret network of radio stations nationwide and quickly grew to paramount importance.[13]

But the C.C. faction's effort to monopolize the Kuomintang's radio intelligence was rendered futile by one of the most dramatic episodes in the history of world espionage: Communist infiltration into the heart of this KMT intelligence apparatus.

The lack of sophistication of the KMT intelligence in the early days was indeed stunning compared with the savvy of the Chinese Communists under the enigmatic spymaster Zhou Enlai. As chairman of the CCP's Military Affairs Committee, Zhou Enlai had already established an intelligence agency for the Communists, the Office of Special Affairs (TeWu Gongzuo Chu) in May 1927.[14] In the summer of 1928 the Sixth Party Congress of the Chinese Communist Party was held in the Comintern headquarters in Moscow. It was decided at the meeting that an overarching intelligence and special operations agency for the CCP should be immediately established, modeled on the Soviet OGPU. For this purpose, a three-man Special Service Committee was set up in the CCP Politburo. Xiang Zhongfa, the newly anointed CCP secretary general, handpicked by the Comintern leadership, was a longshoreman in Shanghai and a boss of the secret society, Hong Bang, or the Vastness Society. He, along with Zhou Enlai and Gu Shunzhang, Zhou's protégé and a former bodyguard of the Comintern's special agent to China, Michael Borodin, oversaw an operational agency called Zhongyang Teke, or the special service section of the Central Committee.[15] This special service section under Zhou Enlai's direct control was put into action in China immediately after the Sixth Party Congress adjourned and the delegates came back to China. The special operations branch was led by Gu Shunzhang, a ruthless genius whose assassination team, the Red Squad, would terrorize Shanghai and other major cities in China in years to come.[16]

But the most astonishing success of the special service section was its secret intelligence branch, led by Moscow-trained Chen Geng. Within a year or two, Chen Geng was able to organize a most impressive mole ring deep inside the fledgling KMT intelligence.[17]

Through bribery, provincial connections, and other means, the CCP and Comintern agents in China were able to break into the web of complicated social and political relationships in the Nationalist apparatus. Undoubtedly, the most telling example of this was the three-man espionage team directly under the control of Zhou Enlai. This team, composed of Li Kenong, Qian Zhuangfei, and Hu Di, penetrated into the heart of the KMT government in 1928.[18] Li Kenong was put in charge of the KMT intelligence in Shanghai; Hu Di controlled the KMT civilian intelligence through various news agencies; and most importantly, Qian Zhuangfei came to head the KMT secret radio intelligence. These three Communist spies formed a special party branch, with Li Kenong as the party secretary. Following Zhou Enlai's instruction, Qian Zhuangfei, who the KMT put in charge of the recruitment of radio operators and decipherers, installed many CCP intelligence agents in Chiang Kai-shek's most secret empire.[19] In the end, Li Kenong became a decoder for Chiang Kai-shek himself in his supreme command post. All sensitive intelligence, including the actual codebook, made its way into the hands of Zhou Enlai and the Comintern agents in Shanghai. This spy ring was not exposed until April 1931, when Gu Shunzhang, Zhou Enlai's deputy, was uncovered in Wuhan by the Nationalists and switched his loyalty to Chiang Kai-shek. The moment Gu defected, Zhou Enlai,

following the Leninist Chekkaesque example of the Soviet Russians, or-
dered the immediate murder of all Gu's relatives—more than ten altogether.
Eight of them were secretly buried deep underground in a garden in the
French concession in Shanghai.[20]

The Gu Shunzhang incident was one of the most crucial events in the
history of the CCP. This incident wreaked havoc on the intelligence agencies of the Chinese Communists. The entire central apparatus of the CCP
and Comintern in China was forced to engage in an overhaul. A brutal
internal struggle, disguised as traitor elimination, ensued in Mao Zedong's
Jiangxi Soviet.[21] Gu's betrayal in 1931 forced the CCP to move its headquarters from Shanghai to Ruijin in Jiangxi Province, where Mao Zedong
had established a "Chinese Soviet Republic." It was from there that the
Communists were defeated in 1934 and fled on their Long March westward,
arriving in Yenan in 1936.

Yet for the Kuomintang, the Gu Shunzhang incident had two important
consequences for the factional struggle to control intelligence. First, the
exposure of massive Communist infiltration into the Zhong Tong effectively dashed the potential monopoly of radio intelligence by the C.C.
group. Now Chiang Kai-shek would not dare to contemplate a cryptographic scheme led by radio engineer Xu Enzeng, the KMT's top Communist hunter then in charge of the Zhong Tong. Instead, Chiang ordered
T. V. Soong's nephew, Wen Yuqing (Y. C. Wen), to work closely in
Chiang's own office as the head of an ultra secret group called the radio
affairs section (Dian Wu Gu). Wen was directly responsible to the generalissimo and exclusively deciphered Chinese codes used by Chiang Kai-
shek's domestic enemies.[22] This arrangement enhanced Soong's stature
within the Kuomintang because now his own man, Wen Yuqing, occupied
a crucial role in Chiang Kai-shek's decision making. T. V. Soong himself
was able to control this cryptographic project since he was the sole financial
backer of Wen's expenditures.[23] Second, because the influence of the C.C.
faction weakened in the KMT after the Gu Shunzhang incident, a brand
new intelligence group emerged, led by Tai Li, who had grown hostile
toward Chen Lifu and his people for, among other things, incompetence
and lack of absolute obedience to Chiang Kai-shek. In late December 1931,
Tai Li established a new intelligence organization called the Group of Investigation and Communication of the KMT Military Committee, or the
Ten Men Group.[24]

This new intelligence organization, composed of ultraloyalists to
Chiang Kai-shek, marked the beginning of Tai Li's great enterprise in build-
ing his secret intelligence network in China in the years to come. In 1934,
Chiang Kai-shek officially appointed Tai Li the director of the Investigation

Department (Diaocha Ke), in charge of military intelligence for his mobile stockade (military command post) in Nanchang.[25]

Tai Li had reason to be sanguine about his rapid rise as Chiang Kai-shek's military intelligence chief, except for one thing: he clearly understood that he could not get Chiang Kai-shek's utmost trust and reliance unless he dominated the art of cryptography that was controlled by Wen Yuqing, director of the radio affairs section and an ardent T. V. Soong henchman.[26] Thus an arduous march toward the monopoly of cryptography in the Kuomintang began, and this would directly lead to America's involvement with Tai Li.

Tai Li had to start from scratch. Immediately after his appointment as the Investigation Department chief, he managed to send four of his men to serve under Wen Yuqing, ostensibly to learn from him.[27] These four men—Zhu Liemin, Liu Baoyan, Yang Shilun, and Wang Huairen—formed the first core group in cryptography of Tai Li's impressive radio interception and deciphering endeavor. Tai Li also found a genius of his own to compete with Wen Yuqing—a reticent and shrewd man named Wei Daming, who was to become the most important person throughout Asia in deciphering Japanese military codes during World War II.

In 1935 the Japanese were becoming increasingly aggressive toward China, and numerous military skirmishes took place in northern China. An all-out southward campaign by Japanese troops seemed imminent. Chiang Kai-shek was therefore anxious to shift his focus away from domestic unification and rooting out the Communists toward resistance to invasion. Subsequently, he summoned Wen Yuqing and bestowed upon him a secret task: to set up an agency focused on intercepting and decoding Japanese intelligence communications. On 1 March 1936, with approval from Chiang Kai-shek, Wen Yuqing established an Inspection and Decoding Office of Secret Telegrams (Midian Jianyi Suo). For this, Wen was given the cover title of division chief of communications under the Ministry of Transportation.

This office was tightly controlled by Chiang Kai-shek and responsible to him personally. Within three to four months, Wen Yuqing broke the secret code of the Japanese foreign ministry; Chiang Kai-shek was elated over the achievements of Wen's office, which subsequently grew in size.[28] By the time Japan staged an all-out war against China in July 1937, the office had more than a dozen secret radio stations intercepting vast amounts of Japanese diplomatic radio communications.[29]

But to Tai Li, now heading the Jun Tong or Bureau of Investigation and Statistics (BIS) under the National Military Council, an old problem remained: Chiang Kai-shek handled his cryptography as a family monopoly. By 1939, only three people could have access to the top secret daily intercept reports from Wen Yuqing: Chiang Kai-shek himself and two of his in-laws, T. V. Soong, Chiang's foreign minister, and H. H. Kung, his finance minister.[30] This created serious consequences in the entire Nationalist military and intelligence apparatus; it not only hampered the strategic planning of military action by Chiang's generals but also accelerated a deadly competition among the many KMT intelligence branches wanting to break this monopoly.

At first, Chiang Kai-shek's chief of staff, He Yingqin (Ho Yingchin) asked Wen Yuqing to give him a copy of the daily intercept reports. Chiang refused to allow Wen to do so.[31] Thus a frustrated He Yingqin was determined to form his own interception and decoding apparatus to compete with Wen's office.[32] Wang Jinglu, division chief of communications under He's general chief of staff office, was ordered to begin intercepting and decoding secret radio communications of the Japanese foreign ministry. However, Wen's office had maintained a sizable advantage and far overshadowed He's achievements.

Starting in 1937, five major intelligence agencies of the Kuomintang regime—the Zhong Tong under Xu Enzeng, the Jun Tong under Tai Li, the Military Intelligence Branch (the Chinese equivalent of the G-2) under Admiral Yang Xuancheng, the Institute of International Studies under Wang Pengsheng, and finally the Inspection and Decoding Office of Secret Telegrams under Wen Yuqing—had begun holding monthly intelligence conferences. Most of the time, Wen's institute upstaged the others, simply because it had the best cryptography.[33] Within the KMT military and intelligence community, this situation embarrassed many and evoked strong responses; all were determined to find a way to end this family monopoly. At the time, the only frontier that could possibly produce a major breakthrough was a most difficult one: the Japanese *military* codes.

In this arena Tai Li emerged as a new star and the biggest threat to the old monopoly. As a first step, Tai Li started dealing with the Americans. In September 1938, after several months of a secret and tenacious search, the Chinese assistant military attaché in Washington, Major Xiao Bo (Hsin Ju Pu Hsiao), a chubby, bright man, approached a middle-aged, bald American in Queens, New York, named Herbert Yardley. Yardley was the father of modern cryptography, the legendary code breaker of Japanese codes during the Paris Conference and the Washington Naval Conference immediately after World War I, and the director of the American Black Chamber (MI-8 of the War Department). Disgruntled and destitute at the time, Yardley accepted a lucrative offer from his Chinese visitor.

Major Xiao Bo was Tai Li's man in Washington. He invited Yardley to go to China and work for Tai Li on a salary of about $10,000 a year.[34] In November 1938, Yardley, using the pseudonym Herbert Osborn, secretly arrived in Chungking, China's wartime capital. Immediately Yardley engaged in organizing what he called the Chinese Black Chamber.[35] Tai Li ordered Yardley to collaborate with Wei Daming in training a core of elite students to break the Japanese military codes.[36] In January 1939 the Chinese Black Chamber began full operations.

The ambitious Tai Li started grandiosely, recruiting all the Japanese experts he could find in China to work under Yardley. In the end, more than fifty scholars and Old Japan Hands joined Yardley's Chinese Black Chamber; about two hundred students were trained in Yardley's system of cryptography.[37] Before long, the Chinese Black Chamber had more than fifty interception stations and more than two hundred radio operators. During Yardley's stay of over a year, the Black Chamber intercepted two hundred thousand secret radio and telegram communications of the Japanese army, of which twenty thousand were studied and evaluated.[38] Finally, a major breakthrough came in mid-1939: Yardley and Wei Daming succeeded in decoding the secret code system of the Japanese Air Force in China.[39]

This was a monumental achievement. Chiang Kai-shek was delighted with Tai Li's success because it allowed China to establish an excellent air warning system against the ferocious air bombing by the Japanese. The fledgling Chinese Air Force and Claire Lee Chennault's China Volunteer Group—better known as the Flying Tigers—became entirely dependent upon intelligence obtained by Tai Li, which enabled them to avoid numerous disasters and achieve more effective evacuations before major Japanese air attacks.

Armed with this success, Tai Li undertook bolder actions to break the hold of Wen Yuqing's cryptographic monopoly. In early spring 1940, Tai Li approached Chiang Kai-shek and suggested that steps be taken to centralize efforts in China to break more of the Japanese codes. Under Tai Li's scheme, all the major agencies were to be merged. Chiang Kai-shek agreed to this on 1 April 1940. A comprehensive cryptographic center named the Office of Technological Research of the Military Council was formed. This was a gamble for Tai Li in his efforts to gain the upper hand in controlling China's cryptography. To Tai Li's surprise and dismay, Chiang Kai-shek chose Wen Yuqing as head of this office, but he also appointed both Wei Daming—Tai Li's man—and Mao Qingxiang, Chiang's confidential secretary, as Wen's two deputies.[40]

Although Wen Yuqing became the official director of the Office of Technological Research, Tai Li was too ambitious to let him run everything. Wei Daming brought in as many Yardley-trained people as possible to occupy major positions in the office. Before long, a clash occurred between Wen Yuqing and Wei Daming over personnel. In early June 1940, a very angry Wen obtained approval from Chiang Kai-shek to go to Hong Kong "for a medical examination." He never came back to Chungking.[41]

After Wen Yuqing's flight, Tai Li intensified his efforts to take charge of the Office of Technological Research. Wei Daming became the acting director and brought in many more of Tai Li's people. However, Tai Li's ambition to control the office backfired and brought forth revived opposition. Tai Li and Wei Daming's aggressive methods of installing their own personnel through the use of blackmail, threats, and other means resulted in a petition sent by many disgruntled anti–Tai Li people to Chiang Kai-shek himself. In March 1941, angry at Tai Li's aggressive actions, Chiang Kai-shek dismissed Wei Daming and appointed his confidential secretary, Mao Qingxiang, as the director of the Office of Technological Research.[42]

Mao Qingxiang was a political appointee without any technical background. After taking his position as director, Mao reshuffled the office personnel by hiring many of his own classmates, mostly young, European-educated liberal arts aspirants. As a result, Mao's actions were deeply resented by the technical experts previously installed in the office by Tai Li. This resentment became open after the attack on Pearl Harbor, when the volume of interception of Japanese radio intelligence increased dramatically. Tai Li's people openly displayed their growing disloyalty to Mao Qingxiang. Furthermore, Tai Li ordered his men in the office to harass and publicly humiliate Mao.

In mid-January of 1942, increasingly antagonized by Tai Li's abrasive assaults, Mao Qingxiang finally appealed to Chiang Kai-shek. Chiang issued a devastating order demanding all those within the Office of Technological Research who were affiliated with Tai Li's Jun Tong to withdraw: "All those who are from the Bureau of Investigation and Statistics are hereby ordered to withdraw from the Office of Technological Research by the end of February."[43]

For Tai Li, who was known for his fanatical loyalty to Chiang Kai-shek, this ultimatum constituted a great humiliation and one of the biggest setbacks in his political career. It was also a clear signal that Chiang Kai-shek might be losing patience with him in the fierce competition for control of cryptography. By the end of January, Tai Li knew that in order to win back face and regroup his people, he must break new ground and do so from a new direction. Once again, he eyed America. Yardley had gone back to the United States and was working for the Canadian government.[44] But the U.S. declaration of war against Japan now made it possible for Tai Li to approach American government agencies.

He had to do this carefully, though, because T. V. Soong had become Chiang Kai-shek's plenipotentiary in Washington and had intimate friendships with the secretary of war, Henry Stimson, and the secretary of the treasury, Henry Morgenthau. Tai Li had to find some American agency outside the influence of Soong to help him. As usual, he ordered his agent inside the Chinese embassy to find an appropriate agency in Washington that would like to cooperate with the BIS on intelligence.

Communist Intelligence and Tai Li's Turn to America

Although bureaucratic competition prompted Tai Li to approach American intelligence, there was another important reason for the eventual rendezvous of Tai Li with U.S. agencies during World War II: the infiltration into China by the Communist International in Moscow and its agents in Yenan.

The Soviet Union had a strong interest in intelligence gathering in China. When the war with Japan had broken out in 1937, Stalin had approached Chiang Kai-shek for cooperation. A joint intelligence project was carried out between the GRU, Stalin's military intelligence organization, and Tai Li's BIS. As a matter of fact, the Soviet Union was the first power to openly side with Chiang Kai-shek. From 1937 to 1939, Stalin sent several thousand Russian military advisers to China, commanded by several of his best generals. In addition, hundreds of the Soviet's best combat airplanes were shipped to China to help Chiang Kai-shek fight the Japanese.[45]

But the signing of the Hitler-Stalin nonaggression pact in late August 1939 fundamentally changed the international alliance pattern in the Far East. Japan's alliance with Germany brought an abrupt end to all hostile military actions between the Japanese and the Soviets. Stalin suddenly abandoned Chiang Kai-shek and withdrew all military aid from China. In the winter of 1939, Stalin invaded Finland and Chiang Kai-shek was instrumental in ousting the Soviet Union from the League of Nations.[46] In April 1941, the Soviet Union and Japan signed the notorious Neutrality Act.

The Chinese Communist Party ostensibly had no direct organizational connections with Stalin; it was only a branch of the Comintern, created by Lenin in 1919, which functioned for the most part as an intelligence agency for the Soviet Union rather than a military command post for world revolution. It is important to know that from August 1935 on the Comintern's international espionage organ, the Department of Overseas Relations (OMS), was headed by Russian delegates who were simultaneously NKVD watchdogs, such as Yezov and Mikhail Trilisser. From then on the espionage agency of the Comintern would be spying directly on behalf of the

Soviet Union.[47] Stalin's startling switch in policy brought Moscow and Yenan closer together. Mao Zedong was virtually the only voice in China vociferously supporting Stalin's pact with Hitler and his subsequent invasion of Poland.

On 1 September 1939, the day Hitler invaded Poland, Mao made a sensational policy statement publicly announcing his enthusiastic support for the German-Soviet nonaggression pact.[48] The *New China Daily,* the Communist party organ based in Chungking under Zhou Enlai, continuously put out articles and policy statements by Yenan and Mao Zedong defending the Soviet Union's pact with Hitler. Mao further praised the Soviet invasion of Poland as a "socialist peace effort" with the purpose of "liberating the eleven million ethnic Ukrainian and white Russians oppressed by the reactionary ruling class in Poland."[49] Zhou Enlai, who was in Moscow from September 1939 to mid-1940, arranged to have Mao Zedong's statement of 1 September translated into Russian by Shi Zhe, a Chinese Communist who had been an intelligence official for the NKVD for nine years. Mao's statement, bound as a pamphlet, was thus widely circulated in the Comintern headquarters in Moscow and was soon translated into German and French by the Communist parties of those countries. The Comintern mouthpiece, the *Communist International,* published a special issue for Mao's speech.[50] On 9 September 1939, the Comintern instructed the Chinese Communists in Yenan that all efforts must be made to attack the "Imperialist Bloc."[51]

Accordingly, in late 1939, the NKVD and GRU began a large intelligence buildup in Yenan. This was established under control of the Russian contingent, while the CCP provided selected Chinese apprentices.[52] At the same time, the Soviets opened a secret intelligence training school in Yenan, code-named the Institute of the Oriental Munich.[53] This top secret intelligence school was set up on the edge of Yenan city by the forbidden Date Garden, where it occupied scores of the famous cave dwellings. In addition, Kang Sheng's much feared Social Affairs Department (SAD), the Chinese Communist Party's intelligence and internal security agency, was also located here.

The school was Moscow's effort to train intelligence officers for Communist revolutions in Asian countries. The full training period was one year. Each class consisted of about three hundred students carefully selected by both the CCP and the Comintern headquarters in Moscow from Communists in China and many other Asian countries. The class of 1942–1943, for example, came from two groups. About 170 of the trainees were selected from the Chinese Communist Party; another one hundred or so were overseas Chinese, Indians, Indonesians, Koreans, Vietnamese, Japanese, and even Africans and Caucasians. The foremost rule of the Institute of the

Oriental Munich was the importance of maintaining utter secrecy about the school's existence, its organizational structure, and the content of its study.[54] Upon graduation, each student was assigned a job behind enemy lines to gather intelligence. During its five years of existence (1939–1943), the Institute of the Oriental Munich in Yenan trained a great number of Communist intelligence officers for the major countries in Asia, and all trained agents were directly controlled by the Russians in Yenan.

But this Moscow tie ought not to be overemphasized. Stalin did not personally like Mao Zedong, who seemed too zealous in his factional infighting.[55] Moreover, Stalin's Great Purge and Moscow's xenophobic attitude had affected various Asian missions to the Comintern, culminating in Stalin's March 1938 ban on all non-Russian-born Communists from directly serving in the Soviet intelligence and defense system.[56] Ironically, this provided Mao Zedong with an excellent chance to turn Yenan into a Mecca for "ethnic Communists." Ho Chi Minh of the Vietnamese Communist Party, Sanzo Nozaka of the Japanese Communist Party, and the chief of the Indonesian Communist Party all left Moscow and flocked to Yenan shortly thereafter.[57]

The duality of the Moscow-Yenan relationship was important. On the ideological and strategic level, Stalin and Mao were closely tied together. But Stalin's Russian chauvinistic spirit antagonized the Chinese Communists. Interestingly, both aspects enhanced Yenan's status in 1938, as is evident in Communist intelligence restructuring.[58] To compete with the independent NKVD/GRU intelligence presence in Yenan, which grew rapidly after the Nazi-Soviet pact, Mao Zedong responded with a swift overhaul and centralization of his wartime intelligence system. In August 1938, Kang Sheng was chosen by Mao Zedong to consolidate Communist intelligence in China. Kang was simultaneously appointed chief of two agencies: the Social Affairs Department (She Hui Bu, political intelligence and internal security) and the Department of Military Intelligence (Jun Wei Qingbao Bu, under the military council of the CCP).[59]

By the time the Japanese attacked Pearl Harbor in December 1941, three spy masters of the Chinese Communist Party had long established a massive triangular intelligence network covering essential parts, Japanese-occupied and not, of China. In Northern China, Kang Sheng operated the home base of Communist intelligence in Yenan, where the NKVD had complete access to intelligence reports at the CCP's Social Affairs Department.[60] In Japanese-occupied Eastern China, Pan Hannian ran a large espionage ring centered in Nanjing and Shanghai, which was deeply interwoven with the Secret Service of the Wang Jingwei puppet regime.[61] In the South and Southwest of China was Zhou Enlai's secret intelligence system based in Chungking, where Zhou had perfect cover as a lieutenant general in Chiang Kai-shek's military council. Under the pseudo–United Front, Zhou took charge of part of the wartime propaganda against the Japanese.

This large intelligence buildup by the Chinese and Soviet Communists based in Yenan was directly aimed at the Kuomintang. For example, Zhou Enlai in Chungking orchestrated a massive intelligence and political penetration into the KMT regime. By January 1942, in Sichuan, Yunnan, and Guizhou alone, five thousand secret agents under Zhou gathered information on "the major aspects—history, policy, personnel and activities— of the Kuomintang government; foremost among these is information about the normal conditions and emergent measures of the central and local government, particularly all the secret service agencies of the KMT."[62]

Tai Li's Bureau of Investigation and Statistics was the chief target of communist intelligence. First ordered into Tai Li's BIS was the Yan Baohang espionage ring organized by Zhou Enlai and Kang Sheng. Throughout the war against Japan, Yan Baohang—a suave, sharp, and very sociable person with valuable connections in Chungking—held high positions in the Nationalist government as cover. At the time he was given this spying task, Yan was working in Chiang Kai-shek's military command post as an adviser with the rank of lieutenant general. With excellent espionage savvy, Yan obtained many of Tai Li's top secret intelligence documents and forwarded them to Moscow via Yenan. In early June 1941, the German military attaché in Chungking, who mistook Yan Baohang for Tai Li's agent, leaked information on the time, nature and scale of Hitler's Barbarossa Operation against the Soviet Union. Zhou Enlai relayed this vital intelligence to Yenan on 16 June 1941, and it was immediately radioed by the NKVD team there to Stalin, who discarded it as "Oriental nonsense" and a possible conspiracy of Western governments to split the German-Soviet nonaggression alliance. When Yan's information proved correct in the early morning of 22 June 1941, a vindicated Yenan received hearty thanks and appreciation from Marshal Voroshilov of the USSR Red Army, in a cable addressed to General Zhu De (Chu Teh), the supreme commander of the Chinese communist military forces.[63]

In late November 1941, Tai Li's well-established cryptographic team detected an imminent Japanese attack on the Hawaiian island of Oahu. This vital piece of intelligence was immediately stolen by Yan Baohang, promptly dispatched to Yenan and then to Moscow. Later, Stalin was so impressed that he sent a personal message to Yan, via General Nicolai Roschin, USSR military attaché to China, thanking Yan for this wonderful intelligence report.[64]

Tai Li panicked in February 1942 when a seven-person Communist espionage ring was uncovered in the nerve center of his intelligence empire, the general station of telecommunications (Dianxun Zhongtai). Six of the agents in his own headquarters, including Lieutenant Colonel Feng Chuanqing, chief operator in charge of hundreds of radio sets and thousands of operators at the receiving end of Tai Li's intelligence system, had formed a secret Communist Party branch right under Tai Li's nose. This team was led by Zhang Luping, a young and attractive woman, who had been sent from Yenan by Kang Sheng's Social Affairs Department in the winter of 1939 and was operating directly under Communist General Ye Jianying in Chungking. According to the Chinese Communist official historian, "This Special Party Branch served as a dagger, stabbing right into the heart of Tai Li's Bureau of Investigation and Statistics." This is in fact an understatement when one considers what Yenan got from Tai Li: "personnel charts of the BIS General Station of Telecommunications, the distribution web of Tai Li's radio sets across the country, and their frequencies, wave length, and code books, etc., were all gradually sent to No. 15 Zenjiayan Road [the compound of Zhou Enlai and Ye Jianying in Chungking]. The secret tasks of several hundreds of radio stations and several thousands of operators were all in the hands of our Party [the CCP]."[65]

The uncovering of the Zhang Luping espionage ring in early 1942 enraged Tai Li. All seven CCP agents were immediately arrested and brutally tortured. Immediate execution for all was proposed by Tai Li, only to be vetoed by Chiang Kai-shek, who called for a reprieve.[66] If Tai Li had until this time only suspected Yan Baohang of espionage activities (which were shielded by Yan's high-level personal connections) the Zhang Luping incident certainly gave him unequivocal evidence of Communist infiltration.[67] Tai Li became determined to modernize and overhaul his internal security and counterespionage system at any cost. Such determination led him to join hands with American intelligence and establish the most controversial unit in the OSS/SACO enterprise—one that would eventually involve many internal security experts from the FBI, the narcotics bureau, the U.S. Navy, and OSS.[68]

Tai Li's Rendezvous with the U.S. Navy

Thus the beginning of 1942 brought Tai Li to the lowest point in his career. He had been kicked out of the Office of Technological Research by Chiang Kai-shek and had uncovered Communist intelligence penetration deep in his own organization. Now another event affected Tai Li at this worst of all possible times: the disastrous breakup of the British China Commando Group. In April, Tai Li expelled the SOE group led by John Keswick from China, resulting in a fierce British propaganda campaign against the BIS and Tai Li himself. This new British media and internal reporting propaganda blitz involved many powerful figures in the Chinese government, particularly the Song (Soong) family, which included Chiang's wife and in-laws, all of whom had been intimate friends of prominent Englishmen like Keswick.

Tai Li's relationship with the Song family was a curious one. On the one hand, all the Song siblings, with the possible exception of the youngest— Song Ziliang and Song Zian—were deeply engaged in the intelligence warfare in China, each maintaining an independent sphere of intelligence operations. The oldest sister, Song Qingling, was a convenient intelligence cover for international espionage throughout the war with Japan: many Comintern agents in the Far East were able to operate under her protection.

Song Meiling (Madame Chiang Kai-shek), T. V. Soong (Chiang's foreign minister), and H. H. Kung (Song Ailin's husband and Chiang's finance minister) each had a personal intelligence agency.[69] Thus every one of them had reasons to dislike Tai Li for the ambitious expansion of his wartime intelligence empire.

Among the Song siblings, however, Tai Li had a cordial relationship with T. V. Soong until the British China Commando Group disaster. Tai Li's man, the assistant military attaché in the Chinese embassy in Washington, Xiao Bo, was for a while simultaneously working for Soong. Soong had on many occasions helped Tai Li to secure foreign equipment and technology. But never did Tai Li completely appreciate T. V. Soong's apparent lack of sophistication. Tai Li always regarded Soong as a highbrowed Brahmin who cared too much about face and never quite understood Chinese political intrigue.[70]

But the China Commando Group incident served as a catalyst for the explosion of antagonism among the Song family against Tai Li. The British China Commando Group breakup was a total loss of face to T. V. Soong and Song Meiling, who had been close friends of John Keswick.[71]

But more important, Tai Li's deep hatred of the British epitomized a far more profound sensitivity in modern China: the changing Chinese views on tradition and modernity. The prominence of the Soong family in China resided to a large degree in the Chinese political snobbery that things Western were necessarily things modern and virtuous. Western connections, mostly American and British, had been the most expedient tool to justify and sustain a peculiar Chinese intellectual and political elitism since 1905, when the authorities in Beijing abruptly abolished the thousand-year-old imperial examination. T. V. Soong and his three sisters were all educated at elite schools in the United States. He graduated from Harvard in economics in 1915; Song Qingling was a Wesleyan graduate; Song Meiling went to Wellesley, and Song Ailin also graduated from an American school.

T. V. Soong's political stature was achieved partly because of his reputation as a master of foreign connections. Even in public life, he acted like a totally Westernized Chinese politician who spoke only English at all times with all people—the only exception being Chiang Kai-shek.[72] In contrast, Tai Li's education was entirely traditional. During his tenure as the head of the Chinese secret police, Tai Li spent an inordinate amount of money building for his agents a large library which only stored Chinese classics, particularly the *Four Books* and *Five Classics* by ancient scholars.[73]

The Song family had connections with the most powerful Western dynasty in the Far East, the Keswick-owned Jardine and Matheson Co. Tai Li's clash with John Keswick, who was then the chief of British SOE in China, was a direct affront to T. V. Soong, who controlled the reports to Chiang Kai-shek from Washington. Soong displayed open and angry contempt toward the rustic yet ruthless Tai Li, who had never studied in the West and had progressed only halfway through Chiang Kai-shek's Whampoa Military Academy in Canton. According to American intelligence reports at the time, Tai Li suffered from a "lack of a Western education and training, his ignorance of English and other foreign languages."[74]

The assault on Tai Li from the British and Song camps started quickly after the ouster of the SOE commando group. The U.S. naval attaché, James McHugh, diligently dispatched voluminous disparaging reports to Washington about Tai Li.[75] This propaganda effort added new absurdities to the already tainted reputation of the Chinese intelligence chief.[76] Recoiling from the enormous publicity assault against his intelligence chief and under great pressure from his in-laws, Chiang Kai-shek was forced to rein in Tai Li and punish him for his lordly behavior in dealing with the British. Right after the China Commando Group incident, Chiang appointed Tang Zong as his personal representative in charge of supervising Tai Li. In July 1942, Chiang Kaishek ordered Tai Li not to deal with any foreign organizations except American ones.[77] To Tai Li, this was not only the gravest humiliation, but also another unequivocal signal of his falling out of favor with the generalissimo.

As early as January 1942, Tai Li had realized that the only way he could possibly get out of his ongoing trouble with various forces was to approach the Americans, who had already declared war on Japan and had a sizable military buildup in China under John Magruder. First of all, in the cryptographic realm, Tai Li decided to regain his prominence by seeking cooperation with U.S. intelligence, particularly the Signal Corps. Second, to combat Communist spies, Tai Li was determined to overhaul his internal security system and modernize his counterespionage schemes. But he had to begin with the basics. He first needed large quantities of high technology equipment, particularly such coveted items as radio direction finders (RDF), in order to weed out spy radios in Chungking. It was clear to Tai Li that he could get these RDFs only from the United States. Third, to counter the propaganda portraying him as a rustic brute incapable of working with foreigners, Tai Li was desperate to work out a new scheme with the Americans to prove otherwise.

Before going to the Americans, however, Tai Li was clearly aware of the necessity of establishing a whole new set of principles in dealing with both his foreign and domestic rivals. First on his agenda was placing a stricter code of conduct on his future foreign partners. Herbert Yardley had been helpful to Tai Li, in part by teaching him some practical lessons about dealing with Americans. Most important was to avoid those who had a penchant to operate the Chinese, rather than to cooperate with them. Tai Li learned from Yardley that many Americans, particularly those who had been living in China for a while, treated it "like the Old West."[78] Throughout his stay with Tai Li, Yardley chronically complained and browbeat the Chinese. Tai Li knew that this must not be repeated in any future dealings with Americans.

In this connection, Tai Li was determined that only those Americans with a strong sense of discipline and self-control would be asked to work with him in the future. This was particularly relevant when it came to the issue of women.[79] When dealing with Yardley, Tai Li's biggest headache was over maintaining intelligence security without offending Yardley's seemingly uncontrollable urge for sexual exploitation outside the BIS compound. At the time, Yardley was famous for purchasing young Chinese girls as sexual slaves and organizing orgies in his own house, thus gaining popularity among some foreign journalists and young American diplomats in the U.S. embassy, where, a young diplomat once flippantly remarked, masturbation was "the favorite indoor sport." Among Yardley's most frequent patrons to his orgies in Chungking was his best friend, Theodore White of Time, Inc.[80] In the end, using threats and loud protests, Yardley had been able to force Tai Li to let him keep his own "comfort" cottage outside the BIS in downtown Chungking.

Second, in light of the fact that the United States had just declared war against Japan and was officially China's ally in a war against a common enemy, Tai Li would cooperate only with American governmental agencies and not with individuals like Herbert Yardley. Third, any new cooperative projects must be based upon the idea of reciprocity. Fourth, all British influence should be avoided. Last and most important, any foreign intelligence agency's cooperative project with Tai Li and his BIS must be completely void of Song (Soong) family influence, particularly from Madame

Chiang Kai-shek in Chungking, who shared pillow talk with the general-issimo, to whom Tai Li was fanatically loyal. In addition, T. V. Soong in Washington, who controlled virtually all high-level contacts with foreign governments, especially the United States, must be kept away. As we shall soon see, one of the most important conditions for Tai Li's agreeing to work with OSS was his insistence that "under no circumstances should T. V. Soong or any other Chinese agency in Washington learn of [the BIS-OSS cooperation]."[81]

Once again, Xiao Bo was Tai Li's choice to do the footwork in Washington. The first U.S. government agency Xiao Bo approached in early 1942 was the Signal Corps of the U.S. Army.[82] This was an unrealistic choice at the time, however, because the MAGIC operation had gotten under way; from the point of view of General George Marshall, complete secrecy about the existence, scope, and nature of this strategic interception and decoding of Japanese military codes had to be protected at any cost. In fact, only a handful of U.S. government personnel closest to the president were aware of this Signal Corps enterprise.[83] What was more telling was the fact that the Signal Corps deeply believed that all Chinese military signal communications were then being intercepted by the Japanese. This belief was held throughout the war by both the U.S. Army and the government. For example, on 30 August 1943, President Roosevelt directly told T. V. Soong in the White House that "our General Staff believes your (Chinese) codes are being tapped by the Japs."[84] The risk of leaking the MAGIC secret to the Japanese through the Chinese was too grave to contemplate. As a result, Xiao Bo's earnest request for cooperation was heard by the Signal Corps but "held in abeyance."[85]

Xiao Bo did not give up. He next went to U.S. Army Military Intelligence (G-2). Much delighted by the Chinese gesture, Sherman Miles started to negotiate with Xiao Bo in early 1942.[86] However, an unexpected event took place in Washington that ultimately halted the BIS–G-2 negotiations: the American post–Pearl Harbor intelligence shakeup—if not witch hunt—found its casualty: Sherman Miles. Miles was fired for opposing a new definition of the role of military intelligence following the Japanese attack on Oahu; he was succeeded by General George Strong.[87] Moreover, there was another aspect to the failure of Xiao Bo's G-2 negotiations. Tai Li was resented by some people in G-2 because of his hostile relationship with Wen Yuqing, who by then was in the United States working for T. V. Soong. At that point, the U.S. Army was preparing—at the request of Lauchlin Currie, the powerful presidential aide at the White House in charge of China affairs—to send Wen Yuqing back to China to serve the U.S. Air Force. This effort by the army was obstructed by General Zhu

Shiming, head of the Chinese military mission to Washington, who most likely had received instructions from Tai Li in Chungking that declared Wen persona non grata in China.[88]

Frustrated at having failed to gain cooperation from the ideal agencies— the Signal Corps and G-2—Xiao Bo then went to talk to his secondary prospects: the fledgling Coordinator of Information (later OSS) under Colonel William Donovan and the Office of Naval Intelligence under Rear Admiral T. S. Wilkinson and Captain Ellis M. Zacharias. However, though surrounded by a group of China Hands—such as Esson Gale, Norwood Allman, Charles Remer, and John King Fairbank—Donovan at the time had no idea who Tai Li was and what his extensive empire in China was like. Rather, Donovan was consumed by COI's own China projects, most notably the Dragon Plan, that were being worked out by his own scholars in the research and analysis branch under William Langer. Consequently, Donovan paid no attention to Xiao Bo's request.

A similar situation occurred in ONI, where Captain Zacharias was spending most of his time plotting how the navy could outrank the army in the mushrooming post–Pearl Harbor intelligence committees in Washington. Moreover, the sole representative of the ONI in China, U.S. Naval Attaché James McHugh, after being deeply humiliated by his failure to provide any inkling of the Japanese attack, was "moving around [in China] in a quiet way" to break, in his own unspecified manner, the monopoly of the China theater by the U.S. Army.[89]

As a result of this complicated situation in Washington, Xiao Bo reported, "Nothing came out of these contacts because both the OSS and the ONI had their own plans."[90] This setback distressed Tai Li in Chungking. Forced to lower his expectations, he went directly to John Magruder in Chungking, hoping to gain cooperation with the theater commander in China. But Magruder by this time had already become a lame duck, and his authority as the U.S. Army's top military officer in China was humiliatingly superseded by Joseph Stilwell.[91] Tai Li's offer of intelligence reports to Magruder in exchange for badly needed radio and cryptographic equipment were met with empty promises from the Army.[92]

Tai Li grew desperate. His search for help from and cooperation with all the corresponding agencies in the intelligence business in Washington seemed an exercise in futility. But then a totally unexpected turn of good luck came about for Xiao Bo. An old connection proved valuable. Xiao Bo had a personal friend of eight years in the U.S. Navy who at the time had very little to do with intelligence and espionage. This naval man was Milton Miles.[93]

Miles, also known in his close circle as Mary Miles after a once-famous Hollywood actress, was no stranger to the China scene. As a young man fresh out of the Naval Academy, Miles had been assigned to the U.S. Navy's Yangtze River patrol and served in China from 1922 to 1927, during which time he learned his meager Chinese.[94] Miles developed a sense of "respect and understanding for the Chinese which explained the ease with which he worked with them during the war."[95] After an eight-year interval, Miles again served in China on the Navy's Asiatic station between 1935 and 1939, when he became an eyewitness to the brutal Japanese invasion of China.[96] In early February 1939, Miles, then in command of the USS destroyer *John D. Edwards* in Swatow harbor near Canton, rushed his ship to the island of Hainan, which was being captured by the Japanese navy. Miles harassed the victorious Japanese with a deliberately confusing "What-the-Hell?" pennant.[97] Soon after that, the Japanese occupied the entire southern coast of China, including the port of Swatow. The Japanese ordered Miles's ship to move out.

Miles soon came back to the headquarters of the U.S. Navy and to a new job in Washington as secretary to the interior control board, where he had the responsibility for writing specifications for new ship equipment.[98] It was here that Miles met Captain Willis A. "Ching" Lee, director of fleet training, a member of the board and instrumental in vigorously promoting a China project that was soon to become known as the Friendship Project and SACO.

Willis Lee also had a keen interest in China, resulting from his duty on the gunboat *Helena* on the Asiatic station from 1910 to 1913.[99] After the Japanese invasion of China in 1937, Lee led an ongoing discussion during coffee breaks with a handful of naval officers who had had some degree of China experience; they traded sharp criticisms of the U.S. government's apathy and inaction toward the China situation. When Miles joined this group in 1939, on several occasions he brought along his family friend, Xiao Bo. Everyone, however, including Xiao Bo, understood these coffee klatches as simple socializing and a leisurely, sometimes boastful, mutual display of knowledge about world affairs—an intellectual exercise in disavowing American provincialism. But empty talk quickly turned serious when China enthusiast Willis Lee was promoted to rear admiral in charge of the interior control board. In the middle of 1941, Lee announced at a board meeting: "We know a lot about the German and British systems of making war, but so far as I can tell from the intelligence reports coming in, we do not know much about what precautions the Japanese are taking against the weapons that we have now. Do they know what we are planning? It seems to me that we should send someone out to China now, someone who may be able to obtain access to the Chinese Intelligence Services and who can find out about Japanese training methods. Also it may be possible to loan the Chinese some of our equipment to use so we can see how effective it is."[100]

Lee further ordered Miles to prepare for such a trip to China. Miles then went to talk with his friend, Xiao Bo, military attaché at the Chinese embassy. Unfortunately, Xiao Bo could barely see Miles and could not spare any time away from helping T. V. Soong arrange a major initiative: the Magruder mission under the U.S. Army. Miles reported back to Lee about the Magruder mission. Immediately, "Lee attempted to attach Commander Miles to the Magruder Mission, [but] he was informed by the War Department that the Magruder Mission was to be a strictly military mission and had no authority for a naval staff."[101] A Miles mission to China was thus killed for the time being and was not reactivated until the morning after the Pearl Harbor attack, when Lee unofficially ordered Miles to get ready to go to China pending clearance from higher authority. Consequently, Miles requested, through his friend, Xiao Bo, approval from the Chinese government to proceed to China.

By late 1941, things seemed very promising for Miles because Lee had been promoted to the post of assistant chief of staff to Admiral Earnest J. King, the commander in chief of the U.S. fleet. Lee immediately placed his China proposal on Admiral King's desk.[102] However, the overall gravity of affairs both in China and the United States right after the attack on Pearl Harbor far outweighed the significance of the Lee-Miles proposal. Miles's request to the Chinese government for approval and Willis Lee's proposal to Admiral King were met with utter silence; no response came for nearly two months. Suddenly, in early February 1942 several fundamental factors put the Lee-Miles proposal on the highest agenda in the Navy.

First and foremost was the formation of Admiral King's Pacific strategy, partly as a rebellious response to the success of the British in forcing the United States to agree to a "Europe First, Asia Second" policy. The British had a great deal at stake in America's decision-making process. The prospect of a close U.S.-China alliance during the war alarmed the British, who possessed vast colonial interests in the Far East. Churchill's strategy was to drag Roosevelt away from any intimate alliance with Chiang Kai-shek lest China emerge from the war victorious and strong enough to threaten Britain's colonial empire.[103] On 10 December 1941, three days after the Pearl Harbor attack, Chiang Kai-shek had proposed to Roosevelt the formation of an ABCD alliance (America, Britain, China, and the Dutch).[104] Days later, Churchill flew to Washington and presented Roosevelt with a counterproposal for an ABDA alliance (America, Britain, the Netherlands, and Australia), specifically excluding China.[105]

Another scheme of the British to isolate China was to push the Americans into establishing a bilateral strategy-planning agency without the participation of China. On 14 January 1942 the Combined Chiefs of Staff (CCS) was formed, consisting of the British and Americans only. Chiang Kai-shek was angered and humiliated, considering that the British military troops in the Far East at the time were suffering from a devastating defeat by the Japanese. Throughout the war, Chiang's tenacious efforts to have China represented in the CCS never ceased.[106]

Perhaps the most important result of Churchill's December 1941 visit to Washington was the acceptance of the "Europe First, Asia Second" strategy. Roosevelt reluctantly acquiesced, though many U.S. military authorities were skeptical about the strategy. Following Roosevelt's instructions, George Marshall sided with the top British strategist, General Sir Alan Brooke, and adopted a policy of "purely defensive attitude in the Pacific."[107]

This aroused deep resentment from Admiral King. In early February, Marshall opposed King's Operation Watchtower in the southwest Pacific, which ultimately led the resolute admiral to decide formally on a military strategy that was of an offensive, not defensive, nature in the Asian Pacific. This decision was both bold and brilliant, and perfectly reflects Admiral King's unswerving personal character and unusual talent for developing an overall strategy. As Samuel Eliot Morison writes:

> A hard man with little humor, he was more respected than liked in the Navy; his eagerness to get things done quickly with no necessary palaver, coupled with an abrupt and often rude manner, infuriated many Americans and dismayed his British opposite numbers. No officer on either side or in any armed service had so complete a strategic view of the war as King's. Neither General Marshall nor any of the British had time or energy to concentrate on the war in the Pacific, but King not only grasped that and the Atlantic War; he had a better strategic savvy of the land phases of the European war than most of the generals. Secretary Stimson hated him, Winston Churchill and Sir Alan Brooke hated him, Admiral Sir Andrew B. Cunningham hated him, many even in the United States Army and Navy hated him. But Tojo, Hitler, and Doenitz had even greater reason to hate King, because, with Churchill, Roosevelt, and Eisenhower, he was a principal architect of Allied victory.[108]

To execute his Pacific strategy, King placed the China theater on a high priority. He envisioned China as an indispensable base for a future landing of allied troops on the Japanese-occupied China coast. This required advance preparation in organizing intelligence networks and cooperation plans with the Chinese military. The only person readily available to accomplish such a task was the man Rear Admiral Willis Lee had recommended weeks earlier, Commander Milton Miles. Immediately after the formation of his Pacific strategy, on 12 February, King pulled out the earlier Lee-Miles proposal and authorized the dispatch of Miles to China.[109]

The second factor followed from the first. To realize Admiral King's Pacific strategy, quick and drastic efforts had to be undertaken to rectify a severe lack of weather intelligence in Asia and the Pacific. The chief of the U.S. Naval Weather Service in the Bureau of Aeronautics, Captain Howard T. Orville, "was most interested in the possibility of setting up small portable weather stations in the interior of China, or any other place possible, in order to get the weather information out of China to amplify his weather set-up at the time, because, during the period 1937–41 most foreigners were pushed out of the interior of China and out of contact with Chinese military circles." Captain Orville instructed Miles: "If you can get even occasional weather from any series of stations in China, it will assist us in completing our Pacific weather map in order that long-range planning can be made for carrier strikes in the Far East."[110]

The third important factor precipitating the Miles mission to China was directly related to the post–Pearl Harbor intensification of turf competition for intelligence control among the U.S. and British intelligence agencies. The creation of the Anglo-American Combined Chiefs of Staff (CCS) in January 1942 had started a British-dominated "committee game," as the well-organized and aggressive British overwhelmed their American counterparts, particularly in the Combined Intelligence Committee.[111] U.S. intelligence agencies, particularly the Office of Naval Intelligence, were hard pressed to elevate the quality and quantity of their intelligence worldwide to compete with their British counterparts in the Combined Intelligence Committee.

China became one of the obvious intelligence areas which ONI decided to reform first. But a cursory look into the ONI-China situation presented an even greater embarrassment to ONI in their contention with the British: much of ONI's intelligence from China came from British sources. This had a lot to do with ONI's sole intelligence channel in China, U.S. Naval Attaché James McHugh.

McHugh was the most senior U.S. intelligence officer in China. By the time of Pearl Harbor, he had spent a total of eighteen and a half years in China. For much of the 1930s, McHugh had dominated U.S. strategic intelligence in China, far overshadowing his rivals, including the curmudgeonly U.S. military attaché in Peiping, Colonel Joseph Stilwell. The sole reason for McHugh's success was his close connection with an eccentric Australian, William Henry Donald, who had been Dr. Sun Yat-sen's adviser as well as Madame Chiang Kai-shek's close friend and the embellisher of her English.[112] This McHugh–Donald–Song Meiling connection made

Fig. 4. Lieutenant Colonel James McHugh, left, U.S. naval attaché and onetime chief of SI/China for OSS, with Lieutenant Colonel William Peers, head of OSS Detachment 101 after Eifler (courtesy of the family of Admiral Milton Miles)

McHugh an important family friend of the Chiangs and provided him with daily access to them through games of bridge.[113] But this relationship had gradually come to an end after the Chiangs broke off their relationship with Donald following the Xi'an incident in 1936, when Chiang Kai-shek was kidnapped by two of his subordinates. McHugh remained a friend of Song Meiling but was increasingly kept at arm's length. As an alternative, McHugh cultivated British intelligence in China and found new sources from inside the British embassy. When Clarence Gauss became U.S. ambassador to China in 1941, he intensely disliked McHugh's presence in the American embassy. As a result, McHugh—still the U.S. naval attaché—left Gauss and moved into the British embassy.

ONI's intelligence from China was further weakened by the utter hostility against McHugh emanating from the rising star of China's intelligence service, General Tai Li. This was because of McHugh's intimate connections with the two forces Tai Li despised most: the British and Song Meiling. Awestruck by the warmth with which Miles was treated by Tai Li, McHugh later lamented that in his years in China he himself had never been allowed into Tai Li's inner circle, even though Chiang Kai-shek was his close personal friend.[114] Furthermore, McHugh was deeply shaken by his failure to predict the attack on Pearl Harbor. It was a humiliating intelligence failure, and he took it personally. In the months after Pearl Harbor, in letter after letter, McHugh apologized for his failure to the secretary of the navy and particularly to ONI headquarters in Washington.[115] As a matter of fact, McHugh was so shaken that he believed ONI was contemplating his dismissal.[116]

By February 1942 it was clear to ONI in Washington that in order not to be frozen out by the British in the Combined Intelligence Committee, a new American source of intelligence in the China theater must be found. The contemplated Miles–Tai Li setup would serve just that need. At the same time, threatened by the newly created Coordinator of Information under Donovan, the U.S. Army and Navy took joint action to check Donovan's expanded influence by creating a Joint Intelligence Committee (JIC), whose main purpose was to prevent Donovan's agency from gaining direct access to the Combined Chiefs of Staff and the Joint Chiefs of Staff.[117] However, in the Joint Intelligence Committee, the Navy badly needed more intelligence about and from China in order to provide an alternative assessment of the situation there, to check and balance the army point of view, and, more important, to obtain an upper hand over both G-2 and COI. The planned Miles–Tai Li arrangement seemed just the perfect scheme.[118]

Armed with Admiral King's 12 February authorization, Miles again went to the Chinese embassy and talked to Xiao Bo, who was in low spirits after having failed to find a willing collaborator for Tai Li in a joint Sino-American intelligence venture. Though the navy's Board of Interior Control and Milton Miles were not exactly what he had been looking for, Xiao Bo was elated at hearing of the high-level nature of the proposed Miles mission to China. He promptly reported back to Tai Li. Before long, a cable came from Chungking announcing that Chiang Kai-shek had personally approved the navy proposal to send Miles to China and that Major

General Tai Li had been designated as Miles's Chinese counterpart. This was the first time that Miles had ever heard of Tai Li. Xiao Bo then informed Miles confidentially that Tai Li was his real boss, but said nothing more.[119]

On 11 March, Admiral Frederick J. Horne, vice chief of naval operations, signed a secret order placing the Tai Li–Miles setup under the chief of naval operations and officially named the project Friendship. An initial $40,000 was allocated for this venture.[120]

In the meantime, Xiao Bo hastily changed the direction of his arduous search for a partner in Washington and focused on this newly created Friendship Project. Following Tai Li's instructions, Xiao Bo and Miles laid out the conditions for cooperation. On 27 March the first document on Project Friendship was drafted by Miles and agreed to by Xiao Bo. This document is an excellent example of international reciprocity. In it, each side laid out its primary aims in the operation and combined them into a mutually understood plan. Essentially, Tai Li's interest in the project was in cryptography and radio intelligence; Miles's was in weather intelligence and "Naval Mine Warfare operating in Chinese Coastal Areas." The document further describes the five specific aims of the project:

> (a) To organize Naval Mine Warfare Unit operating in Chinese Coastal Areas. The Coastal Areas will mainly comprise those that are now occupied and which are more readily accessible from the land via the Chinese Fishing Fleet.
>
> (b) To organize a Radio Intelligence Observation and Analysis Station.
>
> (c) To organize a Weather Information Setup, which will make available to us more information than we now have about weather conditions in the China Coastal Areas.
>
> (d) To organize Lookout and Information Stations, both in occupied and unoccupied China.
>
> (e) To organize a Sabotage Unit for work in occupied China in the Coastal Areas.[121]

Miles continued and set out his requests: "Since the main purpose of the Project is Radio Intelligence and Naval Mine Warfare, I am almost wholly dependent upon the Chinese Government for personnel assistance. At present, it is planned to have only two or three American Naval men to go with me. They should meet me someplace in India, in order to set up the Radio Intelligence Units as soon as possible. Most of the work will have to be done, however, by personnel who know the country better than any Westerner could possibly know it. It is, therefore, necessary that my Project receives the assistance of the Chinese Government to the following extent:"

(a) One hundred per cent cooperation between the Chinese and myself. I expect to keep no secrets and will return one hundred per cent cooperation.

(b) I must know that the persons with whom I am dealing are to be trusted for an all out organization against the Axis. I desire that the persons with whom I am dealing have complete authority, and that they are kept to a minimum in number for safety.

(c) The assistance of the Chinese Secret Service in keeping me informed as to the best operating areas and as to the safety of operation in various areas of importance to my Project.

(d) The assistance of Chinese Naval, or other personnel, to establish Coastal Lookout Stations for Radio Interception, Weather Information, and Lookout Purposes. At first, there will be no U.S. Naval Personnel available to assist on this Project, although the material will be furnished to us as soon as shipping facilities permit. Later U.S. Naval Personnel may become available, if the Chinese deem it necessary and advisable. I hope to organize these Lookout Stations, so that they are Chinese functions, because I believe they would be more effective in collecting information in their Country, than would Westerners.

(e) The assistance of Chinese Secret Service in ports of occupied China, in connection with the placing of sabotage materials inside merchant ships loading for Japan. Materials are being shipped to assist in this part of the Project.[122]

With these points agreed to, an office was set up in the Navy Department specifically for this project. Admiral Lee decided to elevate the Friendship Project to the highest possible level of authority within the U.S. Navy and take it directly "under the wing of the Commander-in-Chief" (Admiral King). Captain Jeffrey C. Metzel, a staff member in Admiral King's office in charge of fleet readiness, was picked as the anchorperson in Washington for the Tai Li–Miles setup.[123]

When everything was ready, Admiral King summoned Milton Miles to his office and personally instructed him as follows: "When you get to China, roam around in the country until you think you know the present situation. Then make your recommendations. In two or three years we will probably need the special help of the Chinese, especially in connection with establishing operating bases along the coast. Do what you can to point up that way. We know you will be successful, good luck!"[124]

On 6 April, two days after the Chinese had delivered an ultimatum to John Keswick for the complete withdrawal of the SOE's China Commando Group, Miles departed New York on a Pan-American Clipper en route to Chungking, together with journalist Edgar Snow.[125] At his stopover in India, Miles met an odd couple, U.S. ambassador to China Clarence Gauss and James McHugh, who were in India arranging an escape site for what they believed to be the imminent Japanese takeover of China's temporary capital, Chungking.[126]

Amid dense gray fog, Miles landed in Chungking on 4 May. Tai Li grandiosely greeted him—a curious gesture because hospitality for foreigners was completely antithetical to Tai Li's nature. Also uncharacteristic was Tai Li's invitation for Miles to visit the ultrasecret BIS lab stacked with modern spying and espionage devices.[127] Even more surprising, Miles was offered a position as a "director" of the lab.[128] A stunned and excited Miles rushed an urgent cable back to Admiral King on 9 May, only five days after his arrival in China: "Project Friendship supported by generalissimo far beyond previous expectation and with department aid in men material am certain of important result. Only urgent request team 10 to 30 officers men be sent now to China for transfer here. Men require select service adverse condition few comfort little foreign food bring available equipment and information start work upon arrival."[129] Immediately the U.S. Navy dispatched to China seven top radio intelligence cryptographers, including Lieutenant D. Heagy, Robert Dormer, chief radio man Clarence Taylor, and Clarence O'Neil.[130]

The Tai Li–Miles match in Chungking sent a shock wave throughout the foreign intelligence communities in China. Particularly bitter about Miles's impressive success in linking with Tai Li's vast intelligence empire were the British. General Sir Adrian Carton de Wiart, Churchill's private representative to Chiang Kai-shek, declared Miles to be "Britain's public enemy number one in the Far East."[131] John Keswick was also "very bitter against Miles."[132]

As for James McHugh, it was a great loss of face to see a newcomer completely superseding him as the most important American in the intriguing world of intelligence and espionage in the Far East. On 11 May a jealous and bitter McHugh cabled ONI headquarters in Washington: "Miles had been given inside track by Generalissimo and will work incognito directly under Gestapo chief."[133] Several months later, a deeply depressed McHugh wrote to Secretary of the Navy Frank Knox: "Commander Miles has gotten off to a flying start and has been taken completely into the confidence of the Chinese Secret Service. He has seen and done things already that I never thought any foreigner would be able to do. . . . Whatever the Navy gets in the way of useful information here in the future will be that which Miles digs out. . . . As for the rest of this show here, it is in the hands of the U.S. Army for better or for worse."[134]

A great enterprise thus began. Although this was indeed a lost golden opportunity for OSS's intelligence operations in China, Donovan was not entirely out of luck. While waiting in India for his China-bound plane, Miles by chance met a fellow traveler to China. Alghan R. Lusey, one of Donovan's secret agents, was en route to Chungking for unrelated secret intelligence business. What Lusey reported back to Washington about Tai Li and the BIS–U.S. Navy cooperation would fundamentally change the direction of Donovan's China plan for OSS's secret intelligence and special operations.

CHAPTER THREE

Donovan's Long March to Chungking

When Donovan was appointed as the chief of COI by Roosevelt to centralize U.S. intelligence, he began with an effort to control shortwave radio broadcasting to foreign countries, then a highly departmentalized endeavor under various bureaucratic agencies—FCC and the departments of state, commerce, the navy, among others. To consolidate these efforts, Donovan ordered Robert Sherwood, stalwart at the time and later a rival, to draft a proposal for COI control of all shortwave radio broadcasting.[1]

Donovan's strong argument for a centralized radio broadcasting system went hand in hand with COI's quick action in securing personnel and equipment for such an endeavor. Colonel Goodfellow was given the power to organize broadcasting centers on both coasts. NBC was asked to lend its experts and machines to COI. On the West Coast, central broadcasting and listening posts were quickly established near Burbank and at Stanford in California. The next logical move was to send someone to the Far East to set up secret radio stations in China to receive and relay COI's home-based broadcasting. For this Donovan turned to his fledgling New York–based secret intelligence division (SI), which was then, because of SOE's William Stephenson connection, under strong British influence through American business tycoon C. V. Starr.

An insurance and newspaper magnate in Shanghai, Starr was the owner of the American International Underwriters and publisher of the largest newspapers in China at the time, *Da Mei Wan Bao* and *Shanghai Evening Post and Mercury.* Starr had a British wife and his best friends were Christopher Chancellor, president of Reuters News Agency, and John Keswick of Jardine and Matheson.

The principal personnel of COI's SI branch in its early stages consisted of Joseph Hayden of the University of Michigan, Esson Gale of the University of California at Berkeley, Ernest B. Price of the University of Chicago, Alghan R. Lusey, and Starr, who fancied himself a fatherly and honorary mentor on China-related affairs for Donovan.[2] With Hayden elevated to COI's planning board, where he took charge of the essential task of training agents for the entire COI, and with Gale having been sent to China, the SI branch was heavily influenced by Starr.

Donovan's Three Wise Men Venture East

In early spring of 1942, Starr, the self-styled intelligence agent, had already worked out an ambitious intelligence plan called "the Counter Japanese Division of the COI."[3] The essence of the plan was to use Starr's own "company men" as COI agents, with himself director of the division. His insurance company and newspapers were to be used as cover to collect intelligence in China. The plan also called for establishing headquarters in New York and in Chungking, while regional offices were to be set up in Washington, San Francisco, London, Zurich, Calcutta, Buenos Aires, Rio de Janeiro, São Paulo, Lima, Kunming, Kugong, Guilin, Yen Ping, Jinhua, Zhengzhou and possibly at Sui Yuan.[4] Furthermore, Starr designated himself director of the New York headquarters and was about to dispatch his protégés, J. Arthur Duff and two assistants, Lusey and L. D. Carson, to China to set up the planned Chungking headquarters for the counter-Japanese division.[5]

Since Lusey had the specific technical expertise in radio, Starr immediately recommended him to Donovan for the radio post. Donovan at once began arrangements for Lusey's China trip. At first, the ever-vigilant State Department was suspicious of Lusey's background and reluctant to validate his passport because of his "unsubstantiated record."[6] Although J. Edgar Hoover of the FBI eventually investigated Lusey and presented the results to Donovan, doubts remained about Lusey in the U.S. high command, particularly in the mind of General Stilwell.[7] On 11 March 1942, Donovan issued an order appointing Lusey the "communications engineer" for COI in the Far East and immediately dispatched him to China to set up a secret shortwave radio system at the other end of the Pacific.[8] As an SI man under Starr, Lusey also had the secret task of facilitating the counter-Japanese division.

Lusey left Washington for China in April 1942. During his long journey to Chungking, Lusey encountered Miles. To Miles, Lusey was a harmless, lighthearted expert in radio communications on his way to China to try his luck; the two became fast friends in India and took the same plane to Chungking. Upon arriving at Chungking, Miles even decided to take Lusey along and introduce him to Tai Li as a friend. But the Lusey mission was not Donovan's only attempt in early 1942 to set foot in the China theater. He had to respond to an entirely unexpected situation: rapidly rising hostility toward COI from the State Department and the army theater commander in China. Perhaps one of the biggest mishaps of U.S.-China relations during this most crucial time in the twentieth century was the unfortunate pairing of two top American officials in China: Ambassador Clarence Gauss and General Joseph "Vinegar" Stilwell, two well-known curmudgeons famous for their short tempers and territorial zeal. The intensity of dislike between the two men is legendary. "There is a definite lack of confidence," one of Donovan's representatives in Chungking reported, "between General Stilwell and the Ambassador. Both of them clearly showed it."[9] Throughout the war, OSS had to tread gingerly between these two sour and jealous men. But at the moment, the one most opposed to Donovan's China plan was Gauss.

Esson Gale, Donovan's first agent to China, ran into stormy resentment from Ambassador Gauss, who had become violently resentful of COI's activities in China in his own sphere of influence as the top State Department official in Chungking. Although Gale's personal behavior contributed to the ambassador's hostility, Donovan and his deputies firmly believed that Gauss's attitude reflected that of the State Department, for "Gauss has the reputation of being very 'State Department.'" Gale's report noted, "It is the old story of the entrenched bureaucracy and its jealousies. The situation extends to the State Department itself."[10] As Donovan's agent reported, Gauss believed that "Gale was sent out to make some secret recommendations about himself" and that the ambassador would accept COI's activities in China "only when it becomes a direct adjunct of his own office." Gauss made it very clear that COI's only acceptable endeavor, such as the filming of Chinese publications undertaken by McCracken Fisher, was operating "the Foreign Information Service of the United States Embassy."[11] Gale took a somewhat philosophical view of his otherwise humiliating relationship with Gauss: "The tempest in a tea pot as to my designation and public status was just a bit of old friend Gauss' occasional bad temper."[12]

As a result, Donovan's field officer despaired over Gauss's intransigence toward COI: "I don't think he likes our organization at all. . . . Any man in our service who wants to work with some scope, freedom of imagination, directness of approach to the Chinese, and generally somewhat independently of mama's apron strings will have a hell of a time in China as long as Gauss is there."[13]

Yet Donovan could not afford to burn his bridge to the China theater by openly confronting Gauss. A great believer in personal charm and charisma, Donovan decided to replace Gale with an agent of gentler outlook, one charming enough to cajole the stiff and territorial ambassador. All things considered, Donovan found the ideal person at the research and analysis branch of COI—the young, bright John King Fairbank. On 2 June 1942, Donovan tested the State Department's reaction by suggesting that Gale be replaced by Fairbank, who would be designated assistant to the ambassador at Chungking and endowed with the innocuous task of procuring open publications in China for the Interdepartmental Committee (IDC). Ten days later the State Department reluctantly approved Donovan's suggestion but then refused to issue Fairbank a diplomatic passport. Two months later, holding a special passport sealed with the words "traveling on official business," Fairbank departed for China.[14] He henceforth acted as a double agent—ostensibly working for IDC under the watchful eyes of Clarence Gauss in the U.S. embassy in Chungking, but in the meantime secretly expanding Donovan's empire of secret intelligence in China.[15]

Yet what concerned Donovan most in China in the first half of 1942 was not Lusey's radio mission, nor Gale's problem with Gauss, nor Fairbank's planned sub rosa activity in Chungking. It was a major intelligence initiative Donovan had intended to pursue in China—the Dragon Plan.

After the attack on Pearl Harbor, Donovan ordered his China scholars in Washington to draw up a comprehensive intelligence plan. Several months of hard labor yielded the Dragon Plan, which in essence was the blueprint for an independent American intelligence system in wartime China, with Donovan in direct control.[16]

The Dragon Plan bore a great deal of British influence because the entire project was to "utilize the services of Mr. C. V. Starr and associates."[17] Donovan had to submit it to the Joint Chiefs of Staff for approval. He received fierce opposition from the military brass, most notably from General George Strong, head of G-2. The core of the army's objection to the Dragon Plan lay in the matter of command. The plan itself was deliberately vague on this touchy issue. Though the plan did require "approval" and "coordination" from the commanding general of the army in the China theater, it was clear that Donovan and his agency would have firm operational control over the plan's field teams. When General Strong was presented with the Dragon Plan and was asked for comment, the anti-Donovan zealot wrote a two-and-a-half-page rejection. While acknowledging the need to improve intelligence gathering in China for the U.S. military mission, Strong dismissed the Dragon Plan and offered an alternative: "An increased number of Americans working under the direct, current instructions of General Stilwell could offer the Chinese intelligence agencies aid in money or material in exchange for information needed by the United States." Where would the "increased number of Americans" under Stilwell come from? General Strong unequivocally stated that they should be G-2 and ONI personnel.[18]

But the inclusion of ONI in General Strong's comments was indeed disingenuous, for the army was not only anti-Donovan but also antinavy. Perhaps nothing irked the army more than the types of intelligence specified in the Dragon Plan, which overwhelmingly specified naval operations: "Information concerning maritime activities in Chinese ports and along the China coast; vessels in port; types of cargo which they are loading and discharging; the speed with which the Japanese proceed in handling the types of material on docks and in storage; the extent to which the capacity of docks and other storage space is being used and so forth. . . . Information concerning the movements of enemy naval vessels in and out of ports and up and down the coast."[19] In the major schism between General Marshall and Admiral King regarding whether or not the United States should take an offensive posture in Asia and the Pacific theater, such open intelligence initiatives favoring naval operations would undoubtedly smack of a navy-OSS secret alliance in offensive strategic planning.

For this reason, Donovan's Dragon Plan was snubbed by the military bureaucratic machine in Washington. By the middle of July 1942, Donovan saw no hope in getting his plan through the Washington maze and therefore resolved to send a high official from COI directly to China in hopes of gaining General Stilwell's endorsement. Doing so would crack the Washington stronghold of opposition from the bottom up. Donovan decided to dispatch the most senior Far East expert in COI, Joseph Hayden, to meet with Stilwell. Hayden, traveling with Fairbank, left Washington for Chungking in August 1942 to sell the Dragon Plan to Stilwell. Hayden's mission could decide whether COI would have any chance to operate in the China theater. Whatever Stilwell decided would determine COI's fate in China.

But the situation in China in the summer of 1942 was by no means as clear-cut as Donovan or Hayden might have thought. General Stilwell was embroiled in a nasty battle with General Claire Lee Chennault regarding command power over U.S. forces in China. Stilwell deeply despised Ambassador Gauss, in part because one embassy staff member who was fiercely allied with Chennault, Naval Attaché James McHugh, sent reports to such Washington dignitaries as Frank Knox and Harry Hopkins suggesting that "the war in this theater would be materially aided by the removal of both General Stilwell and Bissell and their huge staffs" and that Chennault be given full authority in the China theater.[20] Stilwell, in turn, warned everyone not to "open heart" to Colonel McHugh, his long-time rival and new nemesis.

In the meantime, the issue of Burma further agonized the Allies in the China theater. For Chiang Kai-shek and Stilwell, Burma was vital to China's resistance against Japan. But the British, who had their long-term colonial interest at stake in Asia, deliberately sabotaged U.S. and Chinese efforts to control Burma. Even the pro-British McHugh angrily reported to Washington that "the British deliberately lost Burma to Japs to weaken China."[21] Although Chiang Kai-shek and Tai Li had demanded the complete withdrawal of SOE's China Commando Group in April 1942, Keswick's people still tried to operate in violation of Chinese orders. "The British are bidding for reentry into China in every way possible," Miles reported.[22] As McHugh assessed the situation, "The British idea right now in China of utilizing their remaining Commando units is not that of offensive tactics against the Japanese to help the Chinese, but that of trying to help British citizens escape from Hong Kong and Shanghai."[23]

This already intense struggle for control of the China theater would allow no more outside interference. An additional unknown factor like Donovan's organization might aggravate the uncertainty. Hayden's contact with Stilwell in early September right after his arriving in Chungking failed to produce hopeful results for Donovan. Hayden reported that Stilwell was "not predisposed in favor of what we have in mind. . . . General Hearn, his chief of staff, and his local G-2 . . . were even less so." Hayden then went to consult Gauss about the Dragon Plan, which resulted in an equally dismal reception: "His views," Hayden reported to Donovan, "with reference to the possibility of carrying on our work in China are quite definite. 'It can't be done'; and it won't be attempted by anyone connected with his office."[24]

Unexpectedly, Hayden's Dragon Plan received an enthusiastic welcome in Chungking from the other major U.S. player in the China theater—General Chennault, who had developed a revolutionary air strategy that relied heavily on ground intelligence. Chennault's new strategy went against accepted wisdom of the U.S. Army and its air corps; the army followed the Italians and Germans in pursuing the Douhet Theory, that bombardment alone was self-protecting against pursuit attack and that successive waves of bombing over enemy territory would knock out all opposition. Valuable fighting experience in China during the era of the American Volunteers Group, as well as his cooperation with Tai Li's air warning team, had taught Chennault valuable lessons and forced him to challenge his superiors in

Washington. Chennault demanded that the Douhet Theory be revised: any air campaign must operate along with a ground reporting and warning net. Chennault's revolutionary idea was vehemently opposed by the army establishment and remained the core of all his squabbles with the U.S. Air Corps.[25]

In contrast, Donovan's Dragon Plan immediately attracted Chennault because it perfectly fit his strategy; all information the Dragon Plan sought to acquire was related either to Japanese naval installations, battle, and cargo ships, or to Japanese airfields and industrial plants—the exact targets of Chennault's small but highly efficient air force in the China theater. Hayden's meeting with Chennault in China thus went extremely well. Hayden reported to Donovan, Chennault "definitely said that he was interested [in the Dragon Plan] and indicated how extremely valuable quick information concerning enemy air and sea movements up and down the coast would be. For instance, if he could know that ten enemy planes had landed on a field near Hanoi this afternoon he could pounce on them before they took off tomorrow morning.... Chennault's idea is that from his position on the flank and rear, he can strike at everything the Japs send down to the Mac-Arthur-Ghormley area, or could, if he had more planes in China and he can keep on destroying them and their crews."[26]

Chennault's enthusiasm for ground intelligence excited Hayden, who drew the conclusion that "Chennault may be our best entry into this game," and that he "should be supported to the limit." On the practicality of the OSS-Chennault alliance, Hayden elaborated, "I am absolutely confident that with the equipment we have lined up we could give him much information of the highest military value." Further, Hayden reported that Chennault had "fought the Japs more successfully and dealt with the Chinese far more successfully than any other American."[27]

But Donovan did not go after Chennault to execute his China plan. Donovan understood perfectly well that a close alliance with Chennault would enrage the territorial Stilwell, who was bitterly bickering with the equally stubborn air ace, thus jeopardizing COI's chance to operate in China at all. After all, Stilwell had the most powerful connection with the War Department in Washington. Donovan also noted in Hayden's report that "the more 'regular' of the Army outfit [in China] and in Washington are 'horsing' Chennault around a bit,—cramping his style with regulations made without reference to conditions here and without full knowledge of war as it is now being conducted."[28] This worried Donovan, for he had his own battle to wage with the more "regular" army outfit in Washington and did not want to draw more fire by joining hands with another "irregular" like Chennault, who was considered the worst enemy of the War Department and the Washington establishment. Chennault later bitterly put his unhappiness in perspective: "I always found the Chinese friendly and co-operative. The Japanese gave me a little trouble at times, but not very much. The British in Burma were quite difficult sometimes. But Washington gave me trouble night and day throughout the whole war!"[29]

A Triangular Relationship

The most important reason, however, for Donovan's failure to heed Hayden's suggestion for an OSS-Chennault alliance in the fall of 1942 was something entirely unexpected: the extraordinary turn of events regarding Donovan's radio expert, Alghan R. Lusey, who had been in China since May to set up a secret radio system connecting Chungking and Washington.

Lusey met Miles in India and they both reached Chungking in early May. According to separately prearranged schedules, each was supposed to engage a different partner: Miles was to meet Tai Li and Lusey was to meet T. V. Soong's connections in Chungking, including Wang Shijie, the minister of communications. Miles's sudden rise to prominence in American intelligence circles in Chungking convinced Lusey of the value for Donovan of the Miles–Tai Li relationship. Lusey immediately started cultivating his relationship with Miles and promised to help Tai Li and Miles with anything related to radio communications.

When Miles received Tai Li's consent on 23 May to make a trip to the eastern Chinese coast, Lusey asked to join him. Miles and Tai Li agreed immediately. On 26 May, Miles and Lusey, along with a dozen or so of Tai Li's agents, left Chungking in a Dodge truck for Pucheng, Fujian Province, more than a thousand miles east of Chungking, where they were to meet Tai Li in about ten days. When the party arrived at Pucheng and met Tai Li, having crossed Japanese-occupied territories, both Lusey and Miles were surprised to witness the vastness and efficiency of Tai Li's wartime intelligence system. Tai Li's agents from all over the Far East—Shanghai, Fuzhou, Xiamen, Hong Kong, Canton, and even agents from Japan with access to the Japanese Imperial Palace, converged on this obscure village to report to him. Miles recorded his feelings at Tai Li's briefing: "As I listened, my admiration for General Tai's organization and personal ability increased. In fact, by the time we began to make our plans to move on, my belief in Tai Li, as well as in his Secret Service and his guerrillas, had so increased my confidence in the organization I hoped to be able to create that wider plans began to evolve than any that had previously entered my head."[30]

During the visit, Japanese intelligence got a tip from its Chinese collaborators that Tai Li and some Americans were in the coastal area. Before long, eleven Japanese two-engine bombers flew over Pucheng and ferociously bombed and machine-gunned the little town, forcing Tai Li, Miles, Lusey, and their entourage to hide in the nearby rice paddies. If Miles had not by this time formed a clear idea what the "wider plans" he mentioned in his memo might be, Tai Li certainly had. In the rice paddy, an accommodation was reached between the Chinese secret police and the United States Navy, as Miles vividly described:

> General Tai showed no useless anger. He, too, was watching the circling bombers but he had other thoughts in mind. He turned presently toward Eddie Liu [the interpreter] and spoke to him in Chinese.
>
> He referred to me, and used my honorable new Chinese name which in this case, took the form of "Winter Plum Blossom Mister."
>
> "Tell Mei Shen-tung," he said, "that I would like to have him arm fifty thousand of my guerrillas and train them to fight the Japanese. Can he do it?"
>
> I thought I had heard that straight but I listened carefully while Eddie translated. This business of conversing in two languages gives convenient intervals for thinking.
>
> "The United States wants many things in China," he went on, "—weather reports from the north and west to guide your planes and ships at sea—information about Japanese intentions and operations—mines in our channels and harbors—ship watchers on our coast—and radio stations to send this information."
>
> He paused while Eddie Liu translated.
>
> "I have fifty thousand good men. . . . They have been chosen from among those who have most reason to hate the Japanese invader. But they are armed only with what they have been able to make or capture and most of them are almost untrained. But if we are able to give you all you ask for, your operations will need to be protected and you cannot bring in enough men for that. So, if my men could be armed and trained, they could not only protect your operations but could work for China, too."
>
> My mind was filled with a jumble of thoughts as Eddie Liu made his meticulous translation. . . . Here, surely, was a proposition that demanded careful consideration. . . . What a situation, I thought, for a land-locked naval officer! I had reached China—alone—only a month before. Yet here was I, sitting out a bombing attack in a rice paddy with the country's most inaccessible general—one who rarely permitted himself even to meet a foreigner. And more remarkable still, he was actually

offering a most unexpected kind of partnership in a fifty-thousand-man army!

"Would your country allow you," he asked, "to accept a commission as general in the Chinese Army, so that we could operate these men together?"

Could the U.S. Navy use a part interest in fifty thousand guerrillas? From the way the general had phrased his idea it was plain that I would be given some sort of inside track in their control. Training and equipping them would be a big job, of course, but what if we could manage to make it possible for them to gather and report the kind of intelligence we needed for the Fleet?" . . .

"O.K.," I replied.

It is an expression that means the same both in China and in America and no translation of it was necessary.

Out came the general's hand and I took it. This, I knew, was a rare foreign gesture for him to make.

This deal of great importance between Tai Li and Miles, made in such an extraordinary circumstance, overwhelmed Alghan Lusey, who stood beside Miles. Lusey cautioned Miles to be careful and to wait for word from Washington. Miles, however, believed that the generality of Admiral King's order to him—to "harass the enemy"—would cover this deal and that "too often there are no second chances. And in this situation, if I was not, perhaps, the best man for the job, at least I was here. The general had never made any such offer before. He might not again."[31]

Tai Li also approached Lusey for cooperation. By now, Tai Li knew that Lusey was working for Donovan, but only in the capacity of a COI radio propaganda expert, not as a secret intelligence agent under C. V. Starr. What Tai Li wanted most from Donovan was radio equipment and parts, because "the entire Chinese communications system is in grave danger of breaking down due to the lack of essential spare parts with which to keep the existing services going."[32]

A second reason Lusey appealed to Tai Li was that both shared a keen interest in establishing a radio propaganda network in India and Afghanistan.[33] In fact, Lusey went so far as to offer to help Tai Li build a worldwide intelligence system based in India. Tai Li was tantalized by this great promise but warned Lusey that they must keep the British unaware of this OSS-BIS scheme.[34] To ensure Lusey's cooperation, Tai Li even made a deliberate effort to impress Lusey with the intelligence capabilities of BIS. The most coveted information in the summer of 1942 was intelligence on Japanese intentions regarding the Soviet Union, specifically, whether an attack was planned on Soviet Siberia. Tai Li leaked a top secret document showing that Japan would soon attack the Soviet Union.[35] He told Lusey, "Tell Colonel Donovan that I, personally, believe the Japs will attack Siberia before the middle of September; they may delay until October first."[36] Realizing that Tai Li had never given any foreigner any information, Lusey was deeply impressed; he dutifully sent lengthy reports back to Washington and requested most urgent consideration of Tai Li's gesture of cooperation.

However, at this crucial time in the summer of 1942, when the navy was making quick headway in China, Donovan was preoccupied with other things. First, he was still strenuously fighting for the survival of his Dragon Plan in the Joint Psychological Warfare Committee in Washington. Second, his approach to secret intelligence in China was completely dominated by British thinking. William Stephenson in New York and John Keswick in Washington, who had just been kicked out of China, convinced Allen Dulles, now chief of Donovan's New York SI office, that the best way to penetrate China was to recruit agents from the highest circles of Chungking officialdom. In fact, the British had provided Dulles with one name to start with, that of Li Shizeng. Thus the entire SI China branch in the summer of 1942 was busy recruiting the aging KMT octogenarian, who, the British had told Dulles, had a "direct line of communication, by special code, with Chiang Kai-shek."[37]

Third, and most important, Donovan was involved in the first half of 1942 in a bitter dispute with his deputies, notably Elmer Davis, as to the role of propaganda in conducting secret intelligence. To Donovan, moral guidance in propaganda did not exist; Elmer Davis disagreed. During a global war, Donovan argued, it was absolutely justifiable "to fabricate propaganda, rumor and news, and to disseminate the same, whether true or false, to promote or incite resistance, revolution, and sabotage of all kinds."[38] In brief, this argument was waged between amoral lawyers like Donovan, and moralist literati, such as Elmer Davis and Robert Sherwood. William Corson sums up the conflict: "Donovan clearly looked on propaganda as an instrument of modern war, whereas Davis considered its proper function simply the dissemination of facts to friend and foe alike."[39] When both sides exhausted their arguments and remained unyielding, the issue was taken to the White House.

Acting like a good-hearted cop trying to break up a nasty fistfight between wife and husband, President Roosevelt chose the easiest way out, divorcing the lawyers from the literati. On 13 June a military order issued by Roosevelt officially split the Coordinator of Information into two parts: the Office of War Information, or OWI, would "plan, develop, and execute all phases of the federal program of radio, press, publication, and related foreign propaganda activities involving the dissemination of information"—"white propaganda." The Office of Strategic Services, to be headed by Donovan, would handle everything else.[40]

This bitter split in Washington had a severe impact on Lusey's effectiveness in the field. Donovan regarded Lusey as a radio man clearly belonging to the literati group and paid no attention to his communications from Chungking. Lusey's glowing words for Tai Li's organization and his tireless advocacy for a link to the rapidly growing Tai Li–Miles alliance were completely ignored by his Washington superiors.[41] After the COI split, Lusey was left in limbo, not knowing which branch he now belonged to. On 1 August, at Miles's suggestion, Lusey left China for Washington to ascertain for whom he was working and to continue his crusade for a tie with the Tai Li–Miles alliance.[42]

Donovan's Great Awakening and a Bumpy Start for OSS

Upon arriving in Washington on 20 August, Lusey immediately set out to see Donovan, who was exhausted from fighting with the military brass and the literati and frustrated by Hayden's difficulty in dealing with Stilwell in Chungking. Donovan had almost forgotten Lusey and his mission, so he ordered Lusey to sum up what he had to say regarding this "astonishing development in China." Lusey dutifully obliged by writing the following memo to Donovan:

I have reported on this subject, both by cable and by letter, from Chungking, as well as in verbal conversations with you since my arrival.

My recent trip through the provinces in China has convinced me that Tai-lee has the only real intelligence service in China. It is extremely widespread. He has agents in all the main Jap-occupied cities in China, the Philippines, Indo-China, Batavia, etc., as well as Manchukuo, Formosa, Korea, and, at least until recently, in Japan proper.

He has been receiving reports from these agents by very crude short wave transmitters. These transmitters, in many cases, are either out of service, or their efficiency has been greatly reduced due to the lack of spare parts.

His guerrilla and sabotage activities have practically ceased due to the lack of materials. I have [with Miles] worked out a system to greatly improve his communications system, and have promised to try and get him the necessary equipment and materials for communications and sabotage.

Before I left I asked him if he would consider some kind of an exchange arrangement, where we had access to his intelligence organization, or at least to his reports, and we would make reports available here to his representative. Additionally, we would help establish and maintain his communications network and would furnish materials and ideas for his saboteurs.

He told me that he would be glad to consider such an agreement. Upon my arrival here his Washington representative, Major Shao [Xiao Bo], called on me and said he had a cable from General Tai to discuss details of such an arrangement.

His actual radio requirements are small. The Navy Department has already sent part of it to Miles, for General Tai's use. I strongly recommend this arrangement be made. It would make available to us intelligence material that is not and has never been available to the U.S.

If you agree to this plan, I will submit a list of radio material to the communications department. Priority should be secured above everything else for this gear.

I would earnestly request that this memo be kept absolutely confidential from anyone other than the executives in your office. Tai-lee has asked me to be sure that this is done. He has already discussed this with Chiang Kai-shek and has the Gissimo's approval. Under no circumstances should T. V. Soong or any other Chinese agency in Washington learn of it. I am sure this request is unnecessary, but I am simply passing on Tai-Li's request to you.[43]

Lusey was debriefed by Ernest Price of the SI Branch for OSS. During the extensive debriefing, Lusey emphatically made three points that went directly against current OSS thinking with regard to its China operations— points that were to fundamentally change Donovan's modus operandi.

First, "neither American SI or SO operations can have any chance of success in China unless undertaken with the full cooperation of Generalissimo Chiang Kai-shek and General Tai Li." Second, any OSS operations in China "would be foredoomed to failure if they were undertaken in cooperation with the British or even with their knowledge, for the Chinese have become bitterly anti-British." Third, "the Chinese guerrillas are far more capable of carrying on SO activities in their own country than we could ever be, and it would be in our own interest and in the interest of the common cause of defeating Japan if we devoted our energies to giving the Chinese the material assistance which they so badly need, rather than attempt SO operations on our own."[44]

What Lusey had to say fascinated and inspired Donovan. For months, he had been fighting futilely with G-2 in the Joint Psychological Warfare

Committee. His last-ditch effort to get Stilwell's support had obviously failed, for Hayden's report clearly indicated that his Dragon Plan had been cold-shouldered in Chungking by the temperamental general. Now by a seemingly miraculous stroke, the navy had escaped the theater commander's control and could conduct secret warfare independently. This was exactly what Donovan had dreamed of. If the navy could somehow bypass the "imperial" U.S. Army in China, why couldn't OSS? Donovan suddenly realized that he had been moving in the wrong direction by sending Hayden to Chungking to beg for Stilwell's support. Immediately after reading Lusey's debriefing, Donovan cabled Hayden in Chungking telling him to postpone any further contact with Stilwell, pending Donovan's successful shift of gears in Washington.

Lusey's points also fundamentally woke Donovan to the British factor in conducting secret intelligence and special operations in China. Donovan had considered the Anglo connection a matter of symbiosis, something he had cherished since venturing into the intelligence field. But now he realized that the British SOE had not been completely truthful in telling him the story of Keswick's China Commando Group, which alleged that the Chinese were completely antiforeigner, British *and* American, and that the Chinese would be forever unwilling to cooperate with foreign intelligence organizations. The fact that the U.S. Navy had started an impressive operation with Tai Li, who furthermore beckoned in earnest for OSS's cooperation, educated Donovan about the Chungking taint. Donovan daringly decided to ignore the British warning and deal directly with the Chinese.

Moreover, Donovan could afford to do so now because the Joint Chiefs of Staff were about to approve a major demarcation between OSS and SOE vis-à-vis the global intelligence sphere of influence that had been negotiated in June 1942. According to this secret agreement, SOE's area of responsibility covered India, East Africa, West Africa, Gibraltar, the Balkans, the Middle East, Western Europe, Poland, and Czechoslovakia. OSS's assigned territories included China—prominently—as well as Australia, the southwest Pacific, the South Pacific, North Africa, Finland, and the Atlantic islands.[45] In addition, OSS and SOE would exchange liaisons.

What most attracted Donovan in Lusey's reports was Tai Li's claimed irregular army of 300,000 men, as well as his cutthroat image.[46] Born a romanticist, Donovan admired power, war, and ruthlessness. Like Tai Li, he was a strong advocate for unorthodox warfare that would include methods "to harass, confuse, disrupt, deceive, intimidate, frighten, injure . . . to corrupt . . . to fabricate propaganda, rumor, and news and to disseminate the same, whether true or false."[47] His sense of destiny also made him a staunch patriot.[48] Moreover, Donovan's most profound ambition during World War II was to lead guerrilla fighters—an aspiration mostly inspired by British commando tactics. He had sent long memos to Roosevelt recommending such organizations.[49] Partly for this reason, he had also requested his agency be placed under the Joint Chiefs of Staff, hoping that OSS, as a purely military outfit, would someday be allowed to conduct commando raids. Once when his field officer in China became frustrated by inaction, Donovan reminded him that an OSS officer should always behave "like a Lawrence in Arabia."[50] During the heyday of OSS expansion toward the end of the war, one of the major squabbles between Donovan and his chief deputy in the China theater was over the general's stubborn insistence on organizing OSS-controlled Chinese troops into "mounted commandos" and guerrilla groups armed with prick-eared attack dogs.[51]

But for now, Tai Li's roaming and ferocious guerrillas in Japanese-occupied China, as portrayed by Lusey, drew Donovan's attention at once. He was eager to join hands with the mysterious Chinese general in conducting guerrilla warfare. Furthermore, there was the obvious question of compatibility. To Donovan, Tai Li and Miles were an odd pair, expediently put together, each having vastly different goals if viewed from the perspective of tradecraft. When Miles was offered a position by Tai Li as one of the directors of the BIS R&D lab specializing in devices of espionage and secret intelligence, Miles felt awkward; when Tai Li asked him to train 50,000 guerrillas, Miles genuinely thought he might not be the right person.[52] However, each time Miles accepted Tai Li's proposal, despite the apparent incompatibility of his role as a U.S. Navy officer. Only OSS and BIS were compatible counterparts in the true sense, with their common nature as secret intelligence and agencies of sabotage and assassination.

Within days after Lusey's debriefing at the OSS headquarters, Donovan found himself in the Navy Department negotiating with Admiral King's assistant chief of staff, Rear Admiral W. R. Purnell, who had just succeeded Rear Admiral Willis Lee as the chief operator in Washington for the Friendship Project.

Although OSS had enormous problems with intelligence agencies in uniform throughout the war, Donovan had much less trouble with the navy than with the army. One of Donovan's top aides pointed out, "In all this intelligence agency bitterness, the Navy's ONI held a neutral, if not cooperative, attitude toward the OSS," while "the antagonism which Army Intelligence held toward OSS was at such a point that Major General George Veazey Strong and William J. Donovan were no longer on speaking terms."[53] Donovan's open friendship with Secretary of the Navy Frank Knox undoubtedly smoothed things over with the navy.

New to the job, Rear Admiral Purnell listened to Donovan's plea carefully and agreeably, and was easily convinced by the charming and glib Donovan. Purnell then went to talk to Colonel Xiao Bo, Tai Li's representative in Washington, who readily approved the proposed OSS-Navy-BIS alliance. Purnell then proceeded with Donovan to work out the details. The chief concern, of course, was the question of command. To this, Donovan agreed unequivocally that OSS would be subordinated to the navy, since the whole project was based upon Tai Li's liking of one particular naval officer, Milton Miles, without whom OSS or the navy could accomplish nothing.

On 19 September 1942, Purnell and Donovan finalized and signed a "Mutual Understanding Regarding U.S. Strategic Services in China" and a carefully worked out "Organization Chart—Friendship." The "Mutual Understanding" states:

> —After careful consideration of all the factors involved, it is agreed that the best interests of the United States and China will best be served by uniting all Chinese-American Strategic Services in China. To this end, and with the approval of the appropriate representatives of the Chinese Government, Commander M. E. Miles, the U.S. Naval Observer at Chungking, China, is agreed upon as the Coordinator of U.S. Strategic Services, China. Succession to command within U.S. Strategic Service forces in China will be agreed on after joint consideration of recommendations to be submitted by Commander Miles.
>
> —All instructions regarding United States Strategic Services in China and all reports from United States Strategic Services in China will be coordinated by clearing through the Project Liaison Officer in Washington and the Coordinator of United States Strategic Services in China.
>
> —All rapid communications will be handled by the United States Naval Communication System.

Two days later Purnell wrote an official letter of instructions to Miles, to be carried in person by Lusey to China, informing Miles of the Donovan-Purnell "mutual understanding." The letter states that Miles was thereby "assigned additional duties as Coordinator of United States Strategic Services in China" and that Miles's "project designation and use of external and internal addresses will remain unchanged."[54]

Donovan was jubilant at his easy success in negotiating with the Navy. Among other things, the new OSS-Navy-BIS setup could fundamentally change the entire OSS approach toward its penetration into China. Hayden's pathetic lobbying of Stilwell for approval of the Dragon Plan and Eifler's desperately trying to prove OSS's worth in front of a highly skeptical Stilwell all seemed unnecessary now. Donovan had found a back door to operating in the China theater through Miles and Tai Li.

Eifler's Washington operator, James R. Murphy of OSS, immediately notified Eifler in Chungking, "I think everyone agrees that we cannot operate under General Stilwell." Murphy told Eifler what had happened: "When Mr. Lusey returned recently from Chungking we all became convinced that there was only one way in which we could carry on our activities in China, particularly in S.I. and S.O. . . . . It simply involves very close cooperation with the proper Chinese organization which is a counterpart of OSS."[55]

As for Hayden's sales mission at Stilwell's headquarters, Donovan ordered an immediate halt and informed Hayden: "I am convinced that, as a practical matter, there is only one way in which we can expect to carry on our activities in China. That is by designating Commander M. E. Miles who is now in Chungking in the capacity of Naval observer, as the head of all OSS activities in that area." More important, Donovan instructed Hayden to tell Stilwell that "neither the plan nor the personnel involved should in any way be attached officially to him [Stilwell] nor should he be officially responsible for the plan or the personnel."[56]

Donovan also notified another main agent of his in Chungking, John King Fairbank, of the new development and instructed him to directly report to Miles and to "rely upon Miles for any decisions or directions which you may require locally."[57] As agreed upon between Donovan and Purnell, all other OSS missions in progress, including the Tolstoy mission to Tibet, and the Free Thai mission, were to be put under the control of Miles in Chungking.[58]

For OSS, a new day thus began.

CHAPTER FOUR

Of Schemes and SACO

This would have to be handled very carefully, as our whole show would blow up if the Chinese ever found out we were doing anything like this.

—LUSEY to DONOVAN

The hastily manufactured Donovan-Purnell agreement of September 1942 had fundamental flaws that bore grave consequences. While Purnell believed he had dealt well with Donovan, he forgot that Donovan possessed a first-rate lawyer's mind that thrived on conceptual ambiguity. All Donovan wanted from this new alliance was a cover for OSS's independent effort to build a secret intelligence network in China under complete OSS control. As Lusey put it succinctly, "For the present time we must depend on Tai-li's organization for our SI. . . . We are, of course, not content with such an arrangement; we want to build up our own organization."[1] One of Donovan's top aides further explained, "It is necessary that we make use of the proper Chinese organization, for reasons of cover, communications and protection. We must obtain and rely upon the Chinese cooperation almost exclusively until such time as it is possible for us to build up an independent organization."[2]

The SI Plot and Its Aftermath

Donovan conceded command over his SO to Miles only temporarily; OSS intended to use SO people as secret agents for SI. As Donovan told Hayden, "although Miles will be in complete charge, his principal work will be on the S.O. side."[3] As for his SI, Donovan remembered Lusey's membership in C. V. Starr's counter-Japanese division and thus secretly appointed him OSS/China's SI chief. Lusey, Donovan ordered, "will assist

Miles generally, but will also carry on other duties independently. S.I. work will be under his sole supervision and direction."[4]

Most significant was Donovan and Lusey's insistence that this scheme be kept secret from Tai Li, Miles, and Stilwell. As Lusey stated, "none of the [SO] men sent to China as instructors [for Tai Li's guerrillas] should be told they will eventually be used as SI men, or that they will be used for anything except instructing the Chinese SO people; when the time comes for them to do SI work, we will work them in." OSS well understood what was at stake. As Lusey elaborated, "This would have to be handled very carefully, as our whole show would blow up if the Chinese ever found out we were doing anything like this." He assured Donovan, "In my case, of course, the Chinese know that I am to act as your personal liaison with Tai Li. You may be sure that I will never give myself, or our plan away." Lusey further emphasized that "Miles should not be told of our SI plan; not that I don't trust Miles completely, but he is not a permanent member of our organization; he will return to the Navy. For that matter, I am taking an awful lot for granted in saying 'we.' "[5]

Tai Li would have been horrified had he known of such an OSS scheme, for he had been extremely worried about just such a plan. As early as 1 September 1942, Xiao Bo had gone to the OSS headquarters to warn of a possible conflict of command between Lusey and Miles. While acknowledging that "We have no right to suggest and really do not care who is to head American intelligence operations in China, so long as there is a head and different agencies do not attempt to carry on separate and unrelated operations," Xiao Bo emphatically told Colonel Ellery Huntington, Donovan's top aide in charge of SO for the entire OSS, and Ernest Price, SI/China chief of OSS, that what Tai Li "would like is a single agency or a thoroughly coordinated group of agencies operating a single project under the command of a single and responsible head."[6]

In particular, Xiao Bo explained why Miles and Lusey should each have a different role in the new organization. Price reported, " 'Major Shaw' [Xiao Bo] laid all his cards on the table in a way that Chinese seldom do. He said that for a year he had tried to find the agency or agencies, individual or individuals in this country with whom his principals could deal. When Commander M[iles] of ONI came to him a few months ago, he thought that at last here was the man and the agency with whom they could deal. They approved his project and extended to him every facility. They learned to like him and to trust him. L[usey] was taken along merely because introduced by Commander M. The Chinese were uncertain as to L's status but were glad to help him because Commander M endorsed him." In con-

Fig. 5. Alghan Lusey, second from right, with Tai Li, left, Rear Admiral Milton Miles, and a Chinese navy captain during a tour behind enemy lines, 1942 (courtesy of the family of Admiral Miles)

clusion, Xiao Bo strongly suggested to OSS the "advisability of making this mission a part of a single coordinated project for both SO and SI work," and made it clear that his boss in Chungking "would be very pleased if Commander M, with whom [he] already had had dealings and whom [he] trusted and respected, were to be placed as the head of our activities."[7]

Tai Li and Xiao Bo's concern over American command ambiguity in the pending OSS-Navy-BIS alliance compelled OSS officials to immediately propose a conference to discuss these issues raised by Xiao Bo during his meeting with Price and Huntington. After meeting with Xiao Bo, Price listed six major questions to be discussed by OSS, which proved surprisingly prophetic:

1. Can OSS and Navy meet Tai Li's expectation of a complete integration of American intelligence operations?—either Navy over OSS or vice versa, or parallel?

2. Who should head up OSS Operations in China?—Should this be CVS [C.V. Starr]? Should it be Commander M[iles]? In either case, should the head of the organization be given complete liberty to select his American assistants? Should all American personnel necessarily be approved by General Stilwell? By "Major Shaw's" principals?

3. Should OSS operate together in a single command in the field as one team?

4. What if General Stilwell disapproved of the entire project?

5. Relationship of SO and SI Operations—Are, or are not, SO and SI operations in China necessarily closely involved? Should, or should they not, be undertaken as part of a single project, even though under separate vice-commanders in the field?

6. Projects Involving Contiguous Territory—To what extent should the Chinese be apprised of or be allowed to cooperate in projects involving contiguous territory, such as Thailand, French Indo-China, Burma, which must necessarily be initiated in and based on Chinese territory? Must or must we not consider the Chinese as full partners in such operations also?[8]

Unfortunately, the entire Xiao Bo exchange with Huntington and Price remained unheeded by Donovan, who was determined to act secretly and independently in China. Donovan considered Price's questions regarding OSS command problems with the navy and the Chinese too sensitive even to be raised. Donovan was enraged by this meddling Old China Hand from Chicago in his own agency. Right after concluding the Miles/SO–Lusey/SI secret arrangement, Donovan, still angry, started to depose his SI/China chief from OSS. Price was accused of "opposing the policies of Colonel Donovan in China" and was asked to resign. In early October, a disgusted Price tendered his resignation and left OSS.

The fury around Price's unceremonious resignation did not fade away peacefully. On 8 October an angry Price sent a long letter directly to President Roosevelt. He charged that "Colonel Donovan was initiating, directly, a project having to do with China, certain aspects of which seemed to me definitely against our national interests." Price continued:

We cannot . . . carry on espionage or subversive operations in Chinese territory against the Japanese without the knowledge and cooperation of the corresponding Chinese agencies; they would soon discover it in any case, would resent our having attempted it, and would put our agents out of the country, as they did the British. We cannot hope to set up in China a completely independent system of radio or other communications of our own. I would go further and say that for intelligence or subversive operations in China, all plans should be worked out jointly, all operations of each should be known and approved by the other, and all information pooled. On such a partnership basis, I believe we can conduct effective intelligence and subversive operations directed against the common enemy. Without it, we shall be handicapped by Chinese distrust, and by our own inability to conduct such operations on our own.

The central message that Price tried to convey to Roosevelt was that "it is all very well to say that 'we must fight this war with our own men and our own weapons,' but we make ourselves the aggressors if we attempt to do so within the territory of a friendly nation without the full knowledge and consent of its government."[9]

Roosevelt was greatly disturbed by Price's charges about the OSS attitude toward China. On 15 October FDR ordered Lauchlin Currie, the Canadian-born aide he frequently put in charge of China affairs, to make an investigation.[10] Currie talked with Price, who reiterated his charges. Currie then rushed to OSS headquarters in Washington and spoke directly with Donovan and his deputy director in charge of SI, David Bruce. Both men were shocked by the quick and direct involvement of the White House regarding OSS China operations, but they soon regained their composure and responded to Currie's questions. Donovan and Bruce swore that "they would not dream of attempting to carry on military intelligence or espionage activities in China without the full consent of the Generalissimo; that they felt if they were going to get any information worthwhile they would have to work very closely with Tai Li, Head of the Chinese Secret Service, who operates directly under the Generalissimo." Seizing the opportunity, Donovan and Bruce also expressed their discomfort with Stilwell. Currie reported, "Actually they [OSS] were not able to do much as yet [in China] and were dissatisfied with the present arrangement whereby their representatives were responsible in the first instance to General Stilwell."[11]

Currie must have been completely won over by Donovan and Bruce, for the aide reported to the president, "Mr. Price seemed chiefly concerned with getting a job. I think my talk with him obviates the need of a reply to his letter [from FDR]."[12] Donovan and his SI people thus witnessed the quiet ending to this incident. Months later, Lusey, back in China, was notified by the Washington headquarters of this dangerous episode and was told that Currie was "completely satisfied with [Donovan's] assurance that we had made a satisfactory arrangement with Tai Li and did not intend to operate in any other way. Of course, we feel that as time goes on, Tai Li will permit us to have men stationed at various places with his people in the provinces."[13]

Unfortunately, the Miles/SO–Lusey/SI setup started to go wrong in Chungking from the beginning. The duplicity surrounding this project was just as troublesome as Washington's communications about what had been openly agreed upon between the Navy and OSS. While the Donovan-Purnell negotiation was going on in Washington, Miles in Chungking was kept completely in the dark. Even after Donovan, with Purnell's consent, appointed Miles as chief of OSS operations in the Far East, Miles was not immediately notified by cable or radio by Washington. Instead, Donovan and Purnell decided to have Lusey physically carry all the appointment documents back to Chungking.[14] By contrast, Xiao Bo, via secret radio, immediately informed Tai Li of Miles's new designation as OSS chief. Of course, Donovan promptly informed Hayden and Fairbank, both in Chungking, and Eifler of the new development via radio. The only major player not informed was Miles himself. As a result, Miles was baffled by Tai Li's subsequent cold and even slightly hostile attitude when Miles denied knowing anything about attempts by Eifler to enter China proper. For a while, Tai Li believed Miles was acting disingenuously, and was just another kind of SOE-style double-dealer.

The situation suddenly brightened up when Lusey arrived in Chungking on 13 November and presented Miles with Donovan's and Purnell's appointment letters, as well as information on the Eifler group and other projects in the Far East currently run by OSS.[15] Miles immediately showed them to Tai Li and cleared up the misunderstanding. Mindful of Stilwell's possible reaction, Miles conferred with the general immediately on the day Lusey arrived and gained his approval and support for the new arrangement and Miles's new designation. Stilwell "expressed his confidence in Miles and agreed that the project can only be carried out by Miles and by the methods he is using."[16]

While meeting with Stilwell, Miles expressed Tai Li's opposition to Eifler's operations inside China. Stilwell had been skeptical of OSS operations in China from the very beginning and so asked for Miles's opinion about what to do with the tenacious Eifler bunch. Although Eifler and Miles had struck a friendship upon meeting, Miles suggested to Stil-

well that Eifler operate in the Burmese jungle, a proposition Stilwell willingly accepted.

However, the Miles-Stilwell decision to confine the Eifler team to
Burma under Stilwell's control touched a jealous nerve in the British, who
feared development of an independent U.S. intelligence net in the former
Crown colony. John Keswick of SOE, now in Washington as liaison with
OSS, rushed a memo to the OSS headquarters demanding that Eifler
"should know his position and that he should be a sub-mission attached to
S.O.E./India and subject to their direction—they, in turn, being coordi-
nated with British Military Headquarters and the Government of Burma.
This would, of course, mean that he would NOT be directly responsible
to General Stilwell."[17]

Stilwell and Miles also proceeded to rein in OSS's other widely spread,
disorganized missions in the Far East. The Tolstoy-Dolan mission, which
had turned into a propaganda effort for British interests in Tibet, raised
eyebrows among Chinese officials; both Stilwell and Miles believed this had
to be stopped.[18] As to contemplated OSS missions to Thailand and Korea,
Stilwell and Miles agreed to put off dealing with them until later.

On 17 November, Stilwell cabled General Marshall in the War Department, informing him of the decisions made with Miles regarding OSS/
China. First, Stilwell approved the Donovan-Purnell agreement designating
Miles as the chief of OSS in the Far East. Second, Stilwell and Miles would
share the burden of taking care of current OSS missions in various places:
the Eifler group would be working on a specific mission under a directive
from Stilwell, while the Tolstoy-Dolan mission would be under Miles and
the Thai and Korean groups would be dealt with later. However, to satisfy
Donovan, Stilwell agreed that "all of these operations are under the general
direction of [OSS] representative in the Far East," meaning Miles.[19]

The initial enthusiasm from OSS in the Friendship Project overwhelmed
Miles and Tai Li. Donovan's grand strategy was to give them as many SO
men and materials as possible, in exchange for a foothold for future SI
operations. Perhaps not a single U.S. agency during World War II had a
more extravagant method of recruiting personnel and the ability to spend
money unabashedly as did Donovan's OSS. Donovan had authority to conduct "unorthodox war," which certainly allowed for using unorthodox
characters. Thugs, artists, murderers, scientific geniuses, movie stars, cocky
college professors all flocked to OSS. More important was Donovan's Congressional guarantee permitting millions of "unvouched funds" for the purpose of special intelligence.

Immediately after concluding the Donovan-Purnell agreement, OSS

started recruiting and dispatching its personnel to Chungking to join th
Tai Li-Miles establishment. Among them were the famous cartoonist Sau
Steinberg of the *New Yorker;* George Devereux, characterized by Jef
Metzel as "one of the world's most brilliant psychologists, specializing ii
exploiting superstition and taking advantage of mental weaknesses . .
[who] thinks like chain lightening and has 1007⅔ ideas per second;" anc
Frank Gleason, who was "the best grounded man in the U.S. on industria
espionage."[20]

One of the first items OSS offered to Miles was 100,000 single-sho
assassination pistols, called Woolworths and designed by Donovan's "scientific thug" Stanley Lovell. Metzel, the tireless naval general operator in
Washington, was impressed with OSS's enthusiasm, observing that "Col.
D[onovan] is 1000%. Col. Buxton, his #2 is the same."[21] The following
excerpts from Metzel's letter to Miles testify to the extravagance with which
OSS initially invested its money and personnel:

> • Our partners are gathering one Identification Unit complete with per-
> sonnel and gear. In addition to the fingerprint analyst I asked for two
> experienced FBI operatives—good advisors in close tactics and plain and
> fancy detection. . . .
> • Our partners are assembling a propaganda unit for you. Already are
> buying and sending broadcast station, receivers, records, projectors,
> movies, slide films, and leaflets to send ahead.
> • Our partners have deposited to your personal account ten grand each at:
> Chungking, Bank of China
> Kunming, Bank of China
> Calcutta, Bank of India
> Bombay, Bank of India
> Karachi, Bank of India, Australia, and China . . .
> • Our partners are buying you 500 wristwatches, ten to fifty busk
> grades—for coordination and good will. Also all other types of good
> will seed. . . .
> • Our partners are paving the way towards sending Jeeps and other
> useful items by time transportation is unclogged.
> • Our partners are sending ten tons plastic per month.[22]

Miles, in the field, had less reason to celebrate the generosity of OSS.
Starting from mid-1942, when General Stilwell, deeply humiliated over the
Burma fiasco, single-mindedly devoted his energy to the recapture of
Burma, control by theater headquarters over various U.S. intelligence agen-
cies in China quickly evaporated. Besides the normal interservice rivalry

among established intelligence agencies—the State Department, the offices of military and naval attachés, and so on—many newly created civilian intelligence organizations rushed to China, thus adding more turf competition and rivalry to the already chaotic situation. Particularly irksome to Miles was the Board of Economic Warfare (BEW) under Vice President Henry Wallace, who had been embroiled in a bitter turf war with many intelligence agencies, especially those under Jesse Jones of the Commerce Department. BEW was a clumsy clone of the British Ministry of Economic Warfare, a wartime intelligence agency charged with industrial and economic espionage that included making counterfeit money—an action that would have a major impact on the Chinese economy later on. Wallace's overbearing attitude toward the Chinese and the existing U.S. agencies in Chungking angered many, as did BEW's dogmatic and amateurish adaptation of British intelligence concepts and methods. Miles reported to his Navy Department operator: "The Board of Economic Warfare is busy antagonizing the Far East. . . . It is hopeless and makes the Ambassador, the NA [naval attaché], the MA [military attaché], and Chinese MID [military intelligence division] and the OSS all wonder which bureau or office in Washington will win the war single-handed first. If anyone can get the BEW to play ball on that subject we will be less foolish-looking out here. . . . Sounds like a bunch of kids to me."[23]

The initial excitement of being appointed OSS chief in the Far East began to erode from the very beginning for Miles. The first confrontation between Miles and OSS soon came when Joseph Hayden, still in Chungking, sent negative messages to Washington about Miles's relationship with Stilwell. On 8 November, five days before Miles received the detailed documents from Lusey, who was on his way to Chungking, Hayden had dispatched a cable to Washington claiming that Stilwell had seemed annoyed by lack of consultation from Miles about the project and that "Stilwell is not convinced that Miles really has the confidence of the Chinese."[24] This cable circulated widely in Washington. The Navy Department was disturbed by this development and radioed Miles four days later to request confirmation about Hayden's charges; in the same cable, Miles was reminded that "Stilwell's responsibility as U.S. Theater Commander requires he understand before giving precedence [to] your freight [the Hump Tonnage] or backing increased facilities. Suggest conference between Tai Li, Stilwell and you would promote cooperation."[25] Miles was enraged upon receiving this cable and regarded this as a stab in the back by Hayden of OSS. The next day, Miles hurried to see Stilwell, who gave Miles his unequivocal support and personal endorsement. Subsequently, Miles sent an angry cable to Donovan and Purnell in which he launched his counterattack: "Hayden's report of 8th demonstrates the undesirability of allowing miscellaneous people running around out here with too little to do. Situation here concerns only Gissimo, Tai Li, and myself with Stilwell being kept adequately informed. Can see no reason for conjuring phantom monkey wrenches into the works. My orders are clear and Friendship will either produce results or I will ask for my detachment. No further action or thought on matter necessary."[26]

Yet Hayden continued to make trouble in Chungking. As a former teacher, Hayden had many Korean students living there in exile. Since one of the key elements of the Dragon Plan had been to use Koreans in exile to conduct SI and SO for OSS, Hayden continued Gale's failed efforts to organize the Korean community in Chungking. This upset the Chinese, for, as Miles reported, "Tai Li [was] not very hot on Korea."[27] What was most alarming about Hayden's high-profile activities in Chungking was the fact that "Tai Li has become highly suspicious of his [Hayden's] activities," and that "the Ambassador, Stilwell, Gissimo, Tai Li, are unanimous in their disapproval of Dr. Hayden's activities."[28] As a result, Miles stated, "a couple of times I have almost ordered Hayden out of China. I don't want anymore enemies than the Axis can put out in the field,—but if Col. D[onovan] doesn't yank him pretty soon I will either ask for his recall or ask him to take over this job. He has unintentionally antagonized all military and naval officers with whom he has talked. Knowing that he was a direct envoy from OSS, I held back."[29]

If Miles thought Hayden's counterproductive activities in Chungking were unintentional, he soon heard the ominous footsteps of the deliberate Donovan-Lusey SI scheme. Donovan's official letters to Miles defined Lusey's role as follows: "I have asked Mr. Lusey to act as my personal liaison with General Tai Li. However this is not intended to limit your authority in any way as the head of OSS activities, nor will it constitute any division of authority. I believe it would be helpful if arrangements could be made for Mr. Lusey to make periodic trips between Chungking and Washington."[30] This was, of course, part of the OSS plan to secretly operate SI in China.

After Ernest Price's ouster in early October, Allen Dulles, Donovan's SI chief of OSS New York, immediately appointed a former Shanghai judge and businessman, Norwood Allman, as SI chief for the Far East. Allman had been a close associate and admirer of C. V. Starr; his appointment was entirely a result of Starr's recommendation.[31] This Starr-Allman tie enhanced Lusey's SI operations in China, for Allman would be Lusey's direct boss in the United States. Now the chain of command for OSS's SI/China was finally set: Allman in the United States as chief operator, Lusey in China as the field SI commander, who controlled agents like John King Fairbank, S. A. Schreiner, and Clyde Sargent.[32]

Undoubtedly, Lusey's most capable agent in Chungking was the young history professor from Harvard, John King Fairbank, who had various official titles as cover. He accomplished quite a lot in gathering secret intelligence through his vast connections with Chinese officials and intellectuals. Fairbank's SI operations were kept so secret from Tai Li and Miles that almost a year later Miles was still puzzled as to what Fairbank's real mission was. Miles wrote that "Fairbank was our local man out here whose business I don't know what it is, except that he is concurrently the IDC [collection of open publications] man, the Library of Congress man, the Cultural relations man, and in his spare time he snoops."[33]

The first sign of a backfire caused by OSS/China's modus operandi independent of the Chinese and the navy came when Miles discovered that OSS had been using a secret communications channel between Lusey in Chungking and Washington. To the navy, this constituted a direct violation of the 19 September 1942 Donovan-Purnell agreement. Miles protested to OSS and took swift action on 19 November, informing Washington that "from now on all messages Friendship [are to be] in Navy code only."[34]

Moreover, Donovan's own people in Washington were confused. Bafflement arose inside OSS headquarters in late November when Donovan's deputy director, David Bruce, instructed Ellery Huntington to ask Ilia Tolstoy in Tibet to report to Hayden, still in Chungking, instead of to Miles as previously arranged by both Stilwell and Miles and agreed upon by OSS. This bothered Huntington and made him question the practicality of the Donovan-Lusey SI/China scheme. On 22 November, Huntington sent Donovan a memo asking in earnest for clarification:

> 1) In view of the arrangements we have respecting the Chungking Mission, how are we to handle SI men who are sent into this area? 2) We are going to have difficulty with our associates unless some understanding is reached before these are sent out. 3) The somewhat trivial difficulties we have had over Dr. Hayden are in point, and Dave Bruce has just asked me to let him have Captain Tolstoy, who is on his way through, and who was originally intended to report at Chungking. 4) It would seem that a question of policy is involved on which Dave and I should have instructions.[35]

Donovan grew furious over Huntington's request for clarification. Four days later a memo flew back to Huntington's desk from the enraged director: "In regard to your letter of November 22nd. I think the answer to your question is a simple one. Each chief holds and retains the men that belong to him. Naturally one leader will not surrender his men to the other if they are necessary for the carrying out of the mission. It is not necessary to give instructions about this when I expect that you will dispose of trivial difficulties with the same aplomb you always do."[36] Huntington never asked Donovan again about OSS's China policy, with or without aplomb.

Lusey's independent activities in China aroused Miles's suspicion. But Miles detected no hard evidence of OSS's SI scheme until the last days of November 1942, when Lusey reported having worked out a separate plan with Tai Li whereby some SI and SO men would be sent out to China.[37] A couple of days later, Lusey further informed Miles that OSS headquarters was sending to China the Canadian Arthur Duff, who had been working under C. V. Starr's counter-Japanese division. It was clear to Miles that his authority as the number-one U.S. representative had been usurped by Lusey's independent activities. Lusey, as Miles understood through the Donovan-Purnell agreement, was supposed to be his deputy rather than an equal. The worst consequence, of course, was that Tai Li would go over to OSS and abandon the U.S. Navy entirely—after all, OSS and Tai Li's BIS were counterparts in the true sense. Miles finally exploded at the SI team of OSS, composed almost entirely of the Old China Hands: Hayden, Allman, Duff, Gale, and Lusey.

On 2 December, Miles sent a major statement to Washington regarding OSS's unauthorized SI activities in China. The letter circulated widely in the offices of all involved in the Tai Li–Miles–OSS setup:

Lusey got a dispatch about sending a man for SI work to China. The name DUFF was mentioned. I have nothing against Duff or anyone else that I haven't tangled with personally. However, on general principles, I have some ideas on this particular subject.

No SI man is wanted here. The very fact that he is here would put the Chinese on their guard against not only him but our whole Organization out here. Tai Li has to be on guard against people that slip in unseen and unasked, and I am going to help him do it. The job of SI in China is one of TAI LI's worries, and we can not step in here and expect to do any SI work anymore than we would knowingly let the Mexicans send SI men to operate in the USA. The only difference there is that Mexicans might get away with it, while Tai Li would have an SI man spotted the minute he left the US.[38]

Tai Li's dislike of British-styled Old China Hands, such as Gale, Hayden, and Allman, was well known to Miles, who shared much the same feeling.[39] Fearful of being lumped together with the Duff/Lusey gang, Miles expressed his thoughts to Tai Li about Old China Hands in a long letter, in which Miles stated:

> There are too many people who have lived a long time on the China Coast that now have no jobs in America and who think that they are real "experts" on China. Many of these people think that they will be very valuable to the United States if they can only get to China and they don't intend to do China any harm but is [*sic*] patriotically trying to help the United States. They do not think of China as a full fledged nation just the same as the United States. They think that spying is necessary to get information from the Chinese for the United States. It is one of my main purposes in this job to guard the China that I am very fond of from being "infected" with this type of foreigner. I am very critical of persons that have this attitude. If any such attitude exists in any of my men I wish to send them home immediately. Colonel Donovan promised me that if any person that he sent out was not up to my standard I could return him. I am particularly on the lookout against "Old China Hands" for whom I have a well founded dislike.[40]

Miles's objection to Old China Hands should not be construed as an attack on their scholarly knowledge of China; what he objected to was a certain overbearing attitude toward China on the part of many of them. It is important to know that Miles drew a clear distinction between British-styled Old China Hands of the "Orientalist" type and other Old China Hands like Fairbank, Sargent, Schreiner, and David Wight. After the Duff incident, Miles banned Duff from contacting, or "contaminating," his "good" Old China Hands. As to Miles's understanding of the British attitude toward the Chinese, he wrote to Metzel, "As you know, the Americans have enjoyed a lot better prestige than the British—mainly because there is no Hong Kong to rankle, and also because the British are adept at trying to make every other nationality feel inferior to the British. . . . The coastal ports were filled with Old China Hands of every type imaginable. As long as they could stay there they caused no trouble to the foreigners that really knew a lot more about the Chinese and wished to work with them on an equal footing. But those Old China Hands are now starting to descend on us in droves. They are escaping from occupied territories. They are coming back to China as 'Experts' on China. They are not wanted by the Chinese as a whole."[41]

Miles's rage had a devastating impact upon Donovan's China scheme. On 9 December 1942, Donovan was compelled to convene an urgent meeting with Ellery Huntington and Norwood Allman—Lusey's direct operators in Washington—and seriously discuss Miles's protest; no concrete response was given. After the meeting, Huntington drafted a memo directly asking Donovan: "Are we not obligated to clear all projects and personalities with the Navy and our Chinese friends before anyone is sent into the field?"[42] While Donovan wavered, the Navy Department and Tai Li's representative in Washington officially notified OSS that none of its SI projects parallel to Tai Li's efforts would be acceptable. This quasi-ultimatum to OSS declared that: "(1) It is absolutely imperative that all duplicate or parallel efforts between the Chinese and Americans in the Friendship Project should be avoided; (2) Tai Li's SI appeared to be in fine shape and has been effective in getting all information for which we have asked; (3) The Chinese SI radio network is particularly excellent; any new OSS radio setup in Chungking is unnecessary; (4) From now on, ALL American SI coordination would be under the control of ONI's Gregon Williams; (5) Civilians other than Chinese can contribute little to SI in China."[43]

Miles took further action to smother the Lusey SI scheme. He requested that the Navy Department investigate Lusey's real role in OSS. Jeff Metzel of Admiral King's office directly confronted OSS in January 1943 as to Lusey's real status. The tenacious Metzel demanded that OSS let him look at its SI payroll; he subsequently discovered that both Lusey and his assistant Samuel Schreiner in Chungking were paid by SI and that they were reporting only to Norwood Allman.[44] Metzel immediately insisted that OSS change Lusey's SI status.

This was a great loss of face to OSS. But the stakes were too high to clash with Miles at this moment. After considering Metzel's protest, R. David Halliwell of the Washington OSS headquarters obligingly sent a memo to Donovan on 23 January 1943, asking, "Would it not be a good idea to transfer these people [Lusey and Schreiner] formally from SI to SO?" Six days later, Donovan grudgingly assented under Lusey's name.[45] A week after that, Metzel reported to Miles that although Lusey had in the past shown "a double loyalty to you and to his actual boss," the problem had now been rectified; and that "Col. D[onovan] made it clear to Al [Lusey] that you are his boss for all purposes." In brief, Metzel assured Miles that "Al is thoroughly loyal to you."[46]

Miles must have been very satisfied with Donovan's concession and Metzel's assurance, for Lusey remained unscathed and his relationship with Tai Li seemed to grow even stronger.

The British Albatross, the Specter of Communists, and the Birth of SACO

But things were not so simple for Tai Li, who echoed Miles's rage over Old China Hands. However, it would be naive to conclude that Tai Li's antagonism was merely a reflection of China's newly found nationalistic pride or Tai Li's personal misgivings about foreigners. The record of Tai Li's anti-British attitude has never been accurately explained. Most writers who have commented on this have naively attributed Tai Li's antagonism solely to his arrest in Hong Kong by the British police. To Tai Li, the question of Old China Hands rising from the SI attempt of OSS was much more complicated. Rather, it involved two most sensitive aspects of Tai Li's intelligence endeavor: the British and the Communists.

The British approach of using foreign businessmen in China to engage in secret intelligence had been opposed by the Chinese, as in the case of Keswick's China Commando Group. After his ouster from China in April 1942, John Keswick had become SOE's liaison in Donovan's headquarters in Washington. Realizing this, Tai Li grew doubly suspicious of all OSS activities in China. The prime reason he opposed Eifler's operations inside China was that he was sure Keswick was in Washington commanding Eifler's SO teams.[47] Arthur Duff, a Canadian businessman with close British connections, was to be sent into China without Tai Li's approval for secret intelligence purposes; this convinced Tai Li that Keswick was behind a renewed British intelligence effort to penetrate China, only this time under the convenient cover of OSS.

Moreover, essential to the Donovan-Lusey SI scheme in China in the summer of 1942 was the idea of using the Shanghai Europeans, particularly German Jews and Russians. Lusey, in an important memo to Donovan of 14 September, had clearly stated that OSS should draw its SI personnel from people of "German Jewish background," and his "Russian friends" in Shanghai.[48] This was another of Tai Li's taboos. The exiled foreign community in Shanghai had been a hotbed of international espionage unmatched in modern history. It is common knowledge that the Moscow-controlled Comintern had been using Shanghai for espionage. The 1931 Noulen incident exposed the extent of the Communist intelligence network; the famous Richard Sorge spy ring had used Shanghai as the relay base between Tokyo and Moscow. It was not a coincidence that almost the entire Cambridge spy ring, including Guy Burgess, Kim Philby, and Roger Hollis, spent some mysterious time in Shanghai during the 1930s.[49] After the Japanese occupied Shanghai in late 1941, many of these foreigners flocked to Chungking, directly under Tai Li's nose.

Soviet intelligence took advantage of this situation and, using its embassy as a base, launched massive penetration operations in wartime China in close collaboration with Zhou Enlai's agents in Chungking. As the U.S. naval attaché, H. T. Jarrell, reported to Washington, throughout World War II the Soviet Embassy had "by far the largest staff of any diplomatic mission in Chungking. . . . The Soviet need for these people for their Embassy is more than a diplomatic mission; it is a 'fence' from which Soviet influence penetrates all facets of China's political, social and economic structure."[50]

The Soviets had acquired an enormous advantage in intelligence operations because many of their compatriots were residing in Chungking, China's wartime capital. Some of the Russian figures featured in bizarre capacities, representing a wide variety of international interests. Tai Li clearly understood that Charles De Gaulle's chief representative in Chungking, General Zenovi Pechkoff, was dangerously close to Soviet intelligence in China—for very good reason, because Pechkoff's father was the extremely "proletarian" Maxim Gorki, Stalin's model writer specializing in Socialist Realism.[51]

However, to Tai Li, the person who ultimately connected British intelligence with Communist infiltration—further implicating OSS—was Petro Pavlovski. Born a Russian, Pavlovski had lived in China for a long time and been closely associated with the Comintern network in the Far East.[52] Pavlovski's connection with the Comintern was deeply covered during his China years. Only U.S. naval intelligence in China suspected that he might be part of the notorious Shoyet ring, specializing in arms smuggling to the Chinese Communists, an operation directly controlled by the Comintern in Moscow.[53] In 1939, Pavlovski went to French Indochina to become a captain in the French Colonial Army. One year later, he came back to Chungking and linked up with General Pechkoff, who offered him French citizenship.[54]

When the British started to operate the China Commando Group, Pavlovski miraculously became Keswick's assistant in the British embassy in all intelligence operations in China. This was a remarkable feat of intelligence infiltration by the Comintern agent. After the ill-fated China Commando Group, Pavlovski and James McHugh, the U.S. naval attaché then living within the British embassy and working with the British SOE, were responsible for a series of ferocious propaganda attacks on Tai Li. Disguised as intelligence reports, these propaganda materials saturated Washington via McHugh's official channel and are generally known as the McHugh-Petro document on Tai Li.[55] After Keswick was ousted from China, Petro Pavlovski stayed in Chungking and continued his dubious activities.

When assigned a new job in Washington as SOE's liaison to Donovan,

Keswick urgently sought Pavlovski as his aide in OSS headquarters. Donovan immediately issued an order to Pavlovski, still in Chungking, to come to Washington. However, closely watched by Tai Li in Chungking, Pavlovski had become a persona non grata. The U.S. embassy refused to issue him a visa on the grounds that he had no consular or diplomatic status. Ambassador Gauss further insisted that unless the British embassy in Washington requested his visa directly from the State Department, nothing could be done. When Gauss's foe Stilwell was informed of this, he dispatched a secret cable to Donovan in Washington stating that Pavlovski "wants to comply with orders . . . but our Chungking Embassy refuses visa. . . . Your assistance requested in cutting this red tape." Stilwell further assured Donovan that he would help Pavlovski with transportation.[56]

While waiting in Chungking, Pavlovski was delighted to see Hayden, who was asking Stilwell for approval of the Dragon Plan. Hayden reported to Donovan, "He is going to Washington to join the OSS and . . . he wishes to return with me." Sensing strong opposition from Ambassador Gauss, Hayden wisely told Donovan that he would not like to return to Washington with Pavlovski. "This is the last thing that I would wish," Hayden reported to Donovan, and "I doubt whether his association with us would help us with the Chinese."[57] But Donovan certainly thought it would, for he wandered through the Washington bureaucratic maze and finally got Pavlovski a visa to come to the United States.

Thus, to the horror of Tai Li, Petro Pavlovski was now an official OSS agent working again for Tai Li's nemesis, John Keswick; only this time Pavlovski was working for the British in the headquarters of OSS in Washington.[58] This British-Pavlovski-OSS connection completely shocked Tai Li. Yet a bigger blow soon came when Tai Li learned via Xiao Bo that John Magruder, back from China in disgrace and just out of the Walter Reed Army Hospital in September 1942, had immediately become Donovan's special assistant in OSS headquarters.[59] Tai Li's fear seemed perfectly justifiable, for he knew, among other things, that Pavlovski, McHugh, and Magruder were not only uniformly pro-British, they were also all brothers-in-law.[60]

By late October 1942, the situation had become deadly clear to Tai Li: first, there was a British-sponsored plot to operate intelligence teams in China secretly, most likely to take revenge against him and to make deals with the Chinese Communists. Second, this plot centered in Washington was directly controlled by Keswick and Pavlovski, who used OSS as a cover through the Magruder connection.

The most certain confirmation of Tai Li's fears was McHugh's sudden decision to change careers in early October. As we have seen, Miles's impressive success with Tai Li's organization had constituted a major loss of face to McHugh, by far the most long-standing senior U.S. intelligence officer in China. Hopelessly jealous and disgruntled, McHugh submitted his resignation to the Navy, which was accepted by the secretary, Frank Knox, on 28 August 1942.[61] When Keswick, Pavlovski, and Magruder all entered OSS, McHugh suddenly and unexpectedly changed his mind in early October: he decided to stay in China after all. He explained to Knox, "I believe [my decision to stay] offers a better solution than my permanent detachment from here" and that his change of mind was "due to the desires of other organizations, both British and American, to share the bed."[62] Undoubtedly, in Tai Li's mind, McHugh would now be the contact person in China for the Keswick-Pavlovski-Magruder setup in Washington.[63]

At this juncture, OSS was secretly sending Arthur Duff to China, an action Tai Li took as hard evidence of the reinstatement of the China Commando Group in the guise of the Friendship Project that he had worked out with the Navy. Even worse, Duff was instructed by Washington to contact Song Qingling and Sun Ke, the most pro-Communist faction in Chungking, with the chief objective of establishing a smuggling route between Chungking and New York via French Indochina, a plan that recalled the previous Shoyet Ring of arms supplies to Comintern agents in China.

All things considered, Tai Li decided to impose a legal obligation on the U.S. government to regulate Sino-U.S. intelligence operations and stop any future unauthorized OSS secret intelligence efforts in China. Soon after Miles came back from consulting General Stilwell on OSS operations in late November 1942, Tai Li proposed to Miles that a Sino-U.S. treaty be drawn up immediately. Foreseeing the inevitable bureaucratic routine in Washington, Miles initially tried to avoid such a binding agreement. However, upon Tai Li's insistence, Miles caved in. After a series of discussions, Miles prepared a short draft that did not satisfy Tai Li, who thought it too vague. They spent several weeks arguing, compromising, and redrafting a document. The essential issues included the command of Sino-U.S. joint intelligence operations, the training and supply of the guerrillas, and an FBI-style school specializing in counterespionage and internal security. Roy Stratton vividly described the agonizing process: "Miles and Tai Li met daily. Each paragraph took hours of discussion and compromise. Each section had to be translated into Chinese and English so there would be no misunderstanding of its meaning. Both of them, however, were determined to reach a mutually satisfactory agreement, and their work bound them closer together."[64]

In late December 1942, the final draft was sent to Chiang Kai-shek and his chief of staff, General Stilwell. On the last day of 1942, T. V. Soong came down with the draft and held a meeting with Tai Li, Miles, and Lusey. Soong announced that Chiang Kai-shek had approved the draft but that Stilwell, Chiang's Chief of Staff, was devoted to his recapture of Burma in 1943 and would not divert any meaningful hump tonnage to any new and enlarged projects.[65] Because of this, Soong insisted, both President Roosevelt and Generalissimo Chiang Kai-shek would have to sign the document. All present agreed the newly drafted treaty, called the Sino-American Special Technical Cooperative Organization, or SACO, be sent to Washington as soon as possible. On 1 January 1943, Tai Li designated Al Lusey the messenger. Lusey carried the SACO document, along with a letter from T. V. Soong, to Admiral King for an independent air supply line to China, and left for Washington immediately.

Tai Li was most anxious to see the SACO treaty approved. Miles wrote, "Every time we meet he produces a toast to SOCKO! It seems to catch, and is the only American word that I have ever heard him say. He is a grand guy, with one hundred percent loyalty both up and down the line."[66] Ten days later, Lusey arrived in Washington. To prove his newly declared loyalty to the navy, Lusey directly went to see Admiral Purnell and Colonel Xiao Bo at the Navy Department. On the same day, Purnell, Xiao, Metzel, and Lusey held a long meeting. Without much difficulty, Purnell and Metzel immediately realized the possible bottleneck in the final signing of the treaty: the army. As Metzel explained to Miles, "[Although] you can be sure that complete effort will be forthcoming . . . you have got to work on General Stilwell, because everybody from General Marshall down insists that they are giving him everything that can possibly be given and that only he can decide whether your stuff is sufficiently important compared to other things in his area, and his effort, to justify lugging any or all of your freight. . . . So don't relax your work on Uncle Joe."[67]

The SACO draft arrived in Washington at a time when Roosevelt and his top military generals were away in Casablanca meeting with their British counterparts. This wait only added to Tai Li's agony of uncertainty. Moreover, Xiao Bo in Washington indicated that there might be a request for revision of the SACO draft by the U.S. government. To emphasize his seriousness, Tai Li sent a cable to Xiao Bo and instructed him to show it to Purnell. Tai Li raised three major areas of concern: no essential revision of the SACO draft by the U.S. side would be accepted; the British should in no way be involved in SACO; and SACO's command control over SI by OSS was to be absolute. Purnell at once wired a telegram back to Tai Li: "Please be assured of our fullest cooperation and enduring good faith. Any changes made in the SACO agreement are made to assure full understanding now and to prevent future doubt of our frankness; such changes are considered minor so far as the complete plan is concerned. . . . The British are in no way mixed up in our affairs. . . . Our only principle in which Donovan heartily concurs is to send in SI and all other fields only people you request or approve with every individual for any and all duty wholly under SACO command. Our trust in SACO is complete."[68]

After the Casablanca Conference (14–24 January 1943), the Joint Chiefs of Staff began discussing the SACO draft. Vigorous promotion from Admiral King and approval in principle from the White House notwithstanding, General Marshall raised strong objections to the proposal. To the army, there were three major areas in the draft that had to be changed. Key to Marshall's objection was article five, which dictated that the director of SACO would be Chinese and the deputy director American; this constituted an affront to Marshall's idea of maintaining the army's supremacy of command in the China theater. Under the proposed SACO structure, the deputy director would undoubtedly be Miles of the navy, who would then be directly responsible to the Chinese—in this case, Tai Li—not to General Stilwell. Marshall's second objection was related to article ten, which would require a joint Sino-American air survey of the coastal ports and their surroundings. This point again touched on some sensitivity between Marshall and King, since this was obviously a prelude to King's strategy of an early landing of U.S. naval forces on the China coast—a strategy that was at the core of the Marshall-King conflict. Besides, this operation would also involve cooperation between the 14th Air Force under Chennault and the navy in China, a scenario the army had tried its hardest to avoid. Marshall's final objection was to article eighteen, which would require the United States to provide hundreds more radio intelligence specialists to Tai Li's cryptographical team in Chungking. General Marshall's chief concern about this was the maintenance of MAGIC security.

Marshall's unyielding objections raised eyebrows both in the navy and in the White House. But the stalemate continued. A compromise was finally reached in mid-February, which undercut the influence of Tai Li and the navy: the Joint Chiefs of Staff should convey to theater commander General Stilwell the content of the debate and ask for Stilwell's comment and recommendation, which would then be the basis for a final decision as to the fate of SACO. On 16 February, Marshall drafted a cable to Stilwell, co-signed by Admiral King: "Joint Chiefs have made theater commander responsible for psychological warfare in the theater. . . . Accordingly we contemplate charging you with responsibility for Captain Miles's project and placing him together with his OSS and Navy personnel under your command." Marshall then listed his requests for revisions of articles five, ten, and eighteen as conditions for sending the draft from the JCS to Roosevelt for final approval.[69] Marshall was expecting a quick endorsement from Stilwell. Foreseeing Stilwell's concurrence with Marshall, Admiral King simultaneously sent a melancholy cable to Miles in Chungking explaining what changes had been imposed and why, and specifically asking for Tai Li's understanding that all the changes Marshall insisted upon are "necessary for effective support of our cooperative project and will be the foundation for its greater success."[70]

Marshall's proposed changes struck at the core of Tai Li's effort to control and regulate U.S. secret intelligence efforts in China. After Miles informed him of Admiral King's cable, Tai Li reacted violently, particularly at Marshall's proposed change of article five, designating a Chinese director. Tai Li flatly told Miles that before he would submit to General Stilwell's command, he would withdraw from SACO entirely. Tai Li's resolve was well understood by Miles, who immediately warned Admiral King, "Such action [Tai Li's withdrawal] would mean SACO breakdown and grave danger to present military cooperation and future Sino-American friendly relations."[71]

What then happened was a miracle, and it changed the entire situation. Upon receiving Marshall's cable, Stilwell quickly drafted a reply to concur with his mentor in Washington. But Miles rushed into Stilwell's headquarters before the cable was sent. Both men of action, Miles and Stilwell had formed a cordial relationship and respected each other. Besides, it seemed clear to both of them that the chief purpose of SACO was to regulate Donovan's operations in China—a goal they both shared. After learning of Tai Li's violent reaction to the proposed changes and the grave consequences as explained by Miles, Stilwell miraculously redrafted his reply to Marshall. On 21 February, General Stilwell dispatched to Marshall, anxiously waiting in Washington, the following cable:

> After investigation I believe that the Chinese will not accept the SACO agreement if any agency comes between them and Miles. Tai Li's organization is super-secret and super-suspicious. Miles['s] work would be hampered if they knew he was under my command. I have enough confidence in him to recommend that in view of the peculiar and unusual circumstances connected with this matter he be allowed to operate as heretofore, and I believe that any conflict that arises can be adjusted between us.[72]

Undoubtedly this was one of the most important documents in secret intelligence and special operations in the China theater during World War II. It bore far-reaching significance for OSS. Stilwell spared the command control of OSS and gave it to Miles, who was then still in charge of

OSS/China, thus inadvertently creating a gigantic loophole of command over intelligence. Donovan then had an extremely good opportunity for OSS to expand throughout China during the rest of the war. The historian R. Harris Smith has commented, "OSS became accustomed to profound discouragement in its four years in China."[73] But to Donovan the alternative to this discouragement was total elimination of action, as had happened to OSS under MacArthur's command. From now on, thanks to the murky command structure set up by Stilwell and Miles, Donovan was able to maneuver between SACO and the army for survival and expansion. Although OSS would try to break away from Miles's control, Donovan never wanted to leave the SACO structure entirely, for it was a perfect umbrella protecting OSS from the army's encroachment. Yet when SACO became too stifling to Donovan, he could easily claim his allegiance to the theater commander. This resilience and command opacity in China was indeed the biggest attraction for Donovan, and by the end of the war his overwhelming efforts were pulled into China from all other areas.

Stilwell's stunning reply completely disarmed General Marshall and guaranteed a virtual safe passage of the SACO draft. This accomplishment notwithstanding, to make an airtight case, Tai Li urged Miles to proceed to Washington "to review the entire situation" with Admiral King.[74] Armed with Stilwell's endorsement, Miles happily followed Tai Li's instruction and flew back to Washington immediately.[75] Miles quickly got official approval from Admiral King. General Marshall gave his grudging endorsement last, "straight mouthed" and with a bitter smile.[76] Miles then took the intact SACO draft to Admiral Leahy for Roosevelt's final approval. The president gave his verbal blessing to the document but felt that, considering the nature of the proposed organization, it should not be signed by the president as a treaty between China and the United States because any treaty would have to go through a Senate confirmation process and thus be open to leaks. Nor did Tai Li like the word *treaty,* which had become taboo in China; its use would surely conjure an imperialist imposition of obligations upon the sovereign Chinese republic, thus giving the puppets and the Communists good chances to cry out against "treason" and "betrayal" of Chinese national interests. Therefore, the new document was to be known only as an "agreement."

On 15 April in Washington, Secretary of the Navy Knox, OSS Director Donovan, and Milton Miles, representing the United States, along with Foreign Minister Soong, Lieutenant Colonel Sin ju Pu Hsiao (Xiao Bo), representing China, signed the official Sino-American Special Technical Cooperative Agreement, without any changes.

Three months later, on 4 July, Tai Li celebrated the American Indepen-

Fig. 6. Tai Li signing SACO Agreement, 4 July 1943, as Miles looks on (courtesy of the family of Admiral Miles)

dence Day by formally adding his John Hancock to the document. To avoid any misunderstanding, Admiral Leahy wrote a secret memo to Miles:

> You are advised that the Joint U.S. Chiefs of Staff take note of the proposed Sino-American Technical Cooperation Agreement for the conduct and support of special measure in the war effort against JAPAN, and, further, of the exchange of dispatches between General Stilwell and the Chiefs of Staff in which General Stilwell expresses approval of the conduct of American participation in these measures by you di-

rectly under Chinese command. The Joint Chiefs of Staff approve this arrangement and desire that you cooperate with the responsible designated Chinese authorities in every way practicable for the prosecution of war measures against the Japanese.

The President has been informed and has given approval of the plan to place you in direct charge of the American participation, as set forth in the proposed agreement.

On 15 August, Miles and Tai Li in Chungking agreed on an elaborate, detailed Outline of the Working Plan of SACO; it entailed thirty-four specific areas of cooperation in secret intelligence and special operations.[77]

The original Friendship Project was thus replaced by SACO, with Miles in overall command of both the naval contingent and all OSS activities in China. At the signing ceremony in Washington, with OSS personnel and plan under total naval control, and with Tai Li's demands fulfilled, Captain Jeff Metzel expressed his excitement in a typically naval manner: "We're no longer bastard!"[78]

CHAPTER FIVE

OSS in an Army-Navy Game

As a paramilitary organization, OSS was entirely answerable to Stilwell!

—JOHN PATON DAVIES

If Tai Li, Miles, Donovan, Stilwell, King, and Marshall believed that command over secret intelligence and special operations in the China theater had been understood and secured once and for all through SACO, they were mistaken. The signing of the SACO agreement marked only the beginning of a tenacious subversion engineered by their own low-level deputies.

Revolt from Within and
The Shanghai Evening Post and Mercury

It is still a minor mystery why William Donovan agreed to sign the SACO agreement with such alacrity. He was not involved in the essential drafting of the document, nor did he consult his deputies before putting his signature to it. The only logical interpretation might be that Donovan saw a loophole in command in Stilwell's endorsement of SACO. By escaping from the army's control, OSS thus rested its fate entirely on the whims of a naval officer, Milton Miles.

Donovan's subordinates reacted to SACO with utter opposition. Just after Miles's arrival in Washington to expedite the approval process, David Bruce, an SI chief of OSS closely associated with China operations, angrily told Metzel of the navy that "Mary [Miles] has a lot of nerve telling us not to send 'Old China Hands' to China."[1] One month after signing the SACO agreement, Donovan gave a copy to his top scholar on China, Joseph Hayden, and ordered him to provide a review. Realizing that the SACO agreement had already been signed, Hayden pointed out hopelessly that "this agreement is thoroughly bad" and was "open to serious objections from the standpoint of the OSS." He concluded, "I see in this instrument a dangerous weapon which . . . could be used against the OSS both during the war and when the historical record is finally written." The senior scholar's main point was that SACO was bad because OSS should not be associated with a man like Tai Li, whose methods were "assassination by poison and dagger and subtler methods."[2] Yet if Hayden's conclusions were prophetic, his reasoning did not convince Donovan a bit. Donovan simply did not care about Tai Li's methods; on the contrary, Donovan himself was a strong advocate for the same methods of "psychological warfare"—and even more ruthless ones.[3]

Donovan encountered even stronger protest about SACO from the Starr-Allman group in the SI group of OSS in New York, run by those whom Miles termed the Old China Hands. Donovan's decision to put OSS entirely under the command of SACO dashed all hopes for this group, essentially sealing the British attempt to control OSS's China operations. Starr had long planned his own secret intelligence scheme for China, to be directed by his business associates. When the SACO draft arrived in Washington and was endorsed by Donovan in early 1943, Starr strongly opposed it because under the new organization all OSS operations, SO and SI altogether, would be under the control of Tai Li and Miles. On 17 February, while the SACO draft was in front of the JCS for consideration, Starr, together with his associates—Harkson, Allman, and Jones in the quasi-official counter-Japanese division—met with the acting director of OSS, Ned Buxton, and his aide, George K. Bowden. During this meeting, Starr, Harkson, and Allman most strongly protested the SACO setup to OSS and threatened to withdraw from OSS if Miles's command over Starr's people were not removed.[4] However, this time Donovan refused to yield. Eager to operate in China, OSS went along with the SACO proposal. As a result, Starr and Harkson angrily left OSS and quickly went to work on their own China scheme for British secret intelligence.[5]

But Starr did not intend to withdraw from OSS entirely. He left one of his men, Norwood Allman, to continue their independent secret intelligence venture in China. To further counter SACO and maintain the link with Allman, Starr pursued the direct utilization of James McHugh.

McHugh's October 1942 decision to stay in Chungking had met with Tai Li's opposition. Increased pressure soon mounted; Tai Li quickly kicked McHugh out of China. McHugh arrived in Washington in December.[6] Within weeks, he secretly joined OSS and became its Far East SI chief in Washington.[7] His new task was to work with Allman on a new intelligence endeavor in China, only this time it was to be completely sub rosa: neither Tai Li, Miles, nor even Donovan would be fully informed about it. Their new modus operandi was to use Starr's own newspaper, the *Shanghai Evening Post and Mercury,* as a cover under which to operate in Chungking and New York to gather secret intelligence. In addition to getting OSS funding via Allman, Starr himself provided about $15,000 annually for the newspaper. In early 1943 the New York edition of the *Shanghai Evening Post and Mercury* went to print. The FBI became immediately nervous because this appeared to directly encroach its turf. In the end, however, due to high-handed British maneuvering and Starr's assurance that "these activities are in no sense an infringement upon the prerogatives or activities of the FBI and are in fact completely outside the scope or capacity of FBI interests," the Starr group was able to continue its publication in New York.[8]

If Starr had a relatively easy time starting up his newspaper in New York for intelligence purposes, he had absolutely no luck in setting up a Chungking edition. The reason was simple: Starr had entered the domain of General Stilwell, who was a master at using newspapers for intelligence and other purposes. Throughout his tour of duty, Stilwell understood that one of the best ways to gain influence in Washington and Chungking was through control of newspapers, newsmen, and Hollywood actors–turned–army officers. Surrounding Stilwell was a group of reporters and movie stars, among them Theodore White, Clair Boothe Luce, Jack Beldon, and Merian Cooper, the director of *King Kong.*[9] His chief "civilian agent," and a personal confidant, Theodore White of *Time* magazine, had virtually monopolized information gathering on the Chinese government for Stilwell via "news reporting," although White's sometimes daredevil guesswork proved incredibly embarrassing to the government of the United States.

A crisis in Sino-American relations was created by Theodore White in February and March of 1944. At the time, Britain's Admiral Louis Mountbatten had infuriated Stilwell by chastising the latter's effort to open up the Burma Road. Stilwell was in dire need of strong backing from Chungking and Washington. However, at this critical juncture, White provided Stilwell with an explosive piece of "intelligence" that he claimed was from "an absolutely reliable source." White's source, the head reporter of the Central News Agency, had just met with Chiang Kai-shek's envoy to Washington, Ambassador Wei Daoming. White told Stilwell that Wei had been asked by Roosevelt to deliver to Chiang a personal message: "Even if the Burma Road were reopened it could not truck in one tenth the supplies needed to re-equip the Chinese Armies for a large offensive. . . . Perhaps the Burma Road will never need be reopened."[10]

Fig. 7. Theodore White in Chungking, 1944 (courtesy of the family of Admiral Miles)

This enraged Stilwell, who sent a strongly worded cable to Marshall demanding an explanation from Washington. Upon reading Stilwell's cable, Roosevelt was furious. "I have carefully checked the files," Roosevelt wrote to Admiral Leahy on 21 February, "and find that I have no letter even remotely resembling the information given out by Ambassador Wei." He further ordered an investigation: "Frankly, in view of this, I think that we should run down this story, verify it, and get a denial from Ambassador Wei."[11]

General Marshall ordered Stilwell to provide the source of his intelligence and demanded that Stilwell's people meet directly with Ambassador Wei. On 26 February, General Thomas Hearn, Stilwell's chief of staff, cabled Marshall and named White as the source. But White emphatically refused to directly confront his Chinese informant at the Central News Agency and Ambassador Wei. Finally, on 2 March, General Hearn cabled Marshall that White had provided Stilwell with false information.[12] General Marshall then relayed to the White House that the "report as the alleged contents of the letter purported to have been written by the President was erroneous. Hearn's original source in this matter was Theodore White, Time, Inc., war correspondent in China, who evidently attached mistaken conclusions to a story received from his Chinese informant. Due to White's connection and the undesirable publicity that might result, it is considered inadvisable to pursue the matter with White."[13]

Despite this embarrassment, Stilwell did not want to see his own network disturbed by Starr's *Shanghai Evening Post and Mercury,* which already had a dubious connection to British intelligence. After the New York edition went to print in the spring of 1943, Starr designated two of his associates, Frederic B. Opper and Randall Gould, to proceed to Chungking to set up an edition there.[14] Stilwell refused to provide them with air transport, so they had to reach China by ship. After everything was arranged, the State and War departments refused initially to issue them passports. As McHugh and Allman reported, "Even supply of additional personnel to supplement Opper, to say nothing of provision for supervisory trips out from America, has been almost stalemated by War Department and by Far East military difficulties."[15]

Despite its many erroneous claims, the *Shanghai Evening Post and Mercury* achieved very little in gathering secret intelligence for the U.S. government. The newspaper had been under surveillance from day one by Tai Li.[16] Most of its reports did not even come back to Washington; most likely they went to British intelligence in China.[17] Miles, still head of OSS operations in the Far East, knew of the *SEPM* through the Chinese and was wary of it. On 1 September 1943, he declared to Washington, "I have been informed by some Chinese officers that Mr. C. V. Starr is setting up an agency in China which is an offspring of OSS but which is ostentatiously for the purpose of publishing American newspapers in China. I wasn't aware that this had gone through, . . . [but] I personally will try to get along with everybody [in the *SEPM*] as long as they stay out of my hair. The minute they upset my relations with General Tai or [Chiang Kai-shek], I'm going gunning for them."[18]

To the Chinese, this newspaper was yet another unauthorized intelligence operation by OSS in China. Equally telling is that in the minds of those in top Chinese intelligence circles, U.S. intelligence operations in China were sloppy in maintaining secrecy and were not considered entirely reliable. The chief reason for this was the constant leaking of top secret intelligence materials in the newspapers.

To Donovan, Starr's *Shanghai Evening Post and Mercury* posed a constant embarrassment due to its amateurish intelligence activities and sometimes outrageous breach of secrecy. In mid-October 1943, for example, James R. Murphy, head of OSS X-2 (counterespionage) became alarmed that the New York edition of the *SEPM* published articles openly identifying Clyde Sargent and John K. Fairbank as OSS secret agents in China.[19] When the powerful syndicated columnist Drew Pearson poured out intelligence items in his influential columns, the U.S. naval attaché in China protested because Pearson's columns horrified his Chinese informant, who immediately withdrew cooperation and flatly told the attaché: "Frankly how can I possibly give you highly classified information in the face of such leaks? It is not that I do not trust you personally, but if my information leaks out in Washington it could result in the identification of some of our agents and endanger their lives, apart from the fact that it would close important sources to us."[20] It is ironic that Donovan's eventual downfall would have much to do with two of the most outrageous cases of intelligence leakage to the media: the Trohan Leak and the Amerasia case.

Davies's Scheme and the Deconstruction of SACO

The signing of the SACO agreement sent an immediate shock wave through Stilwell's staff circle. Although the general had approved the plan, many of his low-ranking officers were particularly jealous of the navy's success in controlling virtually all non-combat-related intelligence gathering. Almost immediately, sabotage efforts were initiated at the general's headquarters. The chief organizer of such efforts was John Paton Davies, a State Department employee originally under Gauss, who was on loan to Stilwell's headquarters as political consultant.

The coming of John Paton Davies into the OSS picture marked a new stage in Donovan's operations in China during World War II. Davies's chief motive for stepping into secret intelligence was, as he put it himself, to inject "political guidance" into OSS and other intelligence agencies.[21] His secondary motive, however, was purely personal. Shrewd, highly insightful, fluent in Chinese, and often arrogant, Davies had long perceived himself to be a senior member of Stilwell's headquarters. He believed that General Stilwell's decision to let his son, Captain Joseph Stilwell Jr., run secret intelligence at the headquarters was a mistake. This had created an environment in which, as Davies confided to David Wight, Miles's chief assistant, General Stilwell had been too heavily influenced by the younger staff members surrounding Captain Stilwell, who "may not have the proper perspective." Davies told Wight: "The older ones didn't seem to be on the inside as much as might be expected." Particularly troubling to Davies was General Frank Dorn, Stilwell's assistant chief of staff, who Davies chastised as "highly volatile and inclined to the 'vapors' of Young Joe." Davies said Dorn "had evidently taken a fancy" to the general's son. In fact, Davies was so upset about being excluded from the inner circle of the secret intelligence operations under Stilwell Jr. that his pride as a senior China expert in the Stilwell camp was deeply hurt. Davies took it as a personal slight and decided to increase his own influence in the realm of secret intelligence, challenging those, in his own words, "who weren't yet dry behind the ears."[22]

On 16 March 1943, John Paton Davies visited Zhou Enlai, the Communist representative in Chiang Kai-shek's Central Government. Davies expressed to Zhou the idea of reshaping intelligence in the China theater. Zhou Enlai immediately proposed to Davies that a permanent American observers' station be established in Yenan for information gathering.[23] Zhou further indoctrinated Davies about the strength and high capability of the Communists in obtaining intelligence from various sources throughout the China theater. Davies was deeply impressed and decided to pursue connections with the Communists.

To test reactions from Miles's camp, which was so closely tied to Tai Li, Davies on 24 March 1943 went to see David Wight and reported to him about his earlier talk with Zhou Enlai regarding the possibility of cooperation with the Communists in gathering intelligence in northern China. Davies told Wight that the Communists had the best information sources in China. Wight was deeply taken aback by Davies's suggestion that the U.S. Army work with the Communists on intelligence and immediately declared to Davies that "any action of that sort must not be hooked up with us [the navy] in any way." As Wight later reported to Miles, Davies understood the navy's position.[24]

Sensing that no direct objection would come immediately from the Miles contingent, Davies made a formal request to General Stilwell that he request four more foreign service officers for his staff so that the five officials from the State Department, under Stilwell's command, "might supervise political, economic, and psychological intelligence and warfare operations."[25] Three of the requested four officers for this specific intelligence initiative were approved: John Steward Service, Raymond Ludden, and John Emmerson.[26] The "gang of four" from the State Department thus began a tenacious task of secret intelligence cooperation with the Chinese Communists, an alliance that had a most profound impact on Sino-American relations for decades to come.

In order to cooperate with the Chinese Communists, Davies needed a sizable intelligence agency that had both the institutional mandate and the facilities to operate in China. He thought of OSS, which was unfortunately under SACO by now and could not operate in China without the consent of Tai Li and Miles. The next logical move for Davies was to organize another OSS contingent outside SACO—which proved to be an unexpectedly easy task due to one of the biggest miscalculations of the allied war strategy, the lumping together of radically incompatible areas into one war theater: the China-Burma-India theater, or CBI. Regardless of how strict and prohibitive SACO authority might be, its jurisdiction was overwhelmingly confined to China proper. Stilwell, as theater commander of American forces in CBI, could easily escape Chiang Kai-shek's control by simply running his own operations either from Burma or India. To Davies, the solution in the spring of 1943 was to be found in New Delhi, India. British resistance to independent American operations in India was disappearing due to a dramatic episode in World War II history that soon provided Davies with a perfect OSS officer to begin his plan in China: Lieutenant Colonel Richard Heppner, "a presentable young gentleman," to use Davies's words.[27]

Before the war Richard Heppner had been a junior law partner at Donovan's law firm in New York. Then, up until December 1942, Heppner had been Donovan's SO chief in the London OSS office, headed by President Roosevelt's own "double agent," William Phillips. The tense relationship between Gandhi's Indian nationalist movement and the British colonial government in India prompted Roosevelt to dispatch his family friend Phillips to India as a special presidential envoy to inspect the India situation. Phillips took Heppner with him as his aide. The entourage left London in late December 1942 and arrived in Delhi on 8 January 1943. During the four-month stay in India with Phillips, Heppner became acquainted with all the top American military and civilian officials in India, including Generals Stilwell and Merrill, and with John Paton Davies.

In late April 1943, the Phillips mission came back to the United States and presented Roosevelt a devastating report about the colonial policy of the British in India, their peculiar intransigence toward the Indian nationalist movement led by Gandhi, and their unwillingness to fight Japan.[28] Coincidentally, General Stilwell and his entourage, including Davies, were also in Washington for the Trident Conference. By the end of this tour of duty, Heppner wanted to go to the general staff school at Fort Leavenworth, Kansas, and had already asked Donovan to relieve him from OSS.[29]

At this juncture, Davies suggested to General Stilwell in Washington that Heppner be made OSS Chief on Stilwell's staff. This was a startling suggestion, for it would be in direct violation of SACO, which dictated that all OSS personnel affairs in China had to be made jointly by Tai Li and Miles. But to Stilwell, CBI, the Far East, and China were hardly the same concept. The general reluctantly accepted this suggestion from his political

Fig. 8. Colonel Richard Heppner, chief of OSS/China under General Wedemeyer (courtesy of Elizabeth [Heppner] McIntosh)

consultant. On 15 May, Stilwell wrote to the operations division of the War Department, "Major Richard Heppner would be highly acceptable as a staff officer to handle OSS activities. If OSS desires to send him out, air transportation is requested." But there was one proviso to this approval: Stilwell did not want to overtly upset Miles's work in China, so he ordered Heppner to stay at his rear echelon headquarters in Delhi for the time being.[30]

Delighted by Stilwell's approval, Davies immediately went to the OSS headquarters to persuade Heppner to jump on the wagon. Displaying typical State Department cockiness, Davies vividly describes his first impression of Donovan's headquarters: "It was a pungent collection of thugs, postdebutantes, millionaires, professors, corporation lawyers, professional military, and misfits, all operating under high tension and in whispers. I found OSS, then and later, a diverting contrast to Hull's stupefying department [of State]."[31]

Heppner, however, was ambivalent about this new and serious request from Davies. Stilwell's reluctance to send him directly to China worried him, too. He asked his boss, Donovan, what he should do and whether Miles was behind Stilwell's odd decision to put him in India to do a job in China. Donovan told Heppner: "Do not raise any more questions but get ready and go. You may possibly be correct in your suspicion, nevertheless that makes no difference if the plan has been approved."[32] In other words, Donovan was gambling and wanted to push the limit of the SACO agreement: OSS would proceed silently with precisely what SACO prohibited until stopped by protest that, Donovan thought, might or might not come.

Thus in May and June of 1943, Heppner started his adventure anew as the OSS officer in CBI, directly under John Paton Davies. An elaborate code system was worked out specifically for the Davies-Heppner scheme: the army was Lion, the navy Whale, OWI Parrot. Donovan was Charger, Stilwell was Barracuda, Miles was Pickerel or Trout, Chennault Hawk, Heppner Mowgli or Tarzan, Davies Rover or Fido, McHugh Leopard, and Evans Carlson was Bear. As to the Communist-held area, it was Dixie.[33]

If from the very beginning Davies had the idea of using OSS for intelligence gathering in the Communist-held areas in northern China, the same could not be said of Stilwell's regular army staff, even though its members shared with Davies the same jealousies and dissatisfaction toward SACO. A parallel effort was made by these combat-conscious staff members in the army headquarters to use OSS elsewhere in China and Southeast Asia. It began in late March 1943, completely unrelated to north China or the Communists. Instead it involved a U.S. Army plan to conduct combat special operations in Thailand, Burma, and French Indochina.

Originally, Stilwell's strategists thought of using India as a base from which to launch such operations, but fierce British opposition thwarted this idea. On 24 March 1943, Benjamin Ferris, General Stilwell's military aide directly involved in dealing with the British in India, proposed to Stilwell and the War Department the "establishment under theater control of an espionage organization . . . to operate in Thailand, Burma, and French Indochina with military information as primary mission" based in the Chinese border areas of Guangxi and Yunnan. As a matter of course, Ferris asked Stilwell, "Will the Chinese government permit use of their territory for this purpose?"[34] Stilwell's son, who was in charge of conducting secret intelligence, enthusiastically pushed for Ferris's proposal. Young Joe assured Ferris and Colonel Pape, the theater G-2, that the Chinese would certainly grant permission.[35] Indeed, Frank Dorn, General Stilwell's top aide, was dispatched to Chungking to negotiate with the Chinese authorities. Considering the extreme sensitivity of such a plan, General Stilwell, before his departure to Washington for the Trident Conference, instructed his staff to be cautious. He ordered the U.S. Army to negotiate only with General Chen Cheng, not with Tai Li, and specified that Frank Dorn be the only person authorized to conduct such a negotiation. As Stilwell's chief of staff, General Hearn, summed up, "We do not want to get tied up with Tai Li such as happened to Miles. We will figure on operating from areas controlled by Chen Cheng. Such espionage work will have to come under Dorn directly. This by direction of General Stilwell and also because Chinese insist on Dorn being responsible. If project approved group leader should report to Dorn to make arrangements prior to the rest of his group coming out."[36]

Which group should be allowed to carry out this espionage task in Thailand, Burma, and French Indochina? Stilwell's camp had two choices: the OSS team under Eifler already in operation on a much smaller scale and in an experimental stage in the Burmese jungle, or the military intelligence division of the War Department under General George Strong. Since Young Joe was an ardent fan of Carl Eifler, OSS was favored and strongly supported by Frank Dorn. But the issue remained undecided for a while until a strong argument for OSS arose: Donovan's organization had seemingly unlimited financial resources for secret operations, legal or illegal. As General Hearn and Colonel Dickey put it, "OSS has all unvouched funds necessary for India and China."[37] Thus, on 21 June, General Stilwell informed General Ferris that "we are recommending Donovan's organization."[38] Ferris in India had no problem endorsing OSS and abandoning General Strong's MID, as he pointedly stated, "[I] believe Donovan's organization the better. Strong probably jealous and slow on trigger."[39]

But this arrangement met with Davies's strong opposition. First of all, though he certainly did not have any squabbles with Dorn and Young Joe's recommendation that OSS run the proposed army espionage network, Davies did not like to see Dorn and Young Joe choose Eifler for such a task. Davies considered Eifler lacking in political savvy. Second, the U.S. Army's running two parallel secret intelligence operations, one aimed at north China with the Communists and the other aimed at Southeast Asia, would divide intelligence command and might even jeopardize Davies's own authority. Therefore, Davies vehemently opposed Eifler's appointment and strongly pushed Stilwell to have Richard Heppner appointed as chief of all OSS activities in Stilwell's camp, in charge of both the Yenan-oriented and the combat-oriented projects. Once again, General Stilwell agreed with Davies—much to the chagrin of Eifler and the others. In late June 1943, accompanied by Davies and Major Duncan Lee, the enigmatic OSS SI chief of the Japan/China branch in Washington, Colonel Richard Heppner departed Washington.[40] Heppner arrived in India to assume his hush-hush post on 8 July—only four days after Tai Li put his signature, the last one required, on the SACO agreement in Chungking.

This OSS-led espionage plan by General Stilwell's staffers immediately caused tumultuous reactions both in Washington and in Chungking. In Washington, when Donovan informed General Marshall of the scheme, Marshall was pleasantly surprised. Nevertheless, Marshall cautioned Stilwell to get permission from the British first. As for General Strong, Stilwell's decision to use OSS instead of MID constituted an outrage, for Strong not only was the most prominent foe of OSS in Washington but also a proud "regular army" officer who disdained irregular groups like OSS. What Strong feared most was the possibility of OSS emerging triumphant out of Stilwell's theater as the coordinator for a centralized intelligence for the U.S. government. Consequently, Strong at once asked General Marshall to tell Stilwell that MID was "prepared to furnish trained supervisory personnel for operations of decentralized espionage organization under theater headquarters as alternative." General Strong further expressed "doubt of effectiveness of OSS intelligence operations."[41]

When this failed to alter Stilwell's mind, Strong changed his tactics by forming an intelligence research section and putting it directly under the Joint Army-Navy Intelligence Collection Agency (JICA) in India and China. Strong knew that General Stilwell had wished to have an R&A team directly working in his theater headquarters; this research section of JICA could replace a possible R&A setup in Stilwell's camp. General Strong went further and directly informed Colonel Pape, G-2 for the CBI theater rear echelon, that the JICA research group should prevail because "OSS is not capable of doing a professional job in the China, Burma, India Theater of War."

But Strong's hardball politics backfired. Colonel Pape rejected Strong's request and told Stilwell that JICA in CBI "will be largely a transmittal agency because information fragmentary and local collection unprofitable."[42] General John Magruder, now the deputy director of OSS and an eyewitness to General Strong's almost pathological antagonism toward OSS in the Joint Psychological Warfare Committee (JPWC), promptly protested Strong's efforts to the Joint Chiefs of Staff.[43] Strong's proposed research team never materialized and OSS's Heppner was made answerable to Stilwell instead of JICA.

In Chungking, the Heppner-Davies venture resulted in an almost instant protest from Miles, for it obviously constituted a direct breach of the SACO agreement. An outraged Miles, who had neither been informed in the beginning nor consulted later on about Heppner's appointment as OSS chief in the Stilwell headquarters, protested to Stilwell. Davies held firm, flatly rejected Miles's protest, and bluntly told the temperamental Vinegar Joe: "Such suggestion [of Miles] regarding Army officer [Heppner] assigned your staff [is] inadmissible and presumptuous."[44] Utterly defiant of SACO, Davies held that "as a paramilitary organization, OSS was entirely answerable to Stilwell."[45]

Miles's protest over the appointment of Heppner as an OSS officer outside of SACO and under Stilwell also quickly reached OSS headquarters in Washington. Donovan soon realized he had lost his gamble that no strong opposition over the Davies-Heppner scheme would arise. The director now had to face an awkward situation as a result of the Heppner-Davies initiative. Moreover, Donovan's situation was far more complicated. The SACO agreement had just been approved by the White House and the JCS, and signed by Donovan himself. Miles's protest demonstrated that OSS would be a lightning rod for all "thunderstorms" from the White House on down if the Davies-Heppner plan continued.

Furthermore, Davies's ferocious defense of Heppner as an army officer answerable only to Stilwell alarmed Donovan, who had already had a challenge to his authority in the Far East as OSS director from Carl Eifler. To Donovan's dismay and disgust, Eifler had consistently claimed that he was "under the jurisdiction of Commanding General, U.S. Forces in China, Burma and India," and that he was obliged only "to look to OSS for special equipment and funds."[46] Donovan dreaded Heppner becoming another Eifler. It was true that Donovan would not, under ideal circumstances, like being subject to SACO, but he did not like his field teams answering only to the army under Stilwell, either. Donovan loathed being controlled by the army as much as by SACO.

Even worse, Davies's high-handedness in dumping Eifler for Heppner to head the new OSS espionage project infuriated Eifler, who had been assured by Young Joe and Frank Dorn that he would be head of the new group. Davies's insistence on appointing Heppner constituted an arrogant affront to Eifler, who had never been told of either the new appointment or the Davies-Heppner attempt to gather intelligence in Burma, Eifler's turf. In late June 1943, an angry Eifler wired an emotional cable to OSS headquarters in Washington, asking directly, "Does OSS sponsor any project in Burma at present—or otherwise—which is not a part of my group or of which I have no knowledge?" In the same cable, Eifler chastised Donovan:

"As Far East Theater Officer no other project has been called to my attention. This, however, is not very significant since I know of numerous projects that have been launched in the Far East without the branches properly notifying me."[47]

All things considered, Donovan took decisive action. In the last week of July, when the army-navy game was being played out over the controversial Heppner appointment, Donovan, known for making quick decisions, put the emergency brake on the Davies-Heppner scheme. A surprised General Marshall cabled Stilwell and Ferris immediately: "OSS feel that they can take no further immediate steps in China toward implementing your request for espionage; . . . they state they have already had reaction from Navy Department questioning OSS authority to expand in China without sanction from Miles and his Chinese colleague." He continued: "OSS is becoming uneasy about feasibility of branching out in China with activities under Heppner independently of Miles as originally conceived. . . . They now lean to view that Heppner can act only with Miles and Chinese consent and as part of his organization."[48]

With this sudden and dramatic development, Davies's plan via OSS/ Heppner to ally the army with the Communists was temporarily brought to a halt.

The Army's New Stand on Intelligence in China

Antagonistic to SACO and the navy all along, General Marshall took a dramatic step on 29 July, when he secretly cabled Stilwell with a tip about sabotaging SACO: "In any event regardless what informal working agreements may be made with Miles, you request that JCS 245 be amended to clarify your right to base espionage activities in China additional to those required for special operations under the SACO Agreement."[49]

This is a strange instruction coming directly from Marshall. JCS 245, a model of ambiguity, was a plan worked out by the OSS planning group, headed by James Grafton Rogers in early 1943. The full title was "Special Military Plan for U.S. Psychological Warfare Operations Against the Japanese Within the Asiatic Theater." In the original plan, the peculiar Tai Li– Miles–OSS alliance in China and General Stilwell's approval thereof were explained in detail. But Dr. Rogers's planning group added to the JCS 245 draft a final paragraph regarding command control of OSS operations in China: "In order to facilitate the execution of psychological warfare operations in that Theater, the Commanding General, U.S. Army Forces in China, Burma, and India, should be made responsible for the prosecution of all U.S. psychological warfare activities in the Asiatic Theater, and that all OSS personnel and activities should be placed under his control."[50]

At the time the JCS 245 draft was presented, the SACO draft was also waiting to be approved by the Joint Chiefs of Staff. Such language as used by Rogers would put OSS entirely under Stilwell, which was not what Donovan wanted. In a dramatic effort trying to protect OSS's anticipated independence under SACO, Donovan promptly attached a special memo to the Rogers draft of the JCS 245: "I must call to your attention also that our Naval colleagues feel that due to the peculiar situation existing in China (by reason of the complete control of all agencies by the Generalissimo) that the Chief of the OSS Mission there (who is a Naval Officer) should report directly to the Generalissimo and not to the Commanding General, U.S. Army Forces in China, Burma, and India. They suggest that the provision should read 'The Chief of the OSS Mission shall exercise operational military command of this Mission under the Generalissimo Chiang Kai-shek.' "[51] In other words, the director of OSS suggested to the JCS that OSS via Miles should directly report to Chiang Kai-shek, while the chairman of the OSS planning group told the JCS that Stilwell should be in command of all OSS activities in China. Never asking a question, with a masterful stroke of self-contradiction, the Joint Chiefs of Staff approved both.[52]

However, Marshall's instruction of 29 July posed a major challenge to Stilwell. He could easily follow Marshall's tip and take advantage of the command ambiguity that JCS 245 had created by demanding that Miles give up his command over OSS personnel in the Army's theater headquarters. But that would contradict his repeated public statements supporting Miles. Besides, even if Marshall's suggestion ultimately led Stilwell to a victory over Miles, it would appear dishonorable—a victory won on a technicality, not through legal merit. General Stilwell needed more reason than JCS 245 to challenge Miles and SACO.

However, within weeks, Stilwell's attitude toward SACO suddenly turned hostile. The first item that irked the general was the intensification of cooperation between SACO and Chennault's 14th Air Force, as indicated in the vigorous push by Miles and Chennault for an ambitious navy–14th Air Force coastal mining and surveillance project along the Chinese and French Indochinese coasts. This was a long-planned operation desired by Admiral King. Yet the army from the beginning adopted a noncooperative attitude. Even pleas from Admiral King had not been able to alter Stilwell's opposition to this navy–14th Air Force joint intelligence operation. As early as June 1943, virtually all top U.S. naval commanders in Asia and the Pacific theater, including Admirals King, Nimitz, and Halsey, had put Miles in charge of this plan. The stubborn Stilwell, who alone had the control over hump tonnage, repeatedly rejected it as "not adaptable," "insufficient," and "too difficult."[53] Beginning from August 1943, OSS and the naval contingent inside SACO renewed cooperation with Chennault's 14th Air Force in setting up a radio and intelligence network along the coast from Shanghai to Guangzhouwan, and hence to Haiphong, French Indochina.[54]

Yet what was far more troubling to Stilwell was SACO's involvement in intelligence operations in French Indochina and Thailand, which had been a pet peeve of the British against the Americans. These two areas had long invited keen interest from the Chinese, the British, the army, OSS, and the 14th Air Force. Although OSS and SOE regarded these areas as "neutral," the Chinese did not, for, among other things, Chiang Kai-shek had been designated by the Allies as supreme commander in a large area of Asia, including Thailand and French Indochina. As recently as 26 February 1943, Chiang Kai-shek had launched a radio campaign expressing sympathy for "captive nations," including Thailand, and declared that China had "no territorial ambitions in Thailand and harbors no intention of undermining her sovereignty and independence." Roosevelt immediately endorsed Chiang's radio message, while Churchill remained cynically silent.[55]

For Tai Li and Miles, article eight of the SACO agreement specifically provided SACO with legal jurisdiction over operations in "Burma, Thailand, Korea, Taiwan, Annan (French Indochina)." On 28 August 1942, JCS had approved a proposal to recruit, train and equip Thai agents for the purpose of setting up an intelligence network there. Twenty-one Thai agents were approved by OSS in Washington on the condition that their operations be conducted in Thailand and not in China. The French group had an even more dramatic story. In spring 1943, OSS requested that French military authorities in North Africa provide this intelligence organization with French officers for activities in Indochina. Donovan ordered Miles to go to North Africa on his way back to Chungking after the signing of SACO and to contact General Henri H. Giraud, who designated his staff officer, Robert Meynier, the only French submarine officer who did not surrender to the Germans, for this job. Meynier's wife, an Annamite princess who was then interned by the Germans in occupied France, had important contacts in Indochina. On Donovan's request, British and French commando troops stormed the internment camps and made a dramatic rescue of the princess, costing the lives of three British and seven French soldiers. Mrs. Meynier was then taken to London to see the Chinese ambassador, Wellington Koo, who arranged a safe route for her to join her husband in Chungking in the fall of 1943. However, the French Committee of National Liberation in Algiers recognized De Gaulle's leadership. De Gaulle ordered Meynier to report to his chief representative in Chungking, General Petchkoff, who was deeply resented not only by the Chinese authorities but also by virtually the entire resistance movement in French Indochina. Thus the Meynier group was caught in a political cross fire throughout the war. As Eifler later reported, "If openly pro–De Gaulle, it would suffer the resentment of the Chinese and the residents of Indo-china; if it were anti–De Gaulle, it would displease the Theater Commander, the British, and the French Military mission in Chungking to which this group eventually became attached for general direction. The group was finally released to French control by mutual agreement and OSS maintained only minor connections with it thereafter."[56]

When Miles became the head of OSS operations in the Far East, Donovan relied upon him to supervise the ongoing OSS Thai group under Colonel Kharb Kunjara and the French group under Meynier. Both were ordered by Donovan to report to Miles in Chungking. Yet such OSS intelligence initiatives as were carried out by Miles under SACO met with strong British protest. As the most senior U.S. official in the Far East, Stilwell had to hear the constant and nagging objections from the British. As a result, Stilwell had become worried about OSS operations in these two sensitive areas. Meanwhile, Miles, as OSS chief in SACO, was dutifully pushing for Donovan's plans. In a planning meeting in June 1943, a lively exchange between Stilwell and Miles about operating the Thai and French groups illustrated the point:

STILWELL: The British are hostile to the whole idea and we would have to "screw" the British to get them in.

MILES: Donovan backing this?

STILWELL: Donovan is out to screw us. [I] DO NOT LIKE THE WHOLE IDEA. Because I am supposed to be playing an open hand with the British, due to the operations coming up. I think it's just asking for trouble bringing these two groups in. . . .

MILES: Have you any objection to bringing these people into China?

STILWELL: No objection, only wish I could help you. . . .

MILES: Use of Thailanders, Donovan was talking about, know anything about it?

STILWELL: John Davies to bring final decision back on Thailand.

MILES: Have you any objection to operating Koreans?

STILWELL: You have everything except Eskimos.[57]

Fig. 9. Left to right, Colonel Kharb Kunjara, Madame Katiou Meynier, and Tai Li at a banquet in Chungking (courtesy of the family of Admiral Miles)

Yet Stilwell's relationship with the British continued to deteriorate, so much so that General Marshall and General Handy in the War Department lectured him: "While we here must play God Save the King in this matter, you must at least stand up for the ceremony."[58] As a result, during July and August keeping the pesky British happy became General Stilwell's mind-boggling task. Then in late August, when Lord Mountbatten was appointed the new supreme commander in the Southeast Asian Command (SEAC), Stilwell became his deputy. This new theater command structure made Stilwell doubly apprehensive about the strong opposition from the British toward any U.S. intelligence operations in controversial areas such as Thailand and French Indochina. Miles, as the chief of OSS in China, had been du-tifully carrying out Donovan's missions to these areas—the Meynier group and the Thai mission, for example. Now Stilwell wanted to stop all these operations in order to avoid irritating the British further.

The creation of SEAC under Mountbatten further forced General Stil-well to prepare for a major strategic shift and focus his war effort more on China. Foreseeing a stonewalling of his demand for the command of the Chinese army, Stilwell began to envision a bold and risky plan of estab-lishing contact with Communist troops in north China. To achieve this goal, Stilwell had to begin with intelligence operations in the Communist-held areas. Thus in late August 1943, after a brief stage of dormancy, the Davies-Heppner plan was revived. In fact, Stilwell himself presented the idea of conducting intelligence operations in north China with the Com-munists to Donovan and Heppner, and they quickly began to organize. Atop Heppner's list of personnel for this secret endeavor were two marines who had extensive dealings with the Chinese Communists: Colonels James McHugh and Evans Carlson, both in the United States.[59]

But Donovan, worried about the reaction of Tai Li and Miles, took extra care. An OSS team under Davies working sub rosa with the Communists would inevitably invite a fire of destruction on the entire OSS venture in China. Heppner's request for dispatching McHugh and Carlson were po-litely declined by OSS headquarters. Donovan's attitude toward the whole scheme remained lukewarm. As Carl Hoffman informed Heppner: "Gen-eral Donovan is very carefully studying General Stilwell's request and he is in hopes that the opportunity will soon come when something can be done but in the meantime he recommends great care and delicacy in the handling of the matter. As a matter of fact it appears to be smart, until we can move, to try to keep the matter quietly pending and not activate it."[60]

Donovan's wait-and-see policy kept Davies and others in Stilwell's camp anxious. But everyone understood that the key problem was SACO. Upon wistful suggestions by Davies, Stilwell convened an important meet-ing on 12 September 1943 to discuss the OSS and SACO problem. Attend-ing were General Stilwell; his chief of staff, General Hearn; Colonel Pape; John Davies; Joseph Stilwell Jr., now a lieutenant colonel; Lieutenant Col-onel Dickey; and OSS representative Colonel Richard Heppner. The meet-ing began with an update by Davies on the Davies-Heppner plan for intelligence in north China and the SACO stumbling block. Davies's report was filled with personal assaults on Tai Li and Miles. General Stilwell lis-tened quietly. Afterward Stilwell declared, as Heppner reported to Buxton in Washington, that he "felt Miles had a very important function to perform and he had no objections to Miles's connections with Tai Li within certain limitations." But Stilwell was upset by two things: that Miles's involvement in the Thai operations had infringed upon Stilwell's right to operate an SI network in Southeast Asia; and that Miles was helping Tai Li train a police squad (Unit 9). At the end of the meeting, Stilwell voiced four demands: that "Miles abandon his dog in the manger attitude regarding the Army's wish to set up its own OSS SI net in Southeast Asia"; that "prompt steps be taken to amend the SACO Agreement to the extent necessary to Miles under the control of the Theater Commander"; that "any doubt concerning the right of the Theater Commander to carry on SI in China, and SI and other activities in French Indochina and Thailand be removed"; and that Miles be precluded from "engaging in high politics and in activities not directly related to the war effort."[61]

This important meeting renewed vigor for the Davies-Heppner plan. The first step, of course, was to deal with the legal obligations of OSS under SACO. To Heppner, who before the war had been a budding lawyer in Donovan's law office, this was tantamount to a fish finding water. A team in Washington working for Heppner carefully studied all the major documents regarding SACO. The best legal minds in OSS, including Edwin Putzell, Duncan Lee, and James Donovan, drew up a special legal deposition for Heppner's task to crack the SACO legal wall.[62]

Miles's Desertion and a New Deal with Tai Li

Alerted by Stilwell's startling declarations at the 12 September meeting, the navy quickly protested to Donovan regarding Heppner's activities in Stilwell's headquarters. Captain Jeff Metzel in Admiral King's office, Miles's immediate superior in Washington, sent a strongly worded memo to his counterpart in the OSS headquarters on 20 September, demanding the following:

1. Captain Miles's War Diary of 1 August, Page IV-D, indicates that Lt. Col. Heppner has assumed the functions of approving authority on OSS requisitions from Captain Miles. Coupled with the fact that Heppner has neither reported to Miles nor favored him with any communications whatever, you can readily see that the situation is well calculated to interfere with Miles keeping his eye on the ball. None of us can afford to let such an interference continue.

2. I am unable to believe that General Donovan intended any such setup. Please advise him of this and request that he take positive and immediate steps to have Col. Heppner either participate in China The-

ater affairs in a capacity consistent with Miles's status as Chief of OSS Activities there, or to make it clear to all concerned that Heppner is out of the picture in that Theater.[63]

To prevent Donovan from exploding upon reading this memo, Hoffman tried to temper the situation by citing Miles's 15 September "Secret War Diary," in which he described Heppner's lack of courtesy when visiting Chungking. Hoffman attached a note to Metzel's message for Donovan, indicating that Miles still showed some willingness to cooperate with Heppner, despite Metzel's demands.[64]

Donovan, feeling increased pressure both from Stilwell's camp and the navy, realized OSS was in a most dangerous position: the Davies-Heppner appointment had ignited an army-navy contest for turf in China, while OSS had become a pawn of lesser importance. Donovan was not going to let his organization get caught in this army-navy cross fire. His wait-and-see position regarding SACO had to give way to a definite policy. One possibility for OSS was to take an independent stance: either distance itself a bit from the navy or get out of SACO entirely. But any impropriety or mishandling could backfire and endanger OSS's chance of operating in China at all.

In late September 1943, Donovan requested that his top aides work on two urgent issues: preparing SI plans for activity in the Far East and considering whether OSS should divorce from Captain Miles and the SACO agreement. On 5 October a decisive secret meeting was held in the OSS headquarters in Washington, chaired by the deputy director, Colonel Ned Buxton. More than a dozen VIPs of OSS attended, including General John Magruder, Whitney Shepardson, Carl Hoffman, Otto Doering, Duncan Lee, and Donovan's secretary, Edwin Putzell. The meeting first went over Heppner's cable of 13 September on Stilwell's renewed effort to reorganize SACO and OSS. After prolonged discussion, the meeting reached two important conclusions, that "a final divorce by OSS from Captain Miles and the SACO agreement is not recommended at this time," and that instead, "it would be better to seek an immediate amendment of JCS 245 so that OSS can conduct SI activities independently of SACO."[65]

But when OSS requested that the Joint Chiefs of Staff change JCS 245 and clear up its command problems, the result was a total surprise. On 27 October the Joint Chiefs, after stalling a long time, issued a comprehensive, devastating new directive to OSS for its worldwide operations. Known as JCS 115/11/D, the new directive contained a startling clause which read, "all activities [of OSS] within organized theaters or areas are subject to *direct control* by the [Theater] Commander concerned."[66] This sudden, overarching command authority given to a theater commander like Stilwell would completely wipe out any independent status of OSS in the field. In all the war theaters worldwide, the only bright light of hope came from the China theater and OSS's great "necessary evil"—SACO.

Now Donovan badly needed Miles in SACO as a cover for independent OSS activities. But it was too late. The squabbles over the Davies-Heppner plan had frightened Miles; he had deserted Donovan. Why? First, Miles was humiliated over not having been consulted on the Heppner appointment while having just been designated by Donovan as OSS chief in the Far East in SACO. Second, after his arrival at Stilwell's headquarters, Heppner had snubbed, then lorded over Miles, who felt deeply insulted. Third, Heppner's appointment had been widely seen in Chungking as Donovan's plot to check up on the OSS SACO contingent and the Eifler group in Burma. As Miles wrote in his war diary, "Rumors exist that 'Heppner has been sent by Donovan to keep an eye on Eifler and Miles.' I naturally assume that the rumors are not true, but the fact that someone started them makes for disruption in the OSS system."[67] Miles also recorded that "Conversation with Lt. Col. Coughlin of Lt. Col. Eifler's camp indicated that Heppner has not visited Eifler's camp either and appeared in no way interested in the matter. Since Col. Heppner is supposed to be liaison with OSS in the Rear Echelon, I am at a loss to understand what are the meanings of his activities here."[68]

Fourth, and most important, Miles understood the political implications of the Davies connection. Among other things, Davies had told David Wight, Miles's deputy, in late March about wanting to cooperate with the Chinese Communists in intelligence gathering. This would undoubtedly and most seriously damage Miles's relationship with Tai Li, thus derailing the entire SACO project and ending all of the U.S. Navy's operations in China. It is important to note that Miles was by and large nonideological, contrary to how he has been painstakingly portrayed by the official Communist historiography and writings of the far left in the West. Miles was more of a navy man than an ideologue. He valued his relationship with Tai Li more than he cared about anything else.

Feeling cheated and confused, Miles gradually lost his initial enthusiasm for his role as the representative of OSS in the SACO setup. In early August, Miles had spoken of Tai Li's "black book," informing Metzel, "Gen. Tai Li will not countenance cooperating with anyone that is in the little black book—and that includes the British as well as a lot of Americans that are out here now. It does not include the Joe Stilwell or Chennault group—but he does still distrust OSS."[69] Donovan somehow got hold of this message and the last sentence enraged him, for the director believed Miles had been playing Tai Li against OSS.[70]

Relations between Miles and OSS continued to deteriorate. In his diary, which went to the Navy Department as well as the OSS headquarters, Miles spoke of having officers in SACO report to him as naval observer or deputy director of SACO but not as chief of OSS in the Far East. This caused a major uproar in OSS headquarters. A special OSS study was conducted to compile past directives, agreements, and military orders to document that Miles was indeed endowed with responsibilities by OSS as its chief commander in the theater.[71]

In the meantime, Donovan dispatched his aide, Commander R. David Halliwell, to SACO headquarters in Chungking to confer with Miles about implications of the new theater demarcations and to prepare for Donovan's projected visit to Chungking. Upon Halliwell's arrival, Miles held an all-night conference with him. Then Miles stated that he was leaving the next day for India to see Louis Mountbatten. Halliwell felt snubbed. Miles recorded this incident in his diary: "Commander Halliwell seemed to be perturbed at my departing from here without fully conferring with him. I tried to explain to Commander Halliwell that this conference [with Mountbatten] was long standing on engagement book and could not be broken." When Halliwell insisted that Miles postpone this trip, Miles's response would soon ignite a major explosion in Washington: if OSS did not want him to go to India to see Mountbatten, then he would go not as a representative of OSS but as a U.S. naval officer and the deputy director of SACO. Miles arrived in New Delhi on 31 October 1943. His meeting with Mountbatten went smoothly. Four days later Miles held a conference with Stilwell's son, who said that his father had just left New Delhi and had said, "If you see Miles, tell him for me that he is doing all right and that I am pleased."[72]

When Halliwell's report on Miles's statement before his trip reached Washington, Donovan was infuriated. This was the crucial moment when he most needed Miles to represent OSS in SACO, in light of the new JCS directive. On 3 November a high drama started in Washington between the OSS headquarters and the Navy Department. On that day, Donovan sent a letter to Rear Admiral W. R. Purnell, the highest officer directly in charge of the SACO project, proposing to relieve Miles as OSS representative in the SACO setup:

Reading his War Diary and his cables must make as clear to you as it does to me that Captain Miles and OSS are now in an impossible position, not only in relation to General Stilwell but in relation to each other.

Double allegiance and double command with resulting conflicting obligations will not work. Illustrative of this is Miles advising you that he goes to New Delhi as Naval Representative but not as OSS or SACO representative. He cannot divest himself as if it were a coat of his representation of OSS or of the Navy. His obligation to each is a continuing one or it is worth nothing. . . .

So far as intelligence is concerned the situation is further complicated because Miles has given his word to the Chinese that he will not engage in intelligence activities. OSS cannot be bound by this personal obligation he has assumed for the reason that the American and the Chinese intelligence services must each be free to act independently.

Once Captain Miles is released from any obligations to us as our representative, OSS will be able to carry out its obligations to the Theater Commander without conflict. The situation will then be clear and your groups and ours can work together without embarrassment and difficulty. We would be pleased if Captain Miles were to continue with SACO in addition to remaining as your representative.

We will continue to fulfill our obligations under the SACO agreement and will confer with you and our Chinese colleagues as to the advisability either of furnishing a member to sit on the SACO board or having our interest in SACO looked after by Captain Miles. In order to avoid any rumor understanding of our position by him, I would like to send word to him at once stating our views so that he will understand from us that our only purpose is to put our joint effort on a rational and healthy basis.[73]

Donovan wanted to convey four major points to the Navy: Miles was unwilling to represent OSS anymore; Miles's assurance not to conduct secret intelligence in China was unacceptable to OSS; OSS would relieve Miles as its representative, but would like to remain in SACO; and OSS would like to set up a separate SI organization outside of SACO and presumably under Stilwell.

Donovan's letter, particularly the last point, brought an immediate, strong reaction from the navy. Within days, Purnell sent a rebuttal to Donovan, practically contending all his major points. Purnell's reply is worth citing in its entirety:

In reply to your letter of November 3, I agree that certain difficulties present themselves in the matter of our common undertaking in the Far East.

Your letter implies what you told me in our recent conversation, that OSS can serve the United States theater Commander better and carry out its responsibilities under JCS 115/11/D better if it has complete freedom to set up an organization in China outside of SACO. Theoretically I agree. Practically, I do not believe the desired advantages will be realized unless the Chinese agree. It is also my belief that if the change is in any way forced on the Chinese, serious harm will not only be done to the overall war effort, but to long range interests of the United States in China. The proposition requires very delicate handling and no action should be initiated until the Generalissimo understands it and agrees to it. Certainly the concurrence of General Stilwell should be obtained before any actions started to change our relations with the Chinese in their theater.

From your letter and our recent conversation, I take it that you propose to change Captain Miles's appointment, from Chief of OSS Activities, Far East, to Chief of OSS Activities in SACO, and to set up an OSS organization under General Stilwell outside of SACO. Under the SACO agreement, it would make little difference whether Captain Miles is appointed Chief of OSS in SACO or a separate OSS member is furnished, as the organization provides only for a Director appointed by the Chinese side and a Deputy Director appointed by the American side, and a change in the organization requires decision on higher levels. Both Secretary Knox and Miles are signers of SACO, and the Navy's interests therein is substantial, outside of OSS activities. The present set-up of the organization was processed informally through the Joint Chiefs of Staff. I believe any fundamental change should follow the same procedure. From the Chinese point of view, real importance may attach to articles XXVI of the SACO agreement, which requires that organizational changes be discussed by the Director and Deputy Director and submitted for decision to the Generalissimo and President Roosevelt.

Your letter contains a number of statements and implications with which I am not in accord, however, they are largely matters of opinion and I do not believe discussion on this end of the line holds the answer. I think they are the results of misunderstanding, mishandling, inexperience, and mixed nationalities on both ends of a 7000 mile line, and have resulted in what you term the current impossible position between Captain Miles and the OSS.

There is one statement to which I must take exception, "because Miles has given his word to the Chinese that he will not engage in intelligence activities." He is deeply engaged in such activities with full knowledge and collaboration of the Chinese. OSS has neither given nor offered him intelligence officers or other help along this line. Instead SI agents have been sent out independent of him—to his continual embarrassment. I agree that American and Chinese intelligence services should each be free to act independently. As you are aware the Chinese do not agree. Whether or not it will benefit the allied cause to override the Chinese in this matter is something requiring decision on a broad basis, not on the theoretical rights and wrongs of their particular contention.

To release Captain Miles from obligation to OSS as its representative will certainly enable OSS to carry out its obligations to the Theater Commander without conflict with Miles. However, I trust that it will not bring OSS into conflict with much greater obstacles and difficulties. I have confidence in your ability to meet these, but not in that of many others and you have not much time to devote to this personally.

I believe that SACO has great value to the Allied cause, that Captain Miles has done exceedingly well in the face of a multitude of difficulties, and that the matters which are troubling you can be straightened out to the profit of all concerned. I must remind you that it is less than three months since the first load of freight was delivered.

I believe that when you reach the theater and get the first hand appreciation of what is going on, you will be able to arrange a working understanding satisfactory to all concerned, including concession from the Chinese of the essentials of the freedom of action that you want. I consider that the interests of all concerned will be best met by your trip to the theater to determine what the problems are and estimate the situation at first hand, and not rely on pre-conceived Washington decisions. I enclose for your consideration a draft of a message designed to acquaint Captain Miles with the situation and enable him to take preliminary steps to facilitate your achieving a satisfactory solution.[74]

Purnell's reply incensed Donovan. His accumulated rage against the navy exploded. On 8 November he fired back at Purnell:

If you feel that my letter to you of November 3rd calls for such a reply as you have made, then I have nothing more to say except that we do agree upon one thing—that there are difficulties to be met. The question is how to resolve those difficulties. To me the first step is to free Captain Miles from any obligation to act in any capacity for OSS and to have him continue in his present status as Deputy Director of SACO. The tone and content of your letter confirm me in that direction.

You are mistaken in thinking that I wish to designate Captain Miles as Chief of OSS activities in SACO. Such is not my purpose. At this time I suggest no change in the SACO organization and will continue to carry out our agreement. If at any future time a change seems desirable I will, of course, advise with you and with our Chinese colleagues.

I am very interested in your statement that Captain Miles is deeply engaged in intelligence activities with full knowledge and collaboration of the Chinese.

I have found it necessary to make certain fundamental changes in your proposed cable and of course it must come directly from me to Miles.[75]

The next day Donovan dispatched to Miles in Chungking a long cable detailing the situation. The essence of the cable is contained in a single paragraph:

Theater commander must according to our JCS Directives control all activities within his theater. In addition he is authorized to make use of OSS in such manner and to the fullest extent that he desires. Since OSS is now increasingly called upon by the Theater Commander to make available its specialized resources to him, we wish and feel under obligation to support him to the utmost of our ability. We also wish and intend to continue to meet our obligations under the SACO agreement, but your dual responsibilities make it difficult for both of us to operate. I now feel that it is my duty as Director of Strategic Services to relieve you from your difficult position and from any responsibilities to OSS as its representative in order that we may perform the tasks required of us by the theater commander without conflict. It will henceforth be possible for your organization and ours to cooperate without difficulty or embarrassment.[76]

Donovan's claim that OSS had been put under the theater commander was bogus; it was a necessary ruse for OSS to get out of SACO and conduct independent SI activities in China. At the end of the long cable, Donovan officially told Miles that he was coming to China and assured him that "the above is not designed to affect your position as SACO's Deputy Director and does not affect it."[77]

The Donovan-Purnell exchange of fire in Washington inspired panic in Chungking's SACO headquarters. Miles had a most exasperating dilemma. It would not bother him if he no longer represented OSS as its chief in the Far East. After all, this role had been imposed upon him in the first place. But the result of his dismissal as OSS chief representative in the Far East would also inevitably lead to an OSS setup outside of SACO, which not only would be resented by Tai Li but also was technically impossible vis-à-vis the particular articles in the SACO agreement regarding personnel change—Tai Li, director of SACO, had the power to veto any such change and he most certainly would.

Donovan's proposed trip to China was intimidating, for Miles hurriedly demanded Xiao Bo's return to Chungking. If there was anyone on Miles's side who understood all the inner workings, history, and legal issues about SACO and OSS, it was Xiao Bo. On 18 November, while Donovan's entourage was still on its way to China, Xiao Bo's plane landed on the outskirts of Chungking.[78]

In late November the Allied leaders met in Cairo. Donovan was summoned by Roosevelt to report on Yugoslavia.[79] While in Cairo, Donovan and Stilwell discussed the China situation, but Stilwell was preoccupied with his Burma strategy, and Donovan did not want to spend too much time with the general for fear that Stilwell would request more control over OSS activities in China and other areas. Donovan also saw Chiang Kai-shek in Cairo and received approval to go to China. Moreover, Louis Mountbatten approved Donovan's Burma trip to solve Eifler's "loyalty" problem. After Cairo, Donovan's entourage accompanied Roosevelt and Churchill to Tehran to meet Stalin. While in Tehran, Donovan received approval from Stalin to make a trip to the Soviet Union after his trip to the Far East.[80]

On 2 December, Donovan, accompanied by several aides, including Major Hoffman, Commander Halliwell, John Ford—the famous film director, now the chief of the OSS photographic unit—and a Captain McAfee, whom Donovan picked up from General Wedemeyer's headquarters in Delhi, arrived in Chungking. Welcoming them at the airport were Tai Li, Miles, Xiao Bo and Huang Tianmai.[81] Following an excessive exchange of pleasantries, Donovan and Tai Li spent some time swapping spy information with mutual admiration.

This was the first time they had met. The two men each had common interest in conducting unorthodox warfare, utilizing dubious methods, and on their own merits had become equally legendary figures.[82] As a token of esteem, Donovan presented $5,000 from the unvouched OSS fund as a gift to a middle school specifically designed for the orphans of Tai Li's many agents killed by the Japanese.[83] For this, Tai Li was thankful. A luxurious meal and many bottles of the Chinese liquor Maotai were served. After the midafternoon banquet, Miles recorded, "General Tai, Col. Hsiao and Mr. Hwang [Huang Tianmai] disappeared, as also did John Ford and McAfee, leaving us [Donovan, Hoffman, Halliwell, and Miles] alone to do some arguing."[84] The private discussion among the four was mainly about the Thai mission and the French group. Donovan expressed his disappointment to Miles about the lack of progress on these two groups. Miles explained that he had been working on these as hard as humanly possible. The major opposition against the Thai mission, Miles intimated to Donovan, was from the State Department, particularly the recalcitrant Ambassador Gauss. Then

Donovan switched to the Meynier group's projected mission in French Indochina. Miles pointed out that the key to the French mission was De Gaulle's chief representative in China, General Pechkoff, who had not been able to gain Meynier's loyalty or the respect of operatives in French Indochina, and had not even been accepted by the Chinese.

Then Donovan came to the point and stated that he was going to relieve Miles of OSS command in the Far East. Miles countered by saying that the SACO agreement would then have to be revised to change the procedure for personnel removal. The two men began a shouting tirade, but the argument soon turned comical. As Miles later recorded, "We did a tremendous job of arguing and, although I understood most of what they were talking about, I am afraid I enjoyed the situation too much to let it pass as simply as that. To an outsider it would have been amazing to see one poor little Naval Officer being harangued on three sides by expert professional lawyers with a very innocent look on the Naval Officer's face and a continued insistence that he did not understand all those big terms, such as assessments, procurare, assizes, testaments, instruments, pax vobiscums, etc. Finally it was necessary for the simple little Naval Officer to tell them that he had had absolutely no law training and could they tell it to me in common American slang. This they did in about three sentences and it seemed to work, much to the lawyers' relief."[85]

To solve the Thai situation, Donovan spent the entire morning the next day with Ambassador Clarence Gauss, who had been vehemently against SACO's sending the Kunjara group to Thailand. As usual, nobody could change the grumpy ambassador's mind; the talk ended in a stalemate. Returning in the afternoon, Donovan was given a full military parade at the SACO headquarters in Happy Valley, ten miles outside of Chungking. The general's romantic spirit about commandos was revived during his proud inspection of the SACO troops, and he was "very much impressed."[86]

Then Tai Li threw a grand party at his villa for the Donovan entourage, after which serious matters were addressed during a long meeting between Tai Li, Donovan, Halliwell, David Wight, Hoffman, Miles, Xiao Bo, and Huang Tianmai. Donovan's behavior turned lordly when he waved in front of Tai Li a copy of the newly issued JCS directive and declared that the JCS had empowered him to install an OSS organization in China. But Donovan said he did not want to consider a separate OSS setup outside of SACO for another six months; by then if OSS still found the situation unsatisfactory, it would seek to work outside SACO. Donovan then raised his voice and stated to Tai Li that he knew that General Tai could slow down such operations if he wished, but Donovan did not think General Tai would do so because he knew it would be unwise. Tai Li was not used to threats or sarcasm, and he stated coldly that if OSS wanted to conduct intelligence operations outside of SACO, President Roosevelt and Chiang Kai-shek must be consulted first.[87] At one point, Donovan bitterly complained about lack of support from the Chinese and the navy, pointing his finger at Tai Li. Tai Li turned to his aides and said, "You see, he points one finger accusingly at me, but three point to himself."[88] Donovan exploded, crumpled up the JCS paper and threw it on the ground.

Huang Tianmai, forever a diplomat mindful of protocol, immediately murmured into Tai Li's ear that Donovan's behavior was in violation of diplomatic protocol and was extremely impolite; thus Tai Li could legitimately walk away from the negotiation table and call off the talk. Tai Li slowly rose and was ready to leave. Suddenly Donovan realized the seriousness of the situation and quickly yielded. He patted Huang Tianmai's shoulder as an expression of apology and picked up the crumpled JCS paper, putting it into his hip pocket. Tai Li calmly returned to his seat.[89] Within minutes the two empire builders, men of ego and power, were again shaking hands and were all smiles. "Tai Li admitted that OSS could work inside SACO, if the JCS wanted it to, therefore there was no reason for setting up a separate OSS organization in China. Donovan then told Tai Li that he was dissatisfied with Miles, that he had removed him from his job with OSS and was sending Major Hoffman to take it over on a six months trial basis."[90] Upon hearing this, Miles quickly suggested that "since it was impossible for me to be both an OSS officer and a Naval officer, that it also might be impossible for me to be a Naval officer and at the same time Deputy Director of SACO." Donovan blew up again, this time at Miles. As Miles recorded, "At this intimation General Donovan practically bit off my head and there was a general free for all for some minutes in which General Donovan completely lost his temper and the Naval Officer grinned at him."[91]

Donovan clearly realized that he could only afford to neutralize Miles, not antagonize him. If Miles withdrew completely from SACO, OSS would undoubtedly have to go to the army and be subject to Stilwell's control. Miles knew this and used it as leverage to force Donovan to back down. As Miles privately told Metzel, "At any rate, General Donovan said that he had no fault to find with me, except as an OSS Director and that he did not insist upon my being relieved of anything else. Furthermore, that he was perfectly satisfied that I remain as Deputy Director. General Tai added his two cents worth at this time saying that he was also satisfied with my being Deputy Director."[92]

After this tense encounter, Donovan's top aides, Hoffman and Halliwell, spent the entire next day preparing OSS position and project state-

Fig. 10. Major Carl Hoffman with Tai Li at a banquet in Chungking (courtesy of the family of Admiral Miles)

ments, as well as detailed minutes of the meeting. Miles was deliberately kept out of the writing process. On 5 December, Tai Li invited Donovan and his entourage to attend a party at the orphan school. Many glowing speeches were delivered. To illustrate his major point, Tai Li treated the Americans, from OSS and navy camps altogether under SACO, with a specially selected Chinese opera. It was the story of three brothers who were supposed to get along well together but who were generally fighting all the time. Eventually they did join forces and worked well ever after.[93]

Clearly, Tai Li's operatic suggestion did not work immediately. After the opera, all went to Tai Li's house at about 9 P.M. and started arguing again. This time, two sides, OSS and Tai Li, each presented their points in writing—points that had already been extensively discussed two days before. Miles reported to Washington days later, "It was an argument consisting of an out and out fight between General Tai, General Donovan, Colonel Hsiao, and little me, with Mr. Hwang [Huang Tianmai] taking notes."[94] Tai Li's position was that there should be joint control of personnel and materials in SACO; that there should be no separate OSS organization set up in China; and that SACO should continue.

Before the late-night conference, Donovan had presented the OSS position and project statement to Tai Li, without giving Miles a copy. During the conference, Miles mentioned the impropriety of this, at which Donovan flared up and, as Miles remembered, "bit my head off again."[95]

This conference was indeed a startling circus for all involved, particularly considering that Donovan, Tai Li, and Miles all agreed on the fundamental points raised by Tai Li: first, SACO should continue; second, there should be joint control of material and personnel; third, there would be no separate OSS setup. Moreover, all sides shared some fundamental understanding of the problems, particularly over cryptographic work in SACO as promised in article eighteen of the SACO agreement. Donovan even apologetically told Tai Li face to face that "not only as a signer of that Agreement, but also as an American citizen, he felt that the United States had not done its duty with respect to their promise to the Chinese."[96]

The only logical explanation for these outbursts was that of clashing egos and suspicions on all sides. Miles vividly described the scene:

> General Tai was pretty peeved at me for having refused him 300 guns one time for an unexplained use and seemed to have been harboring a considerable grudge because I had not trusted him in the matter. This brought up a lot of angry comments from General Donovan, who insisted that we were not going to turn over any guns to the Chinese unless we knew where they were going. I think it was merely a matter of faulty interpretation. Sin Ju [Xiao Bo] got real angry and his English fell off. He yelled and became unintelligible. General Donovan yelled and became ungentlemanlike. Hoffman butted in and made them all mad. At one time General Donovan stated that we better shake hands and call the agreement off. General Tai said, in Chinese, it was all right with him to call off the agreement, but before Sin Ju could interpret this, Mr. Hwang, the diplomat, stepped in and advised that it should not be translated into English. I believe that was a good thing. Finally it became assured that General Donovan and I were not fighting and that for some reason or other I was still acceptable to the Chinese and to General Donovan and that we had better go home and go to bed. I was very depressed. I did manage, however, to lower my voice as much as they raised theirs. At the end of the conference I was talking in a

whisper which made them all shut up and listen in order to understand me at all. At two o'clock in the morning we all departed.[97]

The conference did produce several concrete results. Donovan fired Miles in writing: "In accordance with my exchange of communications with Admiral Purnell and yourself, you are hereby relieved of your representation of the Office of Strategic Service in any capacity. You are directed to turn over to Major Carl O. Hoffman, U.S. Army, an OSS personnel roster and an updated accounting of OSS finances and supplies."[98] Second, it was agreed that Tai Li should retain his power as the director and Miles as the deputy director of SACO, except that a new OSS representative independent of Miles should directly report to Tai Li: "Navy shall not have the veto power of any OSS personnel reporting for duty and, likewise, OSS shall not have the veto of any Navy personnel reporting for duty. As has been the custom, such personnel will, of course, be cleared with the Chinese."[99]

On the last day of Donovan's trip, 6 December 1943, Tai Li took Donovan to see Chiang Kai-shek and General He Yingqin, Chiang's chief of staff. During the meeting, Donovan told Chiang Kai-shek about relieving Miles of OSS duties, replacing him temporarily with Hoffman, and requesting approval from the generalissimo, who assented. Upon this, with Tai Li present, a jubilant Donovan followed up with a cantankerous question about what the generalissimo thought of General Tai Li. Chiang Kai-shek, smiling, gave Tai Li an unequivocal endorsement.

Donovan was scheduled to fly back to India at 2 P.M. for a similar tough negotiation with Mountbatten about OSS operations there. But General Stilwell's headquarters refused to fly Donovan on time and decided to delay until the next day. The reason given to Donovan by Major General Thomas Hearn, Stilwell's chief of staff, was that the plane had to wait to take Joe E. Brown, a comedian who was entertaining the U.S. Army in China, back to India. Outraged, Donovan threatened to report the incident to Washington. Hearn immediately made a plane available to Donovan, who departed for India three and a half hours behind schedule.[100]

By the end of Donovan's trip, Miles had had the last laugh. He recorded the situation several days after Donovan's departure: "The fights were really unnecessary and very embarrassing. Both Hoffman and Sin Ju got extremely angry at each other in public. Both yelled at the top of their voices. I made them both mad by telling Sin Ju that he had become an American because I had never seen a Chinese lose his temper before in public. At any rate I have kept my mouth shut during the last couple days, my ears open, my eyes open."[101]

After leaving Chungking on 6 December, Donovan arrived the next day at Nazira, where Eifler's Detachment 101 was headquartered. Donovan's inspection aimed to regain Eifler's loyalty, which had almost totally gone to General Stilwell. Eifler was still angry at OSS for lack of supply support, and most recently, for Heppner's superseding him. Donovan's trip to Burma turned into a pompous competition of bravery and chutzpah between himself and Eifler. The highlight was their treetop-level flight in a single-engine plane more than one hundred miles behind Japanese lines.[102] In the end, Donovan decided that Eifler was too individualistic and decided to send him to Washington to do office work. One reason Donovan dared to do so was because of the rumor that General Stilwell would be replaced very soon. Donovan appointed John Coughlin, Eifler's deputy, "to take on *experimentally* for the next two months the job of OSS officer for the Stilwell theater—this to include (1) the immediate Theater needs (2) representative of OSS in SACO (3) Kunming (4) this 101 detachment."[103]

On 10 December, Donovan officially notified General Stilwell of the following six major developments:

(1) Miles had been relieved as the chief of OSS in the Far East, and Hoffman was now taking over.

(2) The generalissimo, Minister of War He Yingqin, and Tai li had approved an intelligence service to be jointly run by the Chinese and OSS under the SACO agreement.

(3) Eifler would be going to Washington for a "brief refresher course in our work" so that he would be in a better position to know the various activities being carried on.

(4) Lieutenant Colonel Coughlin would be the new head of OSS in Stilwell's theater, replacing Heppner, but Coughlin should not be on Stilwell's staff.

(5) Coughlin was also now the OSS representative in SACO.

(6) Heppner would go to the SEAC Theater as the chief OSS representative under Louis Mountbatten.[104]

This was a masterstroke by Donovan. The new arrangement strengthened the OSS position in SACO by forcing the Chinese to agree on OSS's independent status from the navy. It pleased Stilwell by officially appointing John Coughlin as "head of OSS in your theater" but deliberately avoided mentioning who should have direct command control over him. Most important, this arrangement removed two of Stilwell's stalwarts from Burma and China: Eifler and Heppner.[105]

Miles felt a twisted sense of relief. For a long time he had not wanted to be Donovan's representative. Miles sincerely hoped to proceed now with

Fig. 11. Colonel John Coughlin, head of OSS/China during much of General Stilwell's tenure in China (courtesy of the family of Admiral Miles)

his guerrilla training, coastal mining, and weather intelligence. During Donovan's stormy visit to Chungking, Miles was a lone naval officer hopelessly fighting for his own enterprise. He had to endure a most violent assault from OSS. But more humiliating was the apathy, if not betrayal, of Tai Li in defending him and in agreeing with Donovan's high-handed demand of setting up a different unit within SACO. When Miles most needed support from Washington, Rear Admiral Purnell was ill in the hospital, and Metzel stopped communicating with Chungking. As a result, the transition in

Chungking went without much resistance from a deeply weakened and humiliated Miles.

On 7 December, Hoffman jubilantly wired a cable to Metzel in Washington, telling him that "I am now acting as chief of OSS in China."[106] The same day, Miles, Xiao Bo, Halliwell, and Hoffman held a conference to finalize the new arrangements as a result of Donovan's visit. While there was no squabble about the necessity to continue the SACO agreement under the directorship of Tai Li, the four men agreed to a division of functions within SACO:

Navy	OSS
Weather reports	Secret intelligence
Aerial reconnaissance	Counterespionage
Special operations, maritime	Special operations
Mining	(a) physical
Radio interception	(b) morale
Material	Research and analysis
Communication	Material
Training	Communication
Medical	Training
Repair shops	Repair shops[107]

Besides the above division of functions, a tripartite weekly conference would be held for joint action. On 10 December, Miles sent a memo to Tai Li formally informing him of the division of functions:

> You will remember that it seemed advisable to have a special officer from Washington represent the OSS activities of this organization. It was understood that the work of this officer would be separate from the work of the Naval Section of SACO, but that both would report to you as Director of the entire Organization.
>
> Major Hoffman has been designated by General Donovan as his personal representative to handle the OSS work until an officer can be sent out for permanent station. As Deputy Director, I am in accord with this move and recommend the approval of this temporary appointment by you.
>
> It is, of course, understood that the name of the officer nominated for handling the OSS work permanently will be given to you for approval before he is sent out to do the job.[108]

In the meantime, Hoffman began reorganizing the OSS contingent in Chungking. The first action he took was to prevent OSS from having anything further to do with John King Fairbank. "Mr. Fairbank had handled himself so badly that he caused OSS to be under continued suspicion," reported Hoffman, "I cabled Dr. Langer [Fairbank's boss in Washington], that if Mr. Fairbank was connected with OSS in any capacity, it would seriously affect our relations with the Chinese. The unfavorable reports received on Mr. Fairbank were not from SACO Chinese but from Chinese officialdom outside of SACO."[109]

One of the reasons for Hoffman's disavowing Fairbank was the fact that the IDC team under Fairbank had been closely connected with Wang Pengsheng's Institute of International Relations (Guoji Guanxi Yanjiu Suo), another of Chiang Kai-shek's intelligence agencies charged with collecting information from the occupied areas.[110] The reason for this was that Wang Pengsheng's Institute was not only officially bankrolled by British intelligence but also penetrated by Communist intelligence.[111]

On 14 December, Colonel John Coughlin arrived at Chungking to be the permanent chief of OSS within SACO.

The Navy Protests

Miles's relief, however, was short-lived. The new arrangement caused an uproar in Washington. Ever since the issuance of JCS 115/11/D on 27 October 1943, particularly since the Donovan-Purnell exchanges of letters and tempers in early November, the navy had anticipated OSS's quickly altering the SACO situation. The only concern from the navy was that opposition from the Chinese might endanger SACO as a whole. Now, since the Chinese had endorsed the changes, SACO remained intact. But upon carefully reading the communications from Chungking in mid-December, the navy was horrified to realize that OSS actually did not get out of SACO and go over to Stilwell, as anticipated—which would have been all right with the navy.[112] OSS was actually still inside SACO. Worse yet, all signs showed that OSS intended to take over SACO completely.

On 19 December an urgent Navy Department cable asked Miles in Chungking, "Is Coughlin presented as permanent OSS Chief IN or OUTSIDE SACO?"[113] On 21 December, Metzel wrote to Miles, "After all day with Adms R. S. [Schurmann] & P. [Purnell] & Stone re 18 [article eighteen of SACO about cryptography], Halliwell [of OSS] showed up with the amazing news that all is inside SACO. Hoffman dispatches certainly gave no clue." Metzel continued, "We have no light whatever on any new relationships with General Stilwell, whether you continue to deal with him for SACO, or whether Coughlin is to have a separate hookup." What most alarmed the navy was that Hoffman's cables to Washington indicated that OSS did not adhere to the prescribed division of functions, for, as Metzel reported, "One message from Hoffman speaks of OSS cryptographers and weather reporting instructors, neither of which apparent duplication are understood." Metzel further told Miles that "D.N.I. [Director of Naval Intelligence] is certainly not going to tolerate your being pushed completely out of intelligence activities as indicated in the 'division of duties.' " As to the police training school under Charlie Johnston, Metzel warned, "Don't let Johnston get under OSS, or agree to any intelligence lashup not acceptable to Stilwell."[114]

Rear Admiral Purnell was furious over Miles's 10 December memo to Tai Li, agreeing to the division of duties between OSS and navy within SACO. "In view of the fact," the admiral charged, "that Stilwell agreed only to special command setup under General Tai and you, what led you to indicate by your letter to General Tai that you recognize a setup which I have no reason to believe approved by JCS, Cominch [Admiral King], or Stilwell?"[115]

But Purnell was wrong about Stilwell. On 31 December, in direct violation of all open agreements with Miles and the navy, the general issued a secret directive to Carl Hoffman. The comprehensive "Specific Directive to OSS" by Stilwell gave OSS broad secret authority to conduct intelligence on ground rescues of prisoners of war, Japanese psychological warfare, puppet troops, and antiaircraft, as well as engineering intelligence concerning roads, railroads, inland waterways, airfields, ports, landing beaches, and pack transport.[116]

What was more disturbing to the navy and particularly to Admiral King was the conduct of the State Department in a seemingly multidirectional effort to deconstruct SACO. On 6 January 1944, Ambassador Gauss sent a memo to Secretary of State Cordell Hull demanding removal of Miles from his status as naval observer of the embassy, Miles's only public title. Guass's reasoning was rather simple: Tai Li was running a "Gestapo" or "OPGU." It was therefore "most desirable that the Embassy be freed of all official relationship to Army and Navy officers who may have connection with General Tai."[117] But Gauss's real reason to remove Miles was the latter's involvement in the French and Thai groups, which had resulted in diplomatic ill feelings caused by Chungking's De Gaullists, most notably General Pechkoff.

Admiral King and Rear Admiral Purnell decided in early 1944 to react strongly against all new arrangements in SACO resulting from Donovan's recent trip. On 5 January the navy drafted a position statement entitled "Comments on Chungking Conversations of 5 December 1943," which effectively expressed its disapproval of all the new arrangements:

Separation of Captain Miles from position of Coordinator, U.S. Strategic Services in China and appointment of another officer by General Donovan not valid without concurrence of Admiral Purnell. . . . The entire new shake violates JCS-245 which puts the Chief of OSS activities, Asiatic Theater, under the operational command of the Director of SACO. . . . SACO is a military organization commanded by the Director immediately under the Generalissimo, with the Deputy Director second in command. . . . The Navy has furnished more than 90% of the personnel and more than 95% of the material for the entire project and is prepared to continue this in support of SACO as established by the Joint Chiefs of Staff. It is not prepared to turn over personnel nor equipment provided for SACO to the OSS, nor to support OSS organizations set up without authority in defiance of the Joint Chiefs of Staff order number 245. . . . Memorandum of 9 October Chungking Conference clarified nothing and confuses many things. Comdr. Halliwell states Chinese Alternate succeeds Director as head of SACO in his absence, thereby making Captain Miles's position as Deputy Director meaningless. . . . Memorandum completely ignores General Stilwell. Division of duties implies OSS assume command of Naval personnel furnished for fighting, training, and for operations, except Maritime, and takes possession of Naval personnel. Recommend dispatch from Admiral Purnell and General Donovan, or Joint Chiefs of Staff to Captain Miles canceling all changes of command relationship and organization subsequent 1 November, 1943.[118]

With this sudden pendulum swing in the complicated SACO-OSS-navy-army arrangement, Donovan felt the heat quickly. He realized that the navy was determined to use all its resources to overturn what he had gotten from Miles and Tai Li during the trip to Chungking. The situation became so intense on both sides that a massive amount of energy was spent both by OSS and the navy to record what had actually transpired in Chungking and to prepare all the documents, binding and nonbinding, pertinent to SACO. With Donovan still on a global tour, a final showdown in Washington seemed inevitable.

As a first step, Captain Jeff Metzel urgently wired Miles, requesting his return to Washington for a conference. In the meantime, Commander R. David Halliwell, Metzel's OSS counterpart, bombarded the navy with minutes and memorandums related to the SACO situation—documents that thrived on conceptual ambiguities and factually extended interpretations. While everyone was tracking Donovan's whereabouts and calculating his return date to Washington, a prelude of the showdown occurred upon Miles's arrival at the Navy Department on 7 February. Participants at the meeting included Metzel, Miles, Abie Leggett from the Navy, and Halliwell of OSS. After some awkward exchange of pleasantries, Miles and Halliwell immediately intensified the atmosphere by providing different versions of what had happened in Chungking during Donovan's stay. Halliwell's arguments were largely based upon the two conference minutes, dated 5 December and 9 December, which had been agreed upon at the time, and Miles's own memorandum of 10 December to Tai Li confirming all the changes with OSS. Miles's defense was simple: he had been under much pressure to gain a consensus in order to save SACO as a whole; his 10 December memo to Tai Li was an overextension of authority and had already been criticized by Admiral Purnell. As the meeting neared a stalemate, Halliwell asked Miles what he believed the solution was to the navy-OSS fight over operational space and command control. Miles immediately drafted a memorandum, which has since been used by OSS as a major piece of evidence against Miles. Hoffman even added a title to it, "Order by Captain Miles on Only Way SACO Can Operate." Miles's memo read:

1. SACO is a Sino-American Cooperative Military Organization with General Tai Li the Director and in command of all Chinese personnel of the Organization.

2. The Deputy Director of SACO is an American in command of all U.S. personnel attached to the organization and is responsible to the Director for the activities of the Americans.

3. To clarify the status of the Deputy Director, the following essentials of Command are promulgated:

(a) The position of the Deputy Director with respect to the Americans of SACO is equivalent to that of the Captain of a Ship or Commandant of a Shore Establishment.

(b) The Deputy Director shall have an Executive officer who shall be responsible for assisting the Deputy Director in the routine administrative work with the American director and also in liaison with the Chinese side of SACO.

(c) The several American heads of Departments shall be considered assistants to the Deputy Director for matters concerning their specialized branch.

(d) All activities by the American members of SACO to be with the full knowledge and approval of the Deputy Director who in turn is held responsible by the Director of SACO for the conduct of the Americans.

(e) No activities outside of SACO will be carried on by any of the American members of SACO without the express approval of the Director and Deputy Director of SACO in each case.[119]

Soon after the meeting, Donovan returned to Washington from his tour to China, Burma, India, Moscow, and London and was immediately swamped with papers prepared by Hoffman and Halliwell regarding the removal of Miles as OSS chief in SACO and the new setup with Tai Li.[120] On 23 February, Admiral Horne, vice chief of naval operations, presided at a meeting at his office in the Navy Department. Representing OSS were General Donovan, Lieutenant Colonel Otto Doering Jr., who was the deputy director of OSS and Donovan's law partner and stalwart, Commander R. D. Halliwell, and Major C. O. Hoffman; on the navy's side were Rear Admiral W. R. Purnell, Captain Jeff Metzel, and Captain Milton E. Miles.

The meeting started with Admiral Horne's call for a full and candid recount of all the pertinent events leading to the current tension. Admiral Purnell and General Donovan came right to the key to this problem: the role of General Stilwell, and for that matter, the army's ambition to control intelligence gathering in China. Purnell stated that he had been greatly disturbed by the cover sheet of the newly issued JCS 115/11/D directive for OSS that granted "direct control" of all OSS activities to a theater commander such as Stilwell. Because of that, Purnell had personally taken the issue directly to the Joint Chiefs of Staff; the JCS corrected his initial impression and confirmed the fact that "the SACO agreement were now the effective papers of the Joint Chiefs governing the activities of OSS and SACO in China."[121]

Donovan agreed that the key issue was the army and Stilwell. He pointed out that the army should not act independently in intelligence gathering because "General Stilwell was actually the Chief of Staff for the Generalissimo and also Deputy Supreme Commander of SEAC." What Donovan said next shocked all. He confided that General Stilwell had discussed everything thoroughly with him in Cairo about the OSS and SACO situation and that Stilwell's views about OSS and its association with the navy had put Donovan and OSS "in an untenable position." Donovan declared that OSS "did not wish to get in a cross-fire between the Army and Navy."[122]

Donovan then attacked Miles for changing his mind on the newly agreed Chungking setup, to which Miles replied that Purnell had just informed him that he had exceeded his authority by agreeing to it in the first place. Donovan's anger was evident: he pointed out that were it not due to complaints from Roosevelt that America's intelligence gathering from China was insufficient, OSS would be perfectly willing to withdraw from SACO entirely.[123]

Backed by the determination of Purnell and Metzel to overturn the Chungking setup, Miles boldly attacked OSS. He agreed that intelligence in China needed improvement but said that he and the navy in SACO were "unable to provide intelligence on the Chinese as had been requested by Colonel Bruce and Mr. Allman of OSS." Furthermore, Miles stated, "the Chinese objected to the current solution of the problem, for example, (1) that they were confused by the request of OSS for separate housing, (2) that they were confused by the request for different messing, (3) that the entire situation was a continual source of irritation to them."[124] Perhaps the most important charge Miles made was that Colonel Coughlin had been appointed permanent representative of OSS in SACO without Miles's knowledge or consultation. Moreover, the navy was extremely suspicious of Coughlin's triple loyalty to SACO, OSS, and most of all to Stilwell. Miles had earlier told Purnell that Coughlin, despite being an excellent officer and good friend, embodied the "OSS attitude of belligerence to Chinese jurisdiction."[125]

The arguments dragged on endlessly. Admiral Horne finally broke up the fight by asking Miles and Metzel a sensible question: why would the solutions as found by General Donovan in China not work? Metzel's reply was succinct as well as to the point: "A single military command of all American SACO activities was needed."[126] Of course, everybody understood the need for a unified military command; the fundamental disagreement was over who the commander should be. Perhaps the spirit of this meeting was symbolized when Purnell asked Donovan whether OSS agreed to a proposed cable to Chungking; Donovan threw back a resounding "No!" Upon this, Admiral Horne ended the meeting. OSS and the navy continued to go their own ways in China, and the only result was that both OSS and the navy agreed to disagree.

While in Washington, Miles reported to Admiral King on the general picture of the China situation. Eager to gain a quick foothold in the Chinese coastal area, Admiral King decided to speed up mining and aerial surveillance of major ports in eastern China occupied by Japan. For this he wanted Miles and SACO to immediately join hands with Chennault's 14th Air Force. Harassed by OSS, the army, and the State Department, the resolute admiral strengthened Miles's position. King sent a virtual ultimatum to OSS demanding that Donovan cooperate:

> Here is a copy of a directive I propose to address to Captain Miles in order to permit our efforts in China to be directed against the enemy and free them from organization arguments between the two parts of the American side. I request that any instructions you may give to Colonel Coughlin be in consonance with this directive.

Miles is doing essential work of great importance. This directive goes to the ultimate in limiting him to suit your desires. I cannot imperil an essential connection with Tai Li by going further. If you are unable or unwilling to comply with my request in this matter, I understand that you have expressed to Admiral Horne your willingness to withdraw OSS from SACO and I will appreciate your doing so without delay.[127]

On 8 March 1944, Admiral King pointed out in an instruction to the commander of the 3rd Fleet in the southwest Pacific that Miles was "working with the 14th Air Force in offensive mining and operating a weather net in China." He continued, "as our operations advance toward China, he will be able to assist increasingly in many ways. This opportunity should be used to arrange for exploiting the useful possibilities of SACO, particularly in assisting our submarines." Six days later, Miles departed Washington for Chungking via the headquarters of Admirals Halsey and Nimitz and General MacArthur to establish offices of contact with SACO's wide-flung intelligence nets.[128]

With Miles on his way to China, Admiral King made two important decisions regarding his future. First, he went to the White House and persuaded the president to promote Miles to the rank of commodore; second, he fired back at the State Department by relieving Miles from the position of naval observer. Miles got the news of his promotion in India and sent his relief order to Ambassador Gauss in Chungking. On 24 April 1944, Admiral King issued an order establishing a new U.S. naval contingent in China directly under his command. All members of the navy in SACO would now be designated members of the United States Naval Group, China, and the chief would be Commodore M. E. Miles.[129] Puzzled, Stilwell immediately cabled General Marshall to inquire about Miles's sudden new status in SACO.

Rejuvenated, Miles and Chennault immediately began an intense photo intelligence project on mining the China coast—an action that not only would decide the next stage of OSS operations in China but would also give rise to a brand new genre of intelligence activities that still dominates many aspects of U.S. intelligence today—spying from the sky. As for the army and State Department, Miles's return to Chungking with much heavier clout stimulated yet another intelligence enterprise—the long march to Yenan. While the navy and 14th Air Force were going east and south, the army was moving north, toward the Communists. Donovan was once again thrown into yet another army-navy game in China.

CHAPTER SIX

OSS Trisected:
SACO, AGFRTS, and Dixie

Your Honor, General Donovan: My ever longing for you through the
stretching distance is like the endless rolling billows and floating clouds
in the sky.

—TAI LI to DONOVAN

Although the internecine fight between OSS and the navy confused the Chinese, leaving them at a loss as to what to do, Tai Li was
delighted that his command over SACO remained intact. What was more
important was that he finally had a chance to frankly exchange views with
Donovan; the two spymasters came to a deep mutual understanding.

Contrary to popular belief, Donovan and Tai Li deeply admired each
other's pursuit of cloak and dagger in spite of their constant squabbling
over turf and operational control. As Hoffman reported from SACO headquarters, Tai Li and his people "sincerely admired the Director of OSS
before he arrived [at Chungking], and admired him still more after his departure."[1] Tai Li even sent a letter to Donovan right after his visit, apolo-
gizing for the "inadequacy of your reception and entertainment" while
Donovan was in Chungking and further pledging that "I shall exert the
utmost effort in order to develop and stimulate our potentialities to the
highest degree, so that we may jointly deal the very greatest blow to
the enemy."[2] Overwhelmed, Donovan replied to Tai Li, "Your letters recall
to me the very pleasant time I spent with you. The reception and entertainment afforded me were not only most adequate, but were heart warming
in their generosity and sincerity. Equally as important, however, was the
fact that our conferences throughout were marked by an atmosphere of
mutual good faith and a joint desire to do all in the power of each of us to
deal deadly blows to our common enemy."[3]

Yet what satisfied Tai Li more was the fact that OSS seemed to have finally understood the major dilemma for BIS in cooperating with foreign intelligence agencies. Tai Li had put all of his cards in front of OSS and pleaded for understanding as to why China was extra cautious in allowing foreigners to conduct unchecked and independent intelligence forays in China. Major Carl Hoffman, now Donovan's special representative in Chungking for making turnover arrangements, acknowledged: "As I see situation here, there are two Chinese principles which will do much to slow up operations": the principle of Chinese sovereignty and that of internal security.[4]

The issue of sovereignty was obvious, for no government—be it Chinese, American, British, or Soviet Russian—would allow unauthorized foreign secret intelligence activities in its country. On the principle of internal security, Hoffman conveyed Tai Li's message to Donovan: "The Central Government of China believed that its dangers from within are equal to its dangers from without, and the Generalissimo insists on receiving an accounting of the current action of any group of foreigners. There are apparently some very powerful influences inside China who are a daily threat to the Central Government, and if a little aid is unwittingly given them by a foreigner, the results might well be disastrous. . . . Those who thought they had 'the run of China' are finding out that the holiday is over."[5]

With this understanding, OSS received enthusiastic treatment from Tai Li after Donovan's first trip to Chungking in December 1943. When Coughlin and Hoffman both arrived in SACO, Tai Li held luxurious dinner parties welcoming them.[6] Indeed, Hoffman's report seemed to confirm Tai Li's good feeling toward OSS: "I think I can safely say that the Chinese are completely satisfied with OSS. General Tai Li has expressed to me his admiration for Colonel Coughlin. Captain Miles has attempted to raise a question about Colonel Coughlin's not properly reporting to General Tai Li but this is nothing short of an absolute falsehood."[7]

Tai Li's new cooperative spirit was shown in his quickly favoring OSS's requests. First came the historically thorny issue of SI, or secret intelligence. As we have seen, Tai Li's major opposition to OSS was its unauthorized dispatch of agents, normally British-styled Old China Hands, to China without the knowledge of, let alone approval from, Tai Li.

In late December 1943, the new setup of OSS inside SACO clearly gave Tai Li direct control over OSS secret intelligence. After Donovan's departure, Hoffman immediately started to reshape the SI program for OSS in SACO. Captain Hykes was appointed SI chief and the two held a number of meetings to work out a comprehensive program. On 15 December 1943, Hykes submitted to Hoffman an SI plan covering twelve major areas for secret intelligence gathering, largely aimed at occupied China. To implement such a plan, Hykes suggested the immediate establishment of an intelligence school run by OSS inside SACO.[8] Hoffman took the idea to Tai Li, who readily approved it. "Forty-eight hours later," an elated Hoffman reported to Donovan, "the General [Tai Li] made available to us some 350 files on agents. Thirty five agents were selected and school was commenced at once."[9] Hykes was designated head of the school and was greatly impressed by his Chinese students. As he reported, "from the start the students manifested a keen interest, and most of them an aptitude for intelligence work—in general they are a clean cut, intelligent and alert group."[10] On 6 January 1944, at a dinner party welcoming Coughlin and Hoffman, Tai Li enthusiastically offered to give OSS some intelligence materials obtained by his agents and requested that OSS submit a directive specifying the kind of intelligence it was interested in.[11]

In the meantime, OSS also furnished Tai Li with some conceptual innovations in intelligence operations. The first and most important victory was winning Tai Li's acceptance of R&A.

The adventure of OSS's research and analysis in SACO is an extremely complicated story. From the very beginning of Tai Li's cooperation with Americans, he had denied the importance of intelligence analysis. Nowhere in the SACO agreement was the role of R&A defined—in fact, it was not even mentioned. Not until November 1942 had OSS first drafted a formal R&A proposal for the China theater, for collaboration with scholars in China.[12] This first proposal had resulted from R&A/China chief Charles Remer's brainstorming with Stanley Hornbeck, Maxwell Hamilton of the State Department, and Lauchlin Currie and Owen Lattimore of the White House. That proposal was killed. As Remer angrily charged, "It had no chance of success from the beginning because it could and would have been blocked in Chungking and Washington by those who have blocked all later attempts to get something done. In any case it came to nothing."[13]

While John King Fairbank and other R&A people were interacting with many agencies in Chungking quite successfully, Remer encountered resistance from Tai Li and Miles. In the spring of 1943, Remer had contemplated making Fairbank a temporary head of the OSS research and analysis team. But at a meeting in early May, Metzel, Hoffman, and Xiao Bo announced to Remer that Fairbank was not acceptable. Remer's other recommendation that Charles Stelle take charge of the small R&A team in Chungking was also vetoed. The frustration of OSS efforts to establish an R&A effort in China was keenly watched by John Paton Davies, who quickly intervened. "The work of R&A was reviewed by John Davies of General Stilwell's staff," Remer reported to Langer. "I do not know what negotiations may have taken place between General Donovan and General Stilwell but they must have been satisfactory for the plan moved forward." Remer was referring to the ultrasecret Davies-Heppner plan, which touched off an instant reaction from all sides. Remer grew angry because his authority as the chief of R&A had been completely ignored by Donovan and Davies in the appointment of Heppner, who was ostensibly regarded as an R&A man. Remer concluded that "the chief obstacle lay within our own organization." Remer further warned Langer: "The hope has, I believe, been entertained that General Stilwell might take steps that would overcome our difficulties, a hope which is probably ill founded."[14]

Remer was most alarmed by the advances made by competing agencies in setting up intelligence analysis functions in China, as evidenced by the Davies-Heppner proposal. "The State Department," Remer reported to his boss, "has sent a number of additional men to China, some of whom are likely to be assigned to General Stilwell's staff. OEW and OWI [Office of Economic Warfare, under Henry Wallace, and Office of War Information, under Elmer Davis] are sending or have sent additional personnel. It seems that the JICA in the Far East is being organized and set up without our participation."[15] Remer concluded hopelessly that "we are fast losing." On 25 August 1943 a frustrated Remer, humiliated by Davies's intervention into OSS research and analysis, submitted his resignation to William Langer. Remer was to be succeeded by his deputy, Charles Stelle, who would later be chosen by Davies for the Dixie mission to the Chinese Communist stronghold Yenan.[16]

Tai Li's recalcitrant attitude toward R&A had been equally frustrating to Miles. Challenged by the Davies-Heppner plan, Miles started to realize the value of scholars. In September 1943 he announced that "my stand on the Old China Hand situation is naturally somewhat modified." He would now welcome certain OSS agents to do R&A—but not SI—work inside SACO.[17] Miles also urged Tai Li to use public opinion polls as raw material for intelligence analysis.

Donovan clearly understood Tai Li's lack of appreciation of R&A. To Donovan, Tai Li's strength was his ability to collect intelligence in a terrain culturally alien to Americans. This was not enough. OSS knew that any intelligence organization would remain primitive without a strong arm of analysis. The undeniable mission of OSS was to inject research and analysis into existing U.S. intelligence agencies that were overwhelmingly combat-oriented and thus of only tactical significance. It is not an exaggeration to assert that what had truly made OSS a strategic agency was its R&A branch, which was regarded by all as its crown jewel.[18]

During Donovan's visit to Chungking, OSS bombarded Tai Li with sales pitches about the importance of intelligence analysis. As a result, at the 7 December 1943 meeting, Tai Li finally agreed in writing that "there shall be developed under the Director of SACO a special staff for the procuring; analysis; evaluation and distribution of enemy intelligence," and he agreed to provide Chinese personnel to join with the OSS research and analysis team.[19] Subsequently, Hoffman appointed Lieutenant Colonel Herold Wiens as the head of R&A/SACO. On 11 December, Hoffman presented a list of raw materials that OSS wanted Tai Li to provide to R&A.

This new warmth from Tai Li excited William Langer, the OSS chief of R&A in Washington, who immediately instructed his scholars in India, the de facto headquarters of OSS research and analysis in Asia, to prepare for a major setup inside SACO. On 5 January 1944, Colonel Robert Hall, chief of R&A/Far East, arrived in Chungking and inspected SACO. During his visit, the Chinese told Hall that there was a huge amount of unevaluated enemy material collected by Tai Li's agents and that it was stored in several caves in Chungking. Hall reached a formal agreement with Tai Li that a joint research team would be established inside SACO. The specific points included a joint group of American and Chinese researchers would work together; each side would give as well as take (that is to say OSS would supply materials, too); the Chinese would provide all the space needed for the R&A group.[20]

Tai Li appointed his top aide, Lu Suichu, to head the Chinese research team of about ten scholars to help the sole OSS "scholar," Herald Wiens, to work on the voluminous Japanese language materials from various caves. Furthermore, to continue obtaining current enemy publications, Tai Li appropriated for the joint R&A team four million yuan, a handsome sum equivalent to forty-seven thousand U.S. dollars.[21] Tai Li's unprecedented support for the OSS research and analysis effort in China was so impressive that Hoffman reported to Donovan, "That there should be an R&A unit in SACO now has enthusiastic acknowledgement of the Chinese."[22]

OSS Blunders and Tai Li's Renewed Enmity

But while Hoffman and others in the field were painstakingly building a new cooperative relationship with the Chinese in early 1944, OSS was simultaneously destroying this relationship at an even faster pace through a series of unforgivable blunders. Within weeks after Donovan's departure from Chungking, Tai Li started to fundamentally doubt the sincerity of OSS, as well as its competence, in the new cooperation.

The first thing that began to derail the new OSS-SACO relationship was the revival of the Starr group and its sub rosa SI efforts in China. By now the Chinese were certain that C. V. Starr was working for British intelligence. The chief operator this time was Norwood Allman, SI chief for the Far East. Immediately after Donovan's departure from Chungking,

Allman saw a great opportunity to send in his Old China Hands, mostly C. V. Starr's protégés and business associates. This was done without any prior notice to anyone, either in Washington or in Chungking. While Allman's agents thought they were succeeding in China, Tai Li had every one of them under close surveillance from the moment they entered the country, and he briefed Miles on the situation. On 1 January 1944, Miles sent three names—John Smith, Robert "Bud" Smith, and George Frank Adams, all C. V. Starr's men—to Hoffman, and informed him that these were OSS secret agents sent out by Washington. Hoffman also received an angry protest from the Stilwell camp about OSS sending these Old China Hands to China without proper authorization from the army. Infuriated, Hoffman directly protested to John Magruder, the OSS deputy director in charge of all SI worldwide: "As Theater Officer, I have no knowledge of their existence, except that General Dorn [Stilwell's assistant chief of staff] said he would throw them in jail if I could not satisfactorily identify them."[23]

Hoffman's protest prompted a memo from Allman to Donovan saying that "the gentlemen concerned went into this business in good faith and I am sure you will agree that this should be reciprocated on our part." Allman attacked Hoffman: "I further understand that Major Hoffman and associates are tracing down some 12 to 15 other American citizens in the Far East. . . . It occurred to me that the OSS organization in the Far East should spend more time chasing Japs and less time chasing Americans. May I request that orders to this effect be given to all members of OSS who have any connection with Far Eastern affairs?"[24]

Yet Hoffman did not stop and he quickly launched an investigation of Starr himself. This worried the business tycoon a great deal. Three days later, C. V. Starr personally intervened and discussed this rather serious matter with Allman. Allman once again protested to Donovan and pointed out, "I consider this procedure [of Hoffman's] very dangerous to security and respectfully suggest that the good major be called off these people."[25]

This incident, however, was not as explosive as the next one would be. Colonel James McHugh, completely disgraced by Tai Li in China and by General Marshall in Washington, was now back in the United States and was secretly working in the OSS headquarters, along with his brother-in-law, John Magruder. In March 1944, McHugh began to organize his own secret operations in China, disguised as OSS. Once again, the British factor came into play. McHugh decided to dispatch a widely known pro-British businessman as his super agent to work under Tai Li's nose. That man was William B. Christian, formerly general manager for north China of the British-American Tobacco Company.

Christian was opposed not only by many in OSS, including Hoffman, but also by Stilwell, who had become extremely suspicious of the British. The Christian appointment thus was delayed until May, when McHugh most vigorously pushed the issue again. Finally, on 12 May 1944, Donovan appointed Christian his "senior SI officer" in Chungking, without notifying the Chinese. In his order, Donovan demanded that Coughlin provide Christian with "special funds"—starting with $10,000—for his unspecified special activities and informed Coughlin that Christian would be a super agent not controlled by the theater officer but directly by Washington.[26]

The sudden deployment by OSS of secret SI agents in China again coincided with a dramatic turn of events in Asia that made not only the Chinese but also the entire American military establishment in China extremely anti-British. To maintain British colonial interests in Asia, Mountbatten arbitrarily attempted at the beginning of 1944 to implement four strategic changes: stop work on the Ledo Road after reaching Mytkyina; abandon the recapture of Burma as not worthwhile; attack Sumatra in the fall and then work north; and, most important, include Hong Kong in the newly created Southeast Asia Command under Mountbatten. Stilwell was enraged and declared, "The Limies have now shown their hand. This pusillanimous and double-crossing program amply confirms all our suspicions. They are determined to keep China blocked and powerless."[27]

Tai Li was naturally horrified to see the sudden arrival of all these secret agents with British connections disguised as OSS personnel at this particular juncture, when the British were once again making their move to challenge China's potential claim to Hong Kong—an issue that had given Tai Li a reason to oust John Keswick's notorious China Commando Group two years before.

OSS's bad fortune with Tai Li continued. All the agreements Tai Li had made with Donovan and Hoffman during December 1943 and immediately after were based upon the principle of reciprocity, that OSS would both take and give in a mutually cooperative relationship. Donovan and OSS had no squabbles with the arrangement. However, a number of unforeseen reversals ultimately resulted in failures, misunderstandings, inaction, and ill feelings.

First, Tai Li was a constitutionalist, who interpreted the words of the SACO agreement strictly. Donald B. Monroe, OSS's morale operations (MO) chief in SACO, reported at the end of the war, "There was no conscious obstructionism, for the most part, on Tai Li's side. A great deal of the difficulty stemmed from [Tai Li's] own literal interpretation of the SACO articles." Monroe continued: "From the very beginning, General Tai was confused with the OSS chain of command. General Donovan signed the SACO agreement, then sent Major Carl Hoffman out as his personal representative. Hoffman left, and Coughlin appeared on the scene. Already there had been three OSS liaison men, where the navy had continued to have Miles."[28]

If the constant change of OSS commanders inside SACO was merely confusing to Tai Li, Donovan's appointment of Coughlin as the new chief of OSS in China, without consulting Tai Li, did not make him happy either. The ultimate problem lay in Donovan's creative manipulation of chaotic situations in the Asian war theaters. As we have seen, Donovan appointed Coughlin as the OSS chief for CBI, responsible to Stilwell in India as well as to Tai Li in China.[29] This interpretation was never accepted by Tai Li, who insisted that Coughlin's place should always be in China. The fact that Coughlin was constantly absent from China irked Tai Li. Coughlin's permanent deputy, Major William Wilkinson, was never fully accepted by Tai Li as legitimate. As Monroe further explained, "Tai Li complained that the OSS SACO head had only been in China three times."[30]

Tai Li's anger exploded in April 1944 when Coughlin defied orders to stay for a major conference regarding OSS morale operations and R&A operations in China; he abruptly left for India. Tai Li's points were fully explained in his memo to Wilkinson on 26 April 1944:

> I have been instructed that Colonel Coughlin is the representative of OSS in SACO and is the overall responsible person for all the work obligated by OSS in SACO. At this time when SACO activity urgently requires mutual discussion of means for pushing forward the work, I directed Lieutenant Colonel Hsiao Po [Xiao Bo] to request Colonel Coughlin not to depart from Chungking prior to April 6, whatever the urgency. Notwithstanding this, Colonel Coughlin actually left on the morning of April 6, so that he was unable to attend the discussions at 7 p.m. that night for solving the conflicts and problems about the work. The situation in India is critical, but the work of SACO certainly must not be regarded indifferently.
>
> Upon a previous occasion Colonel Coughlin also arbitrarily departed from his duties as representative of OSS in SACO, which is most contrary to the spirit of SACO and most deplorable.
>
> The present activities which Lieutenant Colonel Hall and Major Little propose for OSS in SACO urgently requires discussion and pushing ahead. I firmly believe that General Donovan must have some appropriate disposition for his representative in SACO so as to facilitate present and future progress.[31]

Another point of contention was the joint R&A research project inside SACO. Tai Li's original enthusiasm quickly evaporated as he realized that

OSS could not fulfill its promise for intelligence exchange, which was the basis for his agreeing to set up an R&A team inside SACO in the first place. Magruder in Washington vehemently opposed any intelligence exchange with Tai Li, as agreed upon by Donovan and Robert Hall.[32] This lack of coordination within OSS and the resulting chaos embarrassed Carl Hoffman, for he complained to Donovan directly: "I must admit that I have not been successful in fully supporting General Tai Li since I have been back because one of the important methods of support is the distribution of certain R&A and intelligence reports which would in no way violate the National Security."[33] When Tai Li told Robert Hall, chief of R&A/Far East, that BIS had "caves of enemy materials," he expected a complete free exchange of intelligence with OSS. But due to Magruder's resistance, nothing had come to SACO in months, and all Wiens did was write reports complaining about the lack of cooperation, further angering Tai Li. With no intelligence coming from OSS, Pan Qiwu (Pan Chi-wu), Tai Li's administrative head at the SACO headquarters, implied that OSS should thenceforth share part of the financial burden for obtaining materials, since the Chinese had already committed forty-seven thousand U.S. dollars for R&A/SACO; OSS refused.

Tai Li now felt snubbed by OSS. His enthusiasm for Hykes's SI school soon cooled. Hykes, Donovan's SI chief in SACO, anxiously reported, "I personally see the urgent necessity of coalescing our operations with the Chinese in order to obtain their fullest cooperation and good will, which will assist us materially in our joint projects."[34] Hykes's project was the first to receive a blow. He complained about Tai Li's change of mind, as he reported to Robert Hall, his immediate superior: "During the period 1st January to 31st March, only fifteen intelligence reports were received from General Tai Li," and "delays were becoming the general rule rather than the exception." After submitting his SI plan to Pan Qiwu, Hykes had to wait more than two months to get an "approval in principle" from Chiang Kai-shek. By mid-April 1944 "it was evident," Hykes wrote, "that we had submitted plans that the Chinese were not willing to accept—partly because they contravened Chinese policy, but mostly because the proposals were outside the scope and authority of the SACO Agreement, which was being used as a weapon to impede our efforts and thwart our plans. It appeared that we were completely stymied, and the possibility of joint intelligence operations with the Chinese looked discouraging."[35] Thus, when the Chinese informed OSS that it could not dispatch trained SI agents independently in China, Hykes closed down the SI training school, which only added to the anger and frustration deeply felt by the Chinese, particularly the otherwise amiable Pan Qiwu.

Another problem plaguing OSS was the lack of personnel and equipment; this also contributed to the deterioration of the relationship with Tai Li, who grew doubtful about OSS competence and capability to carry out intelligence and special operations on a scale as demanded by Donovan. When OSS had requested permission to set up an intelligence school, Tai Li granted approval almost instantly. The next day he discovered that OSS could provide only one instructor, Captain D. M. Hykes himself. This not only embarrassed OSS in the eyes of Tai Li, but also provided a weapon for the navy to ridicule OSS. Hykes was forced to borrow navy instructors from Miles, who, in Hykes's own words, "cooperated in an admirable manner."[36]

The same thing occurred in R&A, headed by Herald Wiens, who was the only R&A person in SACO to "cooperate with" the ten Japan experts Tai Li provided for the joint research and analysis team. The official OSS excuse was that it would assign R&A people to SACO only in proportion to the amount of raw intelligence materials Tai Li had. But OSS did believe that Tai Li indeed had "caves of enemy materials." Such an excuse was never accepted by the Chinese.

Yet SACO was not Donovan's only option.

AGFRTS

The lack of OSS personnel and materials for SACO was hardly an isolated phenomenon created simply by red tape, as was often the case at OSS headquarters in Washington. On the contrary, this was a conscious decision to provide a minimum number of personnel to fulfill the OSS obligation to SACO. Obviously, not all the agents sent to China went to SACO. In fact, OSS devoted most of its attention and personnel to a separate enterprise in the Chinese city of Kunming, where General Chennault's 14th Air Force was headquartered.

From the very beginning, Hayden had convinced Donovan that the best chance for OSS in China was to work with Claire Chennault. OSS had not allied itself with Chennault, who was in dire need of ground intelligence, mainly because Donovan feared being caught in a cross fire between Stilwell and Chennault. But in late 1943, the well-informed Donovan knew that a vigorous effort was being made in Chungking and Washington to recall Stilwell. This would dramatically affect the balance of influence in the China theater; it prompted Donovan to pull out as much personnel and resources as possible from SACO and send them over to Chennault.

Another reason OSS considered working with Chennault was the geographical location of the 14th Air Force headquarters. Yunnan Province, where Chennault was located, was a relatively weak spot as far as the influence and control of Chiang Kai-shek and Tai-Li was concerned. Or as Hoffman put it, "In appraising the value of General Chennault's connection, it should be remembered that the Generalissimo's power and General Tai Li's power in the various Provincial governments is quite small but the Provincial Governors or war lords are mostly all good friends of General Chennault."[37] Although no time could be spared to discuss this OSS-Chennault alliance while in Chungking, Donovan finalized his "Chennault solution" immediately after his China trip. On 15 December 1943, Donovan composed an important memo in New Delhi for Heppner and Coughlin. "I am leaving today," Donovan wrote, "and think it wise to put down for your guidance certain instructions that impress me as important in your two theaters." In this memo, among other things, Donovan clearly spelled out his strategy of "using Chennault air raids as cover for our operations." Donovan further pointed out, "We should regard Chennault's position, the area in which he is located, as a definite front and should aid him by whatever means we can, including the use and development of morale operations."[38]

For this specific purpose, Donovan had originally thought to designate a young and bright OSS officer, Lieutenant Commander Edmond Taylor, formerly a newsman, to handle the Chennault connection. But days later, on 18 December, Mountbatten announced the establishment of a "P" Division under British control to centralize command over all quasi-military forces, including OSS, in his theater.[39] For this, the British intercepted Edmond Taylor, arbitrarily changed his orders, and designated him the titular deputy chief of the P Division.[40] Facing this unexpected situation, Hoffman, still in Chungking, took over. He and Colonel Coughlin, the newly appointed chief of OSS in China, visited the 14th Air Force in Kunming on 28 December.

Kunming was the capital of Yunnan Province, under the de facto control of warlord Long Yun, whose loyalty to Chiang Kai-shek's Central Government had always been dubious. The British had long been interested in supporting Long Yun's separatist sentiment because of the geographical proximity of Yunnan and Burma; this strategy had contributed to the disgraceful ouster of SOE in early 1942.

While in Kunming from 28 to 31 December, Hoffman and Coughlin were enthusiastically received by Chennault and his top aides. This sharply contrasted with the army's red tape, pessimistic outlook, and cynicism in the China theater.[41] Chennault was in dire need of ground intelligence to guide his bombing sorties. Quickly, a conference was called to discuss the OSS gesture, during which General Chennault; General Glenn, Chennault's chief of staff; Colonel Jessie Williams, Chennault's A-2 chief of intelligence; and Major Wilfrey Smith, Williams's assistant, expressed their earnest desire to cooperate with OSS. Chennault promised generous support. As Hoffman excitedly reported to Donovan, "They would give us office space, facilities for communications equipment to be installed and wanted personnel and possibly cash with which to hire agents. They wanted an R&A group and an MO group."[42]

Before the OSS-Chennault cooperation could take its first step, OSS had to overcome a major hurdle regarding command: OSS had just promised Tai Li that no OSS activities outside SACO would be conducted. A deal was then struck with Chennault: First, this new group would not be identified as an OSS setup. In fact, it would have a name that would never evoke any connection with OSS. Hoffman utilized his legal talent and offered a strange title: "Air and Ground Forces Resources and Technical Staff," or AGFRTS. "It was," Hoffman confided to Donovan, "the most confused title I could think of at the moment."[43] Second, Chennault insisted that to avoid any protest from Tai Li and Miles, AGFRTS would be commanded by officers from Chennault's staff, although the agents would be provided jointly by OSS and the 14th Air Force.

While negotiations in Kunming went smoothly, Coughlin and Hoffman's success with the 14th Air Force backfired within OSS. First of all, Coughlin's rival, Heppner, believed that OSS was losing its identity and being swallowed up by the 14th Air Force. Compounding this, along with animosity between Heppner and Coughlin, was the issue of R&A personnel required by the proposed AGFRTS. Coughlin chose Lieutenant Colonel Robert Hall, his R&A chief, for the CBI theater; Hall accepted this appointment readily, angering Heppner, who believed Hall was actually his R&A chief. Caught in the cross fire, a baffled Hall was eventually ordered to write lengthy explanations to OSS Washington headquarters proving his lack of ulterior motives.[44] But the issue lingered. Differences between Heppner and Coughlin over the R&A personnel were so wide that many meetings would have to be convened throughout the rest of the year in Washington to settle the issue.[45]

Worse yet, the army naturally felt threatened by the OSS–14th Air Force alliance; this issue only added to the already intense bickering between Stilwell and Chennault. Many in the army, from General Stilwell down, objected to this new setup. The army demanded a revision of the AGFRTS plan, putting it under the control of the G-2. Chennault disagreed and insisted upon the original plan. This tug-of-war lasted into April, when an exhausted Coughlin reported to Donovan that "Air Ground Forces Resources & Technical Staff has finally been approved by the Theater Commander." Coughlin quickly added, "This has come only after a great deal of talking. It took over a week to get the plan written in such a way that General Chennault would approve it, and it took six days to get the Delhi people to approve it."[46] Ironically, John Paton Davies on Stilwell's staff had suddenly turned to support Coughlin's setup of AGFRTS and was vociferously trying to convince doubters of the legality of AGFRTS vis-à-vis SACO. Davies boldly declared that "the validity of the SACO agreement is questionable. It is drawn up as a treaty. But it has not been ratified by the Senate." Davies's motive was pure and simple: to pull apart SACO.[47]

Heppner's concern about being "swallowed" by the 14th Air Force was not without merit. Even after the deal was struck, Coughlin nervously wrote to Donovan: "You are sufficiently familiar with the China situation to know the importance of having a good sponsor—there is no better in China than General Chennault. I have been very careful to be sure that all the important army personnel out here know just who the personnel are that are going into this unit, and why. I am certain that our identity will not be lost out here, and I don't think that it will be lost in Washington. It will be a touchy point with the 14th, as they will be very anxious to claim all credit. However, I think it will work out to the mutual satisfaction of both. Time should tell, and it shouldn't take too long a time."[48]

Coughlin's nervousness was prophetic. In March 1944, even before Stilwell gave his final approval, Chennault had assigned Wilfrey Smith to head AGFRTS. On 1 April, Chennault promoted Smith to the rank of lieutenant colonel. Immediately, Smith ordered fourteen intelligence officers into AGFRTS from the 14th Air Force, two of whom would become major figures in the pages of OSS history: Captain John Birch and Major Paul Frillman. In response, OSS dispatched a total of twenty-two agents into AGFRTS under the leadership of Major Raymond A. Cromley.

Eventually, AGFRTS would become the center of OSS China operations throughout the war in the areas of R&A and MO. The R&A group in Kunming would include such figures as Julia McWilliams, in charge of the sensitive registry office, where all the intelligence reports were stored. McWilliams later married the chief of the OSS presentation branch in the theater, Paul Child, and became the internationally famous chef Julia Child. In support of morale operations, OSS dispatched many scholars and artists, such as William Smith, who drew cartoons, made up rumors, and printed them in leaflets. Chennault's planes would eventually drop tens of millions of these in the occupied areas.

One year later, in April 1945, AGFRTS and all its original members were directly placed under the jurisdiction of OSS as the OSS Zhijiang (Chihkiang) Field Unit. Still under the leadership of Wilfrey Smith, this unit became responsible for a vast SO network in the area between the Yangtze and West rivers.[49]

But the intense competition for turf between OSS agents and those from the 14th Air Force never ceased. Within one year, Heppner noted that Jessie Williams is "a bitter enemy of OSS and has never lost an opportunity to injure us."[50] Captain John Birch, a rising star in the AGFRTS and its succeeding unit, once sent a cable to Chennault asking, "when do I return to Air Force? [I] would rather be a private in the 14th than colonel in OSS."[51] Ironically, had John Birch identified himself as an OSS agent in Shandong Province on 25 August 1945, as he was at the time, rather than an officer of the 14th Air Force, he might not have been killed by Chinese Communist troops.

OSS and the Chinese Communists: The Initial Plan

Donovan's idea of cooperating with the Chinese Communists on intelligence operations had long been established and had much to do with British intelligence strategy. OSS's successful experience with the British SOE in the Balkan Peninsula served a good example for Donovan's operations in China; Churchill's decision to abandon Yugoslavian Nationalist General Michailovic and support the Communists led by Tito was a replica of the Chiang Kai-shek–Mao Zedong dilemma. In fact, Donovan's star agent in Yugoslavia, Walter Mansfield, who had authored an impressive intelligence report on the Michailovic-Tito situation, was quickly transferred to SACO for the sole purpose of surveying the Chinese Nationalist–Communist situation.[52]

British intelligence in China had long been engaged in secret cooperation with Chinese Communist intelligence. Following the Pearl Harbor attack and right after the loss of the British Crown Colony of Hong Kong to the Japanese, SOE began to recruit ethnic Chinese agents in the United States, Canada, and Malaya. SOE trained them in Ontario at special camps, where most of the early OSS agents were also later trained, with the specific purpose of joining hands with the Chinese Communist guerrillas in the Guangdong area for the eventual recapture of Hong Kong.[53]

Not surprisingly, within OSS, all those early enthusiasts desiring to work with the Chinese Communists on intelligence operations were close to the British, particularly the C. V. Starr contingent. As early as 28 January 1943, Starr's representative inside OSS, Norwood Allman, approached the State Department to inquire about the opening of eight new offices inside China. John Service, a third secretary of the U.S. embassy in Chungking, then in Washington, told them that he would like to join OSS since he did not want to go back to China, unless the State Department decided to give him an assignment in the Chinese Communist area in northern China.[54] Delighted, Allman tried to work out a scheme whereby Service would be given an assignment in the Communist area and secretly represent OSS at the same time. Allman shared his idea with Donovan, who immediately went to talk with Service. Service agreed to work for OSS secretly in the Communist area provided Donovan could use his influence to secure his release from the State Department. In early February 1943, Donovan sent an official request to William Kimbel at the State Department asking for Service's attachment to OSS. Kimbel then took this matter to Maxwell Hamilton, head of the Far East section, and George Atcheson, who was attached to the U.S. embassy, but both denied Donovan's request. As Kimbel reported back to OSS, "They stated that it was impossible for a State Department representative to work in this area secretly, i.e., he would have to have the consent of the Chinese Government to be there." Furthermore, Donovan was informed that Service might not be the right person to do the job anyway. "It is not certain," Kimbel told Donovan, "that Jack Service can return to that area. Someone else may be more suitable and better equipped for that duty."[55] John Magruder told a disappointed Donovan that the State Department was right in its decision.[56]

The urgency of intelligence cooperation with the Chinese Communists grew toward the end of 1943 because of the dire American need for highly sensitive intelligence on Chiang Kai-shek's Nationalist government and military. During his trip to Asia in late 1943, Donovan was bombarded by U.S. Army generals demanding such material. "I have been greatly disturbed here," Donovan confided to Heppner and Coughlin, "by the complaints of all concerned, particularly General Wedemeyer, that there is no reliable information on the structure, condition, and quality of the Chinese Army. While we do not intend to carry on intelligence activity within China, it is an essential part of our work to inform the theater commanders of the kind of troops that are to help us." As a result, Donovan instructed Coughlin to adopt two measures immediately. The first was to utilize the SACO channel to spy on the Chinese military. "You will obtain detailed information from the various camp commanders of SACO as to the organization and quality of Chinese troops with whom they are working and have your studies include those who are in the China area."[57] Second, Donovan wanted OSS to approach the Communists, who had been widely known for boasting about their intelligence information on their nemesis, the Chiang Kai-shek government.[58]

To reach the Communist area in the north, the plan had to be discreet and secret. While in Chungking in early December 1943, Donovan held a secret briefing with Tai Li on dispatching an OSS-led SACO intelligence team to northern China. Donovan promised Tai Li that no deal would be struck with Yenan and that Donovan himself would lead the mission. Tai Li agreed.[59] However, when Donovan came back to Washington, he was immediately drawn into the battle with the navy on the dismissal of Miles, a fight that lasted well into March 1944. When this ended, Donovan had to go to London and could not possibly return to China to lead the team to northern China.

As an alternative, somebody else had to be designated team leader, an idea Tai Li neither accepted nor rejected explicitly.[60] The person most qualified was undoubtedly Ilia Tolstoy, whom COI had originally planned to send to north China after he left Tibet. But Tolstoy was intercepted by Tai Li and Miles after SACO came into being. Tolstoy was now the camp commander for Unit 4 at Shanba, the northernmost SACO base. Donovan appointed Tolstoy as chief of the new secret mission to Yenan, and an elite team was trained in the campsite of Detachment 101, waiting to be dispatched to China in late June 1944.

The Davies and Tolstoy Fight Over Dixie

But the OSS-led Tolstoy team immediately found itself blocked by the army, which was then busy preparing an observer group called the Dixie mission for a trip to Yenan. The Dixie mission arose from extremely complex circumstances. The Chinese Communists in northern China sought not only military cooperation—the official purpose of the mission—but diplomatic recognition of the political legitimacy of the Yenan regime.[61] But the general situation in Washington and Chungking was such that the demand for political recognition by the Communists in 1943 was altogether impractical. Davies had written a memo to the State Department in March 1943 only to "convey" Zhou Enlai's request. The only OSS agent who actively lobbied for establishing a diplomatic post in Yenan was John King Fairbank, whose earliest call for this took place in October 1943.[62] Suddenly, around New Year's Day 1944, the entire Stilwell camp intensified its lobbying to pressure Chiang Kai-shek into allowing an army delegation to visit Yenan. The driving force behind this sudden surge of activity was, once again, John Paton Davies.

Why did Davies intensify his efforts to encourage relations with the Chinese Communists? Many reasons have been given, yet one of the most important aspects has been largely ignored: the British factor. In January 1944, Lord Louis Mountbatten arbitrarily readjusted the goals of his SEAC theater, where Stilwell was the deputy supreme commander. The new British aims of the war in Asia focused on "the reoccupation, under British leadership, of colonial Southeast Asia."[63]

In response, Stilwell swiftly redirected his strategy and aimed at Japan's "inner zone." As Davies explained to the White House, "The main American concern is, of course, to strike the Japanese where it hurts most. That is not in Sumatra and Malaya. It is in East China, Formosa, Manchuria and Japan itself."[64] This change in strategy of emphasizing areas north of the former British colonial empire thus necessitated contacting one of the most important forces in north China, the Chinese Communists in Yenan.[65]

As far as OSS was concerned, Davies's increased emphasis on northern China quickly invited criticism, for he was seen as abandoning the other theater areas, especially India, where there was a heavy buildup of OSS personnel. Particularly bitter about Davies's actions was the R&A group in India, headed by the controversial Dr. Cora Dubois.[66]

Getting permission from Chiang Kai-shek for dispatching the Dixie mission was not easy. The tension between Chungking and Washington is legendary on this matter. Stilwell used extreme measures, including banning Chinese officers' visits to the United States, to try and to persuade Chiang Kai-shek.[67] Chiang's reluctant approval for the U.S. Army's observer mission to Yenan was finally granted in June 1944, when Vice President Henry Wallace personally appealed to the generalissimo.

That Wallace promoted the Dixie mission came as no surprise. As chief of the Board of Economic Warfare, an intelligence agency charged with industrial sabotage and financial destabilization, Wallace had had little luck in China; he was shunned not only by the Chinese but also by the embassy and the theater command. Wallace's need to succeed in China was made even more pressing by the devastating success of Japanese economic warfare to destabilize the Chinese economy—in the summer of 1943, for example, the Japanese were pouring out $100 billion in counterfeit Bank of China notes in the southern provinces alone.[68]

Although the Dixie mission was billed as a military observers' team, it was by and large arranged, organized, and controlled by John Davies, a State Department civilian of considerable clout. Davies controlled the selection of personnel for the mission. He recommended to Stilwell that members for the Dixie mission should include a team head, at least three G-2 officers, and some signal corps personnel with radios. Most importantly, John Service, one of the four original staffers Davies had requested for Stilwell in early 1943 to inject "political guidance" into U.S. intelligence operations in China, had to be on the mission. "However," Davies cautioned Stilwell, "I think it would be inadvisable to give any great publicity amongst the Chinese to his [Service's] inclusion in the group."[69]

It was over the matter of personnel for the Dixie mission that OSS dramatically clashed with the army and John Davies. After the public announcement of the Dixie mission, Tolstoy immediately went to Delhi to see Davies and informed him that OSS had already planned a similar mission. Tolstoy inquired whether it would be possible to combine the two into one unit. Upon hearing the brief history of the intended Tolstoy mission to the north, Davies reacted harshly, emphatically telling Tolstoy that any merger with OSS was impossible; Davies further suggested that OSS cancel the proposed project. Tolstoy, though irritated by Davies, requested that he be included in the Dixie mission. Davies flatly refused and told Tolstoy that he "had been a member of SACO and as such was contaminated by Tai Li." Further, "Whether he liked it or not, [Tolstoy] would be considered a White Russian which was also not desirable."[70]

Tolstoy's request alarmed Davies. To preclude any possible OSS attempt to forcibly inject SACO-related OSS agents into Dixie, Davies drafted a long memo blasting SACO and its chief operators, Miles and Tai Li. Davies then gave it to Stilwell's aide, Edwin Cahill, who subsequently circulated it all over Washington; this Davies memo became the standard moral condemnation of SACO.[71]

Tolstoy, however, did not give up. The very day he was snubbed by Davies, Tolstoy cleverly spent the evening charming Stilwell's top aides, including Major General Thomas Hearn, the chief of staff for the CBI theater, showing them films Tolstoy had made on his OSS mission to Tibet. The family connection with the Russian writer Leo Tolstoy, the exotic scenery of Tibet, and Tolstoy's OSS public relations instincts enthralled all in the projection room.[72] Finally, General Hearn said that the films were great, and asked why he, Tolstoy, did not get on the Dixie mission. Unaware of the complex political situation Davies had presented, General Hearn thus inadvertently provided OSS with what it had been wistfully waiting for: a defense, or an excuse, to revive OSS-Communist cooperation in the face of fierce resistance from Davies. As the official OSS interpretation explained, "This was the invitation which caused Tolstoy to proceed to Chungking. Mrs. Davies overheard General Hearn make this remark. John Davies was apparently aware of it but failed to take it up with General Hearn or with Delhi headquarters. Tolstoy believing a Major General (Hearn) outranked a civilian (Davies) and being most anxious for an opportunity to accomplish his Mission, proceeded on the General's invitation without further discussion with Davies."[73]

What transpired next was significant. Following the film show, Tolstoy called on Colonel Creswell of G-2 to arrange for logistics without telling Creswell, an OSS skeptic, what was going on. Although suspicion was aroused, Tolstoy proceeded to Detachment 101 headquarters, where his entire crew was stationed. After consulting with Peers, Eifler's successor, Tolstoy moved the entire group to Kunming. Then he flew to Chungking and directly went to the forward echelon headquarters of the CBI theater command to work out the specifics. At headquarters, Tolstoy conferred with Colonel Dickey, Stilwell's chief of G-2 in Chungking, General Timberman, and General Hearn, who was now back from India. It was a strange meeting of the four. According to OSS official records, "By this time, . . . General Hearn realized that he was getting out on a limb with respect to inviting Tolstoy up and just kept quiet."[74]

However, Dickey and Timberman were not quiet at all. Extremely angry at OSS, Dickey immediately protested. Bypassing Coughlin, he directly contacted the War Department in Washington on 4 August 1944. Dickey's cable, in Coughlin's words, wreaked "havoc" on OSS. The army accused OSS of dispatching an unauthorized mission to the Communist area and declared that the Tolstoy mission "duplicated the Barrett Mission [the Dixie mission was to be led by Colonel David Barrett]." Stilwell's headquarters thus demanded an explanation.[75]

Dickey's protest was taken seriously in the War Department. Numerous army VIPs—including Major General Thomas Handy, the assistant chief of staff, and General McFarland of the Joint Chiefs of Staff—demanded statements from OSS. At the core of the Tolstoy-Dixie crisis was SACO. General C. S. Russell, the deputy chief of theater group at the operations division (OPD) of the War Department, wondered: "General Donovan and OSS is under JCS; in theater OSS under Theater Commander. Shouldn't theater have been consulted?"[76] OSS defended itself from this implication by using the SACO command structure as its cover. Cheston, assistant director of OSS, and Coughlin quickly asserted that OSS was officially under SACO, and SACO was under Tai Li, who had already approved sending an OSS team to the Communist area during Donovan's visit to China in December 1943. As such, there was no need for OSS to consult the army theater commander (Stilwell) because Tai Li was "responsible *only* to the Generalissimo."[77]

Internally, however, Coughlin reported the whole incident to Donovan, saying that "the Tolstoy Mission to date has been very embarrassing to OSS in this theater. I do not feel that OSS is entirely at fault. Had John Davies properly informed Headquarters in Delhi a great deal of embarrassment could have been avoided." Coughlin thus decided that if the stalemate could not be broken within four to six weeks, he would recommend the Tolstoy Mission be dropped and that the personnel be used in other ways, probably in AGFRTS.[78] Yet the stalemate was never broken, and the army would not tolerate any independent intelligence initiatives in north China with the Communists. The Tolstoy mission was squelched.

When assured of their monopoly over command, Davies and the army began to select Dixie personnel. OSS had been widely recognized as a nest for specialization. Although Davies and Dickey vehemently opposed anyone associated with SACO, they needed some OSS agents with certain talents the army could not provide. Eventually, five OSS agents—none "contaminated" by SACO—were among the eighteen original Dixie mission members. One of them, Raymond Cromley, the renowned former *Wall Street Journal* Tokyo bureau chief, had been in China less than three months, as an AGFRTS "super agent" specializing in Japanese order of battle. There was also Charles Stelle, an R&A scholar whose zeal for battlefield gunsmoke far outweighed his academic interests; he had recently joined AGFRTS after leaving the Southeast Asian jungle. Stelle had been part of the ill-fated Long Range Raiders led by the eccentric British general Orde Wingate. He was chosen by Davies as a "target analyst" in the Dixie mission. John Colling joined Dixie initially as an SO man but also was a film documentary expert from John Ford's photographic unit in OSS. Brooke Dolan was a renowned traveler in the Far East; he presumably knew a lot about social and political flora and fauna in the Communist areas.

Fill the India Vacuum

The force and momentum with which Americans forced Chiang Kai-shek to allow Stilwell to send a U.S. military intelligence team to cooperate with the Communists distressed the generalissimo. He was convinced there was a major flaw in the overall command of the China-Burma-India theater. In India, unlike China, Americans resisting his command and control could easily get away with initiating and organizing projects to operate in China via remote control. Nothing exemplified this weakness better than the Dixie mission, which from beginning to end was run out of New Delhi by people like John Paton Davies.

What was even more alarming to Chiang Kai-shek vis-à-vis India was the fact that the British used India as their home base to join hands with Communist intelligence agents and then conducted subversive operations in Guilin and Guangxi provinces to overthrow the central authority in Chungking. Starting in spring 1944, Communist intelligence was trying to instigate one of Chiang Kai-shek's subordinates, Marshall Li Jishen (Li Chi-shen), governor of Guangxi, to rebel against the KMT government. Stilwell's headquarters closely watched this development and was reticent to intervene.[79]

The British military and intelligence authorities were directly involved in this plot. Colonel L. T. Ride, commandant of the British Air Aid Group (BAAG) told American intelligence that Colonel W. P. Thompson, chief of the British Liaison Office for Military Assistance in Guilin, had promised Li Jishen two British airborne divisions for the coup and that Li Jishen had already established direct contact with London.[80] Although the Communists denied any complicity in this attempt, Tai Li's agents had been closely tracking activities of Communist agents in Guilin who were plotting the coup. One of their chief operators directly controlled by Yenan was Dr. Chen Hansheng.

Chen was a highly sophisticated Communist intelligence agent whose colorful résumé included assignments as Richard Sorge's associate in the Sorge spy ring, assistant to Owen Lattimore at the Institution of Pacific Affairs, and most recently the chief organizer of the Industrial Cooperative, a Communist agency in charge of purchasing strategic materials and obtaining cash for Yenan. Based on Tai Li's report, Chiang Kai-shek's National Military Council issued a warrant in March 1944 for Chen's arrest in Guilin. Much to Tai Li's chagrin, Li Jishen tipped off Chen. British intelligence rescued him immediately by flying him to India, where Chen was at once put on the payroll of British intelligence, working as an agent in the Far Eastern Bureau (FEB) of the Ministry of Information (MOI) until the end of World War II.[81]

Chiang Kai-shek confronted a host of challenges: the exasperating command problems caused by Coughlin's absence from China and his virtually permanent presence in India; the Dixie mission, which was largely initiated and organized by the army in India; and the direct involvement of British intelligence agencies with the Communists in subverting Chungking. Together, these factors convinced him to do the unthinkable: penetrate India in order to secure China's rear. In June 1944, immediately after his forced approval for the Dixie mission, Chiang ordered Tai Li to work out a scheme whereby Chinese intelligence could operate in India for "damage control." Within days, a stunning proposal for a large-scale Sino-British intelligence project based in India was sent from Chungking to the chief of British intelligence in India.[82]

To the British, this came as a total surprise. Euphoria notwithstanding, the British thought this offer too good to be true. Mountbatten's headquarters quickly dispatched a cable to the war office in London detailing the situation and requesting an official response. The long cable is worth citing in its entirety:

Although difficult to guess what lies behind Chinese DMI [Director of Military Intelligence] suggestion which is very startling, I suspect following: desire to operate Chinese agents in SEAC, desire to control British organizations in China, desire to gain information which we possess and which Chinese believe is more reliable than their own, desire to strengthen Chungking's slipping grip on Yunnan where British organizations mostly operate, desire to start creation of a counterbalance to Americans and possibly to test our reaction to a unilateral approach.

We are confident Chinese feel they have more to gain than to lose by this proposal and feel that the suggestion coming just before visit of Chinese DMI here has a particular significance.

Very desirable we not turn down Chinese proposal flatly in spite of difficulties foreseen. An atmosphere which shows a cooperative reaction but stressing inadvisability of definite commitments by either of us until project studied more carefully. Meanwhile Military Attache Chungking might draw out Chinese by asking them with whom they would propose we would work with, Chinese DMI, Tai Li, Wang Pung Son [Wang Pengsheng], the Kuomintang Intelligence Service or Overseas Ministry, etcetera. Attache could ask them how many British officers they consider would be required and who the Chinese head of the organization would be. Other useful question to raise would be general discussions on the relationship the Chinese have in mind for this Sino-British intelligence unit in dealing with American Military and Naval Attaches, with Chennault's Air Attache, with Commodore Miles and with OSS. Our Attache could suggest no definite answers are needed or advisable on above points until Chinese DMI visits both Delhi and Kandy. Such an approach shows a willingness to play ball but leaves us sufficient margin to dodge issue entirely, should we find it either undesirable or impracticable. Our further reactions are: this joint Sino-British intelligence office would work in a vacuum unless there was a complete amalgamation of the various Chinese and British intelligence agencies, the proposed order of battle section to be of any value should have access to signal intelligence and this is not safe from security angle, there might be some advantages of a setup similar to the American JICA and such a setup could include Americans, the employment of agents in occupied countries would present some difficulties since Chinese would want either to put their agents into SEAC or have us withdraw our agents from China and we would have grave complications in French Indochina and in the Philippines, there would be advantages in coordination SIS and SOE in China under a single command maintaining closer liaison with Tai Li and Wang Pung Son and finally we remark that War

Office will probably desire to confer with Colonel Mackenzie and Garnons Williams on this entire problem."[83]

Yet in the end, this Sino-British intelligence plan did not materialize after all.

OSS in the Dixie Mission, 1944

In the meantime, the five OSS agents slated for the Dixie mission were immediately overwhelmed by the potential of Yenan as an intelligence base for OSS. Ray Cromley reported to Hall, "There is virtually no spot in Japanese-occupied China in which the Yenan armies do not have permanent agents or guerrilla troops."[84]

The Chinese Communists were certainly cooperative. They had wanted the same things Tai Li did from OSS: American training of intelligence skills and American intelligence equipment. A Yenan training school was immediately approved. At the top of their agenda, the Communists wanted radio gear for their vast yet scattered guerrilla-held areas across the country. Days after the Dixie mission arrived in Yenan, OSS members were approached by an unexpected, curious British permanent resident in the Communist headquarters: Michael Lindsay, who had been a "technical radio adviser" to the Chinese Communists in Yenan since December 1941.

Lindsay had a most enigmatic background. Virtually every intelligence agency within the Nationalist government believed him to be a British secret agent. In 1940, Lindsay was recruited by Mr. Harmon of the British embassy in China as a "press attaché." Harmon was in charge of secret intelligence in China for London, "whose work was that of a most secret nature," reported Gale of OSS.[85]

In 1941, Lindsay suddenly left the British embassy in Chungking. As U.S. Naval Attaché H. T. Jarrel reported, Lindsay then "relinquished the job to Harmon and returned to Peiping in the Spring of 1941, and there married a Chinese." After that, Lindsay went to Yenan to work for the Chinese Communists as a "radio expert." From the time the Dixie mission arrived in July, Lindsay actively sent intelligence reports to British secret intelligence in Chungking under Harmon.[86]

While in Yenan, Lindsay briefed OSS in great detail about the Chinese Communists' communications setup. The Communists requested that OSS supply Yenan with radios to expand the existing system of 657 radio stations run by the Communist 8th Route and New 4th Army. On 28 July 1944, OSS dispatched a thick report, code-named YENSIG 1, to General Stilwell; it detailed the CCP's communications system and its request for

American equipment. The YENSIG 1 proposal stated at the beginning that "this report is the direct result of periodic conferences with Prof. Michael Lindsay." In fact, it was actually written by the British radio expert, not by OSS. Stilwell responded positively.

On 6 September the OSS contingent in the Dixie mission took a significant step. A new document code-named YENSIG 4 described a massive project to supply the Communists with a large quantity of radio equipment. The supplies would go to all fourteen Communist-held areas across China, from Shan-Gan-Ning base area, where Yenan was located, to Jin-Ji-Lu-Yu base area and Jiao Dong base area in the Shandong Peninsula; to Su Bei, E-Yu-Wan, in the east near Shanghai; and to Dong Jiang and Hainan Base areas in the south near Hong Kong.[87] The project called for a complete intelligence communication network for all Communist-controlled territory. Thus OSS began a large intelligence enterprise in cooperating with the Chinese Communists. In the months that followed, large amounts of OSS American radio equipment were flown to Yenan. By 25 April 1945, when OSS became completely independent of the army in operating the YENSIG 4 project, a total of fourteen thousand pounds of lightweight radio sets and parts had been flown to the Communists; fifty-eight thousand more pounds were waiting to be transported.[88] Communists' material requests were so demanding that OSS subsequently had to designate an ordnance man, Willis Bird, the deputy director of OSS in China since fall 1944, to deal solely with Yenan.

Another item the Communists wanted from OSS was cash. As we have seen, OSS was known to have seemingly unlimited unvouched funds. Both the army and the navy had tried to take advantage of this. Yenan badly needed cash, despite its relatively self-reliant economy in the base areas. Yenan's need for American cash stemmed from a peculiar practice by the Communists: cash bribery of the puppet troops for weapons. It was known that Yenan's ultimate goal was not to defeat the Japanese, as all in China believed that Japan would be defeated sooner or later. The final showdown was to be with the Nationalists; this the Communists did not hide.[89] As such, a basic Communist strategy throughout the war was to bribe the puppet troops of the Wang Jingwei regime into turning over Japanese weapons to the Communists. Weapons inflow to Yenan had been the biggest problem for the Communists because of the arms embargo put up by Chungking. These puppet troops were normally sent home after receiving the money, and some of them became professional middle men, making deals with Yenan again and again.

For years, the Communists thrived on bribery. Partly for this purpose, Communist intelligence had established the Industrial Cooperative, which through its vast international network of support gathered and transferred an astonishing $20 million during a period of two and a half years to the Communist headquarters in Yenan.[90] The strategy achieved impressive results, bringing in large quantities of advanced Japanese-made weaponry. Rewards varied, depending on the brand and quality of the munitions. The coming of OSS further enhanced Yenan's appetite for cash to buy weapons from the enemy forces. Throughout the rest of the OSS stay in Yenan, this became a major negotiation item. Specific budgets and market bribery prices were presented to OSS to solicit cash. For example, in January 1945, the rates offered to the puppet troops by the Communists were billed to OSS as follows: twenty U.S. dollars for a rifle, thirty for a pistol, fifty for a grenade launcher, eighty for a light machine gun, one thousand for an artillery gun, and two hundred for a radio set.[91]

The arrival of OSS in Yenan stimulated this "cash and carry" business. The first bargaining chip offered by Yenan was the top secret APPLE project, proposed by another permanently based foreigner in Yenan, Sanzo Nozaka, more commonly known by U.S. intelligence as Okano Susumu, the chief of the Japanese Communist Party and head of the Japanese People's Emancipation League. While Michael Lindsay was selling OSS on the idea of equipping the Communists with radio gear, Okano discussed psychological warfare with Colonel Colling of OSS. Okano told the American that "American propaganda is weak because it has not as yet convinced the people and soldiers of Japan of the truth about this war" and that the United States should not attack the emperor too harshly. Furthermore, Okano told Colling that American propaganda was written in "too high a Japanese language" and that it had to be made clear to the Japanese people that the United States is not run by Jews.[92] Colling was taken by Okano's political savvy and useful advice on America's weakness in propaganda and counterpropaganda.

On 22 August 1944, Okano delivered a surprising statement to Colling and Stelle of OSS, who in turn sent it by top secret cable to Colonel Robert Hall in Kunming: "Okano, rpt Okano, head of Jap Communists willing to send agents for us to Manchuria, Korea, Japan. We will refer to this as APPLE, rpt APPLE."[93]

This was a startling revelation, for the most important part of the original OSS plan had been to penetrate into the inner zones of the Japanese empire—Manchuria, Korea, and Japan proper. Yet the most significant part of the APPLE offer was related to money. Colling and Stelle followed up the cable with a report to Hall detailing the price, which essentially involved payment of "$400,000 in the Japanese Federal Reserve Currency for N.

China." Nervous, Colling and Stelle told Hall, "this is a gamble but we are assured that it is a good gamble."[94]

Surprised by the turn of events in Yenan, Hall replied to Colling and Stelle, "Do not, rpt not, make definite commitments as to amount money available until further details have been given us."[95] In the meantime, Hall asked Washington for further instructions on the rapid developments in Yenan, and added, "these projects will not develop as rapidly as our young men imagine."[96] Nevertheless, efforts to establish APPLE continued. Hall recruited many Japanese Americans, some ardent members of the American Communist Party, to Yenan to work with Okano. Others also came into the project, many of them under the cover of OWI, as in the case of a Hawaiian Communist named Koji Ariyoshi, who later became a major Cold War figure.[97]

Despite warm cooperation from the Communists in Yenan, OSS was severely handicapped in pursuing its operations in the China theater. First of all, the fact that the Dixie mission was under army command was by no means ideal for OSS. Although Colonel David Barrett, head of the mission, was cooperative, all OSS projects, including YENSIG 4, had to have his approval. All communications—cables, acquired materials, and so on—had to be approved by Barrett before being sent. Sometimes problems arose. Cromley's initial shipment of intelligence materials addressed to OSS, for example, was intercepted by the army G-2 and transferred to the JICA library, never reaching OSS.[98]

Moreover, OSS was included in the Dixie mission as a unit of AGFRTS under the direct administrative control of the 14th Air Force, not Coughlin or Donovan. A major crisis befell OSS in September 1944 when Colonel Dickey, Stilwell's G-2, "raised the devil" at OSS over Cromley's efforts to directly transmit intelligence reports to the order of battle division at the War Department in Washington without the prior approval of the theater command or David Barrett. The entire OSS was shaken by this incident. Donovan was disturbed and ordered Coughlin to tell Cromley that "he must clear through regular channels and that his first loyalty is to OSS."[99] General Magruder also was enraged, for he wrote to Donovan, "As to the rat-in-hole transmission by Cromley to a 'secretary' in Lovell's OB division, this should be absolutely forbidden as being wholly irregular." Magruder even suggested conspiracy on part of the army. "There is a remote possibility here of a pattern of penetration of OSS by Lovell [of the order of battle division] via his specially trained experts transferred to us. We can watch this but withhold judgment."[100]

In addition, there was tremendous military and political opposition to proposed OSS projects in cooperation with the Chinese Communists in Yenan. The most obvious antagonism came from Chungking. The other major problem was that the presence of a number of Americans in the Communist-controlled areas of north, central, and south China would undoubtedly evoke Japanese attacks and drive the Communists out of these areas entirely, leading to the loss of intelligence sources for the United States.[101]

Finally, OSS was stuck in a myriad of unsolved policy dilemmas. Many important issues remained unclear and forced some OSS plans to remain tabled. For instance, should the OSS team in the field cooperate with both Nationalist and Communist guerrillas? Cromley was once interested in cooperating with such anti-Japanese quasi-military troops as Father Thomas Megan's fighting guerrillas in northern China. But American policy prevented him from going any further because Father Megan was under the administrative supervision of Tai Li. It would be disastrous if Tai Li knew that his guerrillas were dragged by OSS into a cooperation project with the Communists. Hall thus forced Cromley to abandon the project.[102] A further problem facing OSS in the Dixie mission was the variety of colorful characters in the OSS contingent. Many had their own peculiar demands, which more often than not affected efficiency and morale. For example, both General Stilwell and Ambassador Gauss prohibited any U.S. personnel in China from hiring women secretaries. Tasks such as the order of battle did sometimes require an OSS team to have secretarial staff in typing and copying intelligence reports. Some OSS agents, especially Ray Cromley, demanded a particular "female assistant." Cromley told Hall, "I must have Miss La Donna Andersen here. . . . This is a matter of saving men's lives and winning the war more quickly."[103] Hall's refusal discouraged this OSS enthusiast. "Even General Chennault has been unable to bring a woman secretary over to China," Hall lectured Cromley.[104] Yet only the director himself knew the proper perspective on such things, for Donovan told Coughlin that "Cromley is something of a genius who will probably have to be handled, if his potentialities are to be fully realized, with a little more latitude than the run-of-the-mill good officer who has neither his special talents nor his defects."[105] Such was the general policy of OSS throughout the war.

By far the most serious trouble for OSS concerned the question of command. Like China in the nineteenth century, OSS in World War II was dismembered by all the powers that be. In order to survive, OSS in China had to concede its command to several "sponsors," all of whom had ulterior motives. By the fall of 1944, OSS personnel in China were split into three major spheres of influence: SACO, AGFRTS, and the Dixie mission. Although John Coughlin was Donovan's direct deputy in China with theoretical overall command, he lacked the power to efficiently control OSS either in SACO, where Tai Li and Miles were major detractors, or in AGFRTS, which was actually commanded by a 14th Air Force officer. As far as the Dixie mission was concerned, most of the OSS members reported not to Coughlin but to Spencer in New Delhi, Robert Hall in Kunming, or Dickey. As a result, Coughlin had virtually no direct control of OSS agents in Dixie. There was a dire need for OSS unification of command and Donovan's restoration of integrity.

But OSS/China was not the only U.S. intelligence agency plagued by disorganization, jealousy, confusion, and opacity of command. In fact, by the fall of 1944, the entire American intelligence establishment in the China theater was in chaos. As one high-ranking U.S. intelligence officer commented, "The diffusion of our intelligence activity in China is hopelessly inefficient from our own standpoint and the confusion incident to so many agencies and sub agencies operating in the theater is making us look ridiculous to Chinese officials and most likely to the British as well. It is extremely desirable to end this state of affairs and integrate our intelligence operations in China."[106]

The chance to end this embarrassment came in late October 1944, when General Stilwell was recalled and Lieutenant General Wedemeyer succeeded him as the commanding general of U.S. Armed Forces in China and the chief of staff to Chiang Kai-shek. Wedemeyer had two enormous advantages to help him accomplish the housecleaning: first, the ridiculous CBI theater designation was done away with and Wedemeyer was designated as responsible only for the China theater; second, and certainly more important, is unlike Stilwell, Wedemeyer was a new type of officer, one who had a keen interest in intelligence and was highly competent and organized.

To say Donovan was happy about Wedemeyer's appointment to China is perhaps an understatement; Donovan knew that Wedemeyer had been a great friend to OSS from the very beginning, dating back to the early days of the contentious Joint Psychological Warfare Committee in Washington, where Wedemeyer often served as presiding judge ruling in favor of OSS.

OSS thus entered a new stage in China.

CHAPTER SEVEN

The Miller Faux Pas and Wedemeyer's Ascension

Stilwell's recall in late October 1944 had a profound impact upon the overall plan and ambitions of OSS in China. Part of Donovan's enormous organizational problems with SACO was due to Stilwell's antagonism toward the navy, particularly Milton Miles, as well as strong objections to Tai Li. As a matter of fact, Donovan's December 1943 trip to Chungking to separate OSS from the naval command resulted from desire that OSS not get caught in the cross fire between the army and the navy.[1] The removal of Stilwell from the China theater would certainly tip the balance, thus giving OSS a chance to start anew.

However, at the time of Stilwell's departure, OSS was preoccupied with a disastrous situation of its own making. On 18 October 1944 an important OSS officer, Brigadier General Lyle Miller of the Marine Corps, arrived in Chungking for talks with Tai Li and Miles concerning the SACO-OSS situation. A member of the Washington Planning Group—the brains of OSS—General Miller had been touring Asia on Donovan's orders. While in India and Chungking, conferring with army staff, Miller grew highly critical of army organization in the CBI, finding it "confused and complicated." Miller reported to Donovan: "It will be difficult, if not impossible to integrate an OSS set-up to function without friction."[2] On the morning of his arrival in Chungking, Miller went to SACO and talked with Miles, who briefed the general on the overall situation inside SACO. In the afternoon, Pan Qiwu, Tai Li's assistant and the executive chief for SACO, held a two-hour meeting with Miller, followed by a dinner banquet hosted by Tai Li in Miller's honor.[3]

Four days later a major conference between Miller and Tai Li took place, also attended by the two most senior OSS officers in SACO at the time, Major Wilkinson and Arden Dow. Tai Li expressed the biggest Chinese concern: whether or not OSS intended to stay inside SACO. Sensing that the reason for asking such a question must be related to Chinese confusion over AGFRTS, Miller then took a dramatic step and for the first time officially informed Tai Li that OSS had indeed been operating a separate intelligence organization under the cover of the 14th Air Force, the AGFRTS, but went on to explain that this was only a tactical maneuver required by General Chennault. Moreover, Miller emphasized that OSS of course intended to stay inside SACO. According to Miller, Tai Li "was not surprised, but did seem pleased that it was officially told him. . . . In fact, from this time on he spoke very frankly and seemed to have greater interest in getting the differences between the Chinese and OSS clarified." Tai Li told Miller that his most bitter complaint about OSS was its command structure, which had completely baffled him. While Coughlin was apparently the chief of OSS in China, he was usually in India and rarely in Chungking; Wilkinson had been appointed by Coughlin as his deputy, yet Wilkinson had then appointed Dow as *his* deputy in charge of OSS/SACO affairs. Tai Li insisted that the actual senior OSS representative should be appointed directly by Donovan, not by any intermediate OSS officer, and that when appointed, this officer should be responsible only to Donovan. Miller reported to Donovan, "Tai Li's greatest peeve was against Coughlin. He apparently feels that [Coughlin] is the cause of much of the trouble Tai Li has had with OSS. He stated that he would not under any circumstances have anything to do with Coughlin. That if Coughlin came to Chungking he would not see him."[4] In conclusion, Miller relayed to Donovan the ten main points discussed during his conference with Tai Li and other SACO officials:

1. That Col. Coughlin cannot work with General Tai.
2. That Gen. Tai must be assured by you that OSS intends to remain in SACO.
3. That the Commanding Officer of OSS in SACO be appointed directly by you.
4. That Gen. Tai wants OSS in SACO entirely divorced from the CBI Theater.
5. That Gen. Tai does not care very much whether OSS stays in SACO and certainly will not work with us unless we comply with 3 and 4.

6. That Gen. Tai was more favorably disposed toward OSS after our conversation.

7. That Commodore Miles is furnishing the Navy with intelligence and other information in fastest possible manner.

8. That Gen. Tai is getting practically everything that he hopes to get from United States from Commodore Miles

9. That U.S. Army organizations do not like Gen. Tai and try to have nothing to do with him. (Same for State Department.)

10. Everyone here has a distinct feeling that unless there is an about-face on Tai Li's part little can be accomplished in SACO.[5]

The conference ended most amicably. Miller and Tai Li both shared an open and honest discussion of problems and prospects for future cooperation. Shortly after the meeting, Tai Li, in exuberant spirits, hosted a splendid welcoming party for Miller in the SACO headquarters.

It was during this dinner party that the unimaginable took place, instantly shocking the nerve centers of Chungking and Washington, from Roosevelt on down; the fate of OSS in China was fundamentally altered, both within and outside of SACO, rendering Donovan completely preoccupied with damage control at a time when he should have been making swift policy adjustments in light of the Stilwell recall. An urgent top secret report sent by Dow to Washington immediately after the faux pas describes the disaster:

Very grave diplomatic relations have arisen. A full report is herewith submitted. General L. H. Miller was attended [*sic*] a conference and a dinner on the afternoon and evening of the 22nd of this month by TL [Tai Li]. During the dinner liquor was served and General Miller, both in speech and conversation, spoke most disparagingly of Madame Chiang Kai-shek, her husband, the Chinese people and the country itself. Listed below are the statements made by the General: (1) Again and again Miller demanded that TL afford us the opportunity of being entertained by Sing-song girls. He requested that TL produce such maidens. TL attempted to switch the conversation into other channels but Miller was adamant. (2) Miller asked TL about Chiang Kai-shek's new women and wanted to know if this was the reason for his wife's long absence. (3) The General denied that China is a front rank power. He stated that the country could not even be a 5th or 6th rank power and that they were just about 12th. (4) He stated that China was guilty of "God damn obstructionism." (5) Miller asserted that China would now be under Japanese domination if it had not been for the United States of America guarantees that China is a front rank power and also guarantees China's territorial integrity. According to Miller, 40–50 years will be required for China to assume a leading position. (6) In order to protect China from USSR, it is necessary for China to have our support. (7) Throughout the evening Miller time and again called the Chinese "Chinamen." (8) The General said "you Chinamen must open your eyes and stop sleeping like that idiot over there." Miller designated one of the Chinese guests as an example of what he meant. (9) Miller said that in the Philippines he would get Japanese genitalia and ask the Chinese to a dinner at which they would be served. The General's tirade went on for more than 2 hours, punctuated with a good deal of table pounding and swearing. Both myself and Colonel Tolstoy attempted to break it up but were ordered to remain quiet by both TL and Miller.[6]

This was only a cabled summary of what Miller had said. There were many more crudities that were later recorded by all the OSS officers present at the party.[7] Tolstoy felt ashamed "as a member of the white race," for "he had just seen the most disgraceful thing that he had ever seen in the army." What was even worse was that all present at the party did not believe Miller was drunk when he was on his tirade. "General Miller did not appear drunk," Wilkinson later recorded in his sworn testimony, "He was steady on his feet and his voice was clear."[8]

Tai Li did not understand English. Eddie Liu, Tai Li's interpreter, was stopped from interpreting by Tai Li shortly after the racist tirade began, for Tai Li thought the speech vulgar and distasteful. The next morning, a full transcript of Miller's speech prepared by the Chinese secretary was given to Tai Li, who became rightfully infuriated. The next day's meeting was abruptly canceled by Tai Li, who was "very cool and unreceptive to General Miller" at the breakfast table.[9]

Miraculously, Tai Li did not immediately report this great insult to Chiang Kai-shek. Suppressing his rage, Tai Li informed Miles, who had not attended the dinner because it was "OSS business," that he would take official action but added that "the Generalissimo had been having a considerable number of problems in the last few weeks concerning General Stilwell and General Stilwell's activities and that the American picture in China at the time was not too beautiful." As such, Tai Li did not want to trouble Chiang with an additional problem.[10]

Tai Li's eerie quiet frightened OSS. Miles exercised great restraint in handling this matter, for the issue became one of Chinese versus Americans. The entire OSS contingent sought Miles for help and advice. During the speech, Dow telephoned Miles and asked for advice. Dow asked Miles if it was wise to strike Miller and stop him. Not fully understanding what actually was going on, Miles instructed Dow to remain calm and take careful notes for a future court-martial testimony. Hoping to drop this ugly incident quietly, Miles told Dow the morning after that "unless the Chinese officially pressed charges, nothing would be done about it."[11] Miles himself did not file any report to Washington about this incident.

But the uneasy calm did not last very long. On 26 October 1944, Tai Li hosted a farewell dinner party in his house for Wilkinson, who was scheduled to leave for Washington that night. At the party, Arden Dow, who would succeed Wilkinson, apologized to Tai Li for the Miller incident. Dow recorded the following for Donovan: "I then said that I hoped I could give as equally good cooperation and do as good work as Wilky [Wilkinson] had done. To this General Tai replied, 'I'm afraid it will be impossible, or most difficult, due to the actions and words of General Miller.' "[12] Tai Li then went on to unleash his rage. Dow reported to Donovan the gist of Tai Li's statement: "Within the next day or so TL is going to inform Chiang Kai-shek of the entire incident. Miller is regarded by TL as a personal representative of you, the United States and OSS. He holds that the tirade was conducted in public and that it is indicative of the United States' opinion and also the opinion of OSS. TL refuses to permit the slanderous accusations against his countrymen, China, Madame Chiang Kai-shek and her husband. TL stated that in all probability Chiang Kai-shek will order the withdrawal of the entire SACO from China and will assuredly demand that our entire Organization be recalled."[13]

On the same day, Tai Li summoned Miles and informed him that since Miles was the most senior U.S. officer in SACO, he would be held responsible for the ugly incident and that he might have to order all U.S. personnel to pack up and go home, whereupon Tai Li would kill the SACO project. After being chastised and threatened by Tai Li, Miles broke his silence and immediately wired an urgent cable to Admiral King in Washington, describing the entire incident, in the hope of salvaging the endangered SACO project.[14] The next morning, Admiral King rushed a top secret note to General Marshall, demanding that an immediate investigation be conducted in China by the commanding general of the U.S. forces.[15] Marshall issued a prompt order to the new theater commander in China, Lieutenant General Albert Wedemeyer, en route to Chungking, to investigate.

Miles's cable evoked a strong reaction from Donovan. The antagonism in OSS against Miles was so deep that what ultimately worried Donovan was not the Miller incident per se but rather the prospect that Miles might take advantage of it to oust OSS from SACO entirely. Donovan immediately began a tenacious campaign in Washington to save OSS in SACO. He first delivered an oral apology to Xiao Bo for what had happened—the official written apology to Tai Li from Donovan waited until 14 December.[16] To demonstrate Donovan's resolve to take this matter seriously, OSS, in deep humiliation, sent complete copies of the wires between Donovan, Dow, and Coughlin to General Marshall and Admiral Leahy of the Joint Chiefs of Staff, Joseph Grew and Stanley Hornbeck of the State Department, and finally to President Roosevelt himself.[17]

Internally, however, Donovan cabled a series of instructions to his field officers in Asia, warning them to be most vigilant against Miles's taking advantage of the incident. Nothing is more clear than Donovan's cable to Coughlin. "The crux of the matter concerning the Miller incident," Donovan warned his China chief, "is the fact that a long-standing opponent is endeavoring to use this affair as the means of clearing the field for his own activities. Keeping [sic] this view uppermost in your reasoning."[18] With this instruction in mind, Coughlin intercepted Wedemeyer in New Delhi when the latter stopped there en route to Chungking. Coughlin provided the general with complete details of the incident.

In the meantime, Dow went to see FDR's newly appointed special envoy to China, Major General Patrick Hurley, who confided to Dow that Miles had talked with him about the entire affair. Then something dramatic occurred: Hurley essentially told Dow that panic inside OSS over the Miller incident was not warranted, for nothing serious would happen. Hurley said Miles had a personal motive in ousting OSS from SACO and that he did not approve of Miles's action. A startled Dow at once wired Donovan in Washington: "On October 29th I spoke personally with General Hurley and told him all the details. The General made the following comments:"

1. Until such time as Chiang Kai-shek or TL [Tai Li] notify him officially of the incident, he intends to keep hands off. As yet such official notification has not come to him.

2. Hurley believes that both Miles and TL would like to oust OSS from SACO. Miles is motivated by the desire for greater prestige for himself and also has personal reasons for wanting OSS out of the picture.

3. If official notification of the affair does come, Hurley refuses to allow the incident to be exaggerated beyond its real importance. He intends to treat it as joke with Chiang Kai-shek and Miller drank more than he should and talked out of turn. One intoxicated person is hardly in a position to express your opinion the feelings of our government or the attitude of OSS.

4. Undoubtedly General Miller will be subject to some disciplinary action intended to show China that the United States does not approve of such conduct."[19]

Fig. 12. Left to right, Rear Admiral Milton "Mary" Miles, Consul General Walter Robertson, Ambassador Patrick Hurley, and Tai Li (courtesy of the family of Admiral Miles)

Hurley and Donovan were longtime Republican Party comrades, dating back to their simultaneous service in the Hoover administration. Furthermore, OSS was widely regarded as a Republican establishment, filled with the upper crust of American society. During Dow's visit to the embassy, Hurley requested that Dow convey a personal message to his pal Donovan: "OSS rate #1 in my opinion and . . . I am behind him from Hell to Harrisburg."[20]

It was from Hurley's unusual and timely support that the significance of the Stilwell recall and the formation of a new China theater began to sink in at the OSS headquarters. Donovan suddenly realized that the awkward situation in China under Stilwell was beginning to change in favor of OSS. At the same time a cable from Coughlin in India confirmed Donovan's sudden realization. Coughlin provided another piece of good news: Wedemeyer had the same positive attitude vis-à-vis the Miller incident as did Hurley. "I have given Wedemeyer all of the wires with reference to the Miller case," Coughlin reported, "and have explained the whole matter to him. Wedemeyer was friendly and did not think the matter was as serious as Dow thinks it is."[21]

Donovan received these two cables with great, if not complete, relief. He promptly switched tactics from defense to offense. Donovan began to send reports by Miller himself all over Washington. In one report, Miller admitted only that he had drunk too much upon the insistence of Tai Li, and that the "Sing-song girl" remark was only like "a joke at a bachelor party." Further, Miller flatly denied that he ever cursed the Chinese and characterized them as "fools."[22] On 1 November 1944, Donovan dropped the idea of having Heppner and Coughlin come to Washington for an emergency conference to resolve the Miller crisis, as had been urgently suggested by Dow and another senior OSS officer in the Far East, a Colonel Connely.[23] Five days later Donovan officially requested of Lieutenant General Alexander Vandegrift, the commandant of the U.S. Marine Corps, that Miller be removed from OSS.[24]

Yet on the same day, the army's inspector general, Raymond B. Steiner, completed his investigation of the Miller incident and submitted a comprehensive report to Wedemeyer. The report's conclusions were devastating to OSS. It charged that Miller—a member of the planning board and a U.S. general who was on official business as a representative of the chief of OSS—had made "insulting, embarrassing and profane remarks about the Chinese, China, Generalissimo Chiang Kai-shek and Madame Chiang Kai-shek" and had acted "in a thoroughly disrespectful and disgraceful manner." Miller's conduct in an official capacity was "discrediting to a standard far below that of a general officer of the United States."[25]

Moreover, there was an exceedingly damaging paragraph in the report that prompted Donovan's immediate denial. Paragraph 17 of the report states:

The nature of the work of OSS in SACO has necessitated the closest type of cooperation at all times. The United States Naval Group, China, is a part of SACO. Commodore Miles is the commander of the Naval Group as well as Deputy Director of SACO, and until last December was also in OSS. But due to difficulties, Commodore had to withdraw from OSS to prevent the involving of the Naval Group into them. Now it appears, due to General Miller's offending remarks as a representative of the Chief of the Office of Strategic Services, that the desire of the Chinese to have OSS in SACO is jeopardized and its future is in a delicate balance. We have always felt that the presence of OSS in SACO is to our advantage and now we are in a position where to talk cooperation and sincerity of purpose with the Chinese seems futile. Instead of assistance from the Chief of Office of Strategic Services we have gained added hindrances and responsibilities.[26]

This was tantamount to an indictment of OSS for all the trouble SACO had endured. Donovan countered by writing a memo to Wedemeyer denouncing such language; in the meantime, the Joint Chiefs of Staff requested comments from Wedemeyer on the report. In the hopes of minimizing publicity of the entire affair, Wedemeyer opposed an official court-martial in the field and stated that the impact on the Sino-U.S. relationship would probably not be as serious as indicated by the report because the Chinese had not yet officially protested.[27] Miller was ordered back to the United States immediately. On 27 November, Admiral King delivered to Donovan a copy of the report by the army's inspector general of the China theater and asked Donovan to issue an official apology to Tai Li for Miller's misconduct. The navy was doing its own part in taking "appropriate disciplinary action" against Miller.[28]

The deepening antagonism against OSS created by the report led Coughlin to adopt an ironic viewpoint, in light of the new theater change. "I feel," he stated to Dow on 7 November, "the theater change and the whole Miller foul-up may be the best thing that ever happened to us. It has broken the thing wide open and is a wonderful opportunity for a completely new deal and a more solid foundation and with a better understanding."[29]

Having received Donovan's orders not to return to Washington for a conference, Heppner, Coughlin, and Connely, in New Delhi, responded by detailing to Donovan the increasingly complicated situation created not only by the Miller incident but also by the new designation of the China theater instead of CBI, as well as Wedemeyer's intelligence policy. The issues included the new role for OSS in SACO in light of Tai Li's statement that he did not want to see Coughlin again in China; OSS policy toward the British intelligence sphere of influence in such places as Burma; and a concrete OSS policy for dealing with Wedemeyer. Connely, in a cable sent one day after Donovan's order, stated that "Heppner is very positive that there are certain fundamental questions which must be straightened out with you and that Wedemeyer has given him certain information which must be delivered to you personally."[30] Donovan was intrigued; he wired back the same day, reversing his decision made the day before, "I expect the three of you to return to Washington immediately," and added, "I will return with you should it be necessary for me to do so."[31]

Yet on 5 November, before the three departed New Delhi, Wedemeyer made two dramatic decisions about the future setup of OSS in China. Wedemeyer announced to Donovan, "I would like to have Heppner as my OSS head," and he wanted Donovan to make a personal trip to China. In addition, word also came to Donovan from Heppner that Wedemeyer had "most secret intentions concerning China" in intelligence operations, that he had opened his complete files to Heppner, and that "OSS will be able to function under Wedemeyer's jurisdiction, under a completely different organizational arrangement."[32]

Heppner, Coughlin, and Connely rushed back to Washington to confer with an anxious Donovan. The central issue was Wedemeyer's intention to appoint Heppner as OSS head and intelligence czar in the China theater. This created a dilemma for Donovan. On one hand, he would be happy to comply with Wedemeyer's request; on the other, there was always the question of loyalty. Although Heppner stated emphatically that he had not sought the appointment, Donovan was wary, fearing that his command as OSS director over his field team would be lost if Heppner reported directly to Wedemeyer instead of to OSS headquarters. After all, OSS had been burned once already in the spring and summer of 1944 by the army-navy fight over the Davies-Heppner scheme. After careful consideration, Donovan agreed to Wedemeyer's request, making Heppner the head of OSS in China, but he declined to clarify exactly whom Heppner should directly report to.

Heppner was not happy about this and told Donovan that he would accept the position only on the following conditions:

1. That the OSS "holding company" theory of operations in China be abolished, and that all OSS operations be carried on in the clear under his direct command; that he, in turn, would report directly to General Wedemeyer.

2. That such groups as AGFRTS continue but that they be operated under command of the mission chief and commanding general rather than the 14th Air Force.

3. That OSS headquarters be established at Chungking, with operational headquarters in Kunming.

4. That SACO be perpetuated as long as possible, to buy privileges and immunities by that means.

5. That the new China chief have the right to negotiate with the

new SEAC chief for transfer of certain personnel from SEAC to China and vice versa, and to select branch chiefs.

6. That the new chief of the China theater reserve the right to relieve anyone as he might see fit after first making a careful survey of the situation.

7. That the new China strategic services officer be a permanent and not a temporary assignment.

8. That provision be made for at least three hundred American operations groups, or commando units, in China.

9. That China services of supply for OSS continue to be centered in Calcutta.

10. That every effort be made to obtain a squadron of B-24s to be based in China to accomplish missions and to haul hump supplies.[33]

Heppner's ten conditions would grant virtual independence to OSS/China, away from OSS headquarters; but this seemed to be the only way Donovan could possibly continue any project in China after the Miller disaster. Donovan agreed to Heppner's ten conditions and officially appointed him the chief of OSS in the China theater on 9 December 1944. Coughlin became the chief of OSS in the newly designated India-Burma theater under General Sultan.[34]

During this time, Heppner had started to recruit his own China team. Lieutenant Colonel Willis H. Bird would be the deputy chief of OSS in China, directly under Heppner; Major Richard Farr would be the executive officer; Colonel Paul Helliwell and Colonel John Whitaker would be in charge of SI; Lieutenant Colonel Nicholas Willis would be in charge of SO; Roland E. Dulin would run MO; Paul Child would head the visual presentation branch; Lieutenant Colonel A. T. Cox would be in charge of the operational group; and, most interestingly, a young major named Quentin Roosevelt, Theodore Roosevelt's grandson, would be the liaison between Wedemeyer's headquarters and OSS.[35]

During those ongoing meetings in Washington among Donovan, Coughlin, and Heppner, Donovan agreed to fulfill Wedemeyer's request to make a second trip to China, departing Washington on 26 December 1944. This time, Donovan's agenda would include OSS relations with theater commander; the SACO agreement; present OSS activities under SACO, AGFRTS, and other "illegal" operations (IDC under Katz and Fairbank; the Christian mission; a project code-named Tower, conceived by OSS social butterfly Oliver Caldwell, using Tibetan and Mongolian monk "agents" as the ultimate solution in penetrating Japan's inner zone); and finally and most importantly, intelligence cooperation with the Chinese Communists.[36]

CHAPTER EIGHT

OSS and the Yenan Mystique

History may show that the OSS exerted more influence on Chinese Communist Party policy than any other units of the "Dixie Mission."
—COLONEL IVAN YEATON, CHIEF OF THE DIXIE MISSION

Obviously, from Heppner's conditional acceptance of the position of OSS chief for the China theater, India would now serve only as a logistical supply base for major intelligence operations in China. One of the most secret projects Heppner had in mind was an ambitious intelligence plan in Yenan, the final move of the Davies-Heppner scheme that had originated in early 1943.

While OSS was preoccupied with the havoc caused by the Miller incident and the rapid changes in theater command structure, something significant was developing in the Dixie mission in Yenan. In return for funds from OSS with which to bribe and purchase weapons from the puppet troops, the Communists would provide assistance to OSS in intelligence operations, particularly in the effort to penetrate the Japanese inner zone. Yenan's APPLE project was a result of this agreement, although the overall command structure inside the Dixie mission and possible political difficulties prevented OSS from carrying out the APPLE plan smoothly.

The tumultuous recall of Stilwell and the coming of Wedemeyer in fall 1944 created anxiety within both the Communist high command and the Dixie mission. To test the attitude of the new theater commander, as well as to neutralize the KMT regime, the Communists took a dramatic measure on 3 November 1944, four days after Wedemeyer's arrival in Chungking. John Paton Davies, "father" of the Dixie mission, and its chief, Colonel David Barrett, were summoned to a meeting in Yenan with General Ye Jianying, chief of staff of the Communist army, and Zhou Enlai. Ye and

Zhou presented to Davies and Barrett a proposal for massive military co-operation between Communist troops and American forces in China, aimed at inducing the U.S. high command into a Normandy-style landing at the Communist-controlled port city of Lienyunkang (Lian Yungang) in the strategic border region between Shandong and Jiangsu.[1] This site was vital for the entire Far Eastern war effort due to its railways connecting north and south China. It would also serve as the central point from which air operations could be conducted against Japan, Korea, and Manchuria.

The Communist plan was of a shrewd design, particularly considering its timing. At that moment, the Japanese were launching a ferocious military assault on the Central Government in the south. Chennault's air bases in the advance areas were being lost, and Wedemeyer was concentrating entirely on organizing military counterattacks. For a while, even Kunming and Chungking were in danger of being captured by the Japanese. If the United States agreed to the Communist proposal, a good many U.S. forces and considerable material support would be diverted from the south, most certainly leading to a Japanese elimination of the KMT regime. Moreover, a massive Japanese offensive campaign against joint CCP-U.S. military action in the vital Shandong-Jiangsu area would be guaranteed. In this case, U.S. material support and military equipment would certainly flow into the hands of the Communists. The Japanese would probably move many divisions of their elite Kwantung Army southward from Manchuria, thus easing the pressure of a pending Soviet invasion into that region.[2] But the most immediate goal of the Communists was arms acquisition for a final military showdown with the Nationalist government. As Davies admitted, "the principal need of the Communist Forces is captured Japanese ammunition and light arms." At the end of the proposal, Zhou Enlai added that the CCP's offer was not confined only to the Lian Yungang area and that "if the U.S. decides on a landing in Communist territory, there must be staff talks and other detailed preparations."[3]

This Communist proposal received instant support from Davies, who clearly foresaw the political implications of such a U.S.-CCP collaborative venture. He immediately started arranging for secret staff talks between the U.S. forces and the Communists, as suggested by Zhou Enlai. Instead of recommending that the army carry out this plan with the CCP, Davies proposed utilizing OSS as a clandestine means of cooperating with the Chinese Communists, an objective he had been trying to achieve since the spring of 1943.

But there was one immediate problem—Patrick Hurley was arriving in Yenan on 7 November to mediate a peace between the CCP and the KMT.

Davies decided to keep Hurley in the dark about the secret CCP-OSS project. On the day Hurley arrived in Yenan, Davies sent Wedemeyer a series of "high pitched" reports filled with glowing praises for the Chinese Communists, all with the purpose of neutralizing the new theater commander's opinions.[4] Davies further instructed Heppner, in Chungking, to prepare for a massive OSS-sponsored secret project with the Communists. OSS by now had an enormous advantage in fulfilling Davies's request: Wedemeyer had asked OSS/China to train commando units. Thus Heppner was in charge of a large quantity of arms equipment and a rapidly growing number of military personnel. Starting from mid-November 1944, groups of agents "specially selected and trained in sabotage, demolitions, raids and other special operations requiring a high degree of mobility and striking power" slipped into China sub rosa.[5]

During this period, the Communists became more and more convinced that a massive CCP-U.S. joint effort in landing forces on the China coast was imminent—so much so that Zhu De, the chief of the CCP army, worked out a plan to join with the U.S. Navy. He had it carried in person by U.S. Assistant Naval Attaché Lieutenant H. Hitch, the sole naval officer in Dixie, to Admiral King in Washington. In his personal message to King, Zhu De stated, "At a time when the war in Europe is coming to a successful conclusion and the final victory of the war in the Pacific and Far East has drawn a step nearer, I wish to assure you that the Chinese Eighth Route Army and New Fourth Army together with the people of the liberated areas are willing to carry out to the greatest extent possible cooperation and coordination with any military operations of American forces that may take place in China."[6]

Nor did Yenan's eagerness for cooperation with Americans go unnoticed by Donovan. Though not entirely in control of his China group under Heppner, who had virtual independence from OSS Washington headquarters in accordance with his ten conditions, Donovan was eager to get help from the Chinese Communists to penetrate into Manchuria. In fact, he ordered his R&A scholars in New Delhi to prepare a comprehensive plan for an OSS intelligence project based in Yenan. This plan out of India was called the North China Intelligence Project. "We recommend," the plan began, "that OSS establish a major intelligence organization in North China based at the Communist Border Region capital of Yenan, and operating through four main forward bases in 8th Route Army or guerrilla areas in Shansi, Hopei [Hebei], Shandong, and Jehol, with seventeen advanced teams, and a large number of native agents."[7] This proposed endeavor was the most ambitious, systematic, and imaginative use of

Fig. 13. Colonel David Barrett talking to Zhu De, interpreting for OSS-CCP negotiations, Yenan, December 1944 (National Archives)

intelligence gathering in Communist-held areas, and its direct aim was to penetrate the Japanese inner zone.

Upon receiving word of the CCP's willingness to cooperate, Donovan was exuberant and immediately dispatched the deputy chief of OSS/China, Lieutenant Colonel Willis Bird, to Yenan for a staff talk, as had been suggested to Davies by Zhou Enlai on 3 November. Accompanied by Davies and Barrett, Bird left Kandy, Ceylon, and landed at Yenan on 14 December, joining John Service and Raymond Ludden.[8] The next day Barrett took Bird to see the CCP leadership: Mao Zedong, Zhu De, Zhou Enlai, and Ye Jianying, thus beginning three days of historic clandestine dealings between OSS and CCP, with Barrett and the State Department officials serving as interpreters for Bird. During the three days, extensive plans were drawn and huge deals were made between OSS and the Chinese Communists. Among those Bird could later convey to Wedemeyer in writing were the following:

a. To place our S.O. men with their units for purposes of destroying Jap communications, air fields and blockhouses, and to generally raise hell and run.

b. To fully equip units assisting and protecting our men in sabotage work.

c. Points of attack to be selected in general by Wedemeyer. Details to be worked out in co-operation with Communists in that territory.

d. To provide complete equipment for up to twenty-five thousand guerrillas except food and clothing.

e. Set up school to instruct in use of American arms, demolitions, communications, etc.

f. Set up intelligence radio network in co-operations with 18th Route Army.

g. To supply at least one hundred thousand Woolworth one shot pistols for People's Militia.

h. To receive complete co-operation of their army of six hundred fifty thousand and People's Militia of two and a half million when strategic use required by Wedemeyer.[9]

Bird's overly enthusiastic offer, particularly item (d), overwhelmed the Communists. They had reason to be very happy, for it involved large amounts of OSS-supplied arms and other military equipment. Of particular interest was the OSS promise to give the Communists at least one hundred thousand single-shot "Woolworth" assassination pistols.

The Bird deal with the Communists bore grave policy implications. First of all, it was more of a political than a military maneuver, mainly run by State Department officials in China. In essence, it looked as though OSS had become the private army of a few partisan State Department officials in the China theater. Dean Acheson even gave Willis Bird a State Department commendation for what the lieutenant colonel of OSS had done in Yenan.[10] What was even more startling was the fact that a deal on such a great scale was kept entirely secret from the chief foreign policy official of the U.S. government, the newly appointed ambassador, Patrick Hurley, who was then taking on a most difficult task of mediating the feud between the Nationalists and the Communists in the naive hope that the two sides could still somehow sit together and rule the Chinese people jointly.[11]

But the Bird-CCP secret deal of 15–17 December sabotaged Hurley's mediation mission. Secrecy was particularly vital for Hurley because of the sensitive balance he had to keep between the Nationalists and Communists in negotiating for a coalition government. Any leaks would instantly tip the balance and give the Communists the idea that the United States would

Fig. 14. An OSS agent demonstrating to Communist agents how to use single-shot assassination weapons, Yenan, 1944 (National Archives)

equip the CCP troops anyway, thus providing an excuse for Yenan to withdraw from the talks. During the three-day secret negotiation in Yenan, the question of authorization naturally arose. To the Communists, the OSS offer was indeed heartwarming; nevertheless, their key concern was to what extent OSS had the authority to carry out Bird's extravagant promises. Wistful and eager for action, Bird kept assuring the Communists that approval from higher authorities was not a major problem. Although eager to receive arms and equipment from OSS, the Communists doubted Bird's assurances at first. On the afternoon of 15 December, Bird and General Ye Jianying reached a critical point on the question of plan approval. Ye asked Bird about the likelihood that Chiang Kai-shek would approve the fabulous OSS plan, to which Bird replied that OSS was "very hopeful." The Communists were more realistic about this than the flamboyant Bird. Realizing approval from Chiang Kai-shek was highly unlikely, Ye then asked Bird a most crucial question: if the Central Government of Chiang Kai-shek disapproved of the OSS plan as presented by Bird but the United States government approved it, would OSS proceed to carry it out? According to Bird's own record, his response was equally significant: "Everyone laughed at the question including himself [Ye], and I said something to the effect that army personnel obeyed orders and we would do whatever our government instructed us to do. There were more questions along this line but they were pure speculation and it was always clearly understood that the entire program had to be passed upon by the highest authorities in United States before any steps could be taken."[12]

Bird's answer to Ye Jianying on the afternoon of 15 December was the first time a U.S. military official clearly stated to the Communists that Chiang Kai-shek and the Central Government in Chungking could be considered irrelevant in OSS strategic planning. The only authority OSS needed to carry out the plan was Washington's, not Chungking's. The Communists took Bird's words seriously and immediately began to discuss specifics with the State Department "observers" in Yenan and OSS members in the Dixie mission, with the specific purpose of gaining approval from "the highest authorities in the United States." An elaborate lobbying campaign thus began.

On 10 January 1945 a top secret cable from the OSS team in Yenan to Wedemeyer carried a shocking message: the Communists had informed OSS that Mao Zedong and Zhou Enlai wanted Wedemeyer to arrange to fly one or both of them to Washington to see Roosevelt and explain to him "the present situation and problems of China."[13] The very next day, Zhou Enlai in Yenan summoned the OSS representative for an urgent meeting at which Zhou solemnly told him that the Nationalist government was holding secret peace negotiations with the Japanese "for sell [sic] out of American interest in China" and that therefore the United States should dump the KMT regime. Realizing that Hurley in Chungking was using the navy radio communications system inside SACO, which could monitor and decode all transmissions emanating from Yenan, thus verifying the truth and sources, Zhou emphatically opposed letting Hurley know about this "intelligence." Zhou told the OSS officer that "General Hurley must not get this information as I don't trust his discretion" and that "none of the story should be transmitted via radio."[14]

Zhou Enlai's ploy proved a gigantic mistake. OSS complied with only part of Zhou's demand, not sending a cable to Hurley; but OSS sent Zhou's "intelligence" via radio to Wedemeyer's headquarters in Chungking. What the Communists in Yenan did not know was that unlike the squabbling Stilwell and Gauss, Wedemeyer and Hurley had reached an agreement that they would exchange all pertinent materials in carrying out their military and political missions in China. In fact, to guarantee complete mutual exchange of opinions, the two lived together in one house in Chungking.

The OSS cable quickly reached Hurley, who was furious. Aside from the personal insult to Hurley, it should be noted that the ambassador had been pestered by Zhou Enlai's constant threat of publicizing the documents of Hurley's secret mediation for a KMT-CCP unit. When Zhou's "intelligence" about the KMT's alleged peace deal with the Japanese reached Hurley, he became instantly suspicious of Zhou's motives as well as his source. Hurley pointed out later to Willis Bird and Quentin Roosevelt of OSS that it was comical that the Communists, during the height of CCP-KMT negotiations sponsored by Hurley, would provide such a spurious intelligence report declaring that "it was lamentable that America had been so utterly betrayed by her Ally, the Central Government, and that America had only one friend left in China, namely the Chinese Communists." Hurley became absolutely convinced of the falsity of Zhou Enlai's intelligence source. Quentin Roosevelt recorded that Hurley believed Zhou's information "very clearly gave the measure first, of dishonesty of certain Chinese Communists and second, of the complete unreliability of these peace reports." Hurley later told OSS that he "had received a collection of documents from Yenan describing a contact between a certain individual in Shanghai and Ex-Premier Konoye of Japan. The former had a son who was a friend of a man who held some official position in Chungking. . . . There was not much more meat in the report than this."[15]

On the weekend of 12 January, while in Chiang Kai-shek's compound discussing the Communists' newly hardened attitude regarding his mediation, Ambassador Hurley received a message, according to General McClure, "from the U.S. Navy sources" relating that "the Communists had full and complete information of a U.S. plan to assist them with arms, equipment and U.S. personnel, which would by-pass the Central Government and that the knowledge of this plan to the Communists had made them more or less reluctant to negotiate any further with the Central Government."[16] Alarmed and enraged, the ambassador asked John Paton Davies, just back from Yenan, what had been going on. Always cocky, Davies, still a second secretary in the embassy, told Hurley that he could not say anything to the ambassador because it was a military secret, whereupon Hurley unleashed his accumulated anger and frustration over his disobedient subordinates in the embassy and over their involvement in this complicated situation. To use his own words, Hurley "became a little rough in his language" with Davies.[17] On 14 January an angry Hurley dispatched a curt message to President Roosevelt:

It has taken from the 1st of January until now to find the fundamental cause of the break [between Chiang Kai-shek and the Communist Party]. Here it is:

During the absence of General Wedemeyer from Headquarters, certain officers of his command formulated a plan for the use of American paratroops in the Communist held area. The plan provided for the use of Communist troops led by Americans in guerrilla warfare. The plan was predicated on the reaching of an agreement between the United States and the Communist Party bypassing completely the National Government of China and furnishing American supplies directly to the Communist troops and placing the communist troops under the command of an American officer. My directive of course was to prevent the collapse of the national Government, sustain the leadership of Chiang Kai-shek, unify the military force of China, and as far as possible to assist in the liberation of the Government and in bringing about conditions that would promote a free unified democratic China. The military plan as outlined became known to the Communists and offered them exactly what they wanted, recognition and lend-lease supplies for themselves and destruction of the National Government.[18]

Hurley's explosive message shook the entire Washington establishment. Roosevelt at once instructed Admiral Leahy to have General Marshall launch an immediate investigation. One day after Hurley's cable arrived, Marshall dispatched the entire Hurley message to Wedemeyer and demanded a report on this incident together with Wedemeyer's recommendations for appropriate action. In Chungking, however, Wedemeyer grew furious with Hurley for having dispatched such an important message to Washington without consulting him first. Wedemeyer felt Hurley had broken their gentleman's agreement made earlier that the two would show each other all their cables to Washington before dispatching them. Hurley explained that he could not possibly have done so since Wedemeyer was out of town inspecting the war situation in Burma and Kunming.

Preliminary investigations indicated that the whole incident occurred because of Donovan's proposed visit to China, which had necessitated McClure's sending Bird with Barrett to Yenan for negotiations with the Chinese Communists. But Washington couldn't be told of this because OSS was still legally confined by the SACO agreement. Wedemeyer remained silent for a week without answering Washington. Then on 22 January a confusing report came to Marshall from Chungking. To cover up the OSS connection completely, Wedemeyer avoided explaining the reason and rationale for the proposed cooperation plan with the Communists; in fact,

OSS was never even mentioned. Instead, Wedemeyer emphasized the question of leaking the plan. His major concern was to exonerate his subordinates from charges of having leaked the OSS plan to the Communists. At the end of the cable, Wedemeyer stated, "I recommend that no further action be taken here unless and until further circumstances or developments irrefutably indicate that the plan did leak to the Communists through United States Army sources." Hurley was shown the cable before it was sent, but he and Wedemeyer were "unable to reach agreement concerning the statement of facts."[19] A deeply embarrassed Wedemeyer wished the entire matter could be dropped quietly.

Washington, however, was not satisfied with Wedemeyer's weak explanation. One day later, another urgent cable from Marshall arrived, which bluntly asked Wedemeyer to respond to three points:

> A. was there any plan prepared by U.S. personnel of your headquarters regarding employment of communist troops which contemplated bypassing the Generalissimo? If the above is true, who formulated the plan and what was its status? B. More detail is desired on the specific facts upon which you and General Hurley do not agree as indicated in the last sentence of your message. C. do you believe it advisable for the President to contact the Generalissimo on this matter? If so, along what lines should the President's message be formulated?[20]

Realizing that the matter had reached a point of crisis that could involve the president, thus repeating the situation of Stilwell's disastrous recall, Wedemeyer took immediate action by collecting testimony from all involved. Within two days, Wedemeyer drafted a cable emphasizing that no foul play was involved. As he was about to send it to Washington, however, Willis Bird's long and complete testimony concerning OSS involvement came in on 24 January. This report fully explained the roots of the entire plan to Wedemeyer. His original cable was abandoned with the following words jotted on the cover sheet: "This draft not used in view of additional information obtained."[21] Three days later, after talking with Hurley, Wedemeyer sent a lengthy cable to Marshall. In it Wedemeyer emphatically stressed his policy of supporting the Central Government of Chiang Kai-shek and stating that there had been no conspiracy to bypass Chungking. Then Wedemeyer finally brought up OSS involvement. He explained, "General McClure sent Lt. Col. Willis H. Bird of the OSS with Barrett and directed him [Bird] to explore with the Communist military authorities the feasibility of using a Special Unit for operations in areas under the control of Communist forces." However, Wedemeyer quickly found himself a way out by stating, "I did not know that Lt. Col. Bird, who is the Deputy Chief

OSS China was going to Yenan. General McClure states that he sent Bird in order to forestall a proposal by General Donovan, who was expected in China momentarily, that he and his party be permitted to go." Wedemeyer further listed the eight specific agreements Bird had reached with the Chinese Communists in Yenan. Finally, Wedemeyer offered an apology: "Needless to say I am extremely sorry that my people became involved in such a delicate situation." He added, "I do not believe that this instance is the main cause of the breakdown of negotiations but I am fully aware that unauthorized loose discussions by my officers employed in good faith by General Hurley could have strongly contributed to the latter's difficulties in bringing about a solution to the problem." At the end of the long cable, Wedemeyer informed Washington that Hurley now agreed with this new statement of facts, that Wedemeyer and Hurley had regained their erstwhile harmony, and "each will help the other loyally and completely." Therefore, it was not necessary for President Roosevelt to discuss this matter with Chiang Kai-shek.[22]

After uncovering this OSS/CCP deal, Ambassador Hurley recommended the transfer of John Davies from China to the U.S. embassy in Moscow. Embarrassed, Wedemeyer also fired Barrett from his post as head of the Dixie mission. The only party to escape unscathed in the Hurley explosion was OSS. The question to ask then is this: why did Hurley not play tough with OSS for its essential role in the entire incident? First of all, Hurley was sympathetic to OSS over its abandonment by the army and the State Department officials in China. Hurley and OSS were disgusted by the way the army and State Department officials had quickly fled from sharing responsibility for such an unauthorized deal with the Communists. After uncovering the scheme, both Wedemeyer's men and the State Department officials flatly denied having any connection with Bird's trip to Yenan, while, in fact, OSS believed it had been fully sanctioned by both the army and the State Department. All of a sudden, OSS felt that it had become the abominable "no-man," a possible scapegoat for all the illegality in dealing with the Communists on such a large scale. Davies, in his memoir, went so far as to claim that he had no idea what Barrett and Bird had in mind when the three took a plane together to Yenan on 14 December 1944.[23] Years later, Bird angrily confided to a family friend about how he and OSS had been abandoned by the army and the State Department:

December 1945—22 degree below zero! Fresh from Ceylon. Had to borrow Long Johns from the C.G. [Wedemeyer] and heavy flying suit from Chief of Staff [McClure]. Used the C.G.'s plane—had Col. Dave Barrett to translate—Ray Ludden and Jack Service as the State Department "Observers," spent couple of long days in constant conference with Mao—Chou En-lai—Chu Teh and Yeh Chien-ying. Wild Bill [Donovan] sent me message that Dean Acheson gave me State Department Commendation which he placed in my file. Then it developed Pat Hurley don't [*sic*] know of the trip and raised hell with all kinds of messages to "Frank" [Roosevelt], and very suddenly no one knew how I got there—why I went or what I did there. Birdie caught it again.[24]

Hurley's bias also saved OSS. The ambassador despised people like Barrett, who were from military intelligence of the War Department. On the other hand, Hurley was a great fan of Donovan's OSS. It was widely known in Washington that military intelligence and OSS were hostile to each other. Hurley explained his lenient policy toward OSS to Bird in person a few months later, as reported by Quentin Roosevelt:

> General Hurley stated that in 1943, he had told General Marshall that the MIS, and G-2 were no good and that the OSS would be the greatest of all the organizations born of the War. He then urged strongly that the Chief of Staff take General Donovan, make him a Major General and put him in charge of G-2. During his recent visit to the States the Ambassador was told by General Marshall that his suggestion of two years previously had been correct and that the OSS had a remarkably good record and that he had been prevented from taking Hurley's suggestion only by strong opposition around him. The Ambassador expressed a deep friendship for General Donovan and strong admiration for his organization.[25]

Moreover, Hurley had his own understanding of the part OSS played in the affair. To him, the army and State Department made the policy, and OSS, with its unvouched money and special weapons, was only the gofer and supplementary follower of that policy. In addition, there was a fundamental distinction to make here: while State Department officials like Davies and Service seemed to Hurley primarily interested in helping the Communists in a battle against the KMT regime, OSS was overwhelmingly motivated by the desire to use the Communists to fight the Japanese. As an OSS officer later confided, "our job in OSS was to help defeat the Japanese by all means available, and if we had to use the 'devil' to do it, that we did."[26]

But Hurley was not entirely accurate in his judgment vis-à-vis the role OSS played in the incident. OSS involvement on the U.S. side might be secondary to that of the army and State Department officials, but its impact on the policy of the Chinese Communists was far more profound than others. The Communists were pragmatists; what they really wanted was money with which to bribe the enemy for weapons, as well as weapons supplied directly from the United States. Only OSS made grandiose promises for both, which fundamentally changed the CCP's attitude in the negotiations with the KMT sponsored by Hurley. Colonel Ivan Yeaton, commanding officer of the Dixie mission beginning 31 July 1945, provides the best perspective: "History may show that the OSS exerted more influence on Chinese Communist Party policy than any other units of the 'Dixie Mission.' "[27]

Yeaton's words proved true. Despite Hurley's explosion, the Chinese Communists did not give up on OSS easily. The commotion between Chungking and Washington over the Barrett-Bird secret deal with Yenan immediately killed the OSS plan of supplying the Communists with "complete equipment for up to twenty-five thousand guerrillas." But the CCP understood that OSS was an organization of unvouched money. On 23 January 1945, eight days after the Hurley uproar, General Zhu De, the supreme commander of the Communist armed forces, directly approached Donovan with a truly stunning demand: $20 million in cash. Zhu De's request read:

> In view of the desirability of contributing to the defeat of the enemy by undertaking subversive activities among puppet troops, we make the suggestion that we borrow from the U.S. Army the sum of U.S. $20 million to be used in strengthening subversive activities among puppet troops this year (1945).
> After this money shall have been used, we should make strict accounting to the U.S. Army.
> After victory against Japan is achieved, this army (18th GA) will repay the money used.
> Should you agree to this proposal, gratitude will know no bounds.[28]

Attached to Zhu De's letter to Donovan was an elaborate document entitled "1945 Project and Budget for Undermining and Bringing Over Puppet Forces." It detailed the Communists' past success in bribing the puppets and explained how the $20 million would be spent. According to the budget, the largest part of the money, $7,600,000, would be used by Communist intelligence to launch a massive intelligence penetration into twenty divisions of puppet troops. Only $1,445,000 was specified as outright bribery money for puppet soldiers and officers. Oddly enough, according to the budget, a meager $893,000 was intended to be used to buy weapons from the puppets. A significant sum of $5 million was marked as a reserve fund, which would be used by Communist intelligence for "using

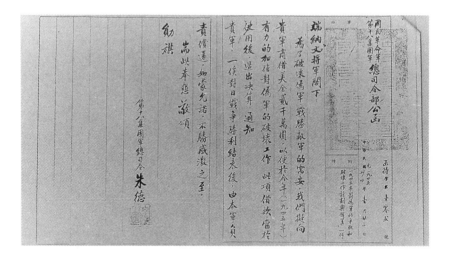

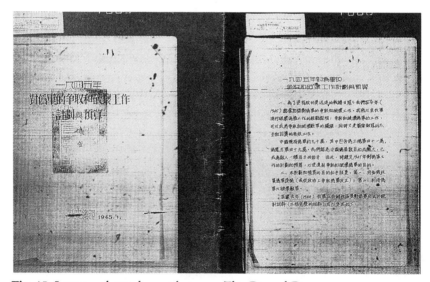

Fig. 15. Letter and attachment between Zhu De and Donovan (National Archives)

puppet officers or soldiers to assassinate Japanese officers of the Army, Navy and Air Forces," as well as for sabotage and demolition.[29]

Someone deep inside OSS must have tipped off Yenan to a heavily guarded secret known only to a few people: the total amount of "special funds" OSS had available for the fiscal year of 1944. Congress in its War

Agencies Appropriation Act of 1944 had authorized OSS $21 million to be spent by Donovan "without regard to the provisions of law and regulations relating to the expenditure of government funds or the employment of persons in the government service."[30] The fiscal year had just started in October 1944. To give the Chinese Communists $20 million as requested would virtually exhaust Donovan's unvouched funds, thus stopping OSS secret intelligence penetration plans worldwide. Indeed, there was no better and more shrewd way to check OSS expansion than this.

Even Donovan was taken aback by Zhu De's request. This was a phenomenal amount of money that could buy enough weapons from the puppets to equip about twenty brigades of Communist troops. Donovan was in an awkward situation. He wanted to strike a deal with the Communists, but their demand was so high that he would have a major problem fulfilling it. As a result, while still in Chungking during his second trip to China in January 1945, Donovan asked his agents in the Dixie mission to inquire whether the Communists would back down a bit in exchange for helping OSS operate in Manchuria. Bad news came quickly from Yenan. On 31 January 1945, Charles Stelle of OSS wired from Yenan to Donovan in Kandy: "The former bargaining demands of the Chinese Communists are now looked upon by them as their minimum demands. . . . They require money in order to buy arms from puppets they believe corruptible."[31] Four days later, Stalin, Roosevelt, and Churchill met in Yalta. The agreements reached there with regard to China would fundamentally change the nature of OSS-CCP relations.

CHAPTER NINE

OSS and Wedemeyer
New Deal for Intelligence

When General Wedemeyer came to China in late October 1944, awaiting him were two fundamental problems that American intelligence operations faced: British intelligence penetration in the China theater, including China proper and French Indochina, and chaos in the intelligence command among the U.S. agencies.

Upon taking over the China theater, Wedemeyer immediately realized the fundamental reason behind Chiang Kai-shek's profound distrust of the British, which in part explained why China had been slow in cooperating with the Allied military strategy dominated by an exclusive Anglo-American high command in Washington and London. "We Americans," Wedemeyer reported to the War Department in an important cable regarding intelligence operations in China, "interpret United States policy as requiring a strong unified China and a China fighting effectively against Japanese. There is considerable evidence that British policy is not in consonance with United States policy. British Ambassador personally suggested to me that a strong unified China would be dangerous to the world and certainly would jeopardize the white man's position immediately in Far East and ultimately throughout the world."[1]

What was even more alarming was that one of the very first requests the British made to Wedemeyer upon his appointment to China was that the United States allow British secret intelligence to place agents on his staff in Chungking to conduct "psychological warfare activities." At the same time, the British SOE unabashedly urged Wedemeyer to authorize air transport of equipment from India to China "for 30,000 guerrillas whom they [the SOE] will organize and train in China." Equally disturbing to Wedemeyer was that the British lied to him about the real activities of BAAG. Urging him to approve the size and scope of BAAG, General Grimsdale, Churchill's military attaché in Chungking, told Wedemeyer that BAAG had been engaged in "rescuing American fliers who are shot down in eastern China." Since almost all of the supposed rescued fliers were Chennault's pilots, Wedemeyer asked Chennault to investigate. Chennault's report unequivocally denied Grimsdale's claim. This and many other reports led Wedemeyer to tell Washington, "British activities in theater are essentially intelligence particularly concerning Chinese political and economic developments. They concern themselves very little with Japanese." In conclusion, Wedemeyer asserted, "in the case of the British I strongly suspect that their activities may be undermining the very United States policy that I am striving so hard to implement."[2] Because OSS had been deeply involved with the British in intelligence matters in Burma, India, Thailand, and China, Wedemeyer needed Donovan to come to the East and directly negotiate with the British.

Wedemeyer's other major problem regarding intelligence in China was the ongoing ugly turf warfare among various U.S. intelligence agencies. "One outstanding weakness in Allied war effort in China," Wedemeyer pointed out to Marshall, "is the fact that there are so many different agencies operating independently and uncoordinated, running at cross purposes, competing for limited Hump tonnage and altogether confusing the situation." The General continued: "For example, there are several intelligence agencies sponsored by the United States including Naval Group, JICA, OSS, AGFRTS, Yenan Observer Section, Military and Naval Attaches, CIC [the Counter Intelligence Corps, the army's version of internal security branch]. Add to these British organizations which have infiltrated into this area and are expanding their activities."[3] Hoping to centralize all intelligence activities, Wedemeyer appointed Colonel Richard Heppner of OSS the "czar" of all U.S. intelligence in China. But such a transition was by no means an easy task.

First on Wedemeyer's agenda was the command of AGFRTS. Ever since Wedemeyer's arrival in late October 1944, OSS members of AGFRTS had been talking about its eventual transfer of command out of the 14th Air Force. Colonel Jessie Williams, Chennault's intelligence chief, vehemently opposed such suggestions and became wary of any possible OSS takeover. In confusion, Chennault wrote to Wedemeyer in November 1944 for assurance of the 14th Air Force's continued command of AGFRTS. Wedemeyer replied to Chennault on 1 January 1945 that he would like to put AGFRTS under the army.[4] Jessie Williams openly dissented.

To strengthen AGFRTS's loyalty to OSS, Donovan, during his second secret trip to China, between 18 and 24 January, conferred with Chennault and inspected AGFRTS. Determined to quell any disobedience, Wedemeyer issued Special Order #38 on 7 February, officially making AGFRTS an OSS unit under the command of Heppner and keeping Lieutenant Colonel Wilfred Smith as the unit head.[5] On 9 April, Heppner decided to drop the name AGFRTS entirely; he changed it to OSS Zhijiang Unit Field Command (Zhijiang Field Unit); it had an operations zone covering South China from the Yangtze to the West River.[6]

The next goal of Wedemeyer's housecleaning efforts was to gain complete command over the OSS contingent inside SACO. The fallout from Bird's Yenan trip and Hurley's subsequent outburst convinced Wedemeyer that an independent channel of communications, such as that of Naval Group, China, was dangerous in carrying out certain intelligence initiatives, particularly those involving the Communists. Wedemeyer decided to put all American personnel inside SACO under his complete control. The first step Wedemeyer took was to gain command over the OSS contingent in SACO; he accomplished this during Donovan's second trip to Chungking, in January 1945.

Tai Li and Miles hoped OSS would still be willing to stay inside SACO. The two anxiously went to the airport to meet Donovan, only to find out that he had effectively snubbed them; changing his schedule without notice, he had already arrived at Chungking with Wedemeyer. When Miles and Tai Li went to see him to discuss the SACO situation, the excited Donovan would speak only about OSS's being placed under Wedemeyer; as a result, Tai Li and Miles never got a chance to talk, and Donovan never mentioned SACO.[7]

The next command matter Wedemeyer tackled proved to be most difficult: U.S. Navy personnel inside SACO. Miles had already lost control over OSS personnel and operations inside SACO.[8] But he would never willingly yield his own navy command to Wedemeyer and the army. Wedemeyer, however, was determined. In early January 1945 he began housecleaning by demanding a written inventory from every intelligence agency in China, including Naval Group China under Miles. Miles grudgingly complied. In the official inventory for Wedemeyer, Miles made the following points loud and clear: first, "the Commander U.S. Naval Group China has two primary functions, one as Commander U.S. Naval Group China and the other as Deputy Director of SACO"; second, "the mission as Commander U.S. Naval Group China is to carry out such duties that the Com-

Fig. 16. Lieutenant General Albert Wedemeyer, third from right, inspecting SACO headquarters, flanked by Colonel Xiao Bo and Lieutenant Commander Charlie Johnston; at left, Tai Li; at right, Rear Admiral Miles (courtesy of the family of Admiral Miles)

mander-in-Chief, U.S. Fleet [Admiral King] directs. The authority for this comes from Commander-in-chief," not Wedemeyer or the army; third, with regard to the relationship with Tai Li, Miles stated, "the only relationship between General Tai Li and U.S. Naval Group China is within SACO. General Tai Li has no command over U.S. Naval Group China outside of SACO"; finally, in a special note at the end of the inventory, Miles emphatically stated that "it is the sincere desire of this command to work in closest possible coordination and harmony with U.S. Army, and to be helpful to the Theater Commander."[9]

On 25 January, the day after Donovan left Chungking, Wedemeyer held a long and important talk with Tai Li, Miles, and Xiao Bo about SACO,

Naval Group China, and Wedemeyer's newly established theater command. During the conversation, Tai Li and Xiao Bo laid out all their concerns and complaints about OSS and the previous army command. In particular, Tai Li charged that OSS had failed to provide its promised supply of equipment—a point OSS in Washington bitterly refuted later. Xiao Bo explained to Wedemeyer the history of SACO and its current function. That historic meeting made Wedemeyer believe that the only way to pull Naval Group China, away from Tai Li was to take the issue to the highest authority in Washington for a revision of the SACO agreement. When back in Washington to talk with the ailing President Roosevelt about the Indochina situation in March, Wedemeyer requested that the Joint Chiefs of Staff make changes in the SACO agreement. For this purpose, Wedemeyer asked Miles to come back to Washington for a conference at the JCS. Miles flew back immediately. After heated debate, Wedemeyer won his case. In early April an amendment to the SACO agreement placing Naval Group China, under the theater command was signed by Secretary of the Navy James Forrestal, and T. V. Soong, now the acting president of the executive branch and concurrently foreign minister of China.[10] The most crucial clauses of the amendment were:

> *a.* The Commanding General, U.S. Forces, China Theater (China and Indo-China) will exercise command and operational control over all personnel and material belonging to American military, quasi-military, and clandestine organizations which are operating or will in the future operate in or from the China Theater.
>
> *b.* Agreements whether written or oral entered into by American personnel of the Sino-American Special Cooperative Organization shall be considered binding insofar as they are in consonance with the present, future and projected policies of the Commanding General, U.S. Forces, China Theater, in his implementation of directives from higher authority.[11]

But there were two major problems. First, Tai Li, the director of SACO, did not agree to this amendment. According to the SACO agreement, the signature of Tai Li was required for any such change. His refusal provided Miles with continuous coverage and protection. Second, Admiral King objected loudly to Wedemeyer's effort to alter SACO. The fleet admiral protested to the Joint Chiefs of Staff, "I am in complete agreement that the Commanding General, U.S. Forces China Theater should be in a position to coordinate the activities of all U.S. forces in the theater. I do not, however, feel that it is necessary to modify the Sino-American Special Technical Cooperative Agreement to accomplish this end." In the end, the amendment gave Wedemeyer "authority" in the China theater over Naval Group China, but King insisted on "direct communications" between himself and Miles.[12] Furthermore, King retained "operational control" over Miles's group.[13] So the dual status of Miles and the ambiguity of command over the navy contingent still lingered on inside SACO.

Third on Wedemeyer's agenda was to claim French Indochina as a sphere of intelligence operations for his China theater. Here, the British and Americans collided head on. At the center of the dispute was the Gordon-Bernard-Tan (GBT) intelligence network. Laurence Gordon, a Canadian and an employee of Texaco Oil Company in Indochina for many years before the war, was a British subject. After the attack on Pearl Harbor, Gordon went to the U.S. War Department in Washington and suggested a plan to organize an intelligence unit in French Indochina. The War Department referred him to the British representatives in Washington, who suggested that Gordon conduct intelligence in China instead of French Indochina. Gordon was sent to India in late 1942 to meet British Brigadier Cawthorne, the director of military intelligence for the British. Cawthorne informed Gordon that because British intelligence was on bad terms with the Chinese, China was out of his area of jurisdiction. Cawthorne favored Gordon's original plan to operate in Indochina and offered to furnish Gordon with radio equipment and funds. Cawthorne agreed not to demand any operational control; he merely wanted to receive copies of all intelligence that Gordon obtained.[14]

Gordon then went to Chungking to see Admiral Yang Xuanchen, the chief of Chinese G-2. Gordon convinced Yang that he was not being directed by British intelligence and said that he would give the Chinese everything he gave the British if permitted to operate in Indochina, where Chiang Kai-shek was officially the Allied supreme commander.[15] Gordon then proceeded south to set up his own intelligence network, hiring only ethnically French agents. As the network grew larger and larger, Gordon obtained the services of two of his former colleagues at the Texaco Oil Company in Indochina, a Harry Bernard and a Frank Tan, both U.S. citizens, the latter a Chinese American.

This network gave Chennault's 14th Air Force much valuable intelligence on Japanese target installations in Indochina. Colonel Jessie Williams rated the Gordon group superior to all other sources combined, including the Meynier group under SACO. Williams appreciated Gordon's service so much that he recommended that AGFRTS give Gordon radio equipment and about one million Chinese yuan out of unvouched OSS funds.[16]

Yet unknown to AGFRTS and the Chinese, the GBT group soon acquired the secret backing of the British SOE's Force 136. On 11 September,

Gordon officially approached Colonel John Coughlin of OSS for joint operations. Although convinced that "Mr. Gordon, strongly pro-British, is thinking in terms of preserving the Empire," Coughlin was tantalized by his invitation, particularly after being shown the complete strength, personnel and intelligence area covered. Coughlin was further told by Gordon that the GBT was also contacting AGAS (Air Ground Aid Service, in charge of rescuing downed pilots) for cooperation in POW rescue missions under Major Witchtrich of MI-X.[17] What Gordon wanted from Coughlin was mostly material supplies, using an independent OSS airplane drop system operating from within China.[18]

The situation regarding French Indochina was confusing and contentious. Coughlin had to walk a thin line between competing authorities on this project, as he cautioned that "the [Gordon] plan, if approved and furnished with the necessary planes, would be cleared in such a way as to receive no objections from the French mission, General Hearn, General Chennault, or the Chinese."[19]

As a first step, in September 1944, Coughlin sent a request for approval to General Stilwell, who was then deeply embroiled in a final showdown with Chiang Kai-shek over military command of Chinese troops. Stilwell designated his chief of staff, General Hearn, to handle Coughlin's request. Mindful of the complexity of the French Indochina situation and the lack of a clear policy from Washington, Hearn warned Coughlin that "the French, although willing to cooperate in every way possible with American or British enterprises, do not look with pleasure on any operation which extends Chinese influence or intrigue into Indochina." Furthermore, Hearn pointed out that "Gordon is a British subject already admittedly working under and for DMI [Brigadier Cawthorne] in India." Hearn concluded: "There is therefore no need for the United States to take over sole sponsorship of Gordon, displacing the existing informal joint sponsorship." However, in light of Coughlin's request, Hearn also made a strange decision: "That AGAS and OSS be instructed and permitted to make such purely practical arrangements with Gordon as may suit their operating needs, and that no commitment be made involving additional hump tonnage for the purpose; and that these practical arrangements not involve the assumption of direct American responsibility for Gordon, but be confined to the grant of specialized equipment, weapons, or money, and the coordinated but independent action of AGAS and OSS agents operating, if these agencies choose, in the same areas as Gordon."[20]

There were two fundamental problems with Hearn's decision. First of all, it authorized the inflow of U.S. equipment without assuming any responsibility for American policy implications—the beginning of a disastrous U.S. intelligence policy toward Indochina. The result was that the British immediately took essential command of the Gordon-Bernard-Tan group. Second, it introduced another element of contention: the pairing of OSS and its rival AGAS in the field without any specific command clarification, which guaranteed a fierce turf battle between the two intelligence agencies, ultimately resulting in the employment of Communist agents, including a man named Ho Chi Minh.

Nevertheless, OSS had obtained a green light to go ahead with the Gordon plan under these ambiguous "practical arrangements." Coughlin designated Major Charles Fenn, a British-born OSS agent, as the liaison with the Gordon-Bernard-Tan network.[21]

When Wedemeyer came to China in late October 1944, he quickly realized that the GBT-OSS setup was not workable because of British control over the project. He immediately launched a tug-of-war with Mountbatten to regain U.S. preeminence in intelligence operations in Indochina. Wedemeyer's major weapon was that his newly designated China theater specifically included Indochina, giving him—theoretically, at least—the upper-hand vis-à-vis intelligence command. Mountbatten, however, insisted that his authority to conduct and command intelligence in Indochina came from an oral "gentlemen's agreement" he had made earlier with Chiang Kai-shek—a story Wedemeyer never believed and directly challenged. As a result, as British Field Marshall Henry Wilson explained to General George Marshall, "Mountbatten has continued to operate on his 'Gentlemen's agreement' ever since and pointed out that of course it will not be found in any records, through which Wedemeyer has been hunting, because it was a verbal agreement."[22]

The issue continued to disturb Wedemeyer. During Donovan's visit to China in January 1945, Wedemeyer held lengthy conferences with the director of OSS on British intelligence gathering in French Indochina. Although Donovan did not completely disapprove of British intelligence, Wedemeyer achieved one major victory by getting him to remain neutral in the ongoing feud between Wedemeyer and Mountbatten. With Donovan still in China, Wedemeyer made the surprise announcement that he would take over the Gordon-Bernard-Tan Group and put it under control of his newly designated intelligence czar, Colonel Richard Heppner.[23]

The British protested most bitterly to Donovan on 29 January, during his meetings in India with U.S. and British intelligence chiefs. Donovan endured the resentment calmly and stated clearly that until the dispute between Mountbatten and Wedemeyer over French Indochina was resolved, coordination between SOE's Force 136 and OSS could not be discussed.[24] The GBT group in the field continued to resist American control. But on

9 March the Japanese military authority in Indochina suddenly arrested all French resistance groups and broke up the entire GBT operations network. Gordon was forced to lead his remaining agents and equipment to Kunming, where OSS immediately moved in and demanded total control. The situation was so tense that Heppner issued the GBT group an ultimatum, demanding that Gordon hand over the entire command to OSS by 1 June 1945. GBT resistance to the OSS demand was so great that even the original OSS liaison, Charles Fenn, ignored Heppner's demand.

In Kunming, Gordon realized that he had lost all of his French contacts, whereupon he instructed Fenn to replace them with a Vietnamese network. Fenn immediately went around Kunming, contacting the exiled Vietnamese community. At this moment, Communist intelligence came into the picture again. While Fenn was searching for new recruits, the Office of War Information in China, an agency tainted with Communist influence, recommended a slim man by the name of Ho Chi Minh, who was then in Kunming.

Fenn first met Ho on 17 March and hired him on the spot as an agent for AGAS. Ho was given the code-name Lucius. Fenn ran the required background checks on Ho. Both French and KMT intelligence agencies had extensive files on him and unequivocally classified him as a Communist. KMT intelligence warned Fenn that Ho and most of his people were Communists and said that "we [OSS] ought to know what we are getting ourselves into." Although Fenn doubted KMT's warning and believed that "naturally they [the Chinese intelligence authorities] have to look at things from the Kuomintang point of view," Fenn nevertheless took the matter to the head of AGAS Chungking headquarters. "The instructions came back," he later recalled, "to 'get a net regardless.' " Thus Fenn and Ho began to work out the details of the new network.[25]

To begin with, Ho asked to meet General Chennault. On 29 March the general met Ho Chi Minh in the 14th Air Force headquarters in Kunming. During the meeting, Ho wanted one particular item from Chennault: an autographed photo of the famous general. Ever photogenic and public relations–minded, Chennault fulfilled Ho's wish. After the meeting, Ho requested that Fenn give him six brand new pistols.[26]

Then Ho traveled back to Vietnam and displayed Chennault's autographed photo to prove his "great friendship" with the famed American general. To fend off factional dissent within his own group, Ho gave each of the opposing group leaders a pistol as a gift in exchange for leadership and respect. From this point on, Ho Chi Minh was able to consolidate his influence among different Vietnamese groups.[27] GBT considered him as merely a local Vietnamese recruit replacing a lost network, but this new role was a great leap forward for the revolutionary career of Ho Chi Minh, the beginning of a momentous Communist revolution that would fundamentally influence the history not only of Vietnam but of the world in decades to come. As Charles Fenn noted:

> Thus it will be seen that these three months since the Jap coup in March 1945 were perhaps the most significant in Ho's career. At the beginning he had been a leader of a party that was but one amongst many: unrecognized by the Americans, opposed by the French, shunned by the Chinese; with no weapons and no equipment. He was also, at the time, cut off from his group by a formidable 600 miles and no chance of flying any part of it. By the end of June, he was, largely thanks to GBT, the unquestioned leader of an overwhelmingly strong revolutionary party.[28]

The effort by Gordon and Fenn to recruit Vietnamese, thus abandoning the previous French-only personnel policy, was largely aimed at replacing the lost network with a strong substitute in order to effectively rebel against the pending OSS takeover. In fact, the new Ho Chi Minh–led network for GBT grew so strong by the beginning of June that Heppner's ultimatum demanding GBT to surrender its command and control to OSS was met with utter defiance. After 1 June, Heppner took the issue directly to Wedemeyer. In a battle for turf, the hard-pressed GBT and its Vietnamese network switched operations so as to come under the command of AGAS. Defecting along with it was the OSS agent that John Coughlin originally assigned to GBT, Charles Fenn.

The loss of GBT to AGAS put OSS in an awkward situation. OSS/China quickly chose an alternative to reestablish its authority on intelligence in Indochina: it dispatched OSS agents to Vietnam to contact the pro-Vichy French groups that were outrightly hostile to Ho Chi Minh and his rising revolutionary movement. From this moment on, U.S. intelligence operations in the field began to have unprecedented and grave policy significance in a situation where there was no clearly defined Washington directive. The OSS alliance with the French group in Vietnam started only as a tactical maneuver in an intelligence turf war for command control, but it immediately became an issue of America's commitment to the French colonial establishment against the rising Communist revolution led by Ho Chi Minh. Ho briefly fantasized that Washington was solidly behind him because of the AGAS connection, but he was soon disillusioned. Fenn recorded Ho Chi Minh's resentment toward OSS: "The first letter I got from Ho reported that OSS had been sending in their own groups who were now co-operating with pro-Vichy Frenchmen, who were more anti-Vietnamese than they were anti-Japanese, so what was the true American policy?"[29] This was indeed the incubation of an American albatross.

Wedemeyer's coming to China as theater commander fundamentally changed the fate of OSS in this complicated part of the world. Sweeping efforts by the well-organized general to centralize intelligence authority achieved admirable results. For the OSS China adventure, an entirely new command outlook emerged under Richard Heppner. When Wedemeyer first took over the China command, OSS had lacked independent status and had been split into three separate missions: SACO, AGFRTS, and the Dixie mission. Within several months, with strong backing from Wedemeyer, OSS gained its full command over operations. Operational Directive #4, issued by Wedemeyer on 7 February 1945, elevated OSS in the China theater to a command level comparable to service of supply in the army, enabling OSS to expand to its fullest capability under Colonel Heppner. More importantly, Wedemeyer tried his best to revise the command setup under SACO to free OSS from what Coughlin called "the SACO straight jacket." Donovan had achieved de facto independence. With the exception of the Dixie mission, where the Bird debacle of December 1944 ultimately precluded a planned OSS takeover of the entire mission, OSS was able not only to consolidate its command but to expand it.

On 9 April 1945, Heppner issued General Order #2, which established two major OSS field commands. Besides reorganizing AGFRTS, under Colonel Wilfred Smith, into OSS Zhijiang Unit Field Command, OSS set up a Xian field unit in north China. A short while later, General Order #6 made the Zhijiang Unit Field Command the Southern Command and the Xian Unit the Central Command. A third new Northeastern Command was also created to operate in Korea. On 9 June, Wedemeyer issued still another order, Operational Directive #20, which allocated a maximum American strength of two thousand men for OSS.[30] With the war's end rapidly coming in the Far East, OSS was ready for a rapid expansion, with lessons learned from the past and a fighting spirit for the future.

CHAPTER TEN

The Great Leap

Donovan's second trip to China in January 1945 was of paramount importance to OSS. The war in Europe was rapidly ending and Donovan had recently submitted to Roosevelt a blueprint for a peacetime centralized intelligence agency.[1] Donovan had established a history office, headed by the Harvard historian Conyers Reed, to document all the achievements of OSS during the war as supporting evidence for the blueprint. Donovan needed an exemplary model to demonstrate to Congress and the White House the absolute necessity for such a centralized agency.

In late December 1944, Donovan prepared a companion blueprint of the China theater as a potential model. That document, entitled "Plan for the Establishment and Use of a Strategic Intelligence Agency in China," was submitted to the China theater commander, General Wedemeyer. In it, Donovan argued first for the strategic significance of China:

China is by far the largest and most important area outside of the Western Hemisphere in which the United States has the predominant interest. This interest is political, military and economic, as the United States wishes to aid in the creation and maintenance of a strong, unified and friendly China. . . . China is, however, surrounded by powers whose interests are not necessarily the same as those of the United States. The most important of these are Russia on the north and west, the British, Dutch and French colonial empires on the south, the Japanese on the east. All of these powers maintain secret intelligence agencies in

China. The United States, on the other hand, has traditionally relied on "open" as opposed to clandestine organizations for the collection of intelligence abroad during time of peace.... The implementation of U.S. policy, therefore, requires complete information, not only concerning China but of the activities of foreign powers in China.... It is, therefore, essential that the United States should have an effective and comprehensive strategic intelligence agency to collect information in China on military, political and economic affairs as well as conduct counter-intelligence.

As to the China setup's relationship with Donovan's proposed central intelligence agency, the document pointed out that "any U.S. strategic intelligence agency in China should, of course, be coordinated with such world-wide strategic agencies as may be established by the United States."[2]

To follow up on this blueprint, Donovan quickly decided to transfer large numbers of OSS agents from the European theater to China. In fact, the immediate purpose of Donovan's second trip to China was to act as an "archangel," ensuring that his agents slipped into China unharmed and undetected. This was not quite realistic because Tai Li, ever vigilant against foreigners, had uncovered Donovan's scheme and informed Miles, who promptly sent off his loud protest to Washington. "It is apparent here," Miles's cable to Captain Metzel stated, "that OSS intends to flood the [China] Theater with agents for various purposes."[3]

The McHugh Roundabout

In fact, one of Donovan's "various purposes" was a daring one: to conduct operations in China jointly with British intelligence. Stilwell's recall and Wedemeyer's strong support for OSS provided Donovan with de facto operational independence in China. This in turn revived one of Donovan's long-held aspirations: to collaborate with the British in collecting intelligence in China. But Donovan had to be very careful this time, because Wedemeyer, while giving OSS much independence, was suspicious of British secret intelligence efforts in China.

During his second visit, in January 1945, Donovan held secret meetings with British secret intelligence in Chungking. These were immediately detected by SACO. Miles quickly sent warnings to Washington: "General conference [between] British and Americans sponsored by Donovan believed in progress in Chungking now. I am excluded and info comes from Chinese who are highly disturbed at possible formation British-American secret service agency in China thus violating the sovereignty of China."[4]

The concrete OSS cooperation plan with the British was to be headed by one of Tai Li's worst enemies, James McHugh, the former U.S. naval attaché who had briefly served as an SI/China chief for OSS.

McHugh's attempt to return to China proved arduous. His brief stay in OSS immediately after his ouster from China was not a fruitful adventure, as he encountered extreme difficulties in organizing China-related SI. He subsequently left OSS in July 1944 and was sent in September of that year to Guam as both the deputy chief of staff and a planning officer for the naval commander there. While in Guam, McHugh was treated cordially but was not used to his full capacity as a senior officer. He became depressed and desired to "get away from here at the first favorable opportunity." Before long, McHugh begged a return to OSS and explained his misery to his friend Lauchlin Currie in the White House:

> I have been cold-shouldered by O.N.I., for whom I had worked for twenty years, ever since my return from China as a result of (a) Mr. Knox having shown my report on Stilwell to the War Dept., (b) Adm. King having blown up when Gen. Marshall protested to him, and (c) Miles and Metzel having taken advantage of the above to do their own finagling and at the same time to keep me out of the Navy picture. Such being the situation, there seemed to be only one other immediate possibility, namely, to return to O.S.S. which I left in good odor despite my private remarks to you. I therefore decided to probe that avenue and wrote to Gen. Donovan and also to my former Branch Chief, Whitney Shepardson, and asked if they still had a job for me in case I returned.[5]

McHugh's bid to come back to OSS received an enthusiastic reply from Donovan, who wrote to him on 8 November 1944: "We are delighted that you want to return with us and will of course be glad to have you. You would fit excellently into the plans which we are making for work in the Far East—particularly in China or the Pacific areas, and I do hope that you will be interested in helping us out in those important fields of operation. If you will let us know when you have written to General Vandegrift, we will pick up the ball on this end and do whatever we can to help you effect the transfer." In the meantime, McHugh utilized all his powerful connections to ensure a transfer to OSS. The first person he approached was his White House connection, Currie, who replied in a supportive but very diplomatic and well-crafted manner, "I am in sympathy with your sentiments regarding your future operations. . . . We will proceed in whatever direction may seem advisable. I am sure that the matter can be worked out to the satisfaction of all concerned."[6]

McHugh had at this time hoped only to work for OSS in Washington, D.C., or New York, but the day he mailed out letters to Donovan and Shepardson, he heard the news of Stilwell's recall from China. He immediately felt a euphoric vindication and followed up his request for returning to OSS with a plea for going back to China. "I am ready," McHugh wrote to Donovan, "to return to China, or India, whenever the opportunity offers."[7] In the first week of December 1944, McHugh officially asked the Marine Corps for a release and transfer to OSS. Thus the former naval attaché was back again with OSS. Donovan quickly designed a new position for McHugh: China chief for OSS economic and industrial intelligence under Ambassador Patrick Hurley in Chungking. Donovan asked Donald Nelson to contact Hurley. Nelson's aide cabled Hurley immediately and assured the ambassador that "McHugh is your kind of man."[8] Unexpectedly, Hurley, Donovan's staunch ally, turned down the request politely.[9]

Thus Donovan's second trip to China became in part a campaign mission for getting McHugh back into Chungking. The director was convinced that the problem lay in the theater, particularly with Wedemeyer and the ambassador. Throughout his stay in China, Donovan tenaciously pushed the McHugh appointment with Hurley and Wedemeyer, but their resistance held strong. One day before his departure from Chungking, Donovan acknowledged that his mission had failed, wiring his deputy in Washington:

> Since I arrived here, I have conferred with both Wedemeyer and Hurley regarding the McHugh matter on three occasions. Other persons besides myself have talked with the Ambassador and the Theater Commander on this question. The Ambassador was very friendly about it. He said he had discussed it with Mr. McHugh and has informed Nelson that he already has a Naval Attaché. I informed him of Nelson's mistake, which your cable points out, and expressed our willingness to make McHugh available. I also stated our position to Wedemeyer. The difficulty, as far as I can make out, has its cause in the McHugh letter concerning Stilwell and not in the Theater. The War Department is still influenced by this letter. Although many people here are friends of McHugh, there are some who are still smarting over the Stilwell incident and would attempt to make trouble for him.[10]

McHugh's anguish was aggravated when Vice Admiral R. S. Edwards, deputy commander-in-chief of the navy, directly informed Cheston that the navy and Marine Corps could not assist on the matter because General Marshall was still upset with McHugh over his 1942 report suggesting that Stilwell be removed from China.[11] McHugh was enraged, and on 26 January 1945 wrote a long memo to Cheston emphasizing the correctness of his original report. McHugh entitled his memo, "Salient Points Concerning Col. McHugh's Report on General Stilwell of Oct. 11, 1942."[12]

McHugh continued his efforts to return to China. He approached Oscar Cox, deputy administrator of the Foreign Economic Administration (FEA), who agreed to "borrow" McHugh from OSS and make him its chief representative in China, with the rank of minister on Ambassador Hurley's staff. In desperation, McHugh promised Cox that "once I reach China any opposition will melt away and that I can work effectively and harmoniously with General Wedemeyer and the Ambassador."[13]

Then an interesting opportunity arose. Stilwell was in Washington, D.C. McHugh went to apologize to Stilwell in person on 16 February. In a dramatic gesture, Stilwell told McHugh to forget the previous ill feelings between them. Surprised, McHugh asked Stilwell, "I would appreciate it if [you] would indicate this [restitution of friendship] to General Marshall." Stilwell "nodded affirmatively with a characteristic gesture."[14] Several weeks later, Hurley came to Washington to find out what had actually gone on at Yalta. Seizing the opportunity, McHugh went to see the ambassador for support in persuading Marshall. Hurley expressed his sympathy and support.[15] When nothing changed, McHugh asked his well-connected friend, Bernhard Knollenberg, the Far East SI chief of OSS, to write to John McCloy, assistant secretary of war, and to Edward R. Stettinius, secretary of state, to put in some good words for him. The State Department approach was curious because McHugh had just tried to have his appointment "put through the State Department in the routine first and then let the Army protest it if they see fit and thus show their hand." His strategy was this: "In such event they [the Army] would have to state their case specifically and thus supply us with a tangible basis for discussion. I believe the whole case to be so petty, however, that they might be loathe to take a position."[16]

On 12 March, McHugh formally wrote to Vice Admiral Edwards. Two days later, Edwards coldly answered: "In reply to your letter of March 12, I regret to say that objection to your assignment to China has not been withdrawn. In view of this fact I do not believe that the Secretary of the Navy will authorize your assignment to the Foreign Economic Administration as suggested in your letter."[17] Furious, McHugh made a last-ditch effort in June by asking Knollenberg to write to Robert E. Patterson, undersecretary of war, requesting a direct confrontation between McHugh and the stubborn general, George Marshall. Patterson rebuffed the request: "I am quite certain that it would be useless to ask General Marshall to see Colonel McHugh. I know something about the background of the matter."[18]

Thus Donovan's McHugh plan was squelched. Two months later, the

war with Japan was over in China. In 1946, McHugh joined the Strategic
Service Unit (SSU), the postwar offspring of OSS, and returned to China,
where he once again encountered a man of much clout, John Keswick of
British secret intelligence. The two jointly embarked on yet another secret
venture in China. In August 1946, Keswick asked McHugh to go back to
Washington to spy on the government of the United States for British Intelligence. Only an excessive demand of payment by McHugh aborted the
plan.[19]

Nevertheless, the failure of McHugh's return to China in 1945 symbolized the end of Donovan's direct involvement in pushing for joint OSS-
British operations in China.

The Question of OSS Inner Zone Penetration

Wedemeyer's sweeping effort to straighten out the messy command situation of U.S. intelligence operations in China did not go forward
in full cooperation with Donovan. The core of Wedemeyer's effort was to
put OSS operations in China tightly under the theater command through
Heppner. This attempt for complete control of OSS/China was soon challenged by Donovan, who was frustrated by the political stalemate in China
and the resultant obstruction of OSS intelligence operations.

After Bird's failed overture to Yenan, Donovan began to contemplate
another means through which OSS could enter north China. Wedemeyer
had taken the position that for the time being no Americans were to go into
north China or Communist-held territories. In early February 1945, however, OSS headquarters in Washington began to challenge Wedemeyer's
edict. Heppner received an elaborate plan from OSS/Washington called
"Special Program for Agent Penetration of Japan's Inner Zone, for Secret
Intelligence Purposes." This plan had been worked out by the planning
group in Washington OSS headquarters. With the war in Europe coming
to a close, the plan proposed using OSS agents in a rapid penetration of
Manchuria and Korea. In a memo to Heppner, Charles Cheston stated that
"this program gives agent penetration of Japan's Inner Zone for secret intelligence the highest priority among all Strategic Services objectives in the
Far East."[20] The most important part of the plan called for establishing a
secret command within Heppner's office in China that would be controlled
in Washington, not in the theater.

Heppner resented this separate secret command under an "SI inner zone
operations officer"; he told OSS headquarters in Washington that such a
scheme would be utterly "unworkable." Heppner further elaborated on the
problems of this sort of program and on his own authority as chief of OSS/

China, responsible to Wedemeyer. "Under our setup," Heppner pointed out, "our Operations Officer is assigned the task of implementing all operational plans, including intelligence plans. To make an exception would, I'm afraid, cause inefficiency and administrative confusion." To remind Washington of the bumpy OSS history in China, Heppner asserted, "In the past, OSS in China has been a very badly administered unit. Because we are held to a strict accountability by General Wedemeyer for the actions of all our personnel, it has been necessary for us to set up a very tight administrative organization in which lines of command and spheres of responsibility are clear. We have machinery which is functioning efficiently. For us to set up a special machinery for special projects will only result, I fear, in putting OSS/China back into the confused position it occupied last year." Heppner ended his protest in a bold and biting tone rarely seen before: "Not the least difficult part of my job is the eradication of inordinate branch-mindedness and the consolidation of various semi-independent OSS enterprises which have produced little and have only brought discredit upon us."[21]

Heppner's complaint was taken seriously in Washington. David K. E. Bruce, one of Donovan's deputies with a special interest in secret intelligence in China, and the planning group were both forced to surrender to Heppner's demand. On 29 March 1945, Donovan grudgingly dispatched a cable informing Heppner that a compromise had been reached. Instead of a separate command remotely controlled by Washington, "the Chief of SI/Washington will request the Chief of the OSS Mission/China [Heppner] to assign an officer in his command the duty of implementing activities under this special program in the China theater." In other words, Heppner would have the authority to choose an officer to do what Washington wanted to do in China. Donovan emphasized the merit of this apparent compromise: "The Planning Group feels and I concur that changes will permit you to overcome your stated organizational problems without sacrificing spirit and intent of program which is to assign one officer under Operations Officer [of OSS/China] the responsibility for successful implementation of program. The Planning Group believes that officer should be free of all other duties."[22]

The result of this compromise was significant. On 9 April, only days after Donovan's cable reached Heppner, he ordered the establishment of a brand new OSS field unit to be based in Xian. The next day, Major Gustav Krause, chosen by Heppner as head of the new base, left Kunming for Xian with forty-six OSS agents. Although the ostensible task of this group was to delay the Japanese drive into Xian from the strategically important Tong Guan, or Tong Passage, the actual chief mission was to organize OSS penetration teams that would soon enter Japanese-occupied north China and gradually work their way to Manchuria, Korea, and Japan proper—the so-called inner zone.

Arriving in Xian, the Krause group took over the Seventh-Day Adventist compound and contacted the headquarters of KMT General Hu Zongnan. Hu gave the Krause unit a warm welcome, memories of which still warm the hearts of OSS veterans.[23] Hu Zongnan further designated his chief of staff, General Fang Hanqi, as the contact person with the OSS group in Xian. Fang and Krause, who both spoke German, became instant friends. Within weeks, the OSS Xian Field Unit took off, as several OSS teams—code-named Jackal, Spaniel, Lion, and Leopard—were dispatched into the field. Notably, these became the first OSS field operations in north China to actually operate since the beginning of the war.

OSS's New Blood: Bishop Megan's Catholic Network

In implementing the inner zone task assigned by Washington, OSS/China encountered a fundamental problem. Obviously, ethnic Caucasians could not sneak into the inner zone; however, to employ Chinese agents provided by either Tai Li or the Communists would undoubtedly embroil the plan in "local" politics, as had been proved by SACO and the stalemated Dixie mission. To solve this problem, Heppner's SI chief, Colonel John Whitaker, devised an ingenious plan, which called for utilizing an excellent civilian anti-Japanese network spread throughout north China: Catholics working under an American bishop, Thomas Megan, whose headquarters was in Huayin, forty-five miles due east of Xian. On 16 May, Whitaker flew to Xian and discussed this plan with Krause. Two days later, Whitaker and Krause went to see Megan and expressed the desire of OSS to utilize his network for intelligence purposes. Megan immediately accepted the invitation and was recruited—along with his many Chinese Catholics throughout north China—into OSS. Krause recorded, "Megan was put under the Hsian [Xian] Field Command and we immediately set to work to give him a front line headquarters and organize his agents by giving them radio instruction and intelligence training. In addition we aided him by putting some of his agents into the field by parachute which speeded his source to a great extent."[24]

The OSS hookup with the Megan group proved effective. Flamboyant, efficient, and deeply respected by his Chinese Catholic followers, the forty-four-year-old Megan immediately impressed the entire OSS team in Xian. As Krause described him, Megan "carried two guns . . . and drove his jeep like mad down the narrow Chinese roads. On several occasions he and I spent time at the front line together—and it was rare when we didn't take pot shots at the Nip—Megan was an excellent marksman and enjoyed himself immensely on these trips. . . . He was extremely active and had a smile with twinkling eyes. . . . He enjoyed a stiff drink of whiskey when he could get it."[25]

The Fighting Bishop, as Megan was known to his many Chinese agents, quickly changed the entire image of OSS in the eyes of many skeptics both in Chungking and Washington. As OSS historical records show, some of the most outstanding achievements of the agency in China came as a result of Megan's extensive agent network and his many pious Chinese followers throughout north China. Megan not only provided OSS with excellent intelligence on the Japanese but also engaged in a new pursuit: counterespionage, or in OSS parlance, X-2. As Krause admiringly recorded, Megan "aided Major Melton [Krause's X-2 chief] in ferreting out 8 Japanese agents operating in and around the Hsian area. He also kept pretty close tab on the British operations in one area. This included the British agent operating in TungKwan [Tongguan] area also."[26]

The immediate success of OSS in Xian under Krause alarmed the Communist intelligence apparatus in Yenan. Megan had long been a foe of the CCP as well as the Japanese. Now Yenan's greatest bargaining chip with the Americans—Communist guerrillas with local connections—began to erode quickly, because American forces were now able to gain intelligence independently in north China through Megan's network.

Communist persecution of Catholics and other religious groups in China was a complicated matter. First and foremost was the ideological struggle of one belief system against another. The moral totalitarianism of Communism does not tolerate loyalty to an outside authority, such as the Vatican. When the ideological zeal of Catholicism was combined with strong anti-Japanese secret activities, the Catholic community in north China gained enormous influence and power among Chinese peasants, thus competing with and soon challenging the organizational efforts of the Communists in the same area.

Yet the Chinese Communists had another important reason for disliking the Megan-OSS hookup. Megan inherited the enterprise from one of the most legendary Catholic bishops in China, the late Father Vincent Lebbe, Zhou Enlai's nemesis ever since Zhou's days in Paris in the early 1920s.

Lebbe was born in Belgium and came to China in 1895 as a priest. In 1912, he became a vice bishop in Tianjin and began publishing an influential newspaper, the *Yi Shi Pao*. A pious shepherd of God and passionate admirer of Chinese culture, Lebbe went back to Europe in 1920 to help the thousands of young Chinese students then on work-study programs in France, Germany, and Belgium. It was there that the ideologies of Catholicism and Communism collided in their mutual pursuits of winning the hearts and minds of the young Chinese students in Europe.

While in France, Father Lebbe became enormously popular by organizing a self-help–Bible study association called the Catholic Family for Chinese Students. Lebbe's popularity in France among many lonely and dislocated Chinese students aroused resentment from the Comintern operatives in France, who were vigorously recruiting agents from the same group of Chinese students. Zhou Enlai was then the leader of the French Comintern–sponsored Chinese Communists. Numerous articles in a Communist propaganda publication, the *Red Light Fortnightly,* of which Zhou was the editor in chief, attacked Father Lebbe and his efforts among the Chinese students. Zhou's magazine vociferously propagandized the party line that "religion is the opiate of the people," and warned that Chinese students in France should not fall into Father Lebbe's trap but should instead all flock together under the flag of Communism.[27]

Undeterred, upon returning to China Father Lebbe continued to organize Christian groups in northern China. After the brutal Japanese assault on China in 1937, Father Lebbe's groups became heavily involved in rescuing and treating wounded Chinese soldiers. His Catholic groups, initially numbering three hundred, became involved in the famous battle between the KMT's 3rd Army 12th Division and the Japanese 20th Division Regiment at Liangziguan in Shanxi Province. Upon being defeated, Father Lebbe persuaded the commanding Chinese general that the local Catholic groups should take care of the 870 wounded soldiers. Having retreated far away from the front lines, the general was touched when every one of his wounded soldiers came back safely.

The tireless Catholic priest led his three hundred nursing teams all over north China until he was struck by fatigue and dysentery and persuaded by his followers to go to Hankou to receive medical treatment. Upon arrival, Father Lebbe became an instant hero. When the Japanese occupied all of north China, Father Lebbe continued running his efficient organization. Hundreds of wounded troops being pursued by the Japanese were hidden in the houses of Father Lebbe's Christian converts.

In the meantime, Tai Li had been establishing several guerrilla bases in north China. In the summer of 1938, Tai Li gave Chiang Kai-shek a proposal for utilizing Father Lebbe's groups. On 4 September, Chiang personally invited Father Lebbe to Hankou for a conference, at which the renowned priest made two suggestions: first, the Nationalists should galvanize resources for propaganda abroad to gain international support; second, they should expand the existing Catholic mercy network. Chiang Kai-shek accepted the second point only and asked Father Lebbe to work out the details of an expansion plan with Tai Li.[28]

Therefore, long before OSS came to China, Father Lebbe had dealt with Tai Li. On 1 October 1938, Tai Li's Bureau of Investigation and Statistics and Father Lebbe's Catholic group jointly established an organization called the North China Frontline Masses-Supervising Service Group of the National Military Council (Junshi Weiyuanhui Huabei Zhandi Dudao Minzhong Fuwutuan).[29] Tai Li named Father Lebbe director of the organization, which included five hundred Catholics. This North China Service Group became an instant success for Tai Li in his plan of expanding guerrilla bases behind enemy lines in that region. Father Lebbe's group utilized almost exactly the same techniques to galvanize local support as the Communists did. Women were organized to form work groups in villages to make clothing and shoes for Tai Li's guerrilla troops fighting the Japanese. Local operas, plays, and magic shows with anti-Japanese themes were performed to gain popular support. Distribution stations for rescue materials, local hospitals, and township factories mushroomed in Zhong Tiao Shan and Tai Hang Shan mountain areas.[30] Father Lebbe's Catholic groups drew hardly any distinction between Communist and Nationalist troops as long as the wounded were victims of Japanese attack, and they aided Tai Li's guerrillas as well as Communist forces in central Hebei under Lu Zhengcao.[31] Tai Li added the task of gathering intelligence on the Japanese and puppet troops in north China to the expanded Catholic groups.

Such successes aroused deep jealousy and resentment on the part of the Communists, who regarded Father Lebbe's popularity as a threat to their own organizing efforts. On 9 March 1940, Chinese Communist guerrilla leader Liu Bocheng kidnapped Father Lebbe.[32] For thirty-five days, the priest endured a gruesome Communist-style "interrogation." The headquarters of the KMT's Fifth Group Army and Hu Zongnan's First War Area, which the North China Service Group had helped, requested that Liu Bocheng release Father Lebbe; Liu flatly denied that any kidnapping had ever taken place. Enraged, Chiang Kai-shek personally intervened. He ordered General Zhu De, commander of all CCP troops, to guarantee Father Lebbe's safety and demanded his unconditional release within twenty-four hours. On 13 April the Communists released a severely tortured Father Lebbe, who was immediately taken to a hospital in Loyang. He was transferred to Chungking on 14 June and died there twelve days later.[33] Thomas Megan succeeded Father Lebbe and became the new head of the North China Service Group.[34] This was the group that OSS recruited in May 1945.

The Spaniel Incident: A Turning Point in
OSS-CCP Relations

The smashing success of OSS in enlisting Megan's cooperation starting in May 1945 was not all the Communists resented. A far more sensitive issue arose when OSS dispatched the Spaniel mission, its code name possibly inspired by Colonel Heppner's dog Sammy.[35] The Americans understood that the CCP maintained extensive connections with the puppet troops in north China.[36] On 28 May 1945, a five-member OSS team led by Major F. L. Coolidge and including Captain R. G. Mundinger, First Sergeant Elmer B. Esch, Pfc. Mort S. Bobrow, and a Mr. Teng, a Chinese agent employed by OSS, were parachuted half a mile away from a Japanese stronghold near Fuping in Hebei (Hopei) Province for the specific purpose of contacting the Communists for possible joint intelligence operations on the puppets.[37] The team was immediately detained by local Communists who had not been briefed about the landing. Two days later, the five were taken for an "efficient and thorough questioning" by an English-speaking agent, most likely from Kang Sheng's Social Affairs Department. On 2 June 1945, this team was taken to communist Political Commissar Cheng Zihua and General Geng Biao (Keng Piao).[38] They immediately decided that the team should be detained indefinitely because Major Coolidge had told them that the American mission was deployed in order to contact the Communist troops in the field for one purpose: to seek help from the local Communists in contacting puppet troops for intelligence and sabotage purposes.

Contacting puppet troops had been a Communist forte throughout the war. Yenan had established an extensive collaborative relationship with not only the local puppet governments but also with the headquarters of Wang Jingwei in Nanjing, via Pan Hannian's intelligence net based in the New Fourth Army in eastern China. When Wedemeyer learned from Donovan in January 1945 that General Zhu De had openly requested U.S. money to bribe the puppet troops into defecting and relinquishing weapons, Wedemeyer realized that the Communists had extensive puppet contacts. But it was equally clear to Wedemeyer that such contacts should not be used as a bargaining chip for U.S. dollars and weapons, which would contribute to an inevitable military showdown with the Central Government. Wedemeyer decided to run his own network in north China, using the CCP's help when and if possible.

The Spaniel mission had originated in Kunming and was dispatched from Xian. A comprehensive report stated the goal and scope of the mission:

This team was organized to work in the area in the general square formed by Chin Chou [Jinzhou], northwest point on the Gulf of Chili, west through Kalgan, south through Ch'ing Yuan, then west to the Shantung [Shangdong] port of Ch'ing-Tao [Qingdao]. It included parts of the provinces of Hopei [Hebei], Shantung [Shandong], Chahar, and southern Jehol. The purpose of the mission was to make reconnaissance of the area indicated, to survey the possibilities of future operations, and to hold conferences with the puppet generals and get their ideas and commitments without committing ourselves. The following subjects are those which were cleared from Theater to discuss with the puppets:

(1). The extent to which they will cooperate with us in setting up an intelligence network in the provinces.

(2). The cooperation they will give in establishing bases in that area from which we can wage Psychological Warfare.

(3). What assistance they will render in sabotaging communication lines, and vital public works in that area.

(4). To what extent they will procure for us plans on fortifications and troop movements.

(5). Definite commitments from the puppet generals and leaders as to the resistance they will make to the Japanese on a given signal:

a. With their present supplies and,

b. With additional supplies from Allies, specifying supplies required in order of their importance.[39]

Unhappy about the independent OSS attempt to contact the puppets, the Communists were determined, for several reasons, not to yield an inch on this matter. The first was obvious: such independent efforts would undermine the credibility of Yenan's claim that the CCP alone knew how to work on the puppets. The second reason was more profound. The Communists and puppets had long cooperated in the vast areas that the Spaniel team intended to cover. An independent OSS intelligence team would discover this relation, leading to immediate condemnation from Washington and Chungking. The third reason was that the Communists feared a connection with OSS would make the puppets fight not only the Japanese but also the Communists. Finally, and perhaps no less important, was that this unannounced OSS team visit in north China posed the greatest threat to CCP propaganda about the Communists' "valiant fighting" against the Japanese.

In retrospect, Yenan's effective propaganda machine worked well. A high-powered radio station, XNCR, aimed directly at North America spread propaganda on the Communists' "fighting" against the Japanese. The fact that the Spaniel team parachuted right into an area of peaceful coexistence between the Communists and the Japanese, only half a mile apart in north China, undercut that propaganda. While impressed with Communist organizational skill and some social reforms, the Spaniel team would eventually and unequivocally report to U.S. headquarters the obvious: "The amount of actual fighting being carried on by the 8th R.A. has been grossly exaggerated. It was their policy to undertake no serious campaign against the Japanese or Puppets. There were occasional ambushes and hit and run raids."[40]

The ostensible reason given for the team's detention of nearly four months was that because no prior notice had been given to Yenan, the Spaniel mission must have ulterior motives to organize people against the Communists. While provided with good food and occasional social entertainment, the OSS team was confined most of the time to virtual house arrest, convinced that "we were being held as prisoners." The team voiced protests on numerous occasions, sometimes violently. One and a half months after their detention, for example, Major Coolidge angrily confronted General Geng Biao. According to the team's diary, "Since we've been here we have told them the complete truth—the obvious inference was that we're complete liars—Coolidge exploded like a delayed July 4th firecracker stating [to Geng Biao] that they had a helluvva nerve doubting the word of an American officer—his explosiveness kept up until Ma [the interpreter] stated that he would discontinue the conversation unless the Major's tone became calmer—but we did score the point that we were very disgusted."[41]

What was even more exasperating to the OSS mission was that the Communists deliberately prevented communication between the Spaniel team and the headquarters of all other American forces in the China theater, so that nobody in OSS knew what had happened to the team: "When we relinquished our arms, when we said we would comply with their desire that we don't use our radio, (which was taken by the communists also), the two generals [Cheng and Geng] both said they would send any message we wished over their radio—since that time we have given them three messages, two to be sent over the radio, the third, a letter, to be sent to Colonel [William P.] Davis [of OSS] by courier—all of them were returned to us with the explanation that they were not necessary. . . . The result of this has been that our headquarters knows nothing whatsoever about the situation."[42] The detention of the Spaniel team, otherwise known as the Fuping incident, set a precedent in Yenan. As Peterkin, the acting head of the Dixie group, reported to Wedemeyer on 11 June 1945, "All communist headquarters have been instructed to arrest and disarm and hold all unauthorized Americans encountered anywhere."[43]

Wedemeyer was duly alarmed because this incident marked the first fundamental clash between U.S. military forces and the Chinese Communists over authority in north China. A particular point of contention was the fact that the Spaniel team had parachuted only half a mile away from a Japanese military installation which coexisted with Communist troops nearby. The capture and arrest of the Spaniel team posed a sharp question to Wedemeyer: did he, as the China theater commander, have the right to authorize U.S. military operations in north China against an enemy of the United States without the Communists' permission? To Wedemeyer, the notion that north China was a Communist-held area was not entirely correct: it was also occupied by the Japanese. As such, Wedemeyer believed he undoubtedly had the right to operate as he had planned.

Wedemeyer later confronted Mao Zedong in person on this issue. Request for permission from Yenan for operation in Japanese occupied territory "is not always feasible," Wedemeyer flatly told Mao on 30 August 1945. It was "in fact generally impossible to do. I have Americans operating all over the China Theater. I do not send information out to other commanders concerning such operations. Americans would contact them when and where possible. They are recognized and accepted as friends and coworkers. Commanders take them right in and treat them kindly."[44]

YENSIG 4

When Wedemeyer learned about the Fuping incident in June 1945, he protested by sending letters and cables to Mao Zedong demanding an explanation and immediate release of the Spaniel team. However, Peterkin intercepted these letters and cables to Mao.[45] At their face-to-face meeting later, Wedemeyer angrily challenged Mao: "Mr. Mao has not had the courtesy to reply to my letters or radios on the release of those four men. . . . I have not had any word from them since May. I wrote letters and radios to Mr. Mao about these four men and have received no information to date. . . . You should have had the courtesy to at least wire me and say, 'Wedemeyer, who are these people that just came into this area?' "[46]

Why did Peterkin and OSS in Yenan decide to withhold Wedemeyer's protest messages? The answer is that they badly needed the Communists' goodwill for the OSS pet project, YENSIG 4, and did not want to let a direct confrontation between Wedemeyer and Mao Zedong ruin their already fragile cooperation with the Communists. The YENSIG 4 project called for a complete intelligence communications network in Communist-controlled territory throughout China. Partly because OSS did not have overall command in Dixie and partly because of the Hurley uproar, YENSIG 4 had been held in virtual abeyance since first proposed in September 1944. After conferring with Roosevelt on the French Indochina situation and dealing with the SACO command, General Wedemeyer took a bolder step in contemplating an OSS takeover of the entire Dixie mission.

On 20 April 1945, Wedemeyer and Heppner held a meeting on OSS projects with the Communists. Heppner was surprised that Wedemeyer agreed to let OSS run SO as well as SI operations in Communist-held areas. A jubilant Heppner immediately wired Donovan, then in Paris, that "probably we will take over Dixie Mission."[47] Heppner further said that Wedemeyer had allowed Colonel Dickey, the theater G-2 and the only leftover staff member from the Stilwell regime, to ship 58,000 pounds of radio equipment to Yenan. Five days later, Wedemeyer issued a directive which officially put the YENSIG 4 project under the sole command of OSS. It stated that "to date 14,000 pounds of an estimated total of 58,000 pounds of equipment has reached Yenan and is in storage there pending its use in YENSIG 4 by OSS. Additional equipment is arriving in Yenan at the rate of three plane loads per week under the present schedule." But there was an important proviso in the directive: "The equipment cannot be turned over to the Communists for their private use. Its use is to be limited to the collection and transmission of intelligence for US agencies and for such administrative messages deemed necessary."[48]

Willis Bird, deputy chief of OSS/China and the major figure in the tumultuous Barrett-Bird episode of December 1944 and January 1945, received this news first. Never forgetting his promise to supply the Communists, Bird interpreted Wedemeyer's proviso regarding transfer of equipment to the Communists liberally, as he wrote to Heppner: "The Yensig plan No. 4 is merely a guide. This has been stressed by everybody concerned so that if there is some slight thing in it that is not agreeable, do not worry over it but just handle it as we wish."[49] To implement YENSIG 4, OSS/China sent its top radio man, Swensen, to Yenan to do a preliminary survey of the guerrilla areas under Communist control.

The capture of the Spaniel mission on 28 May hit the Yenan Communist high command like a bombshell. The Communists began to imagine a conspiracy jointly worked out by the U.S. Army and the KMT aimed at attacking the Communists. Suddenly, on 2 June, the status of the entire Dixie mission was undercut, and the project hardest hit was OSS's YENSIG 4. An urgent cable sent by Peterkin, Swensen and Stelle of OSS was dashed off to Heppner and Whitaker in Kunming:

Communist authorities today stated they are not, repeat not, willing to allow us go ahead setting up communications net until overall plan for intelligence and other operations is formally presented.

What they obviously want is to know completely and exactly just what U.S. Army plans to do in their area. Until complete statement American plans for working in their area is made to them and discussed with them, nothing, repeat nothing, is going to happen up here. There is now some question as to whether communists will cooperate. In any case they will not let us go ahead on anything until everything we plan to do has been formally cleared with them. . . . Swensen will survey situation, make commo [communications] plan and then return on next plane unless advise otherwise.[50]

After consulting with Dickey and Wedemeyer's top aide, General Olmsted, Whitaker replied that "we must not, repeat not, be unduly disturbed by communist attitude" and that "perhaps Chinese there will block our efforts but we believe here they have too much to gain by collaboration." As to Swensen, Whitaker ordered, "Keep your shirt on and your mouth shut."[51] One day later, Stelle was "unofficially" informed by Communist intelligence in Yenan that "4 Americans and 1 Chinese (or Chinese American) of demolitions unit presumably OSS has been disarmed by Communists in East Shansi Area." Alarmed, Stelle warned Dickey and Heppner, "Incidents are highly undesirable at present when Yenan is making decision whether or not to play ball with U.S. Army. Request locations of drops of units already made and permission to tell communists their locations. Recommend no more dropping of such units in or near communist territory."[52] The YENSIG 4 project never got off the ground for OSS. On 27 June 1945, Lieutenant Colonel Charles A. Porter, the chief of the OSS communications branch, wrote a formal memo to Wedemeyer's chief signal officer recommending cancellation of all signal supplies originally allocated for the project, marking the official ending of OSS's ambitious YENSIG 4 project in Yenan.[53]

Donovan's Third Trip to China and the Sudden End of War

One day after the death of the YENSIG 4 project, Wedemeyer, amid emergent Communist intransigence and hostility, arrived at the OSS compound at Xian for a field inspection. His chief purpose here was to receive a complete briefing from Krause on OSS operations in north China.

Wedemeyer's inspection turned into a great morale booster for OSS. As Krause recorded, the general "was extremely pleased with our compound and the manner in which we progressed with our field operations."[54] Wedemeyer himself wrote his staff, "I have to go to an OSS base in Hsian [Xian] to find the best military post in my command."[55]

Despite the difficulty with the Communists, OSS had reason to be proud in June and July 1945. The war with Hitler had ended and large numbers of U.S. military personnel were being transferred from Europe to China, among them many OSS agents. When Wedemeyer took over the theater command from Stilwell in late October 1944, the strength of OSS in China was a meager 106 agents; by July 1945, however, OSS had reached its peak with a total of 1,891 agents in China.[56] Since February 1945, efforts by Heppner and Wedemeyer to reorganize OSS/China had borne sweet fruit. For once, a solid command and branch structure was well established:

Chief, OSS/China	Colonel Richard P. Heppner
Deputy chief	Lieutenant Colonel Willis Bird
Operations officer	Colonel Wm. P. Davis
SI branch	Colonel Paul L. E. Helliwell
Counterespionage (X-2)	Lieutenant (SG) Arthur M. Thurston
SO branch	Lieutenant Colonel Nicholas W. Willis
Morale operations (MO)	Roland E. Dulin
Communications (COMMO)	Major Jack E. Horton
Research and analysis (R&A)	Major Joseph Spencer
Schools and training (S&T)	Captain Eldon Nehring
Field photographic (FP)	Lieutenant Ralph O. Hoge[57]

On 1 August 1945, in light of the rapid growth of OSS in the China theater, Heppner reshaped the field structure by redesignating the Zhijiang Field Unit as the OSS Southern Command and replaced its head, Colonel Wilfred Smith of the 14th Air Force, with OSS loyalist Colonel William R. Peers, the recent commander of Detachment 101 in Burma. At the same time, the Hsian (Xian) Field Unit command was changed to OSS Central Command.

Xian was the focus of OSS energy after the hope of working with the Communists was dashed in June. It became the most important base for penetration into north and northeast China and Japan's inner zone of Manchuria and Korea. The first major Xian-based project was the penetration into Korea. A brand new OSS Northeastern Command was created, based in Tuchao, fifteen miles southeast of Xian, with the sole aim of penetrating into Korea.[58] A new project, code-named Eagle, was established for this specific purpose. One hundred Koreans-in-exile in China under Kim Ku, who was the head of the so-called Korean Provisional Government, were immediately shipped to Tuchao for training under the field commander of the Eagle project, Captain Clyde B. Sargent.[59]

The second major OSS project based in Xian was the Phoenix operation, which involved only the Megan group. Between 29 July and 2 August 1945, five SI teams were dispatched into the field by Phoenix to gather Japanese order of battle intelligence in the Xian-Peiping-Haizhou triangle. The operation soon expanded and achieved remarkable results. According to the official OSS record, "They soon penetrated central Honan [Henan], Shantung [Shandong], southern Shansi [Shanxi], Hopeh [Hebei] and Manchuria. On August 15th, an American non-com, Cpl Bluh, led a mission to Shan-Hsien [Shanxian] in Honan and seized all available Japanese files from the Headquarters there despite enemy fire in the suburbs of the town. The team brought back three bags of documents, books, manual and other miscellaneous items. A second team on the same day successfully seized the Jap files in Yung-chi [Yongqi] in Shansi province."[60] Megan's Catholics took great pride in the rapid development of Phoenix.

The third major OSS operation from Xian was the Chili mission. Major Leonard Clark, formerly of AGFRTS, led the first Chili team to contact Yan Xishan, the de facto ruler in Shanxi. A large quantity of intelligence on Japanese order of battle and troop movements, as well as defense and target data, was collected by the Chili team and given to the 311th Fighter Wing. On 1 August a second Chili team, code-named Alum, led by Captain George S. Wuchinich, was dispatched to replace the original team in Shanxi. The fourth mission, code-named GZ6, was led by Captain William Drummond and operated in the area between the Yellow River and the Yangtze River region. The GZ6 was headquartered in Lihuang in Anhui Province and had four nets supplying information about train movements and the weather for the 14th Air Force.[61]

Yet by far the best OSS mission operating out of Xian was the R2S mission led by Captain John Birch, who was considered by the U.S. military high command as "one of the outstanding intelligence officers in our organization."[62] Birch established twelve intelligence nets with radio contact reaching from Peiping [Beijing] to the Yellow River basin. In particular, Birch's network achieved remarkable results in the Shandong Peninsula and collected much Japanese intelligence.[63]

OSS in China was establishing its effectiveness. Amid great optimism, Donovan arrived in China the first week of August 1945. The entourage included William Langer, the chief of R&A, and David Shaw, an OSS expert on utilizing labor union members as intelligence agents, who also had extensive ties with American Communists in China, such as Israel Epstein. Donovan's group first went to Kunming to inspect OSS headquarters there.

On the morning of 5 August, Donovan and his men flew to Chungking and received a hearty welcome from Wedemeyer, who lodged the director at his own house. That night, Wedemeyer held a luxurious party for Donovan. Wedemeyer announced during the party that he had arranged a meeting between Donovan and Chiang Kai-shek.

The next day, Chiang and Donovan met privately, during which time Donovan requested Chiang's help in the ambitious OSS plan to penetrate into the Japanese inner zone of Manchuria and Korea. Chiang was delighted and offered unconditional help. As Donovan later informed Wedemeyer, "He promised us that he would direct that we be given a selected 1,000 for replacements, and said that he would stir the 1st, 2nd, and 10th War Areas and actually telephoned the 1st War Area before we arrived there."[64]

Donovan's direct channel to Chiang Kai-shek via Wedemeyer bypassed the BIS boss and SACO director, Tai Li, who saw this as an insult. Consequently, Tai Li refused to see Donovan and left town. Donovan nonetheless sent him a brief greeting, dated 6 August: "My Dear General Tai Li: I was disappointed in not finding you here but I understand that pressing matters in the field will detain you there. I am pleased to know that our joint matters are going well, and I wish to thank you for your continued courtesy and help. Looking forward to seeing you in the near future and with all best wishes, I am, sincerely, William Donovan."[65]

The Chinese Communists were extremely interested in Donovan's trip. Long before his party arrived in China, they had learned of his coming. On 6 August in Chungking, David Shaw of OSS held a secret meeting with Song Qingling (Madam Sun Yat-sen), who was closely tied to Communist intelligence. Shaw's official task in OSS was to recruit secret agents among trade unions for intelligence and sabotage. During the seventy-five-minute meeting, Song Qingling pushed one issue in particular: that Shaw should hold a secret meeting with Communist representatives on the possibility that OSS could work with CCP-controlled trade unions in north China.[66] Shaw accepted the invitation.

The next day, minutes before Donovan and his entourage departed Chungking, Shaw received a message from Song Qingling that a meeting with the Communist representatives had been scheduled for 11 A.M. Realizing the gravity of the situation, Shaw at once informed Quentin Roosevelt. A debate ensued. As Shaw related in a followup memo to Roosevelt,

> I immediately reported this to you and told you I intended to talk to these people. You felt that matter was so serious that I should discuss it with Colonel Heppner. I then agreed to go with you to say a few words to Colonel Heppner and General Donovan about the problem.

Colonel Heppner felt that my discussing anything with these people at this time might very well result in the exclusion of OSS from this theater, in view of the delicate situation which confronted OSS as the result of recent discussions carried on by Colonel Yeaton and Yenan. I told Colonel Heppner I had no such desire and such was not my purpose, I was only searching for facts and I would make no commitments concerning American aid, recognition or assistance. General Donovan then told Colonel Heppner that he would take complete personal responsibility for my seeing Mme. Sun's "friends," and that he felt it extremely important for us to have information about north China and the labor movement in that area. He specifically instructed me not to make any commitments of any type, merely to find out facts and to bring back conclusions with this understanding.[67]

Shaw stayed behind in Chungking to conduct the important task of meeting with the Communist representatives at Song Qingling's home. The Communists included Wang Bingnan, Zhou Enlai's deputy in Chungking, and two women: Zhang Xiaomei and Gong Peng (Kung Peng). After making introductions, Song Qingling left and the secret meeting began, lasting about one and a half hours. The most important figure was Gong Peng, who was Zhou Enlai's top aide in charge of intelligence matters with Americans. Gong's major proposals included an immediate meeting between Shaw and Mao Zedong in Yenan. One important issue involved the admission of the Communists to the World Federation of Trade Unions, for which, Shaw said, "there was a very good chance of American support." The Communists then gave Shaw a large batch of English-language materials published by the Communist press in Yenan. Shaw indicated in his report to Quentin Roosevelt that "no promises on either side were made. The association was one of exploratory nature and the conference was kept on that level."[68]

Donovan and his party departed Chungking for Xian on 7 August, one day after the atomic bomb was dropped over Hiroshima. In Xian, the same day, they inspected the crown jewel of OSS under Krause, the redesignated Central Command. "General Donovan, Col. Heppner and party arrived for inspection tour," recollected Krause. "The General was pleased with our entire setup." Donovan reportedly even said that "Hsian [Xian] was the best of all the OSS bases."[69]

While Donovan was in Xian, a thorny issue arose with regard to the Eagle project, involving Koreans under Kim Ku, head of the Korean Provisional Government. This self-styled exiled government had never been recognized by the United States, and some in the State Department were vigorously opposed to it. Kim Ku was looking to Donovan's visit as an effective means of inducing official U.S. recognition. Donovan had not the slightest concern about meeting Kim Ku. Donovan's aide had informed Krause that "the General is intensely interested in Eagle and is anxious that penetration be accomplished at the earliest possible date."[70]

Donovan's hobnobbing with Kim Ku proved instrumental in his own downfall. Days after meeting with Donovan, Kim Ku dispatched a long cable directly to President Truman at the White House. Kim Ku called himself the chairman of the Korean Provisional Government and stated, "It is our hope that American-Korean positive cooperation initiated in China during the last months of the War against Japan will continue and grow."[71] Upon receiving Kim Ku's message, Truman became furious at Donovan and wrote to the director on 25 August 1945, "I would appreciate your instructing your agents as to the impropriety of their acting as a channel for the transmission to me of messages from representatives of self-styled governments which are not recognized by the Government of the United States."[72] Twenty-five days later, Truman dissolved OSS.

While Donovan was in exuberant spirits inspecting his spy stations in Xian, dining lavishly and purchasing Chinese antiques in the most ancient and revered capital of the Chinese past, momentous events were occurring in the Far East. The day after Donovan's arrival in Xian, the Soviet Union declared war on the Japanese empire and the Russian Red Army stormed into Japanese-occupied Manchuria. One day later, the second atomic bomb was dropped over Nagasaki.

All of a sudden, whatever OSS was trying hardest to do—namely, penetrate into the Japanese inner zone—seemed at the same time urgent, and, if not accomplished quickly, inconsequential. Donovan told Wedemeyer, "The entry of the Russians into Manchuria points up my urgent petition that we be no longer delayed in the northern penetration. If we are not in Korea and Manchuria when the Russians get there, we will never get in."[73] On the morning of 9 August, the third day of Donovan's visit to Xian, rumors came in that Japan was about to surrender. In great angst, Donovan decided to go back to the center of American decision making; he left Xian in haste for Washington via Kunming.[74] On the evening of 10 August, Donovan finally succeeded in boarding a special flight from Kunming directly back to Washington; thirty minutes after Donovan's plane took off, intelligence reports came to Heppner in Kunming that the Japanese had surrendered.[75]

Suddenly, a new task befell OSS in China.

CHAPTER ELEVEN

Surrender by Japan and Communist Hostility Toward OSS

The sudden end of the war completely surprised OSS. Immediate action had to be taken in order to have any impact at all on the war history of the United States in China. As Heppner informed Donovan and his party, which had just reached Honolulu en route to Washington, "Although we have been caught with our pants down, we will do our best to pull them up in time."[1]

Heppner showed great resolve and sent an urgent cable to Colonel Davis, chief liaison with Wedemeyer's headquarters in Chungking, asking to secure logistical support from Wedemeyer. This cable outlined the general ambitions of OSS/China "In view of emergency caused by Jap capitulation, request you prosecute the following moves in relation to theater with utmost vigor:"

1. Command teams are available to drop into principal Chinese cities. Urge that airlift be provided in order that these men may raid Jap headquarters and seize vital documents and personalities both Japanese and puppets. These commandos ready to leave tomorrow.

2. Urge theater to provide airlift immediately for placing of OSS teams in critical spots in Manchuria in order that we may be on ground before arrival of Russians.

3. Urge airlift be provided that OSS teams now available be placed in strategic spots in Korea in order that our interests may be protected before Russian occupation.

4. Urge airlift to put OSS teams already available in key localities in China proper in order that American interests and Chinese National Government interest may be safeguarded.[2]

"The Mercy Missions"

On 12 August 1945, Colonel Heppner moved swiftly by ordering OSS teams into strategic spots in three areas: Mukden (Shenyang) and Harbin in Manchuria and Weixian (Weihsien) in Shandong.[3] These teams included SI, SO, medical, and COMMO (communications) personnel and interpreters. Three days later General Wedemeyer issued a comprehensive directive to various special agencies under his control to locate and evacuate POWs in north China, Manchuria, and Korea. To Wedemeyer, this was a job of the highest priority. Although AGAS was mandated with POW rescue work by the War Department, OSS was invited to join the effort, which provided an excellent cover for intelligence penetration into these areas. Nine air sorties were executed from the OSS base in Xian, and the 14th Air Force was ordered to provide the necessary staging facilities. OSS immediately organized eight operational missions, which were coded Magpie (Peiping), Duck (Weihsien), Flamingo (Harbin), Cardinal (Mukden), Sparrow (Shanghai), Quail (Hanoi), Pigeon (Hainan Island), and Raven (Vientiane, Laos).

The Duck mission was sent to Shandong Province on 17 August under Major S. A. Staiger and quickly discovered a big POW camp where 1,038 captured British military personnel, 205 Americans, and 200 troops from other nations—Belgium, Norway, Uruguay, Iran, and Cuba—had been detained.[4] One of the tasks of OSS super agent William Christian was penetrating this camp. The only Chinese operative allowed to enter the maximum security camp happened to be Christian's agent.[5]

The Magpie mission covered the Peiping area and was commanded by Major Ray Nichols of OSS. The mission located 624 Allied POWs. The Pigeon mission, under a young OSS captain fresh out from the European theater, John C. Singlaub, parachuted onto Hainan Island on 27 August, located about 400 POWs, and evacuated them all to nearby Hong Kong.[6] The OSS team to Laos, the Raven mission under Major Aaron Banks, located 143 internees near Vientiane.

A more complicated story unfolded around the Quail mission, under a young Captain Archimedes L. A. Patti; it included five Frenchmen who were not necessarily friendly toward the Vietnamese Communists led by Ho Chi Minh. On 22 August, Patti and his men walked into Hanoi and "liberated" the city; this was the first American military team to confront the Japanese military authority there. However, the connection between OSS and the Frenchmen in the crucial days of August 1945 put Donovan's organization in an extremely precarious position vis-à-vis the Communists and their sympathizers.

In examining the historical documents carefully, we can easily discern that political ideology did not lead OSS to take sides in French Indochina. In fact, OSS was by and large innocent in the whole messy arena where so much American blood would be shed in years to come. For Donovan, getting intelligence was the paramount reason for contacting and/or co-operating with certain groups. By contrast, those who were ideologically motivated were unhappy with the pragmatism and lack of ideology in OSS. As Charles Fenn saw it, "Alternately supporting the Vichy-French, Free-French, Vietminh and other native groups, OSS managed to infuriate even liberal French opinion while at the same time disillusioning the natives as to any real American understanding."[7] Curiously, De Gaulle's special emissary to Vietnam, Jean Sainteny, issued the most biting criticism of OSS: "I often ask myself why OSS, so well endowed with able men, sent into Vietnam only second string underlings, incapable of evaluating the stake and the incalculable results of the drama then taking place in the month of August 1945."[8] Above all, OSS's top priority was to penetrate Korea, Shandong, and Manchuria. In the days immediately following the official Japanese surrender, dramatic episodes took place in each of these areas.

The OSS team drawing the most attention in the waning days of the war was the Eagle mission, designed to cover Korea. The Eagle team was originally commanded by Clyde Sargent and had now been taken over by Lieutenant Colonel Willis Bird, the deputy director of OSS/China. On 16 August the mission boarded a C-47 and headed for Keijo, Korea. While in the air, the mission received intelligence reports that kamikaze planes were attacking U.S. carriers and that the Japanese emperor was unable to enforce his own cease-fire order. The plane was ordered to turn around and return to Xian.

Bird, ever publicity conscious and eager to gain fame by "liberating" Korea single-handedly, added a Mr. Lieberman—an OWI writer—to the Eagle mission in violation of Heppner's specific orders. The entire team then took off from Xian again and landed at Keijo on 18 August. This was the first time U.S. military personnel originating from the China theater had touched Korean soil since the war began. The official record chronicles what ensued: "On arrival, this mission was met with a 'friendly and helpful attitude from the Japanese command,' which informed them that all POWs and civilians were safe and well but that since no instructions had been received from the Japanese Government, the presence of the mission in

Korea was 'embarrassing.' " The Japanese suggested, therefore, that the mission return to China and come back later. Gasoline for the return to China was provided by the Japanese. Eagle flew to Weixian, Shandong, the next day and contacted Duck mission there. On 20 August, OSS Headquarters instructed the mission to return to Keijo immediately and remain there, even if this resulted in temporary internment; but Bird reported that the Japanese had refused to accept the mission even though requested to do so and had ordered it out of Keijo at tank gunpoint. He flew to Chungking on 22 August in order to present in person his opinion that a return to Keijo would mean execution by the Japanese of the twenty-two members of the Eagle mission and the crew.[9]

Then something went terribly wrong. On the afternoon of 22 August, Bird went directly to see Wedemeyer and described the dangerous situation that the Eagle team had encountered in Korea. While Bird was meeting Wedemeyer, however, Lieberman was writing a news story about the first American encounter with the Japanese in Korea. Lieberman accurately recorded something else that had gone on in Keijo between the Americans and the Japanese, something Bird had not told Wedemeyer. As Colonel Davis stated, Lieberman's story "included a couple of paragraphs about Japs entertaining our people with beer and sake and each nationality singing own national songs."[10] Early the next morning, Wedemeyer heard Lieberman's news story over the worldwide OWI radio broadcast and became infuriated. He believed that Bird had disgraced U.S. armed forces in the China theater because Lieberman's story could easily be construed as fraternization with the Japanese troops. Particularly disgusting to Wedemeyer was the fact that Bird had taken an OWI man and photographer along, but no medical supplies or food for POWs. Moreover, the contrast between Bird's report on how hostile the Japanese still were toward Americans and Lieberman's piece on American-Japanese drinking and singing undoubtedly smacked of dishonesty on the part of OSS.

Wedemeyer immediately ordered that all POW rescue efforts in Korea "be reconstituted and completely divorced from Eagle project."[11] Wedemeyer's chief of staff recommended sending Bird back to the United States at once for disciplinary action.[12] Colonel Davis, the most senior OSS officer then in Chungking, panicked at Wedemeyer's rage and wired Heppner, advising him to replace Bird immediately as the head of the Eagle project. Heppner complied, designating Gustav Krause instead. Further, Heppner instructed Davis to "take whatever steps you deem necessary to keep Bird out of contact with all persons outside OSS and theater Headquarters."[13] On the same day, Heppner hurriedly informed Donovan of developments and urged the director in Washington to "take whatever steps may be necessary to protect the organization [OSS]."[14] Donovan sent back an angry reply the next day: "Make sure that action taken [against Bird] for violation of your orders. If necessary send Bird home at once or, in your discretion, prefer charges."[15] Two days later, to tighten control over OSS/China public relations, Heppner appointed Roland Dulin, the MO chief, as public relations officer in charge of all press releases; Heppner also ordered that no OSS personnel be allowed to discuss OSS activities with any member of the press.[16] On 28 August the entire Eagle team was ordered back to Xian for reorganization. Two days later, the mission was canceled because an American corps would shortly occupy the Korean Peninsula.[17] As for Willis Bird no harsh action ever befell him, aside from becoming the laughingstock of Chinese Communist intelligence.[18]

The Killing of John Birch

The second key item on the OSS penetration priority list at the end of the war in Asia was the Shandong Peninsula. In this regard, Bird's escapade in Korea was by no means the biggest problem for OSS. The most profound challenges came from the Communists, both Chinese and Soviet. The first casualty of the Communists' defiance was Captain John Birch.

Birch had devoted himself tirelessly and faithfully to helping the Chinese war of resistance against the Japanese, and he received special recognition from General Joseph Stilwell for his work.[19] A U.S. War Department report reads, "Captain Birch was one of the outstanding intelligence officers in our organization due to his knowledge of China, his knowledge of the Chinese language and finally, to the many, many Chinese friends he had who were marooned behind the [Japanese] lines."[20]

Birch was by no means an ideological zealot, as has been portrayed by American political extremists on both the left and the right. But when fanatics from the far right started their hysterical battle against international communism, they picked Birch as their martyr. Robert H. W. Welch Jr. used the Birch story as a base for anticommunist diatribe; in 1954 he published a widely read biography, *The Life of John Birch,* which devotes most of its pages not to Birch but to political accusations against others.[21] In reality, Captain John Birch had no connection—except a symbolic one—with the John Birch Society, an extremist organization founded by Robert Welch long after Birch's death.

The killing of John Birch by the Chinese Communists was by no means an isolated incident "provoked" by the murdered man, as claimed by some writers.[22] It transpired because the Communists tenaciously tried to keep all American influence out of the geographically important Shandong Peninsula and Northern Jiangsu, which guard the entrance in the Gulf of Chihli (Bo Hai Gulf) to Port Arthur (Lü Shun) and Dairen (Da Lian)—both under Soviet occupation since mid-August 1945; and because the CCP troops were actively searching for the Birch party to prevent it at any cost from meeting the person Captain Birch was instructed to see, General Hao Pengju, formerly a puppet collaborator, with whom the CCP was conducting a hasty and most secret negotiation.[23]

The Shandong Peninsula had been a coveted area for OSS. An earlier report illustrated the reason: "The Shantung [Shandong] peninsula occupies a geographical position of vital strategic importance. It dominates the sea-lanes running into Northeast China and Manchuria from Japan, Central China and Korea. Military forces occupying Shantung would control one of the two major north-south rail routes between Central and North China. Intelligence teams operating from Shantung could cover Hopei, Chahar, Jehol, Manchuria and Korea."[24] Yet the intelligence OSS gleaned from the Shandong area had been extremely meager.[25] The only productive intelligence operation conducted in this area was Birch's R2S.

Throughout the war and with the acquiescence of Japanese occupation authorities, the Chinese Communists had been secretly collaborating with Wang Jingwei's puppet regime and had bought weapons from it to fight the KMT. Mao Zedong understood the United States' desire to penetrate Shandong and northern Jiangsu for the final onslaught against the Japanese homeland, and he was willing to bargain with the Americans. In January 1945, General Zhu De of the CCP raised the stakes to the point of asking the United States for $20 million to equip twenty divisions of puppet troops under Communist control. In turn, the CCP agreed to let Americans use the port of Lian Yungang (Lien Yun-kang) in northern Jiangsu, then under Communist control.

However, under the agreement at the Yalta Conference in February 1945, the Soviet Union was to be given Port Arthur and Dairen in postwar Manchuria (the northeast). This arrangement changed everything. The CCP now refused Wedemeyer's requests for cooperation in allowing Birch to enter Shandong. The War Department considered Birch "the only officer in that area who had a sound knowledge of that section of China."[26] Then the Japanese surrendered on 15 August. As part of the POW rescue operations, Birch was ordered to Shandong Province via northern Jiangsu to survey the former Japanese airfields for the 14th Air Force so that relay air routes for the return of American POWs would be secured. On 20 August the Birch party, consisting of four Americans, seven Chinese, and two Koreans, proceeded to the Shandong Peninsula via Xuzhou (Suchow, in northern Jiangsu). The person they were instructed to contact was General Hao Pengju of the newly designated Sixth Army.

Since 1941, Hao Pengju had abandoned the Chinese cause and worked as garrison commander and governor of the so-called Huai Hai Province for the Japanese under Wang Jingwei's puppet regime. Chinese communist intelligence had extensively penetrated and controlled Hao Pengju's headquarters since 1942. Two of Hao's four division commanders, plus almost his entire staff, had been CCP secret agents for years.[27] Upon the surrender of the Japanese, Chiang Kai-shek, in accordance with the Potsdam Declaration, ordered Hao's puppet troops to stay put and await reorganization by the KMT. Chiang temporarily designated them the Sixth Army, which had already been thoroughly infiltrated and controlled by Communist intelligence. When Birch was asked to contact Hao Pengju, the CCP agents in his headquarters under the direct command of General Chen Yi and Rao Shushi, were pushing Hao to take the entire Sixth Army over to join the Communists immediately, before any peace treaty was signed in Chungking that might preclude such a secret deal.[28] When the cable to Hao Pengju arrived at his headquarters from Chungking, ordering him to cooperate with the incoming Birch party, it was intercepted by CCP intelligence. Fearing any undue influence upon the ongoing secret parley, the CCP promptly dispatched a team belonging to the Eighth Route Army to intercept the Birch party.[29]

CCP troops spotted and detained the Birch party briefly soon after it was forced to proceed on foot because of the rampant destruction of the railways by the Communist troops in the Xuzhou area. Before long, the Communist troops forced the Birch party to stop a second time. Bewildered and upset, Captain Birch was nonetheless able to explain to the Communists that the purpose of his mission was to survey the airfields in eastern Shandong and that as a U.S. intelligence officer he had no intention of meddling in the KMT-CCP conflict. He firmly demanded the party be allowed to proceed. The party was then able to continue unmolested.

On 25 August the Birch party was stopped for the third time at Huangkou station. Birch instructed his deputy, Lieutenant Dong Qinsheng (Tung Chin-sheng), to approach the Communist commander and ask for a pass. The Communist commander responded with a hostile order to surround and disarm the Birch party. Dong went over to tell the commander, "The war is over and we have no more enemies. The Americans have helped us all a lot. Capt. Birch's party is going to Suchow [Xuzhou], under orders, to inspect the airfield. If you want to disarm the Americans, then you may cause a serious misunderstanding between Communist China and America."[30]

Ignoring Dong's plea, the CCP commander ordered his troops to disarm the Birch party. Upon being approached by the Communist soldiers, Birch said, "Peace has come to all the world and still you make trouble here. Why? I will see your responsible officer."[31] In reply, the Communists threatened, "Since you are not willing to be disarmed, you may proceed. If anything happens to you we are not liable." This was understood by the Birch party as an obvious threat.[32]

Nonetheless, Birch insisted on explaining his mission to the commanding officer, but was snubbed and was led by Communist soldiers in a runaround that lasted about an hour, "with no one who would claim the responsibility of commanding officer of the troops who had stopped [the Birch party]" and threatened it. During this long search for the CCP commanding officer, Birch, growing more and more angry, finally took the orderly, who was leading them around, by the back of his collar and shook him, asking, "What is the matter with you, anyway? Are you bandits?"[33]

Surrounded and outnumbered by armed troops, Lieutenant Dong warned Birch to be careful lest they be killed by the belligerent Communists. Having been threatened and frustrated for nearly an hour, Birch said to Dong, in private, "Never mind, you don't know what my feelings are. I want to find out how they intend to treat Americans. I don't mind if they kill me. If they do they will be finished for America will punish them with Atomic bombs."[34]

The run-around in search of the CCP commanding officer continued and Captain Birch and Lt. Dong were led again and again to the same places they had been earlier until a CCP officer who had earlier denied being in command asked Birch and Dong to approach him. Without giving Birch a chance to speak and explain, the CCP officer "then ordered in a swearing manner: 'Load your guns and disarm him [Birch] first.' "[35]

Lieutenant Dong immediately stepped forward and said, "If you are going to disarm him, let me take his gun for you." In answer to this the CCP officer, pointing at Dong, ordered: "Shoot him first."[36] The official investigation report recorded what then happened:

One shot was fired, which struck Lieutenant Tung in the right leg above the knee. As he fell he heard a second shot fired and Captain Birch exclaim "Aye Ya!" and he believes that Captain Birch also fell. The officer then gave the order, "Bring them along," and Lieutenant Tung heard Captain Birch answer: "Wu bu len tso la." (I can not walk anymore.) Both Lieutenant Tung and Captain Birch were picked up and carried a short distance to the edge of a pit and left lying there. Later on it was apparent that Captain Birch had resisted being carried as he

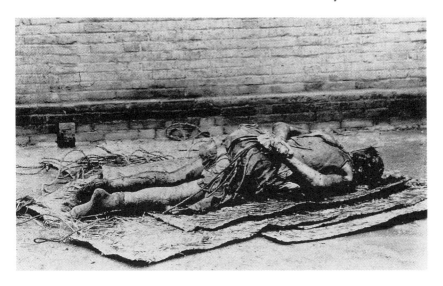

Fig. 17. Body of OSS agent John Birch, mutilated by the Chinese Communists (National Archives)

was found with his arms bound behind his back and his feet tied together.[37]

Birch, who had been wounded by a gunshot to his left thigh, was tied up and dragged to a cinder pile near the railway station and brutally bayoneted to death. William Miller of AGAS, the American officer who conducted the initial on-site investigation, reported to General Wedemeyer that Captain Birch's "face was mutilated [by bayonets] in order to destroy its identity. The job was so thorough that nothing but bone was left. His two false front teeth were also missing. The throat was also wide open from ear to ear indicating either that it was cut or that it had been hit from the side by a dum dum bullet similar to the one that lacerated Tung's leg."[38]

All this happened at about 2 or 3 P.M. The official OSS investigation further reported, "In the evening an old woman came by and saw the two bodies and appeared very frightened. Lieutenant Tung heard her say that they should be buried. He answered, 'I am not dead yet. Help me.' At once, the woman told him that the Communists had not left yet and that he must be quiet. After they left she would come and help him. Later in the evening, he was carried to an air raid shelter. Captain Birch's body was hastily buried by the common people (the Lao Pei Hsing) [Lao Beixing, the common folk]."[39]

An investigation conducted by the U.S. judge advocate of the China theater, dated 13 November 1945, concludes: "Although Capt. Birch's conduct immediately prior to his death indicated a lack of good judgment and failure to take proper precautions in a dangerous situation, nevertheless the actions taken by the Chinese Communist Army personnel fell short of according the rights and privileges due even to enemy prisoners of war and constituted murder. . . . The shooting was done maliciously. . . . The killing was completely without justification."[40]

The killing of Birch by the Communists sent an instant shock wave throughout U.S. forces in China. The entire OSS team of the Spaniel mission was still being detained by the Communists; now one of Wedemeyer's top intelligence officers was senselessly killed *after* the war with Japan was over. Accumulated anger prompted Wedemeyer to take drastic measures. On 30 August he directly confronted Mao Zedong and Zhou Enlai, who were in Chungking for a reluctant and pretentious peace talk. "This is a very serious and very grave incident," Wedemeyer warned Mao and Zhou. "When the American people learn about Captain Birch's death it will have a very disturbing effect." Wedemeyer further pointed out to Mao and Zhou, "I cannot have Americans killed in this theater by Chinese Communists or anyone else."[41] Then Wedemeyer demanded a full explanation and the immediate release of the three other OSS agents in the Birch team who had been captured and since detained by the Communist troops.

During the tense encounter, Mao and Zhou pointed out that the Communists had been friendly to Americans all along, at which point Wedemeyer countered by stating that since May 1945, the Communists had become hostile toward American forces. The angered general then brought up the Fuping incident. "I have not told the American people that Mr. Mao has retained four Americans as prisoners at Fuping since last May," Wedemeyer said. "Why did they [the Communists] capture these men—why did they take them as prisoners? You [Mao] should have had the courtesy to at least wire me and say, 'Wedemeyer, who are these people that just came into this area. Do I have the assurance that these four men will be sent to me immediately?' " Sensing Wedemeyer's rage, Zhou Enlai replied at once, "If you send a plane, you can take them back immediately."[42]

On the morning of 8 September the four detained OSS officers of the Spaniel team woke up and saw "a beautiful windy day." Before long, they heard the sound of an American airplane, signaling the end of their four-month detention.[43] However, what Wedemeyer and the OSS command did not know at the time was that the day after Wedemeyer's protest to Mao and Zhou about the killing of John Birch, the Communists captured yet another OSS team in Shanxi, the Chili mission led by Captain Wuchinich. On 31 August, Wuchinich and his agents found themselves in the no-man's land of a puppet-Communist skirmish. According to the official OSS record, "In their last radio contact Captain Wuchinich reported that the team was holed up in a tower. The radio died and nothing more was heard for weeks."[44]

The Wedemeyer lecture to Mao and Zhou, however, kept the Communists quiet about the Wuchinich capture. Nobody knew where these OSS officers were. The entire OSS was mobilized to make all possible efforts to find them, asking Tai Li and the surrendered Japanese Kempei or military police in the Shanxi area for help.[45] In late September 1945, the whereabouts of the Wuchinich team was finally discovered, and only then did the Communists feel compelled to release them.[46]

The capture and detention of the Spaniel mission, the killing of John Birch, and the capture and detention of the Chili team dashed any illusions OSS/China had had about the Chinese Communists. The flags in the OSS headquarters in Kunming and other places were placed at half mast to mourn the death of Birch. The captures of two OSS field teams were equally indicative of what lay ahead for Donovan's troops in China.

OSS in Manchuria and the Stankevich Ultimatum

The last and most important of the three key areas OSS had targeted was Manchuria. Historians will continue to argue whether the Roosevelt administration "sold out" Chinese Manchuria to Stalin at Yalta. But one thing was certain: whatever motives FDR and his aides might have shared in Yalta, it was disturbing that they did not inform top officials of the Allies, including Chiang Kai-shek, Ambassador Hurley, and General Wedemeyer, about the secret agreement granting the Soviet Union's demand of excessive concessions in Manchuria in exchange for entering the war against Japan. A conspiratorial atmosphere cultivated by the Soviets and British, along with the inaction of a dying Roosevelt, frightened a weakened China, prompting Ambassador Hurley to rush back to Washington in April 1945 and directly confront the president about the Yalta secret agreement. When the tenacious Hurley discovered the shocking document in the Yalta files provided by the White House, he immediately flew to London and Moscow to try to extract pledges from Churchill and Stalin that they would abandon territorial ambitions in China after the war, particularly in such areas as Hong Kong and Manchuria. Hurley pleaded with Churchill that "if Great Britain failed to observe the principles of the Atlantic Charter by continuing to exert control over Hong Kong, the Soviet Union might well make similar demands in regard to North China." Churchill's response to Hurley was rude and violent. The prime minister chided

Hurley that "*first*, Britain was not bound by the Atlantic Charter in regard to its colonies; *second*, Hong Kong would be taken out of the British Empire only over his dead body."[47] Hurley's trip to Moscow was equally frustrating.[48]

A disgraced Hurley came back to China in utter anger and discussed the Yalta agreement with Wedemeyer. When the time came to represent the government of the United States and officially inform Chiang Kai-shek of the Yalta secret agreement, Hurley received the angry reaction he expected. Chiang had gotten wind of such a scheme but had not been formally told. In the mind of General Wedemeyer, the Yalta agreement was no less than an outright betrayal of China's national sovereignty. As Wedemeyer recorded, "I shall never forget his reaction when Ambassador Hurley in my presence performed the highly distasteful task of informing the Generalissimo of the Yalta betrayal of China's national interest."[49]

When Donovan came to China just days before Japan's surrender, Wedemeyer conferred with him about OSS penetration into Manchuria to gather intelligence. Donovan's immediate reaction to the Soviets' entry into the war with Japan was to speed up Manchurian penetration before the Russians could establish firm control there. Heppner certainly understood Donovan's and Wedemeyer's plan. Upon receiving the unofficial news of Japanese surrender, Heppner's first order was to send OSS teams to Manchuria. "Take every step at your disposal," Heppner ordered Gustav Krause, the chief of OSS command in Xian, on 10 August 1945, "in consultation with 14th Air Force and Bishop Meeghan [*sic*] to get agents placed with utmost dispatch in key points in Manchuria concerning which you are informed. You know the reasons for this and I leave it to your discretion to take best methods for speedy implementation."[50]

At almost the same moment, Heppner ordered Colonel Davis "to urge theater to provide airlift immediately for placing of OSS teams in critical spots in Manchuria in order that we may be on ground before arrival of Russians."[51] Quickly, two teams, code-named Flamingo and Cardinal, were organized, targeting at Harbin and Mukden, respectively. But just before their departure the Soviets took complete control of Harbin; the Flamingo mission was canceled, its personnel transferred to the Eagle mission, which also failed.[52]

The Cardinal mission, under Major James T. Hennessy, parachuted near Mukden on 16 August 1945. Two days later, the mission discovered a POW camp in which 1,321 Americans, 239 British, and some Australian, Dutch, and Canadian prisoners had been kept by the Japanese. But the mission's main goal, finding General Jonathan M. Wainwright, who had surrendered to the Japanese in Southeast Asia early in 1942, was not accomplished until

Fig. 18. Lieutenant General Jonathan Wainwright, with cane, thanking Colonel Gustav Krause of OSS/China for liberating him from a Japanese POW camp in Manchuria, August 1945 (National Archives)

27 August. General Wainwright, along with ten other captured generals, including the British General Sir Percival, once Commander of Singapore, the governor of Dutch East India, were immediately flown by OSS to Xian. Wainwright was so grateful to OSS that he recorded a personal thank-you message to Donovan on tape. "This is General Wainwright speaking," the message began. "Greetings, General Donovan. I am speaking from Hsian, China, where I have just eaten my first good American breakfast since the war."[53] Krause noted that the liberated American POWs were so happy that "the entire group was like a bunch of school kids."[54]

After accomplishing their cover task of rescuing the allied POWs, the Cardinal team began its covert operations and tried to establish a firm base in Manchuria. OSS utilized Bishop Megan's Chinese Catholic network, as ordered by Heppner in his 10 August cable to Krause. A large number of these agents parachuted in and around the Mukden area.[55]

OSS activities in Manchuria elicited strong reactions from the Soviets. When the Cardinal team was dropped into Mukden, Soviet troops were on a three-day looting binge. As the Cardinal intelligence report recorded, "Jap-owned buildings and centers were set on fire and/or attacked by local mobs armed with ordnance left behind by some fourteen thousand fleeing civilian Japs. Casualties, killed and wounded, ran into the hundreds on both sides. In numerous cases, roving Chinese mobs beat or killed indiscriminately in the streets at night." During this madness, the mission noted, "Americans are by no means immune from Russian mistreatment, many having been robbed at tommy gun point of their watches, and sometimes of their rings and money." The situation reached such a hostile point that incidents such as "stabbing a B-24 tire, drunken abuse of 'Americanski's,' flagrant insults to American flags, etc." were inflicted upon the OSS team. Protests to the Soviet headquarters and requests for positive identification of the culprits were futile. Although greatly limited in number and resources, the Cardinal team, the only U.S intelligence operation in all of Manchuria at the time, was able to report many important events in that strategic area, including the sudden and unannounced secret entrance of thousands of Chinese Communist Eighth Route Army soldiers into Soviet-occupied Mukden on 7 September 1945; the capture of Henry Pu Yi, the puppet head of Manchukuo and last emperor of China; and the Soviet military occupation of the British-American Tobacco Company.[56]

The presence of any U.S. personnel in Manchuria, particularly intelligence teams, was a direct affront to the Soviet occupation policy. OSS knew that as long as American POWs remained in Manchuria, the Russians would barely tolerate Cardinal's presence. By mid-September 1945, most American POWs and internees had been evacuated. The U.S. Army headquarters in Chungking, under the acting command of Lieutenant General George E. Stratemeyer during Wedemeyer's absence, ordered Major Brady, the new Cardinal head replacing Hennessey, and his OSS team to stay in Manchuria until expelled by force.[57] Under this scheme, protective action had to be taken. Since the United States had no official representation in Manchuria, the army requested the French consulate under a M. Renner in Mukden represent OSS and "American interests" after 19 September 1945.[58]

The Soviets vehemently opposed this arrangement and threatened terrorist action against Renner. On 3 October the French consul used a Cardinal radio set and dispatched an urgent cable to the French embassy in Chungking: "My position at present is extremely difficult . . . involving risks for my own safety and that of my family."[59] On the same day, at 3

P.M., Major General Kavqun Stankevich, the Soviet war commandant at Mukden, issued an ultimatum to the OSS team: "This is to inform you that since you do not have a visa from the Government of the USSR, your papers may not be regarded as official documents. It is therefore ordered that by October 5, 1945 you be outside the boundaries of Manchuria." The Cardinal team stayed in Manchuria right up to the deadline set by Stankevich. Before departing, an angry Cardinal message went to Chungking headquarters: "Immediately upon our departure all United States nationals found in Manchuria will be killed. . . . When did Manchuria become a part of Russia?"[60]

This high-handed Soviet measure shocked the War Department in Washington. General Marshall instantly instructed the commander general of the U.S. military mission to the USSR in Moscow, code-named "Maples," to "register a protest with the Soviet General Staff for Stankevich's order for the expulsion of the OSS group at Mukden." Marshall hinted to Maples how he might phrase his protest to the Soviets: "This group was in Manchuria for the purpose of assisting liberated U.S. citizens, both prisoners of the war and internees. Soviets should be requested to furnish an explanation for their action in demanding the departure of these U.S. personnel from Manchuria in spite of their humanitarian mission, and requested to give assurance that the necessary steps will be taken by them to prevent the recurrence of such an incident." To make sure the protest seemed justified, Marshall ordered Stratemeyer in China to feed Maples details of the episode. "It is desired," Marshall stated, "that Stratemeyer report on the activities of the OSS group in Mukden to Maples as speedily as practicable (information copy to War Department) and state whether in his opinion the activities of the OSS group were such as to justify Stankevich in the issuance of his order."[61]

On 7 October, Stratemeyer sent a preliminary background report to Maples, including a statement that after 19 September "a group of 7 OSS men remained in Mukden. The mission of this OSS group was to collect available information and to protect, insofar as possible, the interests of the United States until authorized American personnel should arrive."[62] Stratemeyer then issued an official report to Maples and Marshall. Stratemeyer wrote that he was somewhat puzzled by the numbers in the OSS Cardinal team: "On October 5th, a group of 14 men was due to leave Mukden for Peiping. OSS team at Mukden was made up of only 7 men and no detailed information is now available as to who was included in the group being evacuated."

Of course, what Stratemeyer might not have known was that the rest of the people in the Cardinal Mission were Megan's Catholic agents, who

Fig. 19. Short-lived warmth between OSS agents and Soviet Red Army soldiers in Manchuria, August 1945 (National Archives)

had not yet been planted in Manchuria by the time Stankevich issued his ultimatum. At any rate, Stratemeyer concluded that "the Stankevich order was not provoked by any overt action by OSS personnel, and that such instructions are without rightful justification. It is noted in connection with this that apparently the basis for the Stankevich order is 'because you do not have a visa from the Soviet Government.' "[63]

However, upon receiving Stratemeyer's information and after consulting with Ambassador W. Averell Harriman, Maples decided not to file a protest to the Soviets. A cable was sent to General Marshall on 12 October to explain:

A study of the reports from COMGEN China on the incident involving the OSS team at Mukden does not indicate that we have as yet built up a very strong case for an official protest to the Russian Government on this incident. . . . The fact that this personnel had departed, leaving only the one team in the area with the primary job of collecting intelligence, could not fail to arouse the antagonism of the Russians. This is particularly true in view of the fact that the Russians are well aware of the nature of OSS activities, having negotiated exchanges of information through this headquarters between OSS and the NKVD. . . . Both the Ambassador and Ritchie agree with my feeling that lodging a strong protest from you with General Antonov on this particular group of men might lead to an exchange of recriminatory correspondence in which we would not be on very sound basis.[64]

Three days later, Marshall issued an instruction to the U.S. commanding generals in China and in Moscow to "take no actions . . . concerning this matter," thus officially ending the overt effort by OSS to collect intelligence for the government of the United States from Soviet occupied Manchuria.[65]

CHAPTER TWELVE

The Last Chapter

OSS's failure to penetrate effectively into Korea, Shandong, and Manchuria was overshadowed by a far more serious drama taking place in Washington. Unaware of the wartime complications that OSS had confronted, the new president, Harry S. Truman, was being influenced by the agency's detractors, who had been unable to derail Donovan and his empire before the death of President Roosevelt. In the months immediately following Truman's entry into the White House, the assaults on Donovan escalated. As Thomas Troy writes, Donovan "had been stymied by the big four [State, War, and Navy departments and the FBI], ignored by the President [Truman], and was unsupported in the Congress. He had been smeared by the press—he harbored Communists, was controlled by the British, was rebuffed by heroes MacArthur and Nimitz, traveled with self-seeking bankers, financiers, industrialists, and socialites, had squandered money, and was marked for a sensational exposé."[1]

Donovan's Downfall

Returning to Washington from China on 14 August 1945, Donovan was surrounded by fires of destruction. Yet the situation in China consumed most of Donovan's time in the weeks to come. He had to deal with a real enemy in the China theater. Meetings were held between OSS and the Chinese ambassador in Washington, and specific plans were drawn. Troy describes the process: "On September 4, [Donovan] reported to Truman that the Chinese ambassador had 'talked [with him] about postwar intelligence.' Wanting American help 'in watching the situation in Korea and Manchuria,' the ambassador 'suggested a working arrangement intelligence wise—with a postwar intelligence agency maintaining liaison with them in China and exchanging information on the Far Eastern area.' ... The President refused to bite."[2]

Sensing that the White House was pessimistic regarding the fate of OSS, Donovan launched a media blitz through many "friendly" reporters and columnists. The achievements of OSS/China were featured prominently, including the rescues of General Wainwright by the Cardinal mission to Mukden and the Doolittle fliers dropped by the Magpie mission to Peiping. The media friends of Donovan and OSS eagerly helped the flamboyant spy chief, who was now in deep trouble in Washington. Troy vividly describes the media frenzy:

> The Donovan case was put forth in blunt laymen's language in five articles written in the *Chicago Daily News* by Wallace Deuel, who worked closely with Donovan throughout the war. Beginning on September 4 the Deuel headlines told the OSS story: "Capital Ax Falling on Our Priceless Secret Spy System"; "Savage Fight Looms for Control of OSS—Its Daring Exploits Paved Invasion Paths"; "OSS Softens Foe Prior to Attack"; "Mata Hari's O.K. but Spying's Done by 'Longhairs' now"; and "If OSS Didn't Exist, It Would Have to Be Invented." ... OSS, said the Associated Press, "pulled another spy thriller from its voluminous collection of war secrets." The *Washington Post* reported "4000 stranded fliers rescued by OSS underground railway." The *New York Times* reported the "U.S. Cloak and Dagger Exploits and Secret Blows in China are now Bared." On September 12 Donovan released the names of twenty-seven OSS men whom he decorated for heroism and courage.[3]

But all of this publicity came too late. Truman had been contacted by the suave Harry Hopkins, who gave the president a deadly report on OSS by a former military intelligence man, Colonel Robert Park. Park had worked at Roosevelt's super secret map room in the White House. The fifty-eight-page Park report is one of the most extraordinary documents in the history of espionage, resulting from political intrigue and presidential betrayal. "The day the late President [Roosevelt] departed for Warm Springs," the Park report starts, "he authorized me to make an informal investigation of the Office of Strategic Services and report on my findings and conclusions."[4] The conclusions of the report were devastating:

1. If the OSS is permitted to continue with its present organization, it may do further serious harm to citizens, business interests, and national interests of the United States.

2. The security of the OSS which should be above question is poor, both here and abroad.

3. Poor organization, lack of training and selection of many incompetent personnel has resulted in many badly conceived, overlapping, and unauthorized activities with resulting embarrassment to the State Department and interference with other secret intelligence agencies of this government. . . .

4. It appears probable that many improper persons have penetrated into OSS—some who cannot handle themselves, some with questionable backgrounds, and some who may be plants for foreign intelligence and counterintelligence agencies. The Communist element in OSS is believed to be of dangerously large proportions. . . .

5. OSS is hopelessly compromised to foreign governments, particularly the British, rendering it useless as a prospective independent postwar espionage agency. Further questioning of British intelligence will evince nothing but praise because the OSS is like putty in their hands and they would be reluctant to forfeit a good tool.

6. If the OSS is investigated after the war it may easily prove to have been relatively the most expensive and wasteful agency of the government. With a $57,000,000, budget, $37,000,000 of which may be expended without provision of law governing use of public funds for material and personnel, the possibilities of waste are apparent. . . .

7. Last November, General Donovan made a proposal for the organization of a new secret world-wide intelligence agency which would control all other U.S. intelligence agencies. There have been suggestions that this proposal was motivated by his personal ambitions. It has all the earmarks of a Gestapo system. . . .

8. All of the activities of the OSS, however, have not been harmful. There are elements and personnel that can and should be salvaged. It has performed some excellent sabotage and rescue work. Its Research and Analysis section has done an outstanding job. These have been the subject of commendatory letters from theater commanders and others.[5]

The accumulated efforts to get rid of Donovan and OSS reached their highest point at the White House on 20 September 1945 at 3 P.M.[6] The White House budget director, Harold Smith, presented President Truman an executive order abolishing OSS effective 1 October 1945 and distributing its functions. Smith recorded the historic moment himself: "When I gave the President the Order on OSS for his signature, I told him that this was the best disposition we could make of the matter and that General Donovan ... would not like it. I showed the President our communication with [Secretary of State] Byrnes and indicated that the State Department was willing to accept certain of the OSS functions while the rest would go to the War Department. The President glanced over the documents and signed the Order."[7]

Thus the Office of Strategic Services came to an abrupt end. Two days later, 1,362 former OSS agents from the research and analysis and the presentation branches were transferred to the State Department's Interim Research and Intelligence Service (IRIS) under Colonel Alfred McCormack, special assistant to the secretary of state for intelligence. C. Martin Wilbur, a historian formerly in R&A, was then designated as chief of IRIS for China; he soon began to establish his organization in Shanghai. The rest of the former OSS agents, 9,028 of them in all, were then assigned to the War Department under a familiar boss, Brigadier General John Magruder, the deputy director of OSS for intelligence. Magruder was given the job against his own wishes but nevertheless went along to take over the OSS rump, now known as the Strategic Service Unit, or SSU.[8]

From SSU to ESD 44

During September 1945, while Donovan was in Washington trying to save OSS, Heppner continued to vigorously push the agenda of OSS in China. Realizing that Communist control was rapidly spreading in north China and Manchuria, he ordered Krause to transfer the essential part of the Xian command station to Peiping on 14 September 1945 in order to establish a new OSS stronghold covering Peiping, Tianjin, Kalgan (Zhang Jiakou), and Harbin—if and when the Soviets retreated from that city.[9] Again, Bishop Thomas Megan went with Krause and rendered crucial help, as those cities in north China were filled with cooperative Catholics. Quickly, a large network of OSS-sponsored agents began to operate in earnest in those cities.

OSS participation in SACO ended pathetically. Although Donovan had been full of big ideas on establishing a joint Sino-U.S. intelligence exchange system in light of the Soviet and CCP assault from late August to mid-September, he was nowhere to be found between the signing of Truman's order on 20 September and the effective date of OSS shutdown, 1 October. During these ten days, Donovan was sleeplessly preoccupied with just one project: microfilming the voluminous OSS secret files in his office, with the help of his loyal aid, Edwin Putzell. Any decision about SACO had to be made by a junior officer on the spot. One day before OSS was officially dissolved, Major L. A. Lovegren, the current representative of OSS in SACO, scribbled a memo to Tai Li:

> Since President Truman has dissolved the OSS, effective 1 October, the SACO agreement is considered to be no longer in effect, and personnel should therefore be withdrawn. I have therefore ordered all of our men in the field to leave their bases. Men in charge of several bases will come to Chungking to report before going to Kunming on their way to America. Other personnel will go direct to Kunming. We shall leave the Valley as soon as all of these men have come through here. I hope that it will be possible for me to meet you again before I leave Chungking, so that I can thank you personally for the cooperation we have received from you and your men. What SACO had been able to do has had a definite share in bringing the war to a successful conclusion.[10]

On 11 October a small and hurried ceremony was held in BIS headquarters, ending the bumpy relationship of almost three and a half years between OSS on the one hand and Tai Li and SACO on the other.

Corresponding to the external organizational changes was the internal reshuffling of personnel in China. Soon after Magruder took over SSU, Heppner was replaced by his executive officer, Lieutenant Colonel Robert J. Delaney, as the chief of SSU in China. By November 1945, the headquarters of SSU in China had moved to Shanghai, where Wedemeyer had also established his command post. On 2 November, Gustav Krause, the station chief in Peiping since September, was ordered to Shanghai to become the second in command of SSU/China, leaving the Peiping post still in full operation.

While reshaping its forces in China to expand intelligence coverage in an entirely new environment, SSU encountered limitations. The primary conflict lay in the different conceptual understandings of the U.S. role in China between army headquarters and SSU. To SSU, the ending of the war with Japan was only the beginning of a systematic effort to establish a long-term clandestine intelligence network for the American government. With the Japanese surrender, the China theater had become extremely important to U.S. intelligence. The State Department, for example, had designated Walter Robertson to rejuvenate its intelligence authority in China. More importantly, SSU had began to make progress in areas long desired by Donovan—Manchuria and north China. With the announced Soviet withdrawal from Manchuria, SSU was ready to reenter that area.

Yet for army headquarters, the end of war meant the beginning of demobilization and gradual withdrawal from China. Its chief mission was dispersing extra materials to the Chinese and auditing its wartime finances before saying a final farewell to China. Not surprisingly, SSU was put under the jurisdiction of General Maddox, chief of the Service of Supply for Wedemeyer. This setup impeded the development of SSU in China. Overall expansion required rapid and generous material and personnel support from the Service of Supply; yet Delaney's requests were rarely honored. Exasperation between Maddox and Delaney grew and reached the breaking point from time to time.

Still, the biggest blow to SSU/China came not from Maddox but from the Chinese Communists and General Marshall. Marshall had retired as the chief of staff for the army after the war ended. Yet on 20 December 1945, Marshall landed in Shanghai on a special mission to mediate between the Communists and the Nationalists—a mission requested by President Truman upon the angry resignation of Ambassador Hurley in late November.

The Marshall mission, as it has been popularly called, tried to put together a couple that had long divorced and now vowed to kill each other at any cost. The key military confrontations between the Communists and the Nationalists took place in north China and Manchuria, the same areas SSU was most interested in. Soon after Marshall's arrival in China, Zhou Enlai protested to Marshall that U.S. secret intelligence was involved in these areas. Uncertain about whether SSU should concede to Communist pressure to withdraw, Marshall consulted the main figures in intelligence at the time.

On 6 January 1946, Marshall had lunch with John King Fairbank, the former OSS agent who had been fired by Hoffman as the R&A chief in China and replaced by Katz in December 1943. Fairbank was now the chief of the U.S. Information Service in China.[11] He voiced a low opinion of SSU. Four days later, Marshall held a meeting with Colonel Ivan Yeaton, head of the U.S. Army Observer Group (formerly the Dixie mission) in Communist Yenan since July 1945. An expert on Communist intelligence, Yeaton had been in China a short while, after a stint as the military attaché at the U.S. embassy in Moscow. In answer to Marshall's question about the nature of Chinese Communism, Yeaton stated that the Communism in Yenan was "pure Marx, Lenin and Mao"; that radio communication between Yenan and Moscow via Vladivostok had been busy; that the only CCP hope for military hardware was to capture surrendered Japanese arms, which could be done only with Soviet connivance; and that the CCP was a formidable armed force of nearly one million seasoned, well-fed fighters, which should not be underestimated.[12] Yeaton then fully endorsed SSU and its continuing operations in north and northeast China—an endorsement partly inspired by his best friend, the legendary writer and British Communist–turned–OSS agent Freta Utley, who was recruited into OSS by C. V. Starr and who had become bitterly anticommunist due to the purge of her Russian husband by Joseph Stalin.[13]

However, Marshall expressed little interest in Yeaton's report. "If he had heard a word I said," Yeaton bitterly wrote in his memoir, "he did not show it. As he finished tying his bow tie, he said, 'Thank you,' and showed me the door." Marshall's disregard of Yeaton's advice should not come as a surprise. As Yeaton noted in his memoir, "The only person he listened to was Chou [Zhou Enlai]." Possessing both charm and intrigue, Zhou was vividly described by Yeaton as a man of deception: "A feature of his which intrigued me the most was his ability to smile with everything but his eyes."[14]

Indeed, Chinese Communist intelligence was fortunate that Marshall admired Zhou. In June 1946, the entire Communist intelligence system was shaken by a blunder committed by Zhou. Early that month, Marshall used his own military plane to fly Zhou to Manchuria for a peace talk. On the return trip to Nanjing, Zhou dozed off on the plane. He accidentally dropped his notebook, which contained much Communist intelligence, including the name and address of Xiong Xianghui, one of the CCP's top spies inside the inner circle of the KMT high command. Xiong's importance alone, Mao Zedong stated, equaled that of several divisions of troops. After he got off the plane, Zhou discovered that he had misplaced the notebook and panicked. He immediately cabled the Central Committee of the Chinese Communist Party in Yenan and requested punishment. In the meantime, Communist intelligence working on the Marshall mission started to prepare for the worst. However, on the afternoon of 9 June, Marshall sent one of his top aides to Zhou Enlai's estate in Nanjing to deliver a "top secret packet." Zhou was not at home at the time the aide arrived. Marshall's aide refused to leave the packet with Zhou's assistants and insisted on giving it to Zhou in person. When Zhou came home and opened the thickly wrapped packet, he was astonished to see his lost notebook, intact, inside the box. Zhou was puzzled that Marshall would give back this notebook. He firmly believed that Marshall had copied it and would give it to Chiang Kai-shek, in which case the CCP agents identified in that notebook should be immediately hidden away. Zhou's escape arrangement for Xiong Xianghui was to send him to the United States to "study" in a university. But Marshall never did give away any information from Zhou's notebook to KMT intelligence. Xiong continued to spy on the KMT for Yenan. The frightening incident proved to be a false alarm, due to Marshall's cooperation.[15]

Finally Marshall encouraged Wedemeyer to stop SSU from operating in north China. Yet Wedemeyer sincerely doubted the odds of success for the Marshall mission. Furthermore, he was impressed by Yeaton's assessment of the Communists during the latter's visit from Yenan to Shanghai in January 1946. Consequently, no immediate action was taken by Wedemeyer on SSU. In the meantime, the Soviets and the Chinese Communists grew closer. The fact that the Chinese civil war was at heart an ideological battle between Communism and noncommunism became increasingly clear.

In late January 1946, U.S. Ambassador Averell Harriman arrived in Chungking and met with Chiang Kai-shek to convey Stalin's demand regarding the Sino-Soviet handling of industrial facilities in Manchuria. Stalin's idea was that the Soviets should control 51 percent of heavy industry and 49 percent of light industry. Chiang flatly refused. Then on 5 March in Fulton, Missouri, Winston Churchill made his famous speech announcing that "an Iron Curtain" had fallen in Eastern Europe. Two days later Truman urgently cabled Marshall in Chungking that Churchill wanted to see him in Washington. The president ordered Marshall back to the United States by 12 March. On 11 March, Marshall left China, believing he had established a solid foundation for mutual cooperation between the Nationalists and the Communists. Two days later, Stalin made headlines by denouncing Churchill's Fulton speech. The next day, Soviet occupation troops pulled out from the strategic city of Sipingjie, the vital link between Mukden and Changchun in Manchuria. Sipingjie fell into the hands of Chinese Communist troops within two days. One day later, on 17 March 1946, Tai Li's airplane crashed near Nanjing, killing the spymaster the Chinese Communists feared most.

The death of Tai Li has evoked suspicions of conspiracy among virtually everyone in the West who studied the history of intelligence in China during World War II. It has elements of a classic Orient Express–style murder: many had the perfect motive. Among the most likely murderers was Communist intelligence. Tai Li had gone to north China to accomplish two things that would nettle the Chinese Communists. First, he went to Peiping to establish an FBI-style police school—complete with counterespionage experts from the FBI as instructors—scheduled to open on 1 April.[16] This counterespionage school would threaten the rampant operations of the Communist underground in major cities in north China. Second, the U.S. Navy had decided to help Chiang Kai-shek build a modern navy. For this purpose, the White House submitted a plan to Congress for support on 4 February 1946. On the vigorous recommendation of Miles and Metzel, the Navy Department, from Secretary James Forrestal and Admiral King on down, was favorably considering Tai Li for the post of the new Chinese navy chief.[17] This was the worst nightmare for the Chinese Communists. The plane, which was carrying Tai Li to bid farewell to the commander of the U.S. Seventh Fleet, Admiral Cooke, crashed on its way to Shanghai.

Top OSS officials claim that Donovan's organization had much to do with Tai Li's death. Stanley Lovell, chief of OSS R&D and Donovan's "scientific thug," in his revealing memoir *Of Spies and Stratagems*, described a bomb of his own design called an anerometer, which could easily be attached to the tail of an airplane and would explode once the plane carrying the device rose five thousand feet above the ground. Lovell states that most of the anerometers were shipped into the China theater and that Tai Li's plane was blown up in the air by such a bomb.[18] Edwin Putzell, Donovan's most trusted aide and the OSS agent most knowledgeable—second only to Donovan himself, perhaps—about the innermost secrets of OSS, claimed that the agency was involved in Tai Li's death.[19]

However, amid this intensified atmosphere Marshall was pushing Wedemeyer to urge the War Department to inactivate the China theater. Wedemeyer grudgingly obliged and submitted a recommendation to the secretary of war, Robert Patterson, that the China theater be inactivated effective 1 May 1946.[20] Knowing that Marshall did not want SSU to stay in China, General Maddox had listed the SSU contingent under Delaney to be among the first to be inactivated.[21] When Wedemeyer's recommendation reached Washington, the Joint Chiefs of Staff—with General Dwight D. Eisenhower now representing the army—promptly vetoed it. But upon his arrival in Washington from China, Marshall directly went to the Joint Chiefs of Staff and got the decision reversed. The JCS decided to accept Wedemeyer's original recommendation and deadline.[22]

The new JCS decision panicked SSU/China. A rescue campaign was launched immediately in Washington. General John Magruder and his deputy, Colonel William Quinn, lobbied the operations division (OPD) of the War Department to save SSU/China. "It was brought to OPD's attention," Colonel Quinn recorded, "that SSU was furnishing practically all the intelligence emanating from the China Theater and also the intra-China radio net of SSU was a valuable asset." As a result, "OPD here in the War Department realized the value at the present time of the SSU China mission." But to convince the mighty and stubborn General Marshall was never an easy task. The Joint Chiefs of Staff and the War Department urged OPD to talk directly to Marshall about the great value of SSU/China—and about the disasters that might result if it were withdrawn. Marshall was forced to compromise and finally agreed that "he was not familiar enough with the situation and desired to leave the decision on the continuance of SSU to General Wedemeyer." SSU had won its first victory, and the second one was easy. When Wedemeyer came to Washington in late March, it took little effort for SSU and OPD to persuade him. An excited Quinn wrote simply that Wedemeyer "decided that the unit should remain."[23]

The exception made to allow SSU to stay in China after the China theater was inactivated was a strong endorsement for Delaney's expansion of operations. Quinn soon instructed Delaney to contact both the Shanghai headquarters of the U.S. Army and the Seventh Fleet of the U.S. Navy under Admiral Cooke to determine the coverage they desired. In the meantime, SSU Washington headquarters asked Delaney to draw up a comprehensive intelligence plan that would include the scope of operations and personnel needs.[24]

On 25 March 1946, Delaney drafted the first comprehensive document, "Plan for Continued SSU Operations After Theater Inactivation." In it he pointed out that "the collection of intelligence in China, particularly North China and Manchuria, is of vital importance to our national interests. . . . Normal peacetime observations will be carried on by the Military and Naval Attachés and members of the Embassy and Consulates, but these agencies are usually understaffed and their diplomatic status makes extensive subversive activity difficult." The plan embodied two crucial parts. First, SSU was to exclusively focus on gathering intelligence in north China and Manchuria; second, SSU should get out of the army command and instead be put under the Third Amphibious Marine Corps. In particular, the plan specified:

> It is proposed that when the China Theater inactivates, SSU Headquarters be moved from Shanghai to Tientsin [Tianjin] to be attached to the Marine III Phib. Corps under cover as liaison with the Chinese. Field teams presently located at Tsingtao, Peiping and Mukden, as well as those proposed for Kalgan and strategic points in Manchuria, will thenceforth feed into Tientsin. SSU installations now maintained at Shanghai, Hankow, Formosa, Canton, Hong Kong, Hanoi, Nanking [Nanjing] will be inactivated. . . . All intelligence will be submitted in raw form to SSU, Washington. . . . All personnel are American. Additional native personnel will be employed to operate agent nets and carry out non-classified administrative duties.[25]

This plan touched Delaney's own Achilles' heel, for it was obviously a defiance of the army. Furthermore, Delaney was caught up a bit in the excitement of being able to stay in China. Months of frustration resulting from the lack of matériel and personnel came to an end in a moment. Delaney attached a letter to the plan, in which he openly accused the army of stonewalling. Wedemeyer's newly appointed G-2 chief, Colonel Ivan Yeaton, tried to prevent Delaney from posting this letter. "Delaney is Irish," Yeaton recalled. "He was in a highly nervous state and thoroughly mad."[26] But Delaney dispatched the documents not only to John Magruder, the SSU chief in Washington, but also to the headquarters of Wedemeyer and to Admiral Cooke. General Maddox in Wedemeyer's headquarters (Wedemeyer was in Washington at the time) became furious not only at Delaney's accusations about the army but also at the suggestion that SSU should get out from under the army's command and operate in north China and Manchuria autonomously. Maddox immediately wired the War Department, protesting Delaney's plan and demanding that SSU take no action until he could directly confront Delaney.[27] Yet Wedemeyer adopted a conciliatory attitude. He explained to Magruder and Quinn that SSU was not alone in complaining about lack of matériel and logistical support. He suggested that Delaney revise the plan so that Marshall would not object to it and SSU's chance to stay in China would not be jeopardized. Thus on 20 April, Delaney submitted a "Revised Plan for Continued SSU Operation," in which the projected areas of intelligence coverage would now include "North China, Manchuria, South China, Formosa, and Indochina."[28]

Delaney's revised plan was a historic document, for it laid the foundation for the new nature of intelligence warfare in China. The primary objective was to observe and counter the Soviet Union's expansion in China and adjacent areas. As to the types of intelligence SSU was to collect, the new plan listed eight items:

a. The strength and disposition of USSR, Chinese Communist, and National Government troops in China, Manchuria, and Asiatic Soviet Russia.

b. The fortifications, armament, supplies, and logistics of Soviet forces, particularly in northern Manchuria and along the Manchurian-Siberian border, and of the Chinese Communist forces.

c. The coastal defenses of Soviet Russia.

d. The strength and disposition of the Soviet navy; the tonnage and contents of Soviet commercial shipping along the east coast of Asia.

e. The airfields of the Soviets, particularly along the Manchurian border, with the strength and disposition of the air force.

f. Roads, railroads, river, telegraph, and telephone communications in Manchuria and Siberia.

g. On all aspects of the Civil War in China.

h. Political and economic conditions in the Soviet and Soviet controlled areas, in China, and in Northern Indochina.[29]

As to the task of counterespionage in China, the new plan stated: "Primary target throughout China will be Soviet Intelligence; secondary target being Chinese Communist Party, Jap, Chinese, British, French Intelligence, etc. with the exception of the representatives in Hong Kong, whose primary target will be British Intelligence. All operations will be aimed at obtaining CE information concerning:"

a. Underground or secret organizations and individuals aiming to injure U.S.interests-military, political and economic—in the Far East.

b. Secret intelligence organizations operating in the China Theater which represent or are sponsored by or under the control of foreign powers.

c. Organizations and operation of enemy espionage organizations to include identity of leaders, agents, techniques, modus operandi, etc.

d. Individuals known or suspected to have engaged or engaged in subversive activities detrimental to American interests.

e. Foreign pressure groups and foreign strategic activities in the Far East, their agency, means of communication, degree of success.

f. Operations of foreign political parties, groups and underground organizations with particular emphasis on their attitudes toward the U.S. and other countries.[30]

Following this blueprint, SSU quickly moved to its target areas and amassed an impressive amount of information on the Soviet Union's formidable intelligence organization as well as its political penetration into China. The outlook of the Communist movement in China and its symbiotic ties with Moscow added a new dimension of intelligence operations for Donovan's apostles. Unfortunately, those voluminous reports by SSU emanating from Manchuria and other major cities in China were underutilized by the U.S. government. They were locked up in archives in the company of silence and rats.[31]

Most curiously, the command authority problem was never touched upon in the new plan, but SSU/China conceded the location of its headquarters—it was going to be in Shanghai instead of Tianjin with the Marines. Still uncertain in spring 1946, General Maddox asked Wedemeyer in Washington to confirm the command status and actual functions of SSU. Washington sent a confusing reply back to Maddox on 10 May 1946. On the one hand, "it was strongly desired by General Wedemeyer and by Colonel Quinn that SSU China continue to work with USAF [U.S. Army Forces] China as in the past." On the other hand, "it is impracticable to attempt a detailed delineation of responsibilities of SSU China in its relationship to US Army Forces China. SSU as an operating agency should be assigned missions by USAF China and should within reasonable limits be permitted to accomplish these missions as they themselves determine. Mission may be assigned direct to SSU by responsible agencies in Washington; the execution of these missions is not to interfere with the execution of missions assigned by USAF China."[32]

Perhaps realizing that the ambiguity in these baffling instructions would inevitably result in disputes over authority, Washington told Maddox in the same cable, "Cases of dispute or of doubt upon the subject of files and on other subjects should be referred to OPD, who will coordinate with SSU Headquarters in Washington."[33] Essentially, this was an explanation of no explanation. By now it was clear to both SSU and Wedemeyer that the hot-blooded Colonel Robert Delaney ought to be removed as head of SSU/China, as originally requested by General Maddox. A new SSU officer then in India, Lieutenant Colonel Amos D. Moscrip Jr., was named Delaney's successor. After being briefed by Washington about the unique situation SSU was in, Moscrip arrived in Shanghai in early May 1946 as the chief of SSU/China. This change of leadership was seen as a Machiavellian dirty trick by the army, designed to do away with SSU entirely. Many in SSU were disgusted by the whole episode. Delaney became a hero among the SSU/China contingent. Consequently, when he left Shanghai on 7 June 1946, some of his loyalists either came home with him, like veteran OSS commander Gustav Krause, or left SSU to join other intelligence agencies in China, as in the case of a marine lieutenant colonel named John H. Cox, who went to head the psychological warfare unit of the Office of War Information (OWI) with a cover as a cultural attaché in the U.S. embassy. Communist intelligence immediately zoomed in on Cox—he was completely manipulated by Chinese Communist secret intelligence, making the psychological warfare unit one of the most dramatic intelligence flops in U.S. history.[34]

Soon after the change of leadership, SSU/China's fate was once again thrown into a whirlwind. SSU had been begging the Seventh Fleet to assume command. Realizing that General Marshall would be the one who had the ultimate say, Admiral Cooke's initial attitude was one of caution. He had always taken the position that as long as the army was in China, SSU should be under its wing, but that when the army had to leave China, SSU should then come under the fleet. Moreover, Admiral Cooke did not want to initiate a request for command over SSU, preferring that the action be taken in Washington. If asked for his opinion, he would then say yes. Cooke expressed this point of view to his intelligence chief, who in turn informed Colonel Yeaton, Wedemeyer's G-2. Yeaton was very understanding upon hearing of the admiral's stance. "He was very happy," Moscrip reported to Magruder about Yeaton's reaction, "stating that everyone wanted SSU to continue in their present capacity as long as possible but [Generals] Gillem and Maddocks were in the position of 'Wanting to clean their skirts' and that our being taken over by Navy would be perfect solution."[35]

In April 1946, General Marshall went back to China to salvage his mediation. He badly wanted to dissociate his mission from SSU. "Both Nanking [Nanjing] and Peiping through Marshall and Byroade [chief of Marshall's Peiping executive headquarters, a Stilwell loyalist] have stated that they want nothing to do with SSU directly, although all admit value of our work," Moscrip reported.[36] Marshall's concerns were profound. His open association with SSU would displease all three sides involved: the Nationalist government because of the sovereignty issue; the Chinese Communists, who traditionally disliked people from OSS and had openly protested to Marshall about SSU's presence in north China and Manchuria; and the Soviet Union, which had amply demonstrated its hostility toward U.S. intelligence operations in Manchuria since August 1945.

After Washington decided to withdraw U.S. Army forces in China after 1 October 1946 and maintain only a military adviser group, General Marshall finally spoke out directly regarding the future of SSU/China. On 7 July 1946 he dispatched a surprising message to Army Chief of Staff Eisenhower and to General Wedemeyer, who was in Washington. In this extraordinary document Marshall stated:

> Some form of China SSU organization after 30 September is desirable for essential intelligence coverage, and its continuation under limited control and full logistic support of Seventh Fleet may be necessary. However realistic steps should be taken to reconstitute it as an undercover agency if possible, particularly if we are to avoid Chinese Government's right to press for a similar unit in United States or avoid Soviet's right to establish similar unit in China.
>
> At present, SSU in China lacks cover as counter espionage agency and is of definite value only as an intelligence unit.[37]

General Marshall's encouraging words quickly reached SSU/China. Before long, Marshall's headquarters officially informed Moscrip of Marshall's approval for SSU/China to come under the command of the Seventh Fleet. The message was simple, even a bit blunt: "General Marshall desires that Seventh Fleet assume control and support of SSU China as soon as practicable in order to disassociate officers in the military advisory and executive groups from connection with an intelligence agency."[38]

This turn of good luck for SSU/China excited Washington. General

Hoyt Vandenberg, the powerful director of the Central Intelligence Group (CIG), created by Truman in January 1946 and the umbrella organization over SSU, directly took over SSU/China affairs and dispatched his personal representative, Captain William B. Coggins, to see Admiral Cooke in Shanghai and General Charles Willoughby (General MacArthur's intelligence chief) in Tokyo in order to work out the specifics. On 15 August, General Vandenberg cabled Marshall and Moscrip, "CIG [is] taking earliest possible steps establish new and efficient undercover organization gradually to replace SSU."[39]

On 30 September 1946 the Seventh Fleet of the U.S. Navy officially assumed limited control and full logistic support of SSU/China, which was renamed External Survey Group 44, or ESG 44. Donovan's people were fascinated with certain words, one of which was *detachment,* borrowed from the British SOE. The word conjured up a sense of working in a special and esoteric spy culture. SSU never felt comfortable with the word *group.* This contingent was commonly called External Survey Detachment 44, or ESD 44.

ESD 44's Washington command would no longer be SSU Washington. Instead, the Central Intelligence Group assumed complete control over ESD 44's finances.[40] The saga of OSS China was thus only one tiny step away from being completely integrated into a brand new era of U.S. foreign intelligence—the era of the Central Intelligence Agency. Nine months later, CIA was created, and ESD 44 under Amos Moscrip became the Agency's first China contingent.[41]

So What?
Conclusions

Three developments are key to understanding the fundamental changes imposed upon U.S. intelligence by World War II. First, the United States' intelligence apparatus began to cover countries all over the world. Second, the federal government began to consolidate the highly departmentalized American intelligence system and establish a centralized, national intelligence agency responsible to a single command. Against this background, the Office of Strategic Services was created. As Donovan pointed out, "In a global and totalitarian war, intelligence must be global and totalitarian."[1] Third, an entirely new concept of intelligence operations, psychological warfare, was introduced.[2]

Donovan's effort to broaden, centralize, and update U.S. intelligence met with fierce opposition from the existing intelligence agencies in the United States and abroad. The saga of OSS/China is an excellent testimony to this high drama of contention.

The experience of OSS in China is a complex one. This unique experience of wartime collaboration with an ally against a common enemy foreshadows most of the fundamental dilemmas of U.S. clandestine operations in foreign countries during the Cold War era. In addition, it was during this encounter with a vast, deeply divided Asian country that nearly *all* branches of American intelligence, civilian and military, competed with extraordinary intensity and tenacity against one another. This ultimately contributed to a considerable extent to the transformation of U.S. intelligence into a centralized organization responsible to only one command.

The experience of OSS in China during World War II, as we have seen, illustrates several major points.

Intelligence Operations Adrift from Foreign Policy

The OSS/China experience illustrates that running intelligence operations in the field without a strong central command in Washington had a profound impact upon the United States' overall foreign policy. The overwhelming emphasis of U.S. wartime attention on the European theater resulted in a remarkable policy indolence toward the China theater among the highest echelons in Washington. Most of the major China policies were initiated not in Washington but by low-ranking field officers in China, and they were announced to Chungking with a rubber stamp from the White House. This situation gave rise to an extraordinary partisan tenor to America's general China policy. At the end of World War II, Admiral William Leahy, chairman of the Joint Chiefs of Staff, pointedly stated: "I could never understand what happened in China. I know at Cairo President Roosevelt assured Chiang Kai-shek of his and America's support in every way. He meant it, too! Over and over he told me we were going to get behind China. But something or somebody got between him and his plans. We were all too busy to push them or to find where the hold-up was. The President mentioned it to me frequently until the time he died. He intended to find out what was happening—why we were not supporting Chiang. But after he died the matter dropped."[3] It was under these circumstances that OSS entered the China scene.

Roosevelt, a Democrat, never fully trusted William Donovan, a fierce Republican. Moreover, Donovan got his job as the chief of COI from Roosevelt through a presidential favor in the spirit of a bipartisan coalition government during a time of global war.[4] Roosevelt considered the appointment inconsequential, even symbolic, and provided little response and instruction. Within a couple of months, Donovan's direct channel to Roosevelt was cut off. Henceforth, virtually all COI (and later OSS) intelligence reports Donovan sent had to go through the president's secretary, Grace Tully.[5] Within one year of its creation, the COI office was severed from its presidential command. On 22 June 1942 it split into the Office of War Information (OWI) and the Office of Strategic Services (OSS). OSS was then put under the command of the Joint Chiefs of Staff, which never took OSS/China seriously enough to provide a clear command structure.

Donovan thus operated his China missions without direct presidential guidance, and OSS/China became an instrument of partisan foreign policies.

Throughout the war, various influential elements, most prominently the low-ranking embassy staffers and the army, coveted the unvouched funds and covert cover of OSS and tried to convert the agency into a "private army" of their own bureaucratic persuasions. This situation fundamentally influenced U.S. war strategy and foreign policy in China, as amply demonstrated in the high drama of the secret dealings between OSS and the Chinese Communists in late 1944 and early 1945.

Interservice Rivalry: Old Story, New Meaning

Almost every piece written to date about the China experience of OSS has emphasized the enigmatic situation in China in which OSS started its endeavor. Richard Smith, for example, pointedly titled his China chapter "The Chinese Puzzle."[6] Most historians have attributed the murkiness of the China theater primarily to the ongoing internal strife among the Chinese, mostly between the Kuomintang and the Chinese Communist Party. Tai Li, Chiang Kai-shek's intelligence chief, has borne most of the blame for American ineffectiveness in intelligence operations. While part of this thesis seemed credible in the past, it grows increasingly inadequate. The newly declassified archives lead us to consider more closely another factor: the extraordinary and heretofore understudied competition for turf among the U.S. intelligence branches themselves in the China theater.

I have attempted in this book to use the case of OSS/China to elucidate this turf war and its consequences. As a newly created intelligence agency eager to set foot in the China theater, OSS was an enthusiastic participant in this internecine competition, associating itself with all sides at one time or another. Examining the case of OSS/China thus provides an excellent vantage point from which to grasp the intensity and tragic aftermath of this struggle.

The lack of unity in the China theater was obvious. Among the U.S. players in China, Stilwell had the personal backing of General Marshall, Miles had that of Admiral King, General Claire Chennault held the favor of Chiang Kai-shek, and the president in the White House personally bestowed his China desk into the hands of Lauchlin Currie and Harry Hopkins. In May 1942, T. V. Soong managed to get General John Magruder kicked out of China through his personal relationships with Henry Stimson and Henry Morganthau. Likewise, Stilwell was capable, through Marshall, of banning U.S. Naval Attaché James McHugh from serving in China forever because of McHugh's secret reports to Frank Knox on the Burma fiasco.

All of this fierce infighting in the field had a devastating impact on the mind-set of the highest echelons of the allied command, for it confused the goals of the war. Both the White House and the Joint Chiefs of Staff wasted an inordinate amount of time and energy mediating the constant quarrels between U.S. generals in the China theater. The question of command made Stilwell and Chennault dire enemies throughout the war; General Wedemeyer and Commodore Miles drove each other to distraction—quite literally in the case of Miles, who came back to the United States suffering from a nervous breakdown just before the war ended; Ambassador Patrick Hurley and the acting commander-in-chief, China theater, General Robert McClure, almost got into a fistfight at a luxurious banquet in their honor. Washington was constantly baffled. Not surprisingly, Admiral William Leahy, chairman of the Joint Chiefs of Staff, always regarded the China theater as "that confused Oriental environment."[7]

This situation has tremendously affected the objectivity of historical writing on wartime China. Accusations and theories defending one side while attacking another have proliferated, as a Chinese saying goes, like bamboo trees after a spring rainfall. McHugh, whose career was ruined by Marshall and Stilwell, and who incidentally was Magruder's brother-in-law, referred to Stilwell as a "small, mean-minded sarcastic man."[8] John King Fairbank, historian and a major OSS/China agent, countered, "Joe Stilwell had all the best American traits of character. . . . [He] was about the best we had to offer to meet China's wartime problems."[9] Miles accused the army and others who challenged his command of being "racist," "mismanaged," and conspiratorial.[10] But in the eyes of his foes, Miles had become a conniver, the ultimate bad guy, "a funny small pig."[11] Barbara Tuchman wrote a biography of Stilwell, yet completely avoided discussing such issues as his relationship with Miles.[12] To defend Stilwell, Theodore White edited and published *The Stilwell Papers* in 1948, but this book did more harm than good to Stilwell's reputation in Washington, for it revealed information that even wrested away the support of Admiral William Leahy—up to that point one of the few naval admirals sympathetic to Stilwell—for the temperamental general.[13]

This infighting ultimately was dragged into American party politics, culminating in Senator Joe McCarthy's notorious speech, "America's Retreat from Victory: The Story of George Catlett Marshall."[14] In a self-defense response to Republicans' partisan charges, the Truman administration put out the equally controversial "China White Papers," which ignored the tragic consequences of the internal bickering among U.S. forces in China and instead blamed the "loss of China" entirely on "internal Chinese forces, forces which this country tried to influence but could not."[15]

The partisan state of the historical record on this wartime period has compromised academic objectivity; it has created in many cases an intellectual travesty in which conclusions and presumptions often precede archival facts. By examining how U.S. foreign policy was actually formed, I have tried in this book to demonstrate that political and ideological considerations were often irrelevant. For in the case of China—where no coherent policy existed—intelligence field operations frequently dictated and preceded policy rather than the other way around.

The OSS story illustrates that competition for command control and intelligence independence in wartime China was the most important factor in many strategic maneuvers by both Chinese and Americans. Contrary to the mainstream interpretation of the wartime Sino-American relation, ideological and political leanings did not play as important a role as did personalities, egos, and, above all, territorial zeal for turf and for control among the allies themselves. Throughout the war, there were more than twenty U.S. bureaucratic agencies and over a dozen independent American intelligence branches in Chungking—Naval Group China, Counter-Intelligence Corps (CIC), Joint Intelligence Collection Agency (JICA), OSS, the embassy, the army, navy and air force attachés, Stilwell's theater command, Chennault's 14th Air Force, the Board of Economic Warfare (under Henry Wallace), etc.—organizationally disconnected, with separate command lines from individual governmental departments in Washington, thus inevitably resulting in an intense bureaucratic competition for independence and command control. OSS, like other U.S. military branches in China, ran afoul of Tai Li not because Donovan cared whether or not Tai Li was the "Gestapo" in China but because Donovan, unlike ONI, did not have a monopoly on cooperation with the Chinese secret police. A U.S. intelligence team sent to Yenan in 1944 had less tactical value for the war effort at the time than political leverage against the recalcitrant, noncooperative KMT. Emerging from all this as the ultimate winner is neither Stilwell, Marshall (the army), Miles (the navy), nor Donovan's people, and certainly not the KMT, but rather the Chinese Communists, whose quiet intelligence penetration achieved stunning effects.

The Dialectics of Chaos

What did all this interservice rivalry mean to the OSS China operation? Instead of being a hindrance, such rivalry provided OSS—a fledgling on the China scene, without high-level political connections in the powerhouses of Washington and Chungking—with blessed opportunities for development. Contrary to popular belief, OSS was by no means a failure in the China theater. The blurred lines of command among the U.S. forces in China, as well as that "confused Oriental environment," gave Donovan golden opportunities to build a solid foundation for his own empire—opportunities OSS had been completely denied in the Pacific theater and found difficult to find in other places, where clear command lines existed.

Precisely because of this disorder, Donovan was able, though with difficulty, to maneuver back and forth among the warring factions of the U.S. forces. During several years of operations in China, OSS cooperated with virtually all of the major players—with Detachment 101 under army commander Stilwell, with SACO under the navy and Tai Li's BIS, with AGFRTS under Chennault of the 14th Air Force, with the Chinese Communists in Yenan on an ambitious project—and finally OSS/China took a great leap forward under the leadership of Colonel Richard Heppner, with General Wedemeyer's direct support. Throughout the war, OSS Director Donovan invested heavily in China; some of his best officers were sent there. Donovan himself made three trips to Chungking.

While suffering from several disastrous blunders—most noticeably the SACO fiasco—at no time was OSS strangled by a force authoritative enough to prevent it from venturing elsewhere in China. After the Dragon plan was cold-shouldered by Stilwell, OSS went to Miles and Tai Li; when the army wanted to kill an independent OSS effort to go to Yenan, Donovan used Tai Li as a shield to protect the plan; as the SACO arrangement grew stifling, Donovan went over to Chennault and eventually back to the army under Wedemeyer; when the army wanted to inactivate SSU in 1946, Donovan's followers wisely and successfully allied themselves with the navy again, under the protection of Admiral Cooke of the 7th Fleet—as ESD 44 of the Central Intelligence Group.

It is true that in the end OSS/China did not become an entirely independent intelligence agency collecting strategic information, but the chances were always there, tantalizing Donovan, who, like Tai Li and Miles, was by nature an empire builder and fierce fighter. When in late December 1943 the energetic director of OSS, returning from China, ebulliently boasted to Lord Louis Mountbatten in India about his (apparently exaggerated) toughness with Tai Li in Chungking, Donovan was indeed enjoying the intricate excitement of the China situation and practically admonishing Mountbatten to take OSS/SEAC seriously or face similar tough treatment.[16]

Of course, this contentious maneuvering for survival and independence was also dangerous. Donovan had to ensure that OSS would not be regarded as guilty of factionalism by association—an extremely difficult task for the field officers in Chungking to handle. As it was, OSS/China did frequently get caught in the cross fires of U.S. factionalism. The navy suspected and loudly accused OSS of pro-army trickery, while army intelligence (G-2) in China under Colonel Dickey almost rejected the OSS plea to join the Dixie mission to Yenan because of its association with the navy and SACO.[17] Nevertheless, like many things Chinese, OSS miraculously thrived on chaos.

The British Connection

Perhaps one of the most understudied areas in the World War II Sino-American relationship has been the British factor and its relation to OSS/China. From the outset, both U.S. foreign policy and intelligence in China were profoundly influenced by the policies of the British, who had vastly different interests at stake in Asia from those of the United States and China.

The objective of the British war effort in Asia was to reclaim its colonial empire. According to John Paton Davies, "The raising of the Union Jack over Singapore is more important to the British than any victory parade though Tokyo." Correspondingly, the British feared a strong China emerging from the eventual defeat of Japan, because, in the eyes of Americans, "China's potentialities in the post-war world cause the present British Government some anxiety. It recognizes that if China emerges from this war strong and unified, China will (1) endanger, as a focus of nationalist infection, Britain's Asiatic Empire; (2) attempt, paradoxically perhaps, imperialistic expansion of its own; and (3) threaten British claims to Hong Kong."[18]

The British themselves frankly confirmed this: "It was desirable that Hong Kong, being a British possession, should be liberated by the British, albeit using Chinese guerrillas in the first assault. There would have to be an all-British follow-up, however, either airborne, sea-borne, or both, otherwise Chiang Kai-shek might claim that the Colony, wrested by the Japanese from the British Empire, had been reconquered by the Chinese."[19] For this very purpose, SOE organized the China Commando Group under Valentine Killery and John Keswick in late 1941, an enterprise that was confronted with ferocious opposition from Tai Li and ended in disaster in April 1942.

In order to avoid making the Chiang Kai-shek regime strong enough to threaten British colonial interests in Asia, London adopted an important method of conducting clandestine operations in China: the use of peripheral forces instead of Central Government forces in China. Those peripheral forces employed by the British were often ones that Chiang Kai-shek worried about most: runaway Chinese provincial governors and Communist guerrillas. Understandably, Chiang Kai-shek abruptly ousted Keswick's China Commando Group for, among other things, SOE's "improperly dealing direct with Provincial governors."[20]

Tai Li was fully cognizant of the fact that SOE trained Chinese Canadians and even Chinese Americans in Ontario for the specific purpose of joining forces with the Chinese Communists in the defense of Hong Kong.[21] All of this resulted in an unshakable hatred and distrust of the British among the Chinese, particularly Tai Li, whose overly zealous anti-British attitude and undiplomatic treatment of Keswick and his SOE contingent in China forced an embarrassed Chiang Kai-shek to censor his secret intelligence chief. Right after the China Commando Group incident, Chiang Kai-shek appointed Tang Zong as his personal representative to supervise Tai Li. In July 1942, Chiang Kai-shek forbade Tai Li to deal with any foreign organizations except the American ones.[22] Tai Li was humiliated. Throughout the war, any attempt by the British to conduct clandestine activities in China met his strongest opposition.

Tai Li's hostility to the British profoundly affected the United States' wartime intelligence gathering in China. Any U.S. agency or individuals associated with the British became targets of Tai Li's crusade. The U.S. naval attaché in China, James McHugh, an ardent admirer of British intelligence, never gained Tai Li's confidence, despite hobnobbing with the shrewd Chinese general. To Tai Li, many such American intelligence officers carried an Anglo taint and were also suspect because of their pro-Communist sentiments. Chief among them was the enigmatic Solomon Adler, who was the chief representative in China for the U.S. Treasury Department during World War II. ONI and SACO completely rejected any British influence. In return, the British denounced Miles as Britain's "public enemy number one in the Far East."[23]

Newly available Chinese and English documents thus furnish us a key to understanding the extraordinary difficulty involved in OSS relations with the Chinese. OSS's embryonic tie with the British cost Donovan dearly in China. After the ouster of SOE from China by Tai Li in April 1942, the British agency immediately dispatched John Keswick and others to carve out spheres of influence in global intelligence operations with Donovan. Under this general agreement, China would now be Donovan's realm. But in the public eye in China, Donovan was only continuing to carry out what SOE had failed to do for Keswick, who had now become the SOE liaison with OSS in Washington. What further confirmed Tai Li's suspicion of the SOE-COI (OSS) symbiotic relationship was Donovan's decision to dispatch to China a group of widely known British-styled Old China Hands, led by Arthur Duff of the C.V. Starr coterie, who would soon be officially working for British intelligence. Naturally, this group of Old China Hands was not welcomed by Tai Li. Eventually, only one among this group, Al Lusey, was accepted in China. Donovan was later forced to terminate all dealings with the Starr group as a condition of gaining favor from Tai Li and ONI. Only after the SACO enterprise went sour for Donovan did he resume employment of Starr's people, in June 1944.[24]

However, Tai Li exaggerated Anglo-American cooperation. Relations between British and U.S. intelligence in wartime China were never free of antagonism. Like Tai Li, the British were intransigent over the creation of an independent American intelligence in Asia. The command of OSS teams in India, the creation of Mountbatten's P Division under overall British control, the contentious intelligence operations in controversial areas like Burma and Thailand, and the fierce dispute between Mountbatten and Wedemeyer over the intelligence sphere of influence in Indochina all testify to the intensity with which the British and OSS clashed during World War II.

There is no better summary of OSS's attitude toward the British than that offered by William Langer, the R&A chief of OSS:

> My feeling in this matter is particularly strong because I have felt almost since the establishment of this organization that the British had a great head start over us and that therefore we would be in constant danger of being frozen out of the picture. No one esteems or respects our British Allies more than I do, but it appears to me to be most dangerous for us to depend upon them in the intelligence field or to accept their control over our intelligence activities. So far as R&A is concerned, we have striven consistently to turn out material as good as or better than that of the British and to bring it to the attention of American commanders so that they would not accept British views or opinions uncritically. It seems obvious that if in the field of secret intelligence the American effort were to be subordinated to British control, the effort would be futile from the outset.[25]

Contrary to popular perception, OSS and its British counterpart, SOE/ SIS, were not an integral entity, as Chinese intelligence believed. The story of OSS in China is permeated with an intense struggle for intelligence independence between the British, committed to maintaining their Far East colonial empire, and OSS, with its different priorities. Curiously, it is in the Far East theater that OSS was able to depart from its British embryonic state and stride toward independence and maturity. The failure of the Chinese to fully comprehend this Anglo-American intelligence struggle in the Far East, and the failure of OSS to effectively articulate it to them, contributed to major strategic blunders on both sides.

OSS Culture: The Question of Command

Throughout the war, OSS was in an adverse environment. General Donovan may have spent more time in Washington's political and power circles fighting for the survival of OSS than in his own headquarters contemplating intelligence plots and penetration.[26] The biggest challenge to OSS came from the Joint Chiefs of Staff over the question of command. Immediately after the split of the COI office into the Office of War Information and the Office of Strategic Services, Army Chief of Staff George Marshall issued a strongly worded statement ordering OSS to straighten out its command question. From June 1942 to October 1943 the Joint Chiefs debated the functions and command of OSS. In September 1943, a directive was issued by the Joint Chiefs of Staff unequivocally putting OSS under the control of theater commanders. The language of the directive was devastatingly clear to Donovan. The Joint Chiefs of Staff announced, "All activities within organized theaters or areas are subject to *direct control* by the commander concerned."[27] Theater commanders themselves—such as Stilwell in the CBI, and not the OSS headquarters in Washington—would have real command over OSS activities.

To OSS, this was tantamount to a death sentence with a reprieve. OSS had to resort to trickery and word games to avoid being overpowered. On 16 September 1943, General Magruder, deputy director of OSS, rushed a memo to the Joint Chiefs of Staff to try to soften their directive by creating linguistic opacity. General Magruder insisted on adding the following wording to the Joint Chiefs of Staff directive: "He [theater commander] is authorized to utilize the organization and facilities of the Office of Strategic Services in his theater or area in any manner and to the maximum extent desired by him."[28] Sugarcoated words notwithstanding, General Magruder skillfully inserted the key word *utilize* to define *direct control*. Utilization does not mean ownership; it suggests only implementation, not decision-making power or complete control. Theater commanders could only *use* the services of OSS, which was ultimately commanded by Donovan himself.

This episode perfectly illustrates what I would call the OSS Culture. In order to survive numerous attempts by the established intelligence community to neutralize it, OSS had to agree on paper with other agencies' orders over it. But in fact, OSS tried to undo such orders by cleverly subverting them through all possible means. This distinction, however, was never clearly spelled out between the Joint Chiefs of Staff and OSS. As a result, Donovan's orders to his field officers were often conflicting and confusing. On the one hand, "no operations or activities of OSS will be permitted in any theater unless plans or proposals shall be first submitted in writing to, and authorized by, the theater commander."[29] On the other hand, Donovan internally made it very clear to his people where their ultimate loyalty should be: "A Strategic Services Officer shall be in command of each Theater Establishment. He shall act in the Theater as the immediate representative of the Director and report directly to him."[30]

The OSS Culture reached its pinnacle in China and was the ultimate reason for the clash between ONI and OSS in their joint intelligence effort in SACO with the Chinese intelligence organization, the Bureau of Investigation and Statistics. The question of command was so overriding that it overshadowed the issue of "non-cooperation from the Chinese." Throughout the war, the need for OSS to succeed in China was enormous. To fulfill that need, OSS had to ostensibly submit itself to the command of the navy, which through Horatio Algeresque "pluck plus luck" touch, had influence with the Chinese through Commander (later Vice Admiral) Milton Miles. But the ensuing SACO endeavor proved disastrous to OSS because Miles used his agreed command over OSS as a means to prevent it from operating in China. Independent OSS efforts under the guise of SACO met with stubborn resistance. All of this led to an open split between the two American intelligence agencies.

This OSS Culture had from the very beginning worried the Chinese. During initial negotiations in 1942 for the Friendship Plan—predecessor to SACO—Tai Li's contact in Washington, D.C., Colonel Xiao Bo, foreseeing a possible conflict of command on the U.S. side, warned OSS that a consolidated command line between ONI and OSS was essential to the success of the Sino-American intelligence endeavor. When Americans in Chungking battled each other, each side tried to use the Chinese to its own advantage. Suspicions ran high and frustration reigned. OSS believed that Tai Li took advantage of the situation and played Americans against each other, but the navy vehemently defended the shrewd Chinese spymaster.

To the Chinese, these two mutually hostile groups of Americans working together in a joint compound created enormous headaches. At a 1944 dinner party held by the Chinese to patch up relations between the two U.S. intelligence agencies, Colonel Xiao Bo expressed to OSS agent George Devereux his exasperation with navy/OSS infighting:

XIAO: Things do not go well. Too many factions. There is the Navy and the OSS.

DEVEREUX: Both are really the same.

XIAO: They *should* be the same but are not.

DEVEREUX: We are all fighting Japan, and in Franklin's words, we ought to hang together lest we all hang separately.

> (This quotation apparently struck Colonel Hsiao [Xiao], who applauded it and repeated it over and over again.)

XIAO: I can do no more than bring boy and girl together. The rest is up to them. I got drunk tonight in order to bring boy and girl together. I cannot marry them, they must marry by themselves.

DEVEREUX: They are already married, are they not?

XIAO: But they don't get along. I got drunk trying to get them together, but I can do no more.

DEVEREUX: A friend of the family can often reconcile a quarreling husband and wife. I had the impression everything was going along well. You realize I am only a lieutenant (jg) and no one tells me anything.

XIAO: Are you Navy or OSS?

DEVEREUX: I am on temporary duty [from the Navy] with OSS.[31]

The central question of command plagued American agencies in their cooperation with the Chinese. For example, it was the overriding issue in OSS dealings with Tai Li's Bureau of Investigation and Statistics. OSS clashed with Tai Li essentially over one issue: command and control of the OSS-trained agents. For Donovan, cooperation with Tai Li and the ONI was only a cover for OSS to establish an independent intelligence network with total OSS command. For Tai Li and Miles, command under SACO had to be shared.

Yenan: Prelude to Supreme Fiction

In this book I have tried to rectify the lack of reading of Chinese sources in the existing literature on OSS/China about Communist intelligence in China. The intelligence buildup by the Comintern and Chinese Communists based in Yenan and Chungking was directly aimed at the Kuomintang regime, particularly Tai Li's Bureau of Investigation and Statistics. As we have seen, the aggressive efforts by the Chinese Communists to penetrate into Tai Li's enterprise succeeded with often devastating results. This discovery furnishes us with a fresh understanding of Tai Li's behavior in his troubled cooperation with American intelligence.

What does this have to do with the story of OSS in China? For Tai Li, the stakes were extremely high for wartime intelligence cooperation with the United States. First of all, after the Zhang Luping incident in early 1942, an enraged and humiliated Tai Li became determined to modernize his internal security. His ensuing tireless efforts to solicit American help were largely motivated by this new task. The first items he requested that ONI ship to Chungking for the Friendship Plan—predecessor to SACO—were radio direction finders to be used in catching the many secret radio transmissions in the Chungking and Kunming areas. He also imposed extreme discipline upon his agents. For security reasons, no one was allowed to get married while working for the BIS. No woman was allowed—even under SACO—in Happy Valley, Tai Li's headquarters in the suburbs of Chungking. Second, Tai Li sought counterespionage expertise. For this purpose, one of the major deals he made with ONI was to establish a counterespionage school (Unit Nine of SACO) that eventually involved the U.S. Narcotics Bureau, the FBI, the U.S. Navy, and OSS.[32] But at the same time, Tai Li grew increasingly wary about people with complicated social, particularly foreign, relationships, when he was approached for cooperation.

As a result, OSS encountered a conflict in goals when cooperating with Tai Li. To OSS, the goal of its operation in China was singular and clear: to penetrate into occupied China and even Japan proper to facilitate the final defeat of Japan. The Communists were seldom a concern to OSS. However, Tai Li's goals were multidimensional. He needed help from the United States not only in fighting the Japanese but also in fending off Communist intelligence efforts against his own organization. U.S. policy makers did not entirely understand his predicament. After all, throughout the war the United States regarded the Soviet Union as a friendly ally. Intelligence operation in and against the Soviet Union by OSS was, in theory, strictly prohibited. The inability of OSS to satisfy Tai Li's multidimensional goals was another reason for the SACO disaster.

By contrast, the navy was successful in cooperating with Tai Li largely due to a mutually agreed upon trade-off of goals. Half of the SACO units emphasized U.S. naval strategies on the eastern and southeastern coast of China, where they collected weather intelligence and spread mines; the other half of the units emphasized radio intelligence and cryptography, which was Tai Li's special interest. In other areas the goals of the navy and BIS overlapped, as in the establishment of intelligence posts deep in the Chinese interior. For ONI such posts served as excellent long-wave weather reporting stations. And for BIS, the counterintelligence value of such posts was obvious: they were located exactly at or near places where the Soviets had their intelligence stations—Urumchi (named Di Hua at the time) in

Chinese Turkestan (Xinjiang), Lanzhou, Xian, and northernmost Shan Pa—for the express purpose of monitoring the Communists as well as the Japanese.

How well did OSS recognize the intensity of the KMT-CCP espionage warfare? The available materials demonstrate that OSS knew very little. A comprehensive "Yenan Intelligence Digest" compiled by the SI branch of OSS in June 1945 includes a very thorough dossier of personalities of the Communists. Kang Sheng, intelligence chief of the entire Chinese Communist Party, who ran an overarching espionage system all over China, was called simply an "intellectual." In the same dossier, Pan Hannian was identified as the "Chinese Communist representative at secret conference in Nanking with the Japanese and the Puppets," but this, noted the report, was merely "claimed by Kuomintang."[33]

The Communists fully exploited OSS ignorance of their intelligence warfare against the Kuomintang. In fact, there is ample evidence that throughout the war, Communist intelligence was able to penetrate OSS operations in China. One of the most damaging episodes involved the deputy chief of OSS in China, whose untimely romantic trysts with his secretary in Chungking prompted Yan Baohang's earnest "help" in arranging a serene house in the suburbs for their rendezvous. As a token of gratitude, the deputy chief asked Yan, the top spy in Chungking for Zhou Enlai and Kang Sheng, to recommend "reliable young people" to enroll into the OSS parachute training school in Kaiyuan, Yunnan. Zhou Enlai instructed Yan to recommend many Communist agents.[34] The Communists were thus able to penetrate into Chiang Kai-shek's crack forces trained by Americans; this ultimately led to the dramatic "mutiny" of one of the three Kuomintang parachute regiments—a force easily taken over by Mao Zedong in 1949.[35]

This inattention to Communist intelligence became even more dramatic in the post-OSS intelligence and information agencies in China. Many Chinese typists and interpreters, particularly in the Yunnan and Shanghai areas, employed by OSS, the Office of War Information, and other agencies, were secret agents working for Yenan. As revealed in recent materials published in China, they stole U.S. documents, organized secret Communist Party activities, often forged intelligence, and fed American intelligence agencies in China falsified information. When George Marshall was in China, Communist intelligence penetration into American agencies ran rampant, and the Communists were even able to pass their forged intelligence and documents favoring Yenan directly to the White House through the U.S. psychological warfare unit in Shanghai, thus successfully manipulating U.S. policy makers.[36]

Fig. 20. OSS-trained Chinese paratroopers in Kaiyuan, Yunnan
(National Archives)

The China experience of OSS during World War II is an important chapter in the history of U.S. intelligence. Yet it has been little studied. Of the limited study done on this topic, much of the writing has been inadequate, mainly based on opinions rather than solid archival research. The newly available archives have provided us with a golden opportunity to correct the traditional black-and-white approach to the extremely complicated scene in wartime China.

OSS/China was a grand experiment of the U.S. government in the philosophy of centralized intelligence. Ever since his humiliating ouster from China in early 1942 by his superiors in the War Department and its Chinese collaborators, General John Magruder, deputy director of OSS for intelligence and the director of SSU, used the China theater as an example to champion his philosophy of a centralized intelligence agency responsible to a single command. The OSS experience in Asia with Tai Li, the British, and other competing U.S. agencies eventually provided General Magruder with unequivocally strong evidence for two crucial arguments during the heated debate over the creation of the CIA: first, the U.S. government should not rely upon any foreign government for foreign intelligence; second, the existing departmentalized intelligence system should be abolished and a single command over intelligence be established. General Magruder's points were taken seriously by the creators of the CIA.

Notes

Preface

1. Memo, Read to heads of all branches and outposts, 28 June 1945, Record Group 226, Entry 154, Folder 3333, National Archives, Washington, D.C. (Hereafter, unless otherwise noted, all files are from RG 226.)

2. Memo, Kermit Roosevelt to Colonel Pruden, 12 November 1948, "Conversation with General Donovan on OSS War Report," RG 218, 1942, 385 (2-8-42) Sec. 1, Part 2, the National Archives.

3. Memo, Hillenkoetter to the Joint Chiefs of Staff, regarding "History of the Office of Strategic Services," 28 September 1949, RG 218, 1942, 385 (2-8-42) Sec. 1, Part 2, the National Archives.

4. Cable, Spencer to Read, 3 January 1945, Entry 99, Box 59, Folder 27.

5. Cable, Read and William Langer to Spencer, New Delhi, 29 December 1944, Entry 99, Box 59, Folder 27.

6. Official lists dated 31 August 1945 of items in Read's History Office delivered to OSS Archives, R. Smith Papers, Box 2, Folder "China," the Hoover Institution, Stanford, Calif.

7. "Quiet End to a Shabby Era," interview of John Paton Davies Jr., by Leonard Gross, *Look Magazine,* 4 March 1969.

8. Lawrence H. McDonald, "The Office of Strategic Services: America's First National Intelligence Agency," *Prologue,* Spring 1991, National Archives and Records Administration (NARA), 7.

9. Bradley Smith, "The OSS and Record Group 226: Some Perspectives and Prospects," in George C. Chalou, ed., *The Secret War: The Office of Strategic Services in World War II* (Washington, D.C.: NARA, 1992), 360.

10. For a general description in English by Western scholars of the gradual release of Chinese Communist Party history documents in China—though none directly related to OSS/China—see Michael Hunt and Odd Westad, "The Chinese Communist Party and Interna-

tional Affairs: A Field Report on New Historical Sources and Old Research Problems," *China Quarterly* 122 (Summer 1990).

11. Pan was an intelligence chief for the Comintern and Yenan who throughout World War II ran an espionage net in cooperation with the Wang Jingwei puppet regime in Nanking and Shanghai. For Pan's deals with the puppet secret intelligence organization, his other wartime intelligence operations, his connection with the Comintern intelligence apparatus, and his purge by Mao in 1955, see Lin Yunhui, et al., *Time of Triumph: History of China, 1949–1989 (Kaige xingjin de shiqi: yijiusijiu-yijiubajiu nian de zhongguo)* [Henan People's Press, 1989], 523–529. Also see Zhang Chengzong, "Struggle of Underground Party in Shanghai Before Liberation, 1937–May 1949" ("Jiefang Qian Shanghai Dixia Dang de Douzheng, 1937–1949.5"); Zhao Zukang, et al., "In Memory of Comrade Pan Hannian," ("Huiyi Pan Hannian Tongzhi"); Chen Xiuliang, "Historical Lessons out of the Case of Comrade Pan Hannian" ("Pan Hannian Tongzhi Anjian de Lishi Jiaoxun"), all in issues 41, 42, and 43 of the *Selected Shanghai Culture and History Materials (Shanghai Wenshi ziliao Xuanji)*, October 1982, January 1983, and April 1983.

12. Shi Zhe, *Alongside the Great Men in History: Memoir of Shi Zhe (Zai Lishi Juren Shengbian: Shizhe Huiyi Lu)* [Beijing: Central Documents Press (Zhongyang Wenxian Chupan She), 1991]; Chen Hansheng, *My Life During Four Eras, (Sige Shitai de Wo)* [Beijing: China Culture and History (Zhongguo Wenshi Chupan She), 1988].

Shi Zhe was a Chinese Communist who went to the Soviet Union in 1925 and subsequently became an agent for the OGPU (NKVD since 1934, predecessor to KGB) for nine years until his dispatch to Yenan in 1940 as a Comintern representative to the 7th Congress of the Chinese Communist Party, which did not convene until April 1945 due to fierce factionalism. While in Yenan, Shi Zhe became Mao's confidential secretary in charge of decoding and drafting all radio messages between Mao and Moscow. Mao also designated Shi Zhe liaison between Kang Sheng and the NKVD intelligence team in Yenan. Incidentally, Shi Zhe was later, in the late 1940s, responsible for the persecution of American Communists within the CCP. For an example, see Sidney Rittenberg, *The Man Who Stayed Behind* (New York: Simon and Schuster, 1993).

Chen, a Comintern intelligence agent associated with Richard Sorge's spy ring in Shanghai and Tokyo, was dispatched by Moscow to New York to aid Owen Lattimore in editing the journal *Pacific Affairs* from 1936 to 1939. During much of World War II, Chen was in China actively working with British intelligence against the KMT. When discovered, Chen was rescued by the British and put on the payroll of British intelligence in India from 1944 to 1946, when Zhou Enlai and Kang Sheng sent Chen back to the U.S. as CCP's liaison with William Foster, chief of the Communist Party of the USA (CPUSA). For Chen's relevance in our OSS/China story, see Chapter 6. For details, see *My Life During Four Eras*.

13. Zhong Kan, *A Critical Biography of Kang Sheng (Kang Sheng Ping Zhuan)* [Beijing: Red Flag Press, 1982]; John Byron and Robert Pack, *The Claws of the Dragon: Kang Sheng, the Evil Genius Behind Mao and His Legacy of Terror in the People's Republic* (New York: Simon and Schuster, 1992).

14. Xiong Xianghui was a CCP star agent working for twelve years as KMT General Hu Zongnan's confidential secretary and was directly controlled by Zhou Enlai. After the Communist takeover, Xiong became Zhou Enlai's top aide in charge of intelligence, directly participating in negotiations with Henry Kissinger during the latter's secret visit to Beijing in 1971.

Yan Baohang was Yenan and Moscow's valued agent inside Chiang Kai-shek's most inner circles in Chungking during World War II. His intelligence work was highly praised by Stalin.

Zhang Luping was an agent of Kang Sheng's Social Affairs Department and the famous operator of a seven-person espionage ring in the heart of Tai Li's intelligence system.

Wang Zhengyuan was the director of Chiang Kai-shek's top secret Military Telephone Station (Junhua tai)—a central switchboard of Chiang's headquarters in charge of monitoring all incoming calls and dialing all outgoing telephone numbers for Chiang—from 1937 to 1949.

In his memoirs, Wang does not identify himself directly as a Communist agent but reveals that seven out of the nine members of the Station were secret agents working for the Communists.

15. Adler was a British-born American. In the 1950s, Senator Joe McCarthy accused him of being a Communist. Soon after, Adler left the United States for England, where he quickly disappeared from public view. Newly available Chinese documents identify him as an adviser for the past several decades in Beijing to the supersecret Chinese Communist Party intelligence agency, the Department of Foreign Liaisons (Zhong Gong Zhong Yang Duiwai Lianluo Bu). See Adler's photo in *Selected Shanghai Culture and History Materials (Shanghai Wenshi ziliao Xuanji),* issue 43, April 1983, Shanghai People's Press.

16. Documents from the Anti-Japanese War include, for example, a reevaluation of the confession materials previously published in the Wen Shi Zi Liao series by captured former Tai Li agents; memoirs and biographies of such key CCP intelligence figures as Kang Sheng (Tai Li's equally ruthless and draconian counterpart in the Communist party), Li Kenong (Kang Sheng's deputy), Song Qingling, Chen Hansheng, Xiong Xianghui, and Ye Jianying (CCP general in charge of military intelligence for Yenan). The author has a relatively complete collection of these Chinese materials.

Other revelations include, for example, that the son-in-law of Chiang Kai-shek's second wife was in charge of the intelligence station for the Comintern in Tokyo and during World War II penetrated into the KMT's Institute of International Studies run by Wang Pengsheng. This institute was Chiang Kai-shek's agency designated to collect intelligence in occupied China and was the prime partner of the British SOE/SIS during World War II, after the disastrous ending of a brief alliance with Tai Li in the affairs of the China Commando Group. Throughout the war this Communist agent further penetrated the Japanese occupation army in Shanghai and ran a large business as a cover for intelligence gathering, ostensibly for the KMT but really for the Communists.

Introduction

1. *PM,* 7 February 1941, Box 4, folder entitled "First Trip to China, Press Clippings," Currie Papers, Hoover Institution.

2. *New York Times,* 7 December 1940; *PM,* 7 February 1941.

3. The CIA historian Thomas F. Troy writes, "Indeed FDR and Donovan were not 'close' in any personal sense of the word. Neither the Roosevelt papers at Hyde Park, nor the Donovan papers show any significant contact between the two men prior to 1940" (*Donovan and the CIA: A History of the Establishment of the Central Intelligence Agency* [Frederic, Md.: Alethia, University Publications of America, 1981], 30–31).

4. *PM,* 7 February 1941.

5. Troy, *Donovan and the CIA,* 39.

6. Ibid., 30.

7. Ibid.

8. Ibid.

9. Ibid., 31.

10. For different interpretations on the origins of this trip, see William Stephenson, *The Man Called Intrepid* (New York: Harcourt Brace Jovanovich, 1976), and Troy, *Donovan and the CIA,* 31, 36, 485.

11. On the identity of Mr. C, see Troy, *Donovan and the CIA,* 31.

12. Ibid., 36.

13. Ibid., 55.

14. Ibid., 417–418.

15. Ibid., 59.

16. "Tab 3," Entry 110, Box 48, Folder 11.

17. Troy, *Donovan and the CIA,* 62.

18. "Memorandum for the President of the United States," 10 June 1941, President's Secretary's Files (PSF), Box 128, Folder entitled "COI 1941," FDR Library, Hyde Park, N.Y. Emphasis in original.

19. Troy, *Donovan and the CIA*, 63.

20. Troy, *Donovan and the CIA*, 63, 69.

Chapter 1. Building an Empire

1. "Memorandum for the President from S. T. E.," 1 August 1941, PSF, Box 128, FDR Library.

2. Letter, Sherman Miles to John Magruder, 11 July 1941, "United States Army, AM-MISCA File: The Magruder Mission to China, July 1941 through June 1942" (hereafter cited as Magruder Files).

3. Memo, Sherman Miles to George Marshall, "Coordinator for the Three Intelligence Agencies of the Government," 8 April 1941, Records of the Army Staff, Army Intelligence Decimal File, RG 319, File 310.11, National Records Center, Suitland, Md.; also Troy, *Donovan and the CIA*, 42.

4. "Report on Some Aspects of the Current Political, Economic and Military Situation in China, March 15, 1941," Box 4, Folder entitled "First trip to China," Currie Papers.

5. Letter, Miles to Magruder, 11 July 1941, Magruder Files.

6. Ibid.

7. Anthony Cave Brown, *Wild Bill Donovan: The Last Hero* (New York: Times Books, 1982), 685; also "American Far-Eastern Policy Studies—Discussion Session #6," McHugh's talk at John Carter Vincent's house at Harvard, 21 April 1959, Box 11, Folder 17, McHugh Papers, Cornell University, Ithaca, N.Y. (hereafter cited as McHugh Papers).

8. "American Far-Eastern Policy Studies—Discussion Session #6," McHugh Papers.

9. "An Official History of the United States Naval Group China," RG 38, Box 1, Folder 1, the National Archives (hereafter cited as Official History Manuscript), 2.

10. Memo for the president from William Donovan, 18 December 1941, PSF, Box 147, FDR Library.

11. "Intelligence Summary," Ammisca, Chungking to MILAD, Washington, 13 December 1941 to 13 March 1942, Magruder Files.

12. William Langer, *In and Out of the Ivory Tower: The Autobiography of William Langer* (New York: Academic, 1977), 181.

13. Langer, *Ivory Tower*, 180–182; see also John King Fairbank, *Chinabound: A Fifty-Year Memoir* (New York: Harper Colophon, 1982), 174.

14. MacLeish would cooperate with Donovan provided that the COI paid for the expenses of materials and manpower and that the COI and the Library of Congress could share operational control over Donovan's research teams. See MacLeish's letter to Donovan on the "Division of Special Information Organization," 29 June 1941, Entry 110, Box 48, Folder 6.

15. Memo for the president from William Donovan, "Report on Research and Analysis Branch," 20 October 1941, PSF, Box 128, FDR Library.

16. Fairbank, *Chinabound*, 174.

17. "Dr. Joseph Ralston Hayden: A Tribute," Entry 110, Box 48, Folder 6.

18. Troy, *Donovan and the CIA*, 26.

19. Fairbank, *Chinabound*, 180.

20. "History of the School and Training Branch, OSS," Entry 99, Box 78, Folder 60.

21. Esson Gale had taught at the University of Michigan and Northwestern University and had an extensive experience in China. See "SI Report to Mr.Wallace," 66, Entry 99, Box 78, Folder 55.

22. Langer, *Ivory Tower*, 194.

23. Memo for the president from Donovan, 23 October 1941, PSF, Box 128, FDR Library.

24. "Conyers Read: SO," 2, Entry 99, Box 78, Folder 57 (hereafter cited as Read).

25. Ibid.

26. "Comparison of June 25 and July 11 Drafts of the Presidential Order," Entry 110, Box 48, Folder 11.

27. "Pencilled Notes of General Donovan on Conyers Read SO History," 18 December 1946, Entry 99, Box 78, Folder 57.

28. Read, 10.

29. Donovan reported to FDR, "Clear was a man whom we took over from the Army to make a survey for our SIS and SO operations in the Far East" (memo for the president, #427, 20 April 1942, PSF, Box 148, FDR Library).

30. Meeting memorandum, Magruder with MacArthur in Manila, 3 October 1941, Magruder Files.

31. Walter LeFeber, *The American Age: United States Foreign Policy at Home and Abroad Since 1750,* (New York: Norton, 1989), 393.

32. Memo for the president, #427, 20 April 1942, PSF, Box 148, FDR Library.

33. Read, 11.

34. Richard Harris Smith, *OSS: The Secret History of America's First Central Intelligence Agency* (Berkeley: University of California Press, 1972), 250.

35. "SI Report to Mr. Wallace," 1–2, Entry 99, Box 78, Folder 55.

36. Ibid., 2–3.

37. Or, as the autograph of Hornbeck's designation on his profusely-used letterhead had it, "PA/H." See Fairbank, *Chinabound,* 177–178.

38. Roy was the editor of the influential *Calcutta Statesman.* Gale found him "on the whole . . . more moderate than might be expected." See "SI Report to Mr. Wallace," 59–60; also see Jonathan Spence, *To Change China: Western Advisors in China 1620–1960* (New York: Penguin, 1969), 357–358.

39. Magruder, *War Diary,* March 1942, Magruder Files.

40. Fairbank, *Chinabound,* 185–186.

41. Memo for the president from Donovan, 19 December 1941, PSF, Box 147, FDR Library.

42. Memo for the president from Donovan, #186, 24 January 1942, PSF, FDR Library.

43. Cable, U.S. Military Attaché, London, to War Department, #68, 31 August 1944, OPD 210.684, India, the National Archives.

44. Charles Cruickshank, *SOE in the Far East* (New York: Oxford University Press, 1983), 154–159.

45. "SI Report to Mr. Wallace," 3.

46. Memo to Colonel Donovan, "Proposed Organization of an American SOS (Special Operation Service)," 13 January 1942, Entry 110, Box 48, Folder 11.

47. "SI Report to Mr. Wallace," 10–11.

48. Chinese-backed Kim Ku would launch a fierce factional opposition, even collaborating with the Korean Communists against Syngman Rhee; Kim was assassinated in 1949. See Tang Zong, *Diaries: My Eight Years as Chiang Kai-shek's Confidential Secretary (Zai Jiangjieshi shenbian ba nian—shicong shi gaoji muliao tangzong riji)* [Beijing: Masses, 1991], 236.

49. Barry Katz, *Foreign Intelligence: Research and Analysis in the Office of Strategic Services, 1942–1945* (Cambridge: Harvard University Press, 1989), Katz does not attempt to cover Donovan's Asia scholars at all for fear that he might lower the standard of the entire study. He maintains a diffidence in his knowledge of Asian affairs (preface, xiv).

50. "What you should know about the OSS," brochure for new members of the OSS, Entry 99, Box 80, Folder 70.

51. "SI Report to Mr. Wallace," 8.

52. Gale once angrily charged, "the motivation [of 'an unexpected opposition to a dynamic policy toward Korea'] was hard to identify but throughout the years there has unques-

tionably been a powerful but obscure influence at work to entirely nullify all efforts to recognize this powerful Korean entity in the moral and military prosecution of the war." See "SI Report to Mr. Wallace," 10.

53. Bradley Smith, *The Shadow Warriors: O.S.S. and the Origins of the C.I.A.* (Berkeley: University of California Press, 1972), 408.

54. Memo to GO, "Chinese Scheme," #W-159, 7 January 1942, Box 4, Folder 1, Preston Goodfellow Papers, Hoover Institution, Stanford, Calif.

55. Untitled memo dated 23 December 1941, Box 4, Folder 1, Goodfellow Papers.

56. Box 4, Folder 1, Goodfellow Papers.

57. Interoffice memo, Langer to Donovan, 3 March 1942, Box 4, Folder 1, Goodfellow Papers.

58. "History: Far East, SI," Part I, 2, Box 6, Folder 17, Norwood Allman Papers, Hoover Institution.

59. Files on Fairbairn, Box 4, Folder 3, Goodfellow Papers.

60. Letter from the OSS Office in the American Embassy in London, Phillips to Roosevelt, 13 August 1942, PSF, Box 38, FDR Library.

61. Memo for the president from Donovan, #186.

62. "SI Report to Mr. Wallace," quotations from 71 and 90, respectively. Wallace's instructions that Gale meet with Keswick and Killery, 4.

63. Ibid., 74.

64. Smith, *Shadow Warriors*, 132.

65. Fairbank, *Chinabound*, 186.

66. Anna Louise Strong, an American with a Ph.D. from the University of Chicago (1908), went to the Soviet Union in the early 1920s. She was chief editor, from 1930 on, of the *Moscow Daily News,* Stalin's major English propaganda mouthpiece. From 1937 to 1949, Strong was China correspondent for the International News Service. Closely tied to the Chinese Communists, she permanently moved to Beijing in 1958 and died there in 1970. Among her many works are *Dawn Out of China* (1949), *When Serfs Stood Up in Tibet,* (1960), *The Rise of the Chinese People's Communes, and Six Years After* (1964); also see "SI Report to Mr. Wallace," 80.

67. "SI Report to Mr. Wallace," 80–81.

68. Ibid., 79–81.

69. Ibid., 67.

70. Smith, *Shadow Warriors*, 132.

71. Cruickshank, *SOE in the Far East,* 13–14.

72. "Paraphrase of secret cable sent by Naval Attache, Chungking, January 27, 1942," and "Interoffice Memo from Wallace Phillips to Donovan, February 11, 1941," Box 4, Folder 1, Goodfellow Papers.

73. John Keswick report to MEW.

74. McHugh report, Box 2, Folder 1, McHugh Papers.

75. "Brief History of OSS/CBI to 26 October 1944," Entry 110, Box 52, Folder 14.

76. LeFeber, *American Age,* 395.

77. "Tab 3" and "Tab 4," Entry 110, Box 48, Folder 11.

78. Memo for the president from Donovan, #186.

79. Memo for Colonel Donovan from DePass, subject: scheme "Olivia," 27 January 1942, Box 4, Folder 1, Goodfellow Papers.

80. Stilwell's cable from Chungking to Goodfellow, #454, 4 April 1942, Box 4, Folder 1, Goodfellow Papers.

81. Roy Stratton, *The Army-Navy Game* (Falmouth, Mass.: Volta, 1977), 52.

82. Smith, *Shadow Warriors,* 131; Thomas Moon and Carl Eifler, *The Deadliest Colonel* (New York: Vantage, 1975), 40. This is a little known, yet highly revealing memoir of Carl Eifler.

83. Stratton, *Army-Navy Game,* 52.

84. Moon and Eifler, *Deadliest Colonel,* 41.

85. Stilwell's own historian later claimed Eifler was "recommended" by Stilwell. See "OSS History in CBI under Stilwell, June 42–October 44," 2, RG 99, Entry 99, Box 58, Folder 24, National Archives.

86. Moon and Eifler, *Deadliest Colonel.*

87. Stratton, *Army-Navy Game,* 52.

88. "SI Report to Mr. Wallace," 12–13.

89. Read, 15.

90. Meeting memo, Magruder with Wavell, 23 December 1941, Magruder Files.

91. Letter, McHugh to Currie, August 25, 1941, Box 1, Folder 8, McHugh Papers.

92. Joseph Stilwell, *The Stilwell Papers,* arranged by Theodore White (New York: Sloane Associates, 1948; rpt. New York: Da Capo, 1991), 26.

93. "Message to Generalissimo Chiang Kai-shek from the President," 14 July 1942, Map Room File, Box 10, Folder 1, FDR Library.

94. Shen Yuan, *Tai Li of Jiang Shan County,* 84–85; Qiao Jiacai, *Selected Writings of Qiao Jiacai* (Taipei: Chongwai Books, 1981), 2: 377–378, 399–402.

95. Magruder's evaluation of Chinese intelligence capabilities was vital in the OSS planning process for China projects when he later became Donovan's deputy director.

96. McHugh wrote in his notes for memoirs, "T. V., whom I have known intimately for over 30 years, was a smooth operator. He cultivated the acquaintanceship of Secretary of the Treasury Morgenthau, Secretary of the Navy Frank Knox, Secretary of Commerce Jesse Jones, and other big shots. He flattered them, ingratiated himself with them by playing poker with some of them and always managing to lose (when he could have taken their shirts off their backs had he chosen to do so) and got on very intimate terms with them." See "Chiang Kai-shek and Stilwell," Box 11, Folder 9, McHugh Papers.

97. McHugh, "Chiang Kai-shek and Stilwell," 6, Box 11, Folder 9, McHugh Papers.

98. Both Magruder and Stilwell held the rank of brigadier general until Stilwell was promoted rapidly to the rank of lieutenant general to suit the "eminence requirement" of his position in China. See Stilwell, *Stilwell Papers,* 26–27.

99. Due to a flight delay, Stilwell actually saw Magruder before Gale did, in early March in India. See "SI Report to Mr. Wallace," 26–27.

100. Quotation from McHugh, "Chiang Kai-shek and Stilwell."

101. Memo for the adjutant general, 15 March 1942, OPD, 210.684, China, RG 165, National Archives.

102. Manuscript by Arthur B. Darling, historical staff, CIA, The DCI Historical Series, HS 1, *The Central Intelligence Agency: An Instrument of Government, to 1950,* chapter 1, "Origins in War," December 1953, 33, RG 263, Records of the Central Intelligence Agency, Office of the Director of Central Intelligence: History Staff, Box 1, National Archives.

Chapter 2. Chungking Fog

1. Stanley Lovell, *Of Spies and Stratagems,* (Englewood Cliffs, N.J.: Prentice-Hall, 1963), 51. Donovan quotation, 83–84. Lovell was the chief of research and development for OSS, responsible for designing spy devices and special weapons. He had extensive cooperation with Tai Li's lab of deadly weapons during the war.

2. Barbara Tuchman, *Stilwell and the American Experience in China, 1911–1945* (New York: Bantam, 1971), 334. Tai Li was so enraged by numerous U.S. foreign intelligence reports from China labeling him the Himmler of China that he once went on a four-hour long shouting tirade of self-defense in front of thousands of Americans and Chinese intelligence officers. See unpublished manuscript by Milton Miles, "The Navy Launched a Dragon," Naval War College, Newport, R.I.

3. Memo, Admiral King to Secretary of the Navy James Forrestal, subject: "Recommendation for Award of Legion of Merit, Degree of Commander, to General Tai Li, Director of the Sino-American Cooperative Organization," FF1/P15, Serial 002109, 30 August 1945, RG 38, Box 39, National Archives.

4. Milton Miles, unpublished manuscript, "General Tai Li," RG 38, Box 40, National Archives.

5. Op-34D-HD, top secret memo for Op-23, subject: Report on General Tai Li, and attachment, 21 January 1946, RG 38, Box 39, National Archives.

6. The best example is Shen Meijuan's *Tai Li: A New Biography (Nie Hai Xiao Xiong—Dai Li Xin Zhuan)* [Beijing: October Literature and Arts, 1992]. While certainly not portrayed as blameless, Tai Li is said to have been "extremely patriotic and anti-Japanese," "caring for his own people," and "antifeudal."

This is a curious publication for two reasons. First, Shen is the daughter of Shen Zui, who once was Tai Li's top aide. After being captured in the Communist revolution, Shen Zui was instructed by Zhou Enlai in the late 1950s to turn his voluminous "confession materials" (jiaodai cailiao) into numerous books and articles. Shen Zui has been almost single-handedly responsible for documenting all of the Communist "verdicts" about Tai Li. In the preface to his daughter's book, Shen Zui belatedly apologizes for the lack of "completeness and objectivity" in his own books. Second, having made many errors in details in the book, Shen Meijuan nonetheless is perhaps the only person in China who writes about Tai Li using documents that can be corroborated with the newly declassified English-language archive materials.

7. Secret memo, Al Lusey in Chungking to Donovan in Washington, 23 May 1942, Box 4, Folder 2, Goodfellow Papers.

8. Upon his first glimpse of Tai Li's Bureau of Investigation and Statistics, Donovan's agent, Al Lusey, reported with awe to Washington that "Tai Lee has the only real intelligence service in China" (memo to Donovan, 8053, in Entry 139, Box 267, National Archives) and that in Tai Li's headquarters "nightly reports are received from Tokyo, Formosa, Korea, Hainan Islands, Manchukuo, the Walled City in Manila, Vigan, in the P.I., Indo-china, Hong Kong, Singapore, Thailand, Mandalay, India, and from all the Jap-occupied areas in China" (secret memo from Al Lusey).

9. Quotation from secret memo from Al Lusey.

10. *Zong Heng,* 1986, no. 1, 42. This is one of the few publications in China overwhelmingly devoted to articles and memoirs by retired high officials about wartime secret intelligence and special operations. Most of the authors were World War II intelligence officers, both in the CCP and KMT.

11. "Note on Conversation with the President on 30 August 1943 from Noon to 12:45 pm," Box 32, Folder "Roosevelt," T. V. Soong Papers, Hoover Institution, Stanford, Calif. Although Soong regarded himself as "something of a cryptographer," his contribution to Chiang's signals intelligence was made possible largely because of one person—his nephew and protégé, Wen Yuqing. A Harvard Ph.D. in physics, Wen Yuqing was the father of China's modern cryptography. The recruitment and financing of Wen gave Soong, who was also a Harvard graduate, new prominence in the factionalized KMT inner circle. Also see Yun Yiqun, "An Expose of T. V. Soong," *Shanghai Cultural and Historical Materials (Shanghai Wenshi Ziliao),* 1980, no. 2, 105.

12. The Zhong Tong was initially named the Office of Investigation of Party Affairs (Dangwu Diaocha Ke).

13. Mu Xin, *Comrade Chen Geng in Shanghai: His Fighting Experience while in the Special Service Section of the Central Committee (Chen Geng Tongzhi zai Shanghai—zai Zhongyang Teke de Douzheng Jingli)* [Beijing: Cultural and Historical Materials, 1980], 34–44.

14. Mu Xin, *Comrade Chen Geng,* 9–10

15. Lin Nong, "Zhou Enlai and Zhongyang Teke" (Zhou Enlai yu Zhongyang Teke), *Military History,* 1991, no. 33.

16. See Mu Xin, *Comrade Chen Geng,* and Lin Nong, "Zhou Enlai and Zhongyang Teke."

17. General Chen Geng later briefly became the supreme commander of the Chinese Communist forces in the Korean War and the vice minister of defense in 1958. He died in March 1961.

18. See Zhou Gu, "Communist Spies in the Heart of the KMT," in *Biographical Literature* 56, no. 1; also see Mu Xin, *Comrade Chen Geng.*

19. Mu Xin, *Comrade Chen Geng,* and Lin Nong, "Zhou Enlai and Zhongyang Teke."

20. See Mu Xin, *Comrade Chen Geng,* and Lin Nong, "Zhou Enlai and Zhongyang Teke." Also see Gu Shunzhang's public reward announcement for information leading to Zhou Enlai's whereabouts, in the Shanghai newspaper *Shen Bao (Shen Pao),* 29–30 November 1931.

21. Li Kenong later became the number two man of the entire CCP intelligence apparatus throughout World War II, serving as the deputy director of the Social Affairs Department under Kang Sheng in Yenan. Qian Zhuangfei was liquidated during the Long March by the CCP for his excessive knowledge of the CCP-KMT intelligence matters. Hu Di was executed by another Communist leader, Zhang Guotao, one of Mao's chief rivals, during the Counterrevolutionary Elimination witch hunt at the E-Yu-Wan Soviet Base in the mid-1930s. For details, see Maochun Yu, "On the Special Service Section of the CCP Central Committee" (Zhongyang Teke Diandi), (Los Angeles) *Press Guardian (Xinwen Ziyou Daobao),* 25 June 1993.

22. Ding Xuzeng, "Chiang Kai-shek's Secret Code-Breaking Intelligence Agencies" (Jiang Jieshi Zhangwo de Mima Qingbao Jigou), *Zong Heng Bimonthly,* Spring 1986, no. 13, 42.

23. Qiao Jiacai, *Selected Writings,* 1: 204.

24. Tang Zong, *Diaries,* 25–28.

25. Qiao Jiacai, *Selected Writings,* 1: 208.

26. McHugh's talk for the Harvard seminar organized by John Carter Vincent, 21 April 1959, Box 11, Folder 17, McHugh Papers.

27. Qiao Jiacai, *Selected Writings,* 1: 208.

28. Ding Xuzeng, "Chiang Kai-shek's Secret Code-Breaking Intelligence Agencies," 44.

29. The office intercepted an average of two hundred to three hundred radio transmissions every day, sometimes as many as four hundred. Of all these intercepted secret Japanese radio transmissions and telegrams, the office could decipher 60–80%. Of this decoded intelligence, the office selected and evaluated thirty to forty messages every day, amounting to about ten thousand Chinese characters in all. See Ding Xuzeng, "Chiang Kai-shek's Secret Code-Breaking Intelligence Agencies," 45.

30. Ding Xuzeng, "Chiang Kai-shek's Secret Code-Breaking Intelligence Agencies," 45.

31. Ibid.

32. See McHugh's talk for the Harvard seminar.

33. Qiao Jiacai, *Selected Writings,* 1: 86.

34. Herbert Yardley, *Chinese Black Chamber,* xzy, xv, 14–15.

35. David Kahn, *The Codebreakers: The Story of Secret Writing* (New York: Macmillan, 1967), 368–369; see also Yardley, *Chinese Black Chamber,* 3.

36. Qiao Jiacai, *Selected Writings,* 2: 208.

37. Ibid.; Shen Meijuan, *Tai Li,* 428; see also Zhang Pengsheng, "The Secret Story of the BIS's Cryptographic Room in Chungking" (Juntong Huolu Neimu), *Chungking Literature and Culture Materials (Chongqing Wenshi Ziliao),* June 1991, no. 35, 235.

38. Qiao Jiacai, *Selected Writings,* 2: 208.

39. Zhang Pengsheng, "The Secret Story of the BIS's Cryptographic Room in Chungking," 236. This remarkable achievement under Wei Daming had international impact, invoking the jealousy and admiration of the British. The British were particularly interested in Tai Li's achievement in late 1940, and in the fall of 1941, British military authorities requested China's help. Tai Li responded with caution, nevertheless dispatching a small, secret, radio

interception and decoding team to Hong Kong and India. See Qiu Shenjun, "The Sino-British Air Force Secret Intelligence Cooperation During World War II," *Zong Heng*, 1986, no. 15, 48–53.

40. Ding Xuzeng, "Chiang Kai-shek's Secret Code-Breaking Intelligence Agencies," 2: 63.

41. Wen stayed in Hong Kong until the Japanese occupation in December 1941. Disgusted with Tai Li's aggressive effort to control cryptography, Wen decided not to go back to China. He subsequently fled to America, and worked as an assistant in T. V. Soong's China Defense Supplies, Inc., in Washington, D.C.

After the Pearl Harbor attack, efforts were made through the White House to send Wen Yuqing to China to work for the U.S. Army; this met with Tai Li's stubborn objection. See letter from Lauchlin Currie to Madame Chiang Kai-shek, 10 February 1942, Box 1, Folder "Madame Chiang Kai-shek," Currie Papers.

42. Ding Xuzeng, "Chiang Kai-shek's Secret Code-Breaking Intelligence Agencies," 2: 63, 65.

43. Ibid., 66. Text of order quoted in Zhang Pengsheng, "The Secret Story of the BIS's Cryptographic Room in Chungking," 239.

44. David Kahn, *Codebreakers*, 369.

45. John W. Garver, "China's Wartime Diplomacy," in James C. Hsiung and Steven I. Levine, ed. *China's Bitter Victory: The War With Japan, 1937–1945* (New York: M. E. Sharpe, 1992), 14.

46. Ibid., 16.

47. Roger Faligot and Remi Kauffer, *The Chinese Secret Service*, trans. Christine Donougher (New York: William Morrow, 1989), 100

48. Niu Jun, *From Yenan to the World* (Fuzhou: Fujian People's Press, 1992), 64–65

49. Han Xinru, *History of New China Daily, 1938–1947*, (Beijing: China Prospect, 1987), 1: 117–121; see also *Selected Works of Mao Zedong* (Beijing: People's Press, 1961), 2: 597–599.

50. Shi Zhe, *Alongside the Great Men in History: Memoir of Shi Zhe*, 131–132.

51. Cable of the ECCI to the Central Committee of the CCP, 9 September 1939, quoted in Niu Jun, *From Yenan to the World*, 64.

52. Shi Zhe, *Alongside the Great Men*, 211.

53. Wang Zhixiu, "Random Memory of the Institute of the Oriental Munich" (Dongfang Munihei Xuexiao Shenghuo Sanji), *Zong Heng*, 1987, no. 19, 72–75.

54. Ibid.

55. For the organizational tie between the Comintern and the CCP, see Li Shengping, "The Comintern and the Chinese Revolution in its Early Stage," *Zong Heng*, no. 7, 154–160. For the January 1935 Enlarged Politburo Congress of the CCP (the Zunyi Conference) during the Long March and Mao's purge of Otto Braun and Zhou Enlai, see Otto Braun's autobiography, *A Comintern Agent in China, 1932–1939*, trans. Jeanne Moore (London: C. Hurst, 1982); also see Maochun Yu, "Otto Braun and Mao Zedong," (Los Angeles) *Press Guardian*, 14 May 1993. For the Yenan Rectification Campaign, see Wang Ming, *The Chinese Communist Party in Its First Half-Century and Traitor Mao Zedong* (Hong Kong: WanHai Language Press, 1980), 11–139; also see Chen Yungfa, *The Shadow of Yenan* (Taipei: Institute of Modern History, Academia Sinica, 1990).

56. Shi Zhe, *Alongside the Great Men*, 86.

57. Ho Chi Minh went to Yenan from Moscow in late 1938 and worked closely for Kang Sheng. See Ho Chi Minh, "The Chinese Communist Party and I," (Hong Kong) *Look Fortnightly (Zhanwang Banyue Kan)*, 16 September 1969, no. 183; also see Jiang Yongjing, *Ho Chi-minh in China* (Taipei: Biographical Literature, 1972); and Charles Fenn, *Ho Chi-Minh: A Biographical Introduction* (London: Studio Vista London, 1973), 136.

Incidentally, Charles Fenn was the OSS officer whom Ho Chi Minh first approached in Kunming in 1945. Fenn was instrumental in establishing the vital connection between Ho Chi

Minh and American forces in China, marking the beginning of America's involvement with the Vietcong.

Sanzo Nozaka was the president of the Central Committee of the Japanese Communist Party who left the Comintern headquarters in Moscow for Yenan in March 1940 in the same plane with Zhou Enlai. He stayed in Yenan throughout the war and was the most visible foreign Communist there.

The Indonesian Communist Party contingent in Yenan was best known for dispatching agents right after World War II to Indonesia to overthrow not only the Dutch colonial rule but also the "bourgeois class" led by Sukharno.

Also in Yenan briefly was Kim Il Sung, who joined the Chinese Communist Party in Manchuria when he was young. During much of the war Kim was working with the CCP on Korean exiles in China. However, Kim Il Sung did not become well known until the final months of World War II, when he went to Soviet Siberia to receive guerrilla and special operations training there. Much of Kim's activities are documented by OSS and SSU intelligence reports.

58. Yenan's importance as the intelligence center for all non-European, particularly East and Southeast Asian, Communist forces, was reaffirmed by the German assault on the Soviet Union in June 1941. This made the Comintern entirely an intelligence apparatus for Stalin. The Intelligence Bureau in the Comintern, established soon after the German blitzkrieg, was now composed of only European Communists; it excluded all Asian participation.

Mao Zedong would plead with Stalin to allow the Chinese Communists to be part of the intelligence bureau, which continued to exist after the Comintern was dissolved in 1943. In his secret visit to Moscow in May 1949, Liu Shaoqi requested that the CCP be allowed to join the intelligence bureau, only to be rejected by Stalin once again. See Shi Zhe, *Alongside the Great Men*, 413–414.

59. Zhong Kan, *A Critical Biography of Kang Sheng (Kang Sheng Ping Zhuan)* [Beijing: Red Flag, 1982], 74–77.

60. Shi Zhe, *Alongside the Great Men*, 219.

61. For Pan's collaboration with Li Shiqun and puppet intelligence, see Lin Yun Hui et al., *Time of Triumph: History of China, 1949–1989 (Kaige Xingjin de Shiqi: yijiusijiu-yijiubajiu de Zhongguo)* [Zhengzhou: Henan People's Press, 1989], 523–529. For other issues related to Pan's wartime intelligence work, see Maochun Yu, "The Mystery Surrounding Pan Hannian" (Pan Hannian Mingyun Zhi Mi), (Los Angeles) *Press Guardian*, 5 March 1993. Also see Zhang Chengzong, "Struggle of Underground Party in Shanghai Before Liberation, 1937–May 1949" (Jiefang Qian Shanghai Dixia Dang de Douzheng, 1937–1949); Zhao Zukang et al., "In Memory of Comrade Pan Hannian" (Huiyi Pan Hannian Tongzhi); and Chen Xiu-liang, "Historical Lessons out of the Case of Comrade Pan Hannian" (Pan Hannian Tongzhi Anjian de Lishi Jiaoxun), in *Selected Shanghai Culture and History Materials (Shanghai Wenshi Ziliao Xuanji)*, October 1982–January 1983, nos. 41, 42, and 43.

62. Zhou Enlai, "On Building a Solid, Strong and Combative Party Organization in the Southwest Provinces," concluding speech at the Southern Bureau Conference, Chungking, January 1942, in *Selected Works of Zhou Enlai*, ed. Documents Compilation Committee of the Central Committee of the CCP (Beijing: People's Press, 1980), 110–111.

63. Cao Jingyan, "Yan Baohang and the Secret Liaison Station of the Chungking Underground Party," *Social Sciences of Changchun (Changchun Shehui Kexue)*, rpt. *Biographical Literature (Zhuanji Wenxue)*, 55, no. 6; also see Shi Zhe, *Alongside the Great Men*, 212.

64. Yan Baohang further proved indispensable to Stalin's final military advance in Manchuria at the end of the war. Yan, in 1945, before the Soviets declared war on Japan, went into the KMT's top secret safe and filmed crucial intelligence on the order of battle, military deployment, and army rosters of the Japanese Kwantung Army in Manchuria. See Cao Jingyan, "Yan Baohang and the Secret Liaison Station."

65. Shi Wenqi, *Biography of Zhang Luping (Zhang Luping Zhuan)* [Beijing: China Youth, 1985], 114, 132, 138, 142. Quotations from 142 and 138, respectively.

66. The seven were locked up in Tai Li's Xifeng prison in Guizhou for several years and were summarily executed on 19 December 1944, when a Japanese military assault of the Guizhou area seemed imminent. See Shi Wenqi, *Biography of Zhang Luping,* 180, 224–228.

For thirty-nine years, a systematic coverup by the CCP has led to harsh treatment of all those who know anything about the Zhang Luping case. All seven were denied the rank of "revolutionary martyr" and were branded "counterrevolutionaries." In 1983 the CCP Central Committee decided to grant "political rehabilitations" to the seven World War II intelligence agents, and Marshall Ye Jianying personally verified the existence of such an infiltration team to Tai Li's agency. See Ye's handwritten note in the opening pages of *Biography of Zhang Luping.*

67. Both Tai Li and General He Yingqin, Chiang's chief of staff, were suspicious of Yan Baohang; they thought he was a Communist agent but could not take further action, partly due to Yan's personal connection with Madame Chiang Kai-shek. See Cao Jingyan, "Yan Baohang and the Secret Liaison Station."

68. See unpublished manuscript by Milton Miles, "The Navy Launched a Dragon," chapter 28, Naval War College.

69. See, for example, the British "most secret" report, "Notes On General Aspects of Military Intelligence in China," Box 1, Folder 9, McHugh Papers; and Li Maosheng, *Biography of H. H. Kung (Kong Xiangxi Zhuan)* [Beijing: China Radio and Television, 1992].

70. Tang Zong, *Diaries,* 340.

71. See Keswick's 17 November 1942 handwritten note to Soong in T. V. Soong Papers, Box 30.

72. Li Maosheng, *Biography of H. H. Kung,* 170; also see Yun Yiqun, *T. V. Soong and H. H. Kung (Song Ziwen he Kong Xiangxi)* (Wenshi Ziliao Xuanji, Shanghai, #2, 1980).

73. See Shen Yuan, *Tai Li of Jiang Shan County,* and Qiao Jiacai, *Selected Writings.*

74. G-2 report, #89-d-45, Naval Group China Files, Box 39, RG 38, National Archives. For further reading on traditional and modern educations in Republican China, see Yeh Wen-hsin, *The Alienated Academy: Culture and Politics in Republican China, 1919–1937* (Cambridge: Harvard University Press, 1990).

75. At the time, McHugh was living in the British embassy compound in Chungking, not the American, and was closely working with the SOE.

76. According to Washington intelligence reports, for example, Tai Li had murdered his mother twice.

77. Tang Zong, *Diaries,* 271, 295; also see minutes of meeting between Wedemeyer and Tai Li, 30 January 1945, Entry 148, Box 14, Folder 194, "SACO."

78. "What but necessity or some political or criminal activity would drive a white man like myself to Chungking?" Yardley wrote in *Chinese Black Chamber,* 7.

79. This was a strategically important issue in the realm of intelligence in China during the 1940s. Many of the most flagrant security blunders, made both by the Americans and Chinese, were direct results of intelligence officers' susceptibility to sexual attraction to female agents of hostile forces. Throughout the war, all of Tai Li's BIS agents were banned from getting married; womanizing was strictly prohibited by Tai Li in the BIS and SACO, at least in theory. The only person who got away with the violation of Tai Li's rule on marriage was General Wei Daming—Tai Li's cryptographic chief and most valued officer.

The newly declassified OSS files provide a fresh understanding of the role of many OSS women agents in an intelligence agency. The military authority in the Asian theater was forced to deal with such "unfitting" and unheard-of issues as sexually integrated billeting, promotion standards, equal rights, sexual harassment, and lesbianism. The fact that the chief of research and analysis of the OSS, CBI, was a brilliant anthropologist who was also a lesbian caused an uproar in the OSS.

80. Yardley, *Chinese Black Chamber,* xvii, 182; also see David Kahn, *Codebreakers,* 368–369.

81. Memo for Colonel Donovan from L. R. Lusey, subject: Tai Li, undated, Entry 139, Box 267, Folder 3934, National Archives.

82. Minutes of meeting between Wedemeyer and Tai Li, 30 January 1945.

83. Throughout Marshall's career as the top U.S. Army general, the protection of the MAGIC secret was a prominent theme, which on numerous occasions, including the Pearl Harbor investigation and the 1944 Dewey-Roosevelt presidential campaign, jeopardized his own military and political career. For a vivid description of this dramatic topic, see William R. Corson's heretofore rather underappreciated book, *The Armies of Ignorance: The Rise of the American Intelligence Empire* (New York: Dial, 1977), 209–214.

84. Note on conversation with the president on August 30, 1943, T. V. Soong Papers. There may be a great deal of truth to this, because, as reported by Donovan's radio expert, "the Japanese are intercepting everything, commercial, press, Government and broadcast, that is being handled to and from Chungking by radio." See Report to Donovan from Al Lusey, subject: enemy intercept, Undated, Entry 139, Box 267, Folder 3934.

85. Minutes of Meeting between Wedemeyer and Tai Li, 30 January 1945.

86. Ibid.

87. Corson, *Armies of Ignorance,* 151–161.

88. Letter from Lauchlin Currie to Madame Chiang Kai-shek, 10 February 1942.

89. Letter, McHugh to T. V. Soong, 15 March 1942, Box 6, Folder "McHugh," T. V. Soong Papers.

90. Minutes of meeting between Wedemeyer and Tai Li, 30 January 1945.

91. Magruder's fall from grace in China also had much to do with the personnel shakeup in the G-2 headquarters in Washington. It was General Sherman Miles who in the summer of 1941 picked Magruder to go to China, bypassing Stilwell, the other China Hand in the U.S. Army. With the dismissal of General Miles as the G-2 boss, Magruder lost his rear-echelon connection in the War Department.

92. Secret memo from Al Lusey; also see the related memos in Magruder Files.

93. Xiao Bo had been acquainted with the Miles family for years. See Wilma Miles's unpublished biography of Milton Miles at the Naval War College; I also interviewed Mrs. Miles, August 1992, Bethesda, Md.

94. Wilma Miles, unpublished biography of Milton Miles; also interview Mrs. Miles.

95. Oscar P. Fitzgerald, "Behind the Lines in Asia During World War II: Commodore Milton E. Miles's Mission to China," the Duquesne History Forum, Department of the Navy, Naval History Division, Washington, 2 November 1973, p. 3.

96. Ibid.; also see the voluminous reports by Miles from China about the Japanese attacks in the Far East in the Malaya desk of the foreign intelligence branch of the ONI, RG 38, Entry "The Office of Naval Intelligence," National Archives.

97. Milton Miles, *A Different Kind of War,* 103–105.

98. Fitzgerald, "Behind the Lines in Asia," 3. This job proved to be very useful to Miles in the years to come when identifying and ordering radio and other espionage equipment to be shipped from the United States to China.

99. *Biography of Willis A. Lee Jr.,* Chief of Naval Information, Naval Yard, Washington, D.C.

100. Official history manuscript, Miles Files, Chapter 1, 2. RG 38, Box 1, Folder I, "Personal," National Archives.

101. Ibid.

102. Fitzgerald, "Behind the Lines in Asia," 4.

103. Memo, John Paton Davies to Ambassador Gauss, "Anglo-American Cooperation in East Asia," 15 November 1943; and Cruickshank, *SOE in the Far East,* 160.

104. "Memo of Meeting with Generalissimo," 10 December 1941, Magruder Files.

105. Corson, *Armies of Ignorance*, 180–182.

106. See the voluminous files in this regard in the papers of Lauchlin Currie and T. V. Soong at the Hoover Institution, and the Chiang-Roosevelt correspondence at the Roosevelt Library in Hyde Park.

107. Samuel Elioit Morison, *History of United States Naval Operations in World War II* (Boston: Little Brown, 1947), 164–165.

108. Ibid.; quotation from 35.

109. Official history manuscript, 4.

110. Ibid., 10.

111. The CCS had two subcommittees; the other one was the Combined Planners Committee. Challenged by the British superior coordination of command, General George Marshall convened the first meeting of all U.S. participants in the CCS on 9 February 1942 (Corson, *Armies of Ignorance*, 180–82).

112. See McHugh's unpublished memoir, Chapter 4, Box 1, McHugh Papers.

113. McHugh, "A Memorandum for a Book: The Unknown Era," Box 11, McHugh Papers.

114. Official history manuscript, 19–20.

115. See, for example, McHugh to Frank Knox, February, 1942: "What I have wondered about is whether I had misled our people as to the real strength of the Japanese." Also see McHugh's letter to Captain Ellis Zacharias, assistant director of naval intelligence, Box 1, Folder 9, McHugh Papers.

116. McHugh's career at the ONI ended when General Marshall excoriated Admiral King after McHugh secretly reported "from the Navy's point of view" to Secretary of the Navy Frank Knox on General Stilwell's military fiasco in Burma in October 1942. General Marshall banned McHugh from serving in China forever in spite of McHugh's continuous plea for mercy. Because of Marshall's stubborn insistence against his return to China, McHugh was forced to work secretly for the OSS and served as its chief of secret intelligence, Washington desk.

117. Corson, *Armies of Ignorance*, 163–164. The JIC was a heavily bureaucratic entity and largely a committee game played by the army and navy against the OSS, which was represented in the committee mostly by General John Magruder. Donovan cleverly bypassed it by requesting direct command authority under the JCS and by strengthening his own planning group, the R&A. See JIC Files, in M1642, Roll 6.

118. Interview by Oscar Fitzgerald of Vice Admiral George C. Dyer (ret.), September 14 1973. Admiral Dyer served on Admiral King's staff from January 1942 to February 1943 as intelligence officer in the plans division. He later served as navy representative in the JIC, which extensively used the SACO intelligence reports from Miles. See Fitzgerald, "Behind the Lines in Asia," 12 and 21. See also Ernest King and Walter Muir Whitehill, *Fleet Admiral King: A Naval Record* (New York: Norton, 1952), 541; and William Leahy, *I Was There* (London: Victor Gollancz, 1950), 395.

119. Official history manuscript, 4.

120. Chief of Naval Operations Serial 0302823, 11 March 1942, Naval Historical Division, Navy Yard; also the official history manuscript, 5.

121. Memo for Major Hsiao, serial 0303623, 27 March 1942, RG 38, Miles Papers, Box 1, Folder 3, "Personal," National Archives.

122. Ibid.

123. Captain Metzel proved to be Miles's most important aide in securing the rear within the intriguing circle of the Washington politicos. From March 1942 until the very last day of SACO, 30 September 1946, Metzel fought tenaciously for the smooth operation of SACO, often with blunt determination and pungent naval pride, against forces from the army, OSS, and occasionally the White House. The official history of U.S. Naval Group China states, "To [Metzel], more than any other one man, with the possible exception of Commander

Miles, must go the credit for the success of the Naval Group in China" (official history manuscript, 9).

124. Official history manuscript, 9; for a slightly different description of King's instruction see Miles, *A Different Kind of War,* 18.

125. Miles, *A Different Kind of War,* 24.

126. Gauss was considered territorial by many; his first words to Miles were, "What is the purpose of your going to China? We already have a Naval Attaché there, and it is not necessary to have an additional naval officer there as observer. We do not need you." McHugh ultimately smoothed things over. See official history manuscript, 14.

127. Official history manuscript, 24–27.

128. This proved to be the very beginning of a highly sophisticated R&D joint venture between Chinese and Americans, including the development by Stanley Lovell and Carl Eifler of OSS of weapons and surveillance devices of dubious morality.

129. Cable, Commander Miles to Cominch [Admiral King], 9 May 1942, Miles Files, R.G 38, Box 2, National Archives.

130. Memo for Major Hsiao, 4 Nov 1942.

131. Miles, *A Different Kind of War,* 260.

132. Official history manuscript, 23.

133. Cable, McHugh to Washington, 11 May 1942, Box 2, Miles Files, RG 38, National Archives.

134. Letter, McHugh to Frank Knox, "Secret and Personal," 1 August 1942, Box 1, Folder 9, McHugh Papers.

Chapter 3. Donovan's Long March to Chungking

1. Sherwood first stressed the importance of such a matter: "The short wave radio is a vital strategic weapon, political and military in character. Its use must be directed by the coordinated intelligence of all services and departments. The right programs must be directed from the right stations to the right regions at the right hours, with emphasis on the fact that the U.S. A. is speaking to the world with unanimity." Moreover, COI pointed out, "there is likely to be confusion because of the desire of various government agencies to have in their own hand control, partial or complete, of short wave radio broadcasting to foreign nations. It is therefore important that the agency charged with responsibility for such broadcasting shall have clearly defined authority and accountability. Parallel or possibly competing efforts along the same line by other agencies, or censorship by other agencies, would seriously hamper operations. It would be as though the State Department had its own private tank corps, independent of the Army, or as though no Navy ship could move without the O.K. of the Department of Commerce." See memo, Sherwood to Donovan, 10 July 1941, Entry 110, Box 48, Folder 11.

2. Allman, "History: Far East, SI," 6, Box 6, Folder 17, Allman Papers.

3. OSS Data on Starr Project, Roll 91, A3304.

4. The London office of Starr's counter-Japanese division was designed to "maintain closest contact with Reuters, Jardine & Matheson, Butterfield & Swire, Lloyds, as many insurance men as possible, British intelligence agents, the Chinese Embassy, Hong Kong & Shanghai Bank, China Inland Mission and send all information via Embassy pouch." By this time, John Keswick of Jardine and Matheson had become SOE's chief for the China Commando Group, and Vallentine Killery of Butterfield and Swire had become the chief of SOE's Oriental mission.

5. Duff was born in China of Canadian missionary parents. A longtime associate of Starr's, Duff had been the director of Reliance Motors in Shanghai until December 1941, when the Japanese took over. Lusey had been in China for several years as a newspaperman, advertising agent, and radio engineer (personnel data on Starr's project, Roll 91, A3304).

6. Memo, William Kimball to Mr. Newson, 11 March 1942, Roll 69, A3304.

7. Memo, Hoover to Donovan, Roll 69, A3304, R69; also Hayden to Donovan re: conversation with Stilwell, 8 November 1942, Roll 137, A3304.

8. Donovan's order to Lusey, 11 March 1942, Roll 69, A3304.

9. Cable, Hayden to Donovan, 6 October 1942, Box 1, Folder 9, McHugh Papers. Miles once suggested to Washington that Gauss be replaced by Admiral Harry Ervin Yarnell as ambassador to China. See Miles to Metzel, 20 November 1942, RG 38, Miles Papers, Box 2.

The ensuing battle between the army and State Department, however, mainly focused on the issue of State Department personnel in the embassy "loaned" to Stilwell—John Paton Davies, John Service, David Barrett, and others—which in part was responsible for the rise of an "imperial" army headquarters and a weakened embassy, the rectification of which would later occur under a tough-minded new ambassador, General Hurley.

10. Gale to Hayden, 6 May 1942, Roll 41, M1642.

11. Memo, Robert Aura Smith of COI to Hayden, 4 May 1942, Roll 41, M1642.

12. Gale to Hayden, 6 May 1942, Roll 41, M1642.

13. Robert Smith to Hayden, 4 May 1942, Roll 41, M1642.

14. William Kimball memo, 13 August 1942, Entry 92, Box 30, Folder 18.

15. Fairbank's dual role was not discovered by the State Department until mid-November, as William Kimbal, Donovan's liaison with the department, reported to R&A chief William Langer and Donovan on 13 November 1942: "Some confusion and undue suspicion is being aroused [in the State Department] by the fact that many of Fairbank's cables deal with subjects which are completely foreign to the work of the Interdepartmental Committee. They refer specifically to his cable to IDC, No. 1173, which deals with expansion of personnel, funds, etc., obviously for activities which would have no relation to Interdepartmental Committee functions. These cables are received at State through regular channels and pass through the hands of the Far Eastern Division. Question is being aroused on the part of those several people who are not familiar with Fairbank's dual status. Potential embarrassment to Fairbank's activities may be in the making" (memo, Kimbal to Langer, Donovan, and David Bruce, 13 November 1942, Entry 92, Box 30, Folder 18).

16. For a complete text of the Dragon Plan, see Roll 64, A3304. The microfilmed text is of poor quality, but the text can be found in Entry 180.

17. Allman, "History: Far East, SI," Part I, 23, Box 6, Folder 17, Allman Papers, Hoover Institution.

Note that the copy at the National Archives has been sanitized by CIA, with all pages regarding OSS's Starr connection taken out. See the same title in Entry 99, Box 78, Folder 55.

18. Memo for Colonel Solborg, from G-2, 13 July 1942, Roll 64, A3304.

19. Dragon Plan, Roll 64, A3304.

20. McHugh's secret reports to Frank Knox, 5 and 11 October 1942, Box 1, Folder 9, McHugh Papers.

21. McHugh's secret report to Knox, 11 June 1942, Box 1, Folder 9, McHugh Papers.

22. Miles to Metzel and Legget, 20 November 1942, Box 1, Folder 9, McHugh Papers.

23. McHugh to Knox, 11 June 1942, Box 1, Folder 9, McHugh Papers.

24. Hayden to Donovan, 6 October 1942, Box 1, Folder 9, McHugh Papers.

25. McHugh to Knox, 9 July 1942, Box 1, Folder 9, McHugh Papers.

26. Hayden to Donovan, 6 October 1942, Box 1, Folder 9, McHugh Papers.

27. Ibid.

28. Ibid.

29. Letter, Chennault to Miles, 4 March 1958, Box 1, Folder 41, Miles Papers, Hoover Institution; also, Miles's unpublished manuscript "The Navy Launched a Dragon," chapter 24, 311, Naval War College.

30. Miles, *A Different Kind of War,* 47–48.

31. Ibid., 53.

32. Memo, Lusey to Donovan, 24 August 1942, Entry 139, Box 267, Folder 3934.

33. In his secret report to Donovan, Lusey severely criticized the top intelligence officer of the U.S. government in India and Afghanistan and wanted him replaced: "Major Gordon Enders, the Military Attaché at Kabul and the sole U.S. intelligence representative, is a bag of wind. He is well known in China for that. He thinks or tries to make one think, that he has everything in control; everyone eating from his hand. As a matter of fact, I think every one from the British to the Japs are fooling him." Lusey further reported that "I have several more vague indications that the Chinese and Indians are carrying on some kind of undercover skull-duggery" (letter, Lusey to Donovan, written on his way to China. Roll 69, A3304). Undoubt-edly, Tai Li's interest in setting up an intelligence net was a result of his vigilance against the British, especially on matters related to British influence in Tibet and Chinese Turkestan.

34. See cables between Lusey and Washington on the subject, Roll 138, A3304.

35. Tai Li gave this document to Admiral Yang Xuancheng, G-2 chief of Chinese Army, to leak to Lusey. Yang told Lusey that he personally believed this document. It is curious to note that Yang Xuancheng was known as the only official in the Chinese high command to openly disbelieve that Japan would attack the Soviets. See Huang Zengfu, "Admiral Yang Xuancheng, International Military Intelligence Expert" (Guoji Junshi Qingbao Zhuanjia Yangxuancheng), *Hunan Culture and History (Hunan Wenshi),* 1991, no. 42, 99–105.

36. Memo, Lusey to Donovan, undated (probably August 1942), subject: Russo-Japanese, Entry 139, Box 267, Folder 3934.

37. Memo, Allen W. Dulles to Hugh R. Wilson, 20 May 1942, Entry 139, Box 267, Folder 3934. Li Shizeng was best known for starting a large Study Abroad Movement after the May 4th Movement of 1919, resulting in many young Chinese students going to Europe, particu-larly France and Germany. Among those Chinese students in France and Germany were Deng Xiaoping, Zhou Enlai, Zhu De, Chen Yi, and Nie Yongzhen, who were recruited by the Comintern. Many, including Zhou and Deng, subsequently were sent to Moscow to receive training in the Lenin School. Li was decidedly an ally of T. V. Soong. During much of World War II, Li was a freelance diplomat for Chiang Kai-shek and closely associated with Allen Dulles. In 1948, Chiang appointed Li an adviser to the presidential palace of the Nationalist Government (Zhongtongfu Zizheng). When the Communists took over China in 1949, Li went to Switzerland, Dulles's wartime intelligence base. Li went to Taipei in 1956 and died of natural causes in 1973.

38. Memo, Donovan to J.P.W.C, subject: response to J.W.C. 45/D, forwarded on 31 October 1942 and included as an Enclosure to SECRET, J.P.W.C. 45/1. Also see Corson, *Armies of Ignorance,* 182–183.

39. Corson, *Armies of Ignorance,* 183.

40. Military Orders to establish OWI and OSS, 13 June 1942, Entry 110, Box 48, Folder 6.

41. For example, Lusey wrote to Donovan on the eve of his departure with Miles to the east coast to meet Tai Li at Pucheng: "I have developed some astonishing and valuable infor-mation [about Tai Li]. . . . I am being taken more and more into the confidence of General Dai Li's organization. . . . Dai's organization is very efficient and we can use it to great advan-tage" (letter, Lusey to Donovan, 23 May 1942, Box 4, Folder 2, Goodfellow Papers).

42. Miles once wrote to his superior in Washington regarding the sorry state of bureau-cratic feuding between OSS and OWI, "I am sorry that OSS and OWI are so separated back there, because in China it looks as tho the two are in the propaganda business together. Mac Fisher [of OWI] out here and I are the best of friends, and as long as he heads up OWI we can work fine together without getting in each other's hair" (letter, Miles to Jeff and Abie, 20 November 1942, RG 38, Miles Papers, Box 2, National Archives).

43. Memo for Colonel Donovan, from A. R. Lusey, subject: Tai-Li, undated, Entry 139, Box 267, Folder 3934.

44. Report of debriefing with Mr. X [Lusey] on 21 August 1942, dated 27 August 1942, Entry 139, Box 267, Folder 3934.

45. Four people—Colonels Goodfellow and Garland Williams of the United States and

Colonel Taylor and John Keswick of Great Britain, just ousted from China—participated in the negotiations. See record of discussion regarding collaboration between United States and British SOE, 17 June 1942, and JCS 86/1 "Agreements Between OSS and British SOE," 26 August 1942, record of JCS 30th meeting, Item 4, Roll 94, A3304.

46. Price briefing of Lusey, 21 August 1942, Entry 139, Box 267, Folder 3934.

47. Memo, Donovan for JPWC, 24 October 1942, forwarded 31 October 1942.

48. During the hectic days of the North African Invasion, he started his daily staff meeting by reading aloud a chapter of a history of the War of 1812. One time after reading the war history, Donovan told his subordinates, "They haven't burned the White House yet. You know, boys, no one in their senses would have bet a dollar that the United States would survive. England had every facility to destroy us completely, yet here we are. Our country, I believe, has a destiny and a meaning in human history that no nation has ever before possessed. Nothing can ever stop us, but the will of God" (Lovell, *Of Spies and Stratagems,* 186–187).

49. Memo, Donovan to Roosevelt, #94, 22 December 1941, Entry 110, Box 48, Folder 5.

50. Memo, Donovan to Richard Heppner, 2 February 1945, Entry 154, Box 170, Folder 2941.

51. Due to Donovan's demand—over complaints from Colonel Richard Heppner, chief of OSS/China—a large number of horses, mules, and dogs were prioritized into the coveted hump tonnage and flown over the Himalayas to China. On his third trip to China in August 1945, Donovan took great pride and satisfaction in inspecting his mounted commandos and dog guerrillas. See photos of Chinese troops with dogs and cables between Heppner and Donovan on the subject in Roll 45, M1642.

52. Miles, *A Different Kind of War,* 43.

53. Lovell, *Of Spies,* 167–168.

54. "Instructions Regarding Additional Activities," Purnell to Miles, 21 September 1942, RG 38, Miles Papers, Box 2, National Archives.

55. Murphy to Eifler, 22 September 1942, Entry 139, Box 267, Folder 3934.

56. Letter, Donovan to Hayden, 21 September 1942, Entry 139, Box 267, Folder 3934.

57. Memo, Donovan to Fairbank, 21 September 1942, Entry 139, Box 267, Folder 3934.

58. Memo, "FE4—Friendship," RG 38, Miles Papers, Box 2, National Archives. Donovan later considered the Tolstoy mission useless. See Donovan's penciled note on Conyers Read's SO history, 18 December 1946, Entry 99, Box 78, Folder 57.

Chapter 4. Of Schemes and SACO

1. Secret memo, Lusey to Donovan, 14 September 1942, Entry 139, Box 267, Folder 3934.

2. James Murphy to Eifler, 22 September 1942, Entry 139, Box 267, Folder 3934.

3. Donovan to Hayden, 21 September 1942, Entry 139, Box 267, Folder 3934.

4. Memo, Donovan to Fairbank, 20 September 1942, dated 21 September 1942, Entry 139, Box 267, Folder 3934.

5. Secret memo, Lusey to Donovan, 14 September 1942, Entry 139, Box 267, Folder 3934.

6. Memo, Ernest B. Price to Hugh R. Wilson, subject, interview with "Major Shaw," 2 September 1942, Entry 139, Box 267, Folder 3934.

7. Ibid.

8. Price, "Questions to Be Considered Before Suggested Conference with Major Shaw," 2 September 1942, Entry 139, Box 267, Folder 3934.

9. Letter, Price to FDR, 8 October 1942, PSF, safe file: OSS, Box 4, Folder "OSS," FDR Library.

10. Memo, FDR to Currie, 15 October 1942, PSF, OSS, Box 4, FDR Library.

11. Memo for the president, from Currie, re: letter from Ernest B. Price, 29 October 1942. PSF, OSS, Box 4, FDR Library.

12. Ibid.

13. Memo, James Murphy to Lusey, 22 December 1942, Roll 69, A3304.

14. On 12 October 1942, Miles was notified by the Navy Department, via cable, of only his new title as OSS chief in China; he was not given any details at all. Cable #131255, from COMINCH to ALUSNA Chungking, 12 October 1942, RG 38, Miles Papers, National Archives.

15. Cable, Miles to CominCh, 14 November 1942, NCR 8710-s, RG 38, Miles Papers, Box 2, National Archives.

16. Cable, Hayden to Donovan, 17 November 1942, Roll 137, A3304.

17. Memo, Keswick to Huntington, 26 October 1942, RG 38, Miles Papers, Box 2, National Archives.

18. See the extremely anti-Chinese, pro-British correspondence from Ilia Tolstoy, the team's leader, to General Marshall, 16 May 1943, RG 493, Record of China-Burma-India Theater of Operations, U.S. Army (CBI), Record of Commanding General (Stilwell), Personal Messages Files, Box 1, Suitland Archives Center, National Archives. Regarding the Tolstoy mission to Tibet, Miles wrote to the Navy Department that he was trying to "find out what I am expected to do with these Tibetan explorers. Maybe they can help me launch a battleship up there next year. I wonder where we stand there. The British are jealous of their control of Tibet, and we don't want anything to do with its control and the Chinese do. And the Tibetans don't want anyone in there" (Miles "letter to Jeff and Abie," undated but certainly before December 1942, RG 38, Miles Papers, Box 2, National Archives).

19. Memo, Donovan to Brigadier General John R. Deane, assistant chief of staff, 22 December 1942, Roll 41, M1642.

20. Memo, Metzel to Miles, 7 February 1943, RG38, Miles Papers, Box 1, Folder 1, National Archives.

Steinberg became a crony of Miles and grew even more famous after the war in the world of cartoon illustration. Steinberg and his many cartoons also featured prominently in Miles's book, *A Different Kind of War*.

21. Ibid. OSS possessed about half a million of the Woolworth pistols at the time. Many of these assassination guns slipped into China during World War II, eventually falling into the hands of the Chinese Communists, who were in dire need of weapons due to Chiang Kai-shek's blockade. The pistols thus greatly enhanced the business of political assassination.

22. Metzel letter to Miles, 20 October 1942, RG 38, Miles Papers, Box 2, National Archives.

23. Miles to Metzel, 2 December 1942, RG 38, Miles Papers, Box 2, National Archives.

24. Hayden to Victor (Donovan), 8 November 1942, Roll 137, A3304.

25. Cable, CominChi to Miles, 12 November 1942, RG 38, Miles Papers, Box 2, National Archives.

26. Cable, Miles to Donovan and Purnell, 16 November 1942, NCR 00149-S, RG 38, Miles Papers, Box 2, National Archives.

27. Cable, Miles to Donovan and Purnell, 14 November 1942, NCR 8710-S, RG 38, Miles Papers, Box 2, National Archives.

28. Miles to Metzel, 2 December 1942, RG 38, Miles Papers, Box 2, Folder 3, National Archives.

29. Miles to Jeff [Metzel] and Abie [Leggett], 20 November 1942, RG 38, Miles Papers, Box 2, National Archives. Realizing that Hayden had just published a book highly critical of General MacArthur's Philippine defense policy, Miles decided to punish the "busybody" scholar by sending him to MacArthur's headquarters in Australia. Donovan eventually agreed to Miles's decision and Hayden was ordered to Australia in late December.

30. Letter, Donovan to Miles, 21 September 1942, Entry 139, Box 267, Folder 3934.

31. Allman, "History: Far East, SI."

32. Clyde Sargent was a Ph.D. candidate in the history department at Columbia University. In China, he was writing his dissertation, which was a translation of a section from the

Chinese text of Former Han history (Qian Han Shi). Sargent soon joined the army and became a chief operative in training Korean exiles in Xian for the eventual penetration of the Japanese inner zone.

33. Letter, Miles to Metzel, 1 August 1943, RG 38, Miles Papers, Box 2, National Archives.

34. Cable, Miles to Cominch, 19 November 1942, RG 38, Miles Papers, Box 2, National Archives.

35. Memo, Huntington to Donovan, 22 November 1942, Entry 139, Box 267, Folder 3937.

36. Memo, Donovan to Huntington, 26 November 1942, Entry 139, Box 267, Folder 3937.

37. Memo, Miles to Tai Li, 19 December 1942, RG 38, Miles Papers, Box 2, National Archives.

38. Letter, Miles to Metzel, 2 December 1942, RG 38, Miles Papers, Box 1, Folder 3, National Archives.

39. Ibid.

40. Memo, Miles to Tai Li, 19 December 1942, RG 38, Miles Papers, Box 2, National Archives.

41. Letter, Miles to Metzel, 2 December 1942, RG 38, Miles Papers, Box 1, Folder 3, National Archives.

42. Memo, Huntington to Donovan, 9 December 1942, subject: Far East—OSS Activities through channels other than Captain Miles. Entry 139, Box 267, Folder 3937.

43. Memo, Metzel to Huntington, 11 December 1942, RG 38, Miles Papers, Box 2, National Archives; also in Box 1, Folder 9, McHugh Papers.

44. Metzel to Miles, 7 February 1943, RG 38, Miles Papers, Box 1, Folder 1, National Archives.

45. Memo, Halliwell to Donovan, 23 January 1943, Entry 139, Box 267, Folder 3937.

46. Metzel to Miles, 7 February 1943, RG 38, Miles Papers, Box 1, Folder 1, National Archives.

47. Eifler was supposed to be stationed in Chungking at the U.S. embassy with a cover assignment as assistant military attaché.

48. Memo, Lusey to Donovan, Entry 139, Box 267, Folder 3934.

49. This topic is worth a study in itself. For a cursory look at the Shanghai connection with British intelligence, see William J. West, *Spymaster* (New York: Wynwood, 1990), on Roger Hollis's sojourn in Shanghai.

50. Memo, Jerrel to the director of naval intelligence, subject: "Some Notes on Foreign Diplomatic Representation in Chungking," 27 August 1945, RG 38, Alusna Letters—1945, ONI-FE-China/Malay Desk, National Archives.

51. See *Intelligence Report,* secret, ONI-215-400, Serial 65-S-46, subject: Soviet personalities in China, 10 November 1946, 40. RG 38, Entry ONI, Box 2, Folder "Nanking-Secret-2," National Archives. General Pechkoff's relationship with the Soviets was one of the major reasons for China's reluctance to abandon an alliance with De Gaulle's partisan enemy, General Giraud. The Giraud–De Gaulle internecine struggle further complicated all the China-based intelligence operations in French Indochina under Tai Li and OSS. Pechkoff stayed in Chungking as De Gaulle's chief of the French military mission in China until the fall of 1943, when he was sent to Algeria. In June 1944 he became the ambassador of French Committee for National Liberation to China. After the war, Pechkoff headed the French military mission to Tokyo.

52. See card file on Pavlovski in folder entitled "Russia's Espionage in China," RG 38, Records of the Office of Chief of Naval Operations-ONI, Foreign Intelligence, Far East, Box 2, National Archives.

53. Shoyet was formerly a U.S. Army officer who had been "for some time a dealer in illegal arms acting on instructions of the Comintern." Shoyet disguised his arms as railway

materials to ship to Pavlovski, who worked as a railway engineer. See card file on Shoyet in folder entitled "Russia's Espionage in China," RG 38, Record of the Office of Chief of Naval Operations-ONI, Foreign Intelligence, Far East, Box 2, National Archives.

54. Card file on Pavlovski, "Russia's Espionage in China."

55. OSS report, from Calcutta, subject: Tai Li operations in China, 26 June 1944. This was an intelligence report largely based upon Arthur Duff's testimony to Carl Hoffman. Entry 148, Box 25, Folder 368, Chungking-SO-Op-2.

56. Cable, Stilwell to Donovan, 29 September 1942, RG 493, Records of American Military Mission to China, AMMISCA VI (Magruder Mission), outgoing Messages, file # 1199, Suitland Record Center, National Archives.

57. Memo, Hayden to Donovan, 6 October 1942, Box 1, Folder 9, McHugh Papers.

58. Smith, *Secret History,* 248. Petro Pavlovski was eventually expelled from Washington due to strong protest from the Chinese embassy.

59. Memo, Magruder to Captain Pugliese, 9 June 1945, Roll 71, M1642. This is a biographical sheet submitted by Magruder himself for promotion.

60. Each had married a daughter of Jacob Gould Schurman, a former president of Cornell University (1892–1920) and former U.S. minister to China. See card file on Pavlovski, "Russia's Espionage in China."

61. Letter, Knox to McHugh, 28 August 1942, Box 1, Folder 9, McHugh Papers.

62. Memo, McHugh to Knox, 5 October 1942. Box 1, Folder 9, McHugh Papers.

63. OSS records indicate that months later McHugh "was practically given the bum's rush from China" and that some believed it was because McHugh had "carried on some sort of nefarious activity over there and the Chinese pounced on the first thing they could get" (memo, Hoffman to Metzel, requesting more information on why McHugh was suddenly kicked out of China, 3 November 1943, Box 1, Folder 9, McHugh Papers).

64. Stratton, *Army-Navy Game,* 49–50.

65. Ibid.

66. Memo, Miles to Purnell, Metzel, and Legget, 1 January 1943, RG 38, Miles Papers, Box 2, National Archives.

67. Metzel to Miles, 3 January 1943, RG 38, Miles Papers, Box 2, National Archives.

68. Cable, Purnell to Tai Li, 27 January 1943, RG 38, Miles Papers, Box 2, National Archives. Arthur Duff was on his way from India to Chungking at this moment, and Tai Li's people had been most closely watching his every step, as a surveillance schedule later shown by Tai Li to Miles's radio chief R. A. Kotrla indicated (memo, Kotrla to Miles, Subject: List of CNAC Passengers other than Chinese traveling to and from China, 3 October 1943. RG 38, Miles Papers, Box 2, National Archives).

69. Cable, War Department to AMMISCA, NR.2146, 16 February 1943, RG 38, Miles Papers, Box 2, National Archives.

70. Cable, King to Miles, 16 February 1943, RG 38, Miles Papers, Box 2, National Archives.

71. Cable, Miles to King, 21 February 1943, RG 38, Miles Papers, Box 2, National Archives.

72. Stilwell to AGWAR, 21 February 1943, RG 493 record of China-Burma-India theater of operations, U.S. Army, record of commanding general, personal message file, Box 1, Suitland Record Center, National Archives.

73. Smith, *Secret History,* 284.

74. Cable, Miles to King, 21 February 1943, RG 38, Miles Papers, Box 2, National Archives.

75. When Miles arrived in Washington, Donovan, excluded so far from active participation in the drafting of SACO, treated Miles to "lunch at the 1925 F Club and dinner at General Donovan's wood-guarded residence in Georgetown." This was the first time Miles had seen Donovan personally and the impression was certainly positive; Miles described Donovan as "a big man—fast, alert, brilliant, and quick in making decisions." Donovan even gave Miles a

tour of OSS headquarters, during which Miles found some of the OSS officers "racist" and incompetent (Miles, *A Different Kind of War*, 116–119).

76. Ibid., 115.

77. Memo, Leahy to Miles, RG 38, Miles Papers, Box 2, National Archives.

78. Miles, *A Different Kind of War*, 116.

Chapter 5. OSS in an Army-Navy Game

1. Miles, *A Different Kind of War*, 118.

2. Hayden's report to Donovan, regarding "A Certain Agreement," Box 1, Folder 10, McHugh Papers.

3. See Donovan's definition of SI and SO, Corson, *Armies of Ignorance*, 182–183.

4. Meeting memo by Bowden to Donovan, 22 February 1943, Entry 99, Box 78, Folder 55.

5. Smith, *Shadow Warriors*, 133.

6. William M. Leary, "Portrait of an Intelligence Officer: James McHugh in China, 1937–1942," in William B. Cogar, ed., *Naval History: The Seventh Symposium of the U.S. Naval Academy* (Wilmington, Del.: Scholarly Resources, 1988), 261.

7. McHugh's employment within OSS headquarters at this time was kept ultrasecret. In 1992, I discovered an innocuous "OSS Request for Travel Order," dated 11 January 1943, in the McHugh Papers in Ithaca, New York. It was a travel order for McHugh, whose title was listed as "Chief, SI, Far East, Washington, D.C." See the document in Box 2, Folder 4, McHugh Papers.

This means that Donovan had secretly hired McHugh because the official request for McHugh's employment in OSS was not given to Secretary of the Navy Frank Knox until 6 September 1943.

8. Report by McHugh and Allman, "Survey of Accomplishments of *Shanghai Evening Post and Mercury* Enterprise to Date," 1 July 1944, Box 2, Folder 1, McHugh Papers.

9. Later purged by Stilwell for his criticism, Cooper was banned from serving in China by General Marshall (Smith, *Secret History*, 259).

Chennault was also press-conscious and was surrounded by star reporters like Joseph Alsop, who became a master of image building.

10. Cable, Hearn to Marshall, in RG 218, records of the Joint Chiefs of Staff, chairman's [Leahy's] files, Box 21, Folder 137 "Misc. Memos, 42–44," National Archives.

11. Memo, Roosevelt to Leahy, in RG 218, records of the Joint Chiefs of Staff, chairman's [Leahy's] files, Box 21, Folder 137 "Misc. Memos, 42–44," National Archives.

12. Cable, Hearn to Washington, in RG 218, records of the Joint Chiefs of Staff, chairman's [Leahy's] files, Box 21, Folder 137 "Misc. Memos, 42–44," National Archives.

13. Memo, Marshall to Leahy and White House, in RG 218, records of the Joint Chiefs of Staff, chairman's [Leahy's] files, Box 21, Folder 137 "Misc. Memos, 42–44," National Archives.

14. Opper died in April 1994. The *New York Times* obituary related: "A native of Manhattan, Mr. Opper, who was known as Fritz, graduated from Amherst College and started his journalistic career with a news service in Washington and a Scripps-Howard newspaper in Toledo, Ohio. He went to the Far East to report for United Press and the Japan Times. After Pearl Harbor, the Japanese imprisoned him in Shanghai. He was freed in a prisoner exchange. Mr. Opper became the Far East correspondent for ABC after the war and, in 1946, the network's bureau chief in London. He joined Radio Free Europe in 1953 and retired in 1972" (*New York Times*, 19 April 1994).

Gould had served as editor for *Shanghai Evening Post and Mercury* and *Ta Mei Wan Pao* until the attack on Pearl Harbor, when the Japanese took over Shanghai. Until 1941 he was also chief Far East correspondent for the *Christian Science Monitor*. Gould was closely associated with T. V. Soong and Hu Shih.

15. McHugh and Allman report.

16. Bradley Smith claims that *SEPM,* as an intelligence organization, was unknown to Chinese intelligence (*Shadow Warriors,* 133), but that may not be true, for Tai Li and Miles constantly discussed and made jokes about the newspaper.

17. The McHugh-Allman report states, "They [seek] to turn over vital information to the places where it would do the most good in China, making little effort to send it back to America. That is how things have worked out for the most part."

For British MI6's direct effort in running the *Shanghai Evening Post and Mercury* intelligence network in China, see Smith, *Shadow Warriors,* 258.

18. Stratton, *Army-Navy Game,* 109.

19. Memo, L. C. Irvine to Murphy, 19 October 1943, Entry 92, Box 30, Folder 18.

20. Secret memo, Henry T. Jarrell to director of naval intelligence, subject: security, 17 January 1945, RG 38, ALUSNA letters, ONI-FE. China/Malay Desk, National Archives.

21. John Paton Davies Jr., *Dragon by the Tail: American, British, Japanese, and Russian Encounters with China and One Another* (New York: Norton, 1972), 285–286.

22. Quoted in Stratton, *Army-Navy Game,* 88–89.

23. U.S. State Department, *Foreign Relations of the United States* (FRUS), 1943, 214–216.

24. Quoted in Stratton, *Army-Navy Game,* 88–89.

25. Davies, *Dragon by the Tail,* 286.

26. But this was only the overt staff for such a project. Within a couple of months, Davies would have frequent secret contact with two Marines: Lieutenant Colonel James McHugh, now back in Washington, and Evans Carlson, the first U.S. official ever to visit the Communist headquarters in Yenan in 1938.

27. Davies, *Dragon by the Tail,* 286.

28. Phillips report, Entry 110, Box 52, Folder 14. The report was kept secret until 2 September 1944, when Senator Albert B. Chandler of Kentucky made it public. The next day the *New York Times* ran the full text.

29. Robert Warren interview with Heppner, 1944, Entry 110, Box 52, Folder 14.

30. Memo, Stilwell to OPD, 15 May 1943, Entry 110, Box 51, Folder 2.

31. Davies, *Dragon by the Tail,* 287.

32. Cables between Heppner and Donovan, 24 and 25 June 1943, Entry 110, Box 51, Folder 2.

33. Memo, "Special Code to Be Used in Communications with Heppner and Davies," Entry 146, Box 192, Folder 2723.

34. Ferris to Stilwell, 24 March 1943, RG 493, record of China-Burma-India theater of operations, U.S. Army (CBI), records of commanding general (Stilwell), personal message file, Box 1, Suitland Record Center, National Archives.

35. Stilwell Jr.'s cable to Ferris and Pape, 2 April 1943, RG 493, record of China-Burma-India theater of operations, U.S. Army (CBI), records of commanding general (Stilwell), personal message file, Box 1, Suitland Record Center, National Archives.

36. Hearn to Stilwell and Ferris, 2 April 1943, RG 493, record of China-Burma-India theater of operations, U.S. Army (CBI), records of commanding general (Stilwell), personal message file, Box 1, Suitland Record Center, National Archives.

37. Cable, #576, by Thomas Hearn and Dickey, undated, RG 493, record of China-Burma-India theater of operations, U.S. Army (CBI), records of commanding general (Stilwell), personal message file, Box 1, Suitland Record Center, National Archives.

38. Cable, Stilwell to Ferris, 21 June 1943, RG 493, record of China-Burma-India theater of operations, U.S. Army (CBI), records of commanding general (Stilwell), personal message file, Box 1, Suitland Record Center, National Archives.

39. Cable, Ferris to Pape, #585, 19 June 1943, RG 493, record of China-Burma-India theater of operations, U.S. Army (CBI), records of commanding general (Stilwell), personal message file, Box 1, Suitland Record Center, National Archives.

40. After the war, Duncan Lee was found to have been a Communist agent inside OSS;

he soon fled to Canada. To this day, Donovan's inner circle is certain that Lee was a Communist mole (interview with Edwin Putzell, 23 May 1994). In October 1995, when the National Security Agency released the second batch of the Venona intercepts of Soviet KGB communications during World War II, Lee was further identified as a source for Soviet intelligence.

41. Marshall to Stilwell, #584, 19 June 1943, RG 493, record of China-Burma-India theater of operations, U.S. Army (CBI), records of commanding general (Stilwell), personal message file, Box 1, Suitland Record Center, National Archives.

42. Cable, Pape to Stilwell, re JICA, 22 June 1943, RG 493, record of China-Burma-India theater of operations, U.S. Army (CBI), records of commanding general (Stilwell), personal message file, Box 1, Suitland Record Center, National Archives.

43. Memo, Magruder to General John Deane, Secretary of JCS, 15 June 1943, Entry 146, Box 192, Folder 2723.

44. Cable, Davies to Stilwell, re Miles's opposition to Heppner appointment, #622, 2 July 1943, RG 493, record of China-Burma-India theater of operations, U.S. Army (CBI), records of commanding general (Stilwell), personal message file, Box 2, Suitland Record Center, National Archives.

45. Davies, *Dragon by the Tail,* 285.

46. Memo, from Lieutenant Commander R. David Halliwell to Donovan, subject: open questions on Eifler mission, 22 March 1943, Entry 146, Box 192, Folder 2723.

47. Memo, from Carl Hoffman to Colonel Buxton and Commander Halliwell, subject: cable no. 48 from Eifler, 23 June 1943, Entry 146, Box 192, Folder 2723.

48. Marshall to Stilwell and Ferris, #695, 28 July 1943, RG 493, record of China-Burma-India theater of operations, U.S. Army (CBI), records of commanding general (Stilwell), personal message file, Box 2, Suitland Record Center, National Archives.

49. Cable, Marshall to Stilwell, 29 July 1943, RG 493, record of China-Burma-India theater of operations, U.S. Army (CBI), records of commanding general (Stilwell), personal message file, Box 1, Suitland Record Center, National Archives.

50. Appendix to enclosure A, "Estimate for U.S. Psychological Warfare Operations Against the Japanese Within the Asiatic Theater, Statement of the Problem," by James Rogers, Entry 99, Box 80, Folder 70.

51. Enclosure B, memo from Donovan to JCS, subject: "Special Military Plan for U.S. Psychological Warfare Operations Against the Japanese Within the Asiatic Theater," 15 February 1943, Entry 99, Box 80, Folder 70.

52. Joint Chiefs of Staff, JCS 245, "Special Military Plan for U.S. Psychological Warfare Operations Against the Japanese Within the Asiatic Theater," Entry 99, Box 80, Folder 70.

53. See, for example, cables between Marshall and Stilwell, 13 and 23 June 1943, RG 493, record of China-Burma-India theater of operations, U.S. Army (CBI), records of commanding general (Stilwell), personal message file, Box 1, Suitland Record Center, National Archives.

54. "Proposed OSS Plan for a Radio and Intelligence Network for Use with the 10th and 14th Air Forces in China in Combating Japanese Shipping and Plane Movements, based on the Request Made by Brigadier General Davidson in a Conference with the Communications Branch," Entry 146, Box 192, Folder 2723.

55. Bruce Reynold, "A Tangled Web: The OSS China-Based Thailand Operation," unpublished article, prepared for the August 1991 Meeting of the Pacific Coast Branch-American Historical Association, Kona, Hawaii, 12.

56. Eifler memo, "Stilwell's Reports Ju. 1942–Oct. '44," in Troy Papers, RG 263, Box 12, Folder 98, National Archives.

57. Minutes of meeting held Wednesday, 16 June 1943, at General Stilwell's home, subject: OSS, Entry 110, Box 51, Folder 2.

58. Cable, Marshall to Stilwell, 2 July 1943, RG 493, Record of China-Burma-India Theater of Operations, U.S. Army (CBI), Records of Commanding General (Stilwell), Personal Message File, Box 3, Suitland Record Center, National Archives.

59. Letter, Hoffman to Heppner, 25 August 1943, subheading "Jimmy-Carlson," Entry 146, Box 192, Folder 2723.

60. Ibid.

61. Cable, Heppner to Buxton, 12 September 1943, Entry 146, Box 192, Folder 2723.

62. See, for example, Donovan's memo for Heppner on "Jurisdiction over United States Forces in Foreign Lands," in Entry 146, Box 192, Folder 2723; also in the James Donovan Papers at the Hoover Institution. Putzell was Donovan's confidential secretary. Duncan Lee was for a while Heppner's aide in Stilwell's camp, before he was accused of being a Communist agent. James Donovan had a most colorful legal career: chief counsel for OSS during World War II, chief counsel at the Nuremberg Trial, and later the defense lawyer for the Soviet spy Rudolf Abel.

63. Memo, Metzel to Hoffman, 20 September 1943, Entry 146, Box 192, Folder 2723.

64. "Secret War Diary," 15 September 1943, Entry 148, Box 24, Folder 360; also memo, Hoffman to Otto Doering, subject: "Heppner's Relations with Mary," Entry 146, Box 192, Folder 2723.

65. Memo, Putzell to Donovan, "Conference Concerning SI Plans for the Far East," 5 October 1943, Entry 146, Box 192, Folder 2723.

66. JCS Directive 115/11/D, RG 218, CCS 385. (2-8-42) Section 1, Part 7, National Archives.

67. "Secret War Diary," 1 August 1943, Section I: Personnel, 1. Entry 148, Box 24, Folder 357.

68. Memo, to Otto Doering, subject: "Heppner's Relations with Mary," Entry 146, Box 192, Folder 2723.

69. Miles to Metzel, 1 August 1943, RG 38, Miles Papers, Box 2, National Archives.

70. Donovan to Hoffman, 30 August 1943, Roll 71, M1642.

71. See, for example, Report by Lieutenant William Brewster to Major Carl Hoffman, subject: status of "Mary," 20 October 1943. Entry 139, Box 192, Folder 2547.

72. "Secret War Diary," 1 December 1943, Entry 148, Box 24, Folder 365. Miles's trip to India was mostly about securing a smooth supply line between India and Chungking. His meeting with Mountbatten caused alarm in the U.S. Army contingent under General Albert Wedemeyer, who was Mountbatten's deputy supreme commander and was much antagonized by Mountbatten's insistence that all clandestine forces in India, both American and British, be subject to overall British control. On the insistence of Heppner, who was then living in the same bungalow as Wedemeyer, Wedemeyer expelled Miles's representative in New Dehli, Hal Williams.

73. "SACO," Entry 148, Box 14, Folder 194.

74. Ibid.

75. Ibid.

76. Ibid.

77. Ibid.

78. "Secret War Diary," 1 December 1943, Entry 148, Box 24, Folder 365.

79. Smith, *Secret History,* 258.

80. Brown, *Wild Bill Donovan,* 411–412.

81. Huang Tianmai was Tai Li's private "foreign minister." Huang had lived in Europe as a diplomat for the Nationalist government. He had a long-standing personal feud with Yang Jie, Chiang Kai-shek's one-time ambassador to Moscow. Huang was thrown into jail by Chiang Kai-shek as a result of Yang Jie's accusation that he had embezzled public funds. Tai Li appealed to Chiang and had Huang Tianmai released from jail, thus gaining a stalwart. Yang Jie later joined Communist intelligence and was assassinated by Tai Li's followers in Hong Kong in the late 1940s.

82. However, in a later interview, Tai Li's chief interpreter at SACO, Eddie Liu summed up Tai Li's view on Donovan: "It would be erroneous to say Gen Tai thought either highly or lowly of Col. Donovan. He might have had a lot of respect for the colonel as an intelligence

officer, but I know he didn't have a high opinion of him in relation to his knowledge of the particular situation in China at that time" (quoted in Stratton, *Army-Navy Game,* 134–135).

83. Brown, *Wild Bill Donovan,* 416–417.

84. Letter, Miles to Metzel, 10 December 1943, RG 38, Miles Papers, Box 1, National Archives.

85. Ibid

86. Ibid.

87. There has been much historical speculation about what Tai Li actually said here. There are two popular versions. In the first, from Edmond Taylor, *Awakening from History* (Boston: Gambit Incorporated, 1969), 347, General Donovan says, "I said to him [Tai Li], 'General, I want you to know that I am going to send my men into China whether you like it or not. I know that you can have them murdered one by one, but I want you to know that will not deter me.' "

The second version is from Oliver Caldwell's *A Secret War,* which was accepted by Roy Stratton's *Army-Navy Game,* 130–132:

TAI LI:	If OSS tries to operate outside of SACO, I will kill your agents.
DONOVAN:	For every one of our agents you kill, we will kill one of your generals.
TAI LI:	You can't talk to me like that!
DONOVAN:	I am talking to you like that!

The intensity of the meeting between Donovan and Tai Li has been grossly exaggerated. Neither of the above versions is true. Conversations such as these never took place. The first version came from Donovan's bluffing Mountbatten over opening up India to OSS operations. The second does not come even close to any archival record. Caldwell's book is highly unreliable and Caldwell himself admits in the book that he knew this conversation only from a secondary source. Moreover, had such conversation really taken place, Miles, Donovan's prominent detractor, who was actually at the scene, would likely have noted it in his detailed book, *A Different Kind of War.*

American newspapermen were essentially responsible for propagandizing Donovan's "toughness" with Tai Li during his trip to China.

88. Miles, *A Different Kind of War,* 169.

89. Qiao Jiacai, *Selected Writings,* 2: 315–316.

90. Stratton, *Army-Navy Game,* 130–132.

91. Miles to Metzel, 10 December 1943, RG 38, Miles Papers, Box 1, National Archives.

92. Ibid.

93. Ibid.

94. Ibid.

95. Ibid.

96. Memo, Miles to Knox, Subject: SACO agreement, Article XVIII, 9 December 1943, RG 38, Miles Papers, Box 1, National Archives.

97. Miles to Metzel, 10 December 1943, RG 38, Miles Papers, Box 1, National Archives.

98. Stratton, *Army-Navy Game,* 130–131.

99. Memo of conversations, Chungking, China, 5 December 1943, Roll 89, A3304.

100. Stratton, *Army-Navy Game,* 130–131

101. Ibid.

102. Brown, *Wild Bill Donovan,* 412–413.

103. Memo, Donovan to Hoffman, from Nazira, undated, Roll 89, A3304.

104. Memo, Donovan to Stilwell, 10 December 1943, Roll 89, A3304.

105. According to Heppner's own account, his appointment to Mountbatten's theater

was a "cover and deception" measure secretly worked out by Stilwell and Donovan during the Cairo conference, with the aim of diverting British interference and hamstringing Stilwell's own "purely American activities" (interview of Heppner by Warren, 9, Entry 110, Box 52, Folder 14).

106. Cable, Hoffman to Metzel, 7 December 1943, RG 38, Miles Papers, Box 2, National Archives.

107. "Minutes of Conference Held as a Result of Instructions by General Tai Li and General Donovan During Their Meeting of December 3rd and 4th, 1943," 9 December 1943, RG 38, Miles Papers, Box 2, National Archives.

108. Memo to Tai Li, 10 December 1943, RG 38, Miles Papers, Box 2, National Archives; also the same document in Roll 89, A3304.

109. Hoffman's log of tour of duty in China, Roll 89, A3304

110. Fairbank had been constantly warned by Miles to stop any association with Wang Pengsheng (Fairbank, *Chinabound*, 218).

111. After the expulsion of the China Commando Group by the Chinese in 1942, SOE turned to Tai Li's rival, Wang Pengsheng, for cooperation. Eventually the British were responsible for one-third of the institute's entire budget (Cruickshank, *SOE in the Far East*, 151).

The Shanghai station of Wang Pengsheng's intelligence organization was run by a senior Communist intelligence officer by the name of Lu Jiuzhi, who had been Richard Sorge's assistant in Tokyo and at the time was the son-in-law of Chiang Kai-shek's second wife, Ms. Chen Jieru.

112. Proposed JCS cable to Stilwell via Admiral Horne, 10 November 1943, RG 38, Miles Papers, Box 2, National Archives.

113. Cable to Miles, 19 December 1943, RG 38, Miles Papers, Box 2, National Archives.

114. Metzel to Miles, 21 December 1943, RG 38, Miles Papers, Box 2, National Archives.

115. Purnell to Miles, undated, RG 38, Miles Papers, Box 2, National Archives.

116. Secret "Specific Directive to OSS," received from General Stilwell by Major Hoffman, 31 December 1943, Entry 110, Box 52, Folder 11.

117. Gauss's secret letter to Hull, subject: status of Captain M. E. Miles, U.S.N., naval observer of the embassy in China, 6 January 1944, RG 38, Miles Papers, Box 1, National Archives.

118. Headquarters of the commander in chief, United States Fleet, Cominch file, "Comments on Chungking Conversations of 5 December 1943, RG 38, Miles Papers, Box 2, National Archives.

119. Draft SACO minutes, 7 February 1944, prepared by Halliwell and presented to Metzel on 11 February 1944, RG 38, Miles Papers, Box 2, National Archives.

120. While in Moscow, Donovan was treated lavishly by his counterpart at the NKVD, General Fitin. See Brown, *Wild Bill Donovan*, 422–424.

121. Aide memoir of SACO meeting with Admiral Horne, by Halliwell, 24 February 1944, RG 38, Miles Papers, Box 2, National Archives.

122. Ibid.

123. Ibid.

124. Ibid.

125. Cable, Miles to Purnell, 17 December 1943, NCR 7737, 171115Z, RG 38, Miles Papers, Box 2, National Archives.

126. Aide memoir of SACO meeting, 24 February 1944.

127. Stratton, *Army-Navy Game,* 133. Note that Stratton misdates the document as 12 December 1943. Donovan did not express his idea of withdrawing from SACO to Admiral Horne until the 7 February 1944 meeting.

128. Stratton, *Army-Navy Game,* 147–148.

129. Miles, *A Different Kind of War,* 207–208.

Chapter 6. OSS Trisected

1. Report by Carl Hoffman on SACO, 13 December 1943, Roll 89, A3304.

2. Letter, Tai Li to Donovan, 10 December 1943, Roll 115, M1642.

3. Donovan's reply to Tai Li's letters of 10 December 1943 and 6 January 1944, dated 10 March 1944, Roll 115, M1642.

4. Report from Carl Hoffman on SACO, 13 December 1943, Roll 89, A3304.

5. Ibid.

6. Hykes's report to Hall, 4, Entry 84, Box 2, Folder "SACO Papers."

7. Hoffman's log of tour of duty in SACO, 22 and 27 February 1944, Roll 89, A3304.

8. Memo for Major Hoffman, 15 December 1943, documentary attachment No. 1, in memorandum to Lt. Col. Robert Hall from Hykes, subject: review of S.I. activities under SACO, December 1943–April 1944, dated 14 April 1944, Entry 84, Box 2, Folder "SACO Papers."

9. Hoffman's log of tour of duty, 11, Roll 89, A3304.

10. Hykes's report, 2, Entry 84, Box 2, Folder "SACO Papers."

11. Hykes's report to Hall, 4, Entry 84, Box 2, Folder "SACO Papers."

12. "Plan for the Establishment of a Research Group in China to Collaborate with the Office of Strategic Services," and Doering's proposed messages to Xiao Bo, 1 December 1942, Roll 41, M1642.

13. Memo, Remer to William Langer, 30 August 1943, Entry 54, Folder 1.

14. Memo, Remer to Langer, 5 May 1943, Entry 54, Box 1 Folder 1.

15. Ibid.

16. Resignation letters of 25 and 30 August 1943, Remer to Langer, Entry 54, Box 1, Folder 1.

17. Memo, Miles to Metzel, 20 September 1943, Entry 146, Box 192, Folder 2723.

18. Magruder called R&A the "major core" of OSS. See Magruder's memo to Donovan, subject: organization of intelligence, 11 September 1943, Entry 110, Box 52, Folder 13.

19. Minutes of meeting, 9 December 1943, Entry 148, Box 2, Folder 51.

20. Memo, Hall to Wiens, 2 February 1944, Appendix B, in Wiens's report to Hall, subject: history of R&A in SACO through 1 April 1944, Entry 84, Box 2, Folder "SACO Papers."

21. Wiens's report to Hall, subject: history of R&A in SACO through 1 April 1944. Entry 84, Box 2, Folder "SACO Papers." In December 1943, one U.S. dollar was worth 85.4 Chinese yuan (fabi) in Chungking. See Shi Yufu, *A Brief History of Chinese Money and Finance,* (Tianjin: Tianjin People's Press, 1984), 312.

22. Hoffman's log of tour of duty in China, 16.

23. Memo, Hoffman to Magruder, subject: John Smith, Robert Smith, George Frank Adams, 2 February 1944, Roll 41, M1642.

24. Memo, Allman to Donovan, 21 February 1944, Roll 41, M1642.

25. Allman's note, marked urgent, 24 February 1944, Roll 41, M1642.

26. McHugh's note to Donovan and Donovan's memo to Coughlin, subject: Mr. William B. Christian, 12 May 1944, Roll 41, M1642.

27. Letter, Stilwell to Hearn, 11 January 1944, RG 493, record of the China-Burma-India theater of operations, U.S. Army (CBI), records of the commanding general, personal messages file, Book 5, Suitland Record Center, National Archives.

28. History notes, author unknown, Section II, Entry 154, Box 170, Folder 2941.

29. See Donovan's explanation to Hoffman in his letter from Nazira, Roll 89, A3304.

30. It is important to note that the army hated SACO so much that in September 1944, General Sultan made it mandatory for Coughlin to establish his headquarters in Delhi. See history notes, Section II, Entry 154, Box 170, Folder 2941.

31. Memo, Tai Li to Wilkinson, translation, 26 April 1944, Entry 154, Folder 3410, "SACO–Tai Li."

32. See, for example, Hall's agreement with Tai Li on setting up R&A/SACO, condition number 2.

33. Hoffman's log of tour of duty, 14.

34. Memo, Hykes to C. N. Weems, subject: exchange of intelligence with General Tai, 18 May 1944, Entry 148, Box 17, Folder 244.

35. Hykes's report to Hall, April 1944.

36. Ibid.

37. Hoffman log of tour of duty, 20.

38. Memo, Donovan to Heppner and Coughlin, 15 December 1943, Entry 110, Box 51, Folder 2. Donovan's stay in New Delhi had one important mission: to indoctrinate Heppner that the loyalty of an OSS officer should not be to the army, but to the OSS director. For this purpose, Donovan warned Heppner not to use his connections with the theater army generals, namely Stilwell and Wedemeyer, against Coughlin, an OSS loyalist.

39. "Directive from Supreme Allied Commander to All Quasi-Military Organizations and Irregular Forces in the South East Asia Theater," 18 December 1943, Entry 54, Box 1, Folder 1. This so-called P Division was under the control of the British Captain G. A. Garnons Williams, R.N.

40. See Warren interview with Heppner. Taylor eventually was kicked out by the British.

41. When Hoffman visited Stilwell's camp on 8 December, he was bombarded by Colonel Joseph Dickey, the theater G-2, with an anti-Miles tirade. Hoffman wandered about Stilwell's headquarters amid the huge staff and lobbied Generals Frank Dorn and Thomas Hearn for cooperation. Though the spirit was cordial, enthusiasm and concrete offers were not forthcoming. At one point, when Hoffman offered the enthusiastic help of OSS, Hearn, Stilwell's chief of staff, cynically told Hoffman that if OSS could not reap results, not to worry, because "the Army has been here two years and haven't done anything yet" (report from Carl Hoffman on SACO, 13 December 1943, Roll 89, A3304).

42. Hoffman's log of tour of duty, 20–21.

43. Ibid.

44. Letter, Hall to Langer, from New Delhi, 29 January 1944, Entry 54, Box 1.

45. See, for example, memo, Langer to Donovan, subject: problems of R. and A. outpost, 25 December 1944, Entry 110, Box 47, Folder 486.

46. Secret memo, Coughlin to Donovan, 28 April 1944, Entry 146, Box 82, Folder 1167.

47. Memo, Davies to Coughlin, 24 April 1944, Entry 146, Box 82, Folder 1167.

48. Letter, Coughlin to Donovan, 28 April 1944, Entry 146, Box 82, Folder 1167.

49. Memo, Heppner to Donovan, re: promotion of Wilfrey Smith, 10 July 1945, Roll 42, M1642.

50. Memo, Heppner to John O'Gara, deputy director—personnel, OSS, 8 April 1945, Entry 168, Box 16, Folder 222.

51. Claire Chennault, *Way of a Fighter* (New York: G. P. Putnam's Sons, 1949), 260.

52. The Mansfield report of 22 May 1945 and attached documents, Entry 99, Box 67, Folder 212.

53. Charles Cruickshank, *SOE,* 152–162

54. Memo, Allman to John Wiley, 28 January 1943, subject: John S. Service, RG229, Entry 92, Box 241, Folder 24

55. Memo, Kimbel to Donovan, subject: north China, 11 February 1943, RG229, Entry 92, Box 241, Folder 24.

56. Note from Magruder to Donovan, 19 February 1943, RG229, Entry 92, Box 241, Folder 24.

57. Memo, Donovan to Heppner and Coughlin, 15 December 1943, Entry 110, Box 51, Folder 2.

58. Zhou Enlai, for example, had mentioned CCP's intelligence capability to Lauchlin Currie in 1941 and also certainly told John Paton Davies, who even advised SACO people that the CCP had the best intelligence in China.

59. Memo, Cheston and Coughlin to Thomas Handy, 10 August 1944, RG 165, OPD 210, 684 China, "Dixie Mission."

60. Ibid.

61. Zhou Enlai first brought up the establishment of an American diplomatic post in Yenan to Lauchlin Currie in 1941. Zhou suggested it to Davies in March 1943.

62. See, for example, urgent cable from Fairbank to Langer and Kilgour via Gauss, 11 October 1943, RG 263, CIA Files, the Murphy Collection, Box 16, Folder "4202-China-1940."

63. Davies memo to the White House, 16 January 1944, subject: coordinated attack on Japan's inner zone, OPD 210, 684, China, RG165, "Dixie Mission."

64. Ibid.

65. Memo, Davies to the White House, 15 January 1944, subject: observers' mission to north China, OPD 210, 684, China, RG165, "Dixie Mission."

66. See, for example, Cora Dubois's "Comment on [Davies's] 'American Policy in Asia,'" Roll 41, M1642. Cora Dubois was the only woman in OSS heading a major R&A outpost. Her brilliance as an anthropologist, as well as her lesbianism, caused her trouble in the patriarchal world of the U.S. Army.

67. Files on the subject in RG 165, OPD 210, 684, China, "Dixie Mission."

68. Hearn to Marshall, 9 July 1943, RG 493, Records of the China-Burma-India theater of operations, U.S. Army (CBI), records of the commanding general, personal messages file, Box 2, National Archives.

69. Memo, Davies to Stilwell, undated, most likely February 1944, regarding personnel recommendation for Dixie, RG 493, records of the China-Burma-India theater of operations, U.S. Army (CBI), records of the commanding general, personal messages file, Box 5, National Archives.

70. Memo, Coughlin to Donovan, 18 September 1944, subject: Tolstoy mission, Entry 148, Box 3, Folder 58, "Secret File."

71. The Cahill dispatch, 23 July 1944, RG 493, records of the China-Burma-India theater of operations, U.S. Army (CBI), records of the commanding general, personal messages file, Box 5, National Archives.

72. Ilia Tolstoy was Leo Tolstoy's grandson.

73. Memo, Coughlin to Donovan, 18 September 1944, subject: Tolstoy mission, Entry 148, Box 3, Folder 58, "Secret File."

74. Ibid.

75. Ibid.

76. Note by General Russell, entitled "SACO-Sino-American Special Technical Cooperation Organization," RG 165, OPD 210, 684, China, "Dixie Mission."

77. Memo, Thomas Handy to A. J. McFarland, subject: Lieut. Colonel Ilia A. Tolstoy's Mission to China, 10 August 1944, RG 165, OPD 210, 684, China, "Dixie Mission." Emphasis in original.

78. Memo, Coughlin to Donovan, 18 September 1944.

79. Letter, Hearn to Gauss, 17 August 1944, RG 493, records of the China-Burma-India theater of operations, U.S. Army (CBI), records of the commanding general, personal messages file, Box 4, National Archives.

80. Secret Cable, Hearn to Stilwell, 1 September 1944, RG 493, records of the China-Burma-India theater of operations, U.S. Army (CBI), records of the commanding general, personal messages file, Box 4, National Archives.

BAAG was the British counterpart of AGAS. In October 1942, AGAS was created as a ground intelligence and POW/flyer rescue agency. Although China was exclusively America's area of operations, the exception was made for BAAG to be attached with AGAS in Guilin. After the ouster of SOE's China Commando Group, BAAG became the prime British agency in China instigating warlord revolt against the Nationalist government, as in the case of Li Jishen, and harboring Communist intelligence activities in Guangxi and Guangdong area. The

AGAS base in Fuhai, Yunnan, also turned into a British headquarters from which to operate intelligence activities in Thailand and Burma.

81. Chen Hansheng, *My Life During Four Eras: A Memoir.* For the Sorge connection see 54–58, 60–61; for Chen's dispatch from Moscow to New York to work at Lattimore's magazine, see 63–65; for his assignment for Industrial Cooperatives, or Gung Ho, see 67–74; for the warrant see 76; for the rescue by British intelligence, see 76–77.

82. Top secret cable, Merril to Sultan, 7 July 1944, RG 493, records of the China-Burma-India theater of operations, U.S. Army (CBI), records of the commanding general, personal messages file, Box 4, National Archives.

83. Copy of cable, SEAC to war office, secretly obtained by Merrill from the British, as transmitted from Merrill to Sultan, top secret, 7 July 1944, RG 493, records of the China-Burma-India theater of operations, U.S. Army (CBI), records of commanding general (Stilwell), personal messages file, Box 4, Suitland Record Center, National Archives.

84. Cromley's report, subject: Yenan as the major order of battle China base of operation, SINOB-RP-33, 30 July 1944, top secret, Entry 148, Box 7, Folder 103 "Dixie."

85. Gale SI report, 81, Entry 99, Box 78, Folder 55.

86. See Jarrell's report to director of naval intelligence, entitled "Some Notes on Foreign Diplomatic Representation in Chungking." RG 38, Alusna Letters—1945, ONI-F.E.-China/Malay Desk. National Archives.

87. YENSIG 4, subject: proposed radio intelligence network, 8 September 1944, Entry 148, Box 11, Folder 162 "Yensig."

88. Cable, Willis Bird to Heppner, NR 928, 25 April 1945, Entry 148, Box 11, Folder 162 "Yensig."

89. For example, Mao Zedong publicly announced on 22 December 1944 over Yenan radio that "the real target for Yenan to attack is so far the Fascistic part of the Chungking regime" (intercept translation of Yenan radio broadcast, item "News Comments," 20:10 OHT, 22 December 1944, Entry 148, Box 7, Folder 103 "Dixie").

90. Chen Hansheng, *My Life During Four Eras,* 67–73.

91. Secret document of the Communist headquarters in Yenan, "1945 Project and Budget for Undermining and Bringing Over Puppet Forces," January 1945, Yenan, Roll 41, "OSS/China," M1642.

92. Colling's report to Barrett, subject: comments of Japanese Communist leader on American psychological warfare, 29 July 1944, Entry 99, Box 68, Folder 219.

93. The cover paragraph states, "This message is for Col. Hall only, and is presented, pursuant to his instructions, to him only, and in its original form and without paraphrase; no other copies made, original destroyed, together with cipher text" (top secret cable from Colling and Stelle to Col. Hall only, August 22, Entry 148, Box 7, Folder 103, "Dixie").

94. Top secret memo, Colling and Stelle to Hall, subject: APPLE project, Entry 148, Box 7, Folder 103 "Dixie."

95. Cable, Hall to Colling and Stelle, 25 August 1944, Entry 148, Box 7, Folder 103 "Dixie."

96. Memo, Hall to chief, SI branch, OSS, Washington, D.C., subject: Dixie mission and two proposed projects, 26 August 1944, Entry 148, Box 7, Folder 103 "Dixie."

97. In August 1951, Koji Ariyoshi was arrested by the FBI and was convicted two years later of conspiring to overthrow the government of the United States with violence. In June 1953, Ariyoshi was sentenced to five years in prison. See *Remembering Koji Ariyoshi: An American GI in Yenan,* edited by Hugh Deane, China Series, Number 5, US-China People's Friendship Association, Los Angeles, 1978.

98. Hall to Cromley, 27 August 1944, subject: matters OB, China and Cromley, Entry 148, Box 7, Folder 103 "Dixie."

99. Memo, Donovan to Coughlin, 5 October 1944, Roll 40, M1642.

100. Memo, Magruder to Donovan, 7 October 1944, Roll 40, M1642.

101. Memo, Barrett to Hall, 7 August 1944, Entry 148, Box 7, Folder 103 "Dixie."

102. Memo, Hall to Cromley, 27 August 1944, Entry 148, Box 7, Folder 103 "Dixie."

103. Memo, Cromley to Hall, 31 July 1944.

104. Hall continued, "Women to China has been one of the hottest issues in the theater for two years and many of the ambitious have acquired badly burned fingers. Both General Stilwell and Ambassador Gauss bitterly oppose it. It is not a profitable issue to stick your neck out on" (Hall to Cromley, 27 August 1944).

105. Letter, Donovan to Coughlin, 5 October 1994, Roll 40, M1642.

106. Colonel W. H. Bales, FE comment, October 1944, RG 38, Entry ONI-China/Malay Desk, Box 2, Alusna Letters, 1943–1944, National Archives.

Chapter 7. The Miller Faux Pas and Wedemeyer's Ascension

1. See, for example, "Aide Memoir of SACO Meeting with Admiral Horne," by R. David Halliwell, 24 February 1944, RG 38, Miles Papers, Box 2, National Archives.

2. Memo, Miller to Donovan, from Delhi, 13 October 1944, Roll 127, M1642.

3. Miller's report to Donovan, from Chungking, 23 October 1944, Roll 127, M1642.

4. Ibid.

5. Ibid.

6. Top secret cable, Dow to Donovan, 26 October 1944, Roll 127, M1642.

7. For a complete set of documents on the Miller incident, see Roll 127, M1642, and Entry 148, Box 44, Folder 670.

8. Wilkinson, "Sworn Statement," 4 November 1944, Entry 148, Box 44, Folder 670.

9. Dow's report to Coughlin, 25 October 1944, Entry 148, Box 44, Folder 670.

10. Quoted in ibid.

11. Miles's sworn testimony, subject: inquiry into case of General Miller between Commodore Miles and Major Steiner, Entry 148, Box 44, Folder 670.

12. Dow's report to Coughlin on the events in SACO from 25 to 26 of October, Entry 148, Box 44, Folder 670.

13. Top secret cable, Dow to Donovan, 26 October 1944, Roll 127, M1642

14. Top secret cable, Miles to King, 26 October 1944, Roll 127, M1642.

15. Top secret memo, King for Marshall, 27 October 1944, Roll 127, M1642.

16. Letter, Donovan to Tai Li, 14 December 1944, Roll 127, M1642.

17. See the subject file, "Miller Incident," Roll 127, M1642. Also Donovan's correspondence with Roosevelt on this matter in the PSF files in the FDR Library in Hyde Park.

18. Cable, 109 (Donovan's code name) to Coughlin, 28 October 1944, Roll 127, M1642.

19. Cable, Dow to Donovan, information Coughlin, 29 October 1944, top secret, Roll 127, M1642.

20. Ibid.

21. Cable, Coughlin to Donovan, 29 October 1944, Roll 127, M1642.

22. Report to Coughlin for Donovan from Miller, 29 October 1944, top secret, Roll 127, M1642.

23. Cable, Donovan to Connely informing him of the decision that it would not be necessary for Heppner, Coughlin, and Connely to travel to Washington, 1 November 1944. Roll 127, M1642.

24. Memo, Donovan to Vandegrift, 6 November 1944, Roll 127, M1642.

25. Report of investigation, Office of Inspection General, China Theater, 5 November 1944, Roll 127, M1642.

26. Ibid.

27. Memo, Wedemeyer to JCS, 10 November 1944, subject: investigation conducted in compliance with WARX 53122, Roll 127, M1642.

28. Memo, King to Donovan, 27 November 1944, Roll 127, M1642.

29. Letter, Coughlin to Arden Dow, 7 November 1944, Entry 148, Box 44, Folder 670.

30. Cable, Connely to Donovan, 2 November 1944, Roll 127, M1642.

31. Cable, Donovan to Heppner, Coughlin, and Connely in New Delhi, 2 November 1944, Roll 127, M1642.

32. Cable, Heppner to Donovan, 5 November 1944, Top Secret, Roll 127, M1642.

33. Memo, author unknown, "Reorganization of OSS Under Colonel Richard P. Heppner," Entry 154, Box 170, Folder 2941.

34. Ibid.

35. Ibid.

36. Ibid.; for Caldwell's projects, see his memos, "Activation of the Tibetan Project" (2 November 1944) and "Utilization of Buddhist Contacts in Connection with OSS/MO Activities in China" (27 October 1944), in Entry 148, Box 44, Folder 668.

Chapter 8. OSS and the Yenan Mystique

1. Davies memo, "Chinese Communist Preliminary Estimate of Cooperation which They Could Offer a Hypothetical American Landing at Lienyunkang," Yenan, Shensi, 3 November 1944, RG 493, record of China theater of operations, record of commanding general, Box 7, Folder "Radios-Eyes Alone—Communists, Wires re 3 November–10 December 1944," Suitland Record Center, National Archives.

2. Stalin had told the British two weeks earlier that the Soviet Union would enter the war soon. Churchill summoned Wedemeyer to Cairo and told him this. Wedemeyer reported to Washington on 24 October 1944 after meeting with Churchill, "Russia will definitely enter the war against Japan as soon as practicable after Germany's capitulation. Russia presently has approximately 30 divisions in the Far East and could add 30 more before initiating operations against the Japs. The movements of such a force to the Far East would require about three or four months" (Wedemeyer to Marshall, TOPSEC, 24 October 1944, RG 218, Leahy Papers, Box 3, Folder 13 "China-Burma-India, 1944." National Archives).

3. Davies report on the Lienyunkang plan, 3 November 1944.

4. Davies's reports, "The Chinese Communists and the Great Powers," "How Red Are the Chinese Communists?" "Will the Communists Take Over China?" "The Policy of the 8th Route Army Toward Japanese Prisoners," in RG 493, records of the China theater of operations, records of the commanding general, Box 7, Folder "Radios-Eyes Alone—Communists, Wires, re 3 November–10 Dec. 1944," Suitland Record Center, National Archives.

5. Memo, Barrett to McClure, 12 December 1944, RG 493, records of the Chinese theater of operations, record of Office of the Commanding General, "Eyes alone messages, Subject file, Box 7, F Radios—eyes alone—Communists, Misc., 12 December 1944–25 January 1945," Suitland Record Center, National Archives.

6. Letter, Zhu De to Admiral King, 5 December 1944, RG 38, Miles Papers, Box 40, Folder "Chinese Communists," National Archives.

7. "North China Intelligence Project—Draft proposal for a major OSS secret intelligence operation in North China and from North China into Manchuria and Korea prepared by Lieut. (sg) Guy Martin, Dr. Charles B. Fahs, Major Philip X. Crowe, Major Joseph E. Spencer, Lieut. Thomas J. Davis," OSS, New Delhi, India, 5 January 1945, Entry 99, Box 68, Folder 219.

8. The time of Bird's arrival was crucial for the sake of later developments. The army insisted—falsely—that it had presented this plan to the Central Government before Bird's secret visit to Yenan. General McClure talked to General Chen Cheng, the minister of war, on 19 December 1944.

9. Memo, Willis Bird to chief of staff, subject: Yenan trip, 24 January 1945, Entry 148, Box 7, Folder 103, "Dixie."

10. Letter, Bird to Betty McIntosh, 23 May 1979.

11. Wedemeyer's chief of staff, General Robert McClure, was cognizant of the scheme and had tentatively talked with Hurley and T. V. Soong, both of whom thought it was most difficult if not impossible to get approval from Chiang Kai-shek. While Wedemeyer was away

inspecting troops in the front, McClure nevertheless secretly authorized the Barrett-Bird-Davies trip of 14 December 1944 without telling either Hurley or the Nationalist government. McClure nervously tested the reaction of the Nationalist government by vaguely suggesting the use of Communist troops to General Chen Cheng, Chiang Kai-shek's minister of war, on 19 December, after the OSS/CCP deal became a fait accompli. Chen Cheng never approved such a suggestion (minutes of meeting with General Chen Cheng, #3, eyes alone E. Top secret, RG 493, record of the China theater of operations, record of Office of the Commanding General, Eyes alone messages, Subject file, Box 7, Folder "Radios—Eyes Alone—communists, Misc., 12 December 1944—25 January 1945.")

12. Memo, Willis Bird to chief of staff, subject: Yenan trip, 24 January 1945, Entry 148, Box 7, Folder 103 "Dixie."

13. Top secret cable, Evans, signed Cromley, to Wedemeyer for Dickey, 10 January 1945, RG 493, records of the China theater of operations, record of the commanding general, eyes alone messages, Box 7, Folder "Radios-eyes alone-wires re Communists-Important Messages, In, 10–23 January 1945," Suitland Record Center, National Archives.

14. Cable, Evans, signed Cromley, to Wedemeyer, 11 January 1945, RG 493, records of the China theater of operations, record of the commanding general, eyes alone messages, Box 7, Folder "Radios-eyes alone-wires re Communists-Important Messages, In, 10–23 January 1945," Suitland Record Center, National Archives.

15. Memo, Quentin Roosevelt to Heppner, subject: Colonel Bird and Major Roosevelt's visit with General Hurley, 8 May 1945, Roll 41, M1642.

16. McClure's aide memoir, "Plans for operations in communist territories," RG 493, records of the China theater of operations, records of the Office of the Commanding General, "Eyes Alone Messages, Subject file, Box 7, F Radios—eyes alone—Communists, Misc., 12 December 1944-25 January 1945," Suitland Record Center, National Archives.

17. Report, Quentin Roosevelt to Heppner, 8 May 1945.

18. Memo, Leahy to Marshall, 15 January 1945, RG 218, Leahy files, Box 21, Folder 136, "Miscellaneous memorandum, 1945–1946," National Archives.

19. Cable, Wedemeyer to Marshall, 22 January 1945, RG493, records of the China theater of operations, records of the commanding general, Box 7, Folder "Radios—eyes alone—wires re Communists—Important Messages in, 22–25 January 1945," National Archives.

20. Cable, Marshall to Wedemeyer, 23 January 1945, RG 493, records of the China theater of operations, records of the Office of the Commanding General, Box 7, Folder "Radios—eyes alone—wires re Communists—Important Messages out, 22–25 January 1945," Suitland Record Center, National Archives.

21. Draft cable, Wedemeyer to Marshall for his eyes only, RG 493, records of the China theater of operations, records of the Office of the Commanding General, eyes alone messages, Box 7, Folder "Radios-eyes alone-wires re Communists-Important Messages, Out, 10–23 January 1945," Suitland Record Center, National Archives.

22. Cable, Wedemeyer to Marshall, 27 January 1945, RG 493, records of China theater of operations, record of the commanding general, Box 7, Folder "Radios—eyes alone-wires Re Communists-Important Messages, Out, 22–25 January 1945," Suitland Record Center, National Archives.

23. Davies, *Dragon by the Tail,* 383.

24. Letter, from Bangkok, Willis Bird to Betty McIntosh, 23 May 1979.

25. Memo, Roosevelt to Heppner, subject: Colonel Bird and Major Roosevelt's visit with General Hurley, 8 May 1945, Roll 41, M1642.

26. Letter, Archimedes L. A. Patti to Mr. and Mrs. McIntosh, 3 July 1979.

27. Yeaton, *Memoirs of Col. Ivan D. Yeaton, USA (RET) 1919–1953* (Stanford, Calif.: Hoover Institution, 1976), 95–96.

28. Letter, Zhu De to Donovan, 23 January 1945, Entry 190, Box 583, Folder 435.

29. CCP Yenan Headquarters, "1945 Project and Budget for Undermining and Bringing

Over Puppet Forces" (yijiusiwu nian dui weijun de zhengqu he pohuai gongzuo jihua yu yusuan), January, 1945, Roll 41, "OSS/China," M1642.

30. Memo, chief, special funds branch, to Donovan, subject: *Congressional Statement on Administration of Unvouchered Funds,* 29 March 1944, Roll 27, OSS Budget Files, M1642.

31. Cable, Donovan to Magruder, Doering and Cheston, from Kandy to Washington, relaying Stelle's cable, 31 January 1945, Roll 38, A3304.

Chapter 9. OSS and Wedemeyer

1. Wedemeyer to War Department, top secret, 29 December 1944, RG 218, Box 3, Folder 13 "China, Burma, India, 1944," National Archives.

2. Ibid.

3. Ibid.

4. History notes, Entry 154, Box 170, Folder 2941.

5. Memo, Heppner to Donovan, 10 July 1945, subject: promotion of officer, Lt. Col. Wilfred J. Smith, Roll 42, M1642.

6. General Order #2, OSS/China headquarters, 9 April 1945, Exhibit P, in "OSS-Section V," RG 493, records of Allied & U.S. Army commands in the China-Burma-India theater of operations (World War II), records of the China theater of operations, U.S. Army (CT), records of the general staff, G-5, (civil affairs) section, formerly classified reports—special agencies in China, Box 61, Suitland Record Center, National Archives.

7. Cable, Donovan to Doering and Cheston, 28 January 1945, R38, A3304.

8. It is important to keep in mind that up to now, OSS authority to operate in China had been in SACO only. Technically speaking, it was illegal for Wedemeyer even to appoint Heppner as the China theater chief for OSS; because OSS was officially part of SACO, Tai Li's consent was required for any appointment of any commanding officers.

9. "Index: Naval Group China," records of China theater of operations, records of the commanding general, formerly top secret "Black Book" on China, Black Book #2, Box 16, Folder "Black Book-China #2," Suitland Record Center, National Archives.

10. "Amendment I—Agreement to Supplement the SACO Agreement," Exhibit #3 in "OSS-Section V," RG 493, records of Allied & U.S. Army commands in the China-Burma-India theater of operations (World War II), records of the China theater of operations, U.S. Army (CT), records of the general staff, G-5, (civil affairs) section, formerly classified reports—special agencies in China, Box 61, Suitland Record Center, National Archives.

11. Ibid.

12. Memo by the commander in chief, U.S. Fleet, and chief of naval operations to the Joint Chiefs of Staff, top secret, JCS 1290/1, page 5, special distribution, FF1/A16, Serial: 00737, 24 March 1945, RG 493, records of the China theater of operations, records of the commanding general, Box 19, Folder "JCS Minutes, 1944–1946, Misc.," Suitland Record Center, National Archives.

13. Note that the amendment gave Wedemeyer operational control over only the personnel and material of Naval Group China, not operations initiatives.

14. Coughlin memo, 20 September 1944, "Gordon and His GBT Group," Entry 148, Box 44, Folder 669.

15. Ibid.

16. Ibid.

17. The chart of GBT Group, as of 1 September 1944, as presented to Coughlin by Gordon, Entry 148, Box 44, Folder 669. MI-X was the equivalent of British MI-9, in charge of POW rescue, but also serving as a ground intelligence service.

18. Coughlin memo, "The Gordon Plan," 20 September 1944, Entry 148, Box 44, Folder 669.

19. Ibid.

20. Memo, Hearn to Sultan, 4 November 1944, Entry 148, Box 44, Folder 669.

21. History notes, author unknown, Entry 154, Box 170, Folder 2941.

22. Aide memoir for General Marshall from British Field Marshall Henry Wilson, undated, RG 493, record of the China theater of operations, record of the commanding general, Box 20, Folder "State, War, Navy Coordinating Committee Minutes Book I (1)," Suitland Record Center, National Archives.

23. History notes, Entry 154, Box 170, Folder 2941.

24. Minutes of meeting, 29 January 1945, SEAC Files, Entry 110, Box 51, Folder 2.

25. Charles Fenn, *Ho Chi-Minh: A Biographical Introduction* (London: Studio Vista, 1973), 78, 80

26. Ibid., 78–79.

27. Ibid., 78–80.

28. Ibid., 82.

29. Ibid., 80.

30. The strength of OSS as of October 1944 was 106 and reached a peak of 1,891 in July 1945.

Chapter 10. The Great Leap

1. Donovan drafted a plan on 10 October 1944 entitled "The Basis for a Permanent United States Foreign Intelligence Service." On 18 November 1944, a comprehensive package internally called the Donovan plan was submitted to the president. See files on Donovan's efforts to establish a centralized intelligence agency, Roll 117, A3304.

2. RG 493, Black Book-China-Book 5, Vol. II., records of the China theater of operations, records of the commanding general, Box 16, Folder "Black Book—China, Book 5, Vol. II," Suitland Record Center, National Archives.

3. Top secret cable, Miles to Cominch, 20 January 1945, RG 38, Miles Papers, Box 2, National Archives.

4. Top secret cable, Miles to Metzel, 20 January 1945, RG 38, Miles Paper, Box 2, National Archives.

5. Letter, McHugh to Lauchlin Currie, 2 November 1944, Box 2, Folder 1, McHugh Papers.

6. Letter, Currie to McHugh, 17 November 1944, Box 2, Folder 1, McHugh Papers.

7. Letter, McHugh to Donovan, 26 November 1944, Box 2, Folder 1, McHugh Papers.

8. Cable, E. A. Locke to Hurley, 28 December 1945, Roll 71, M1642.

9. Cable, Hurley to secretary of state for Donald Nelson, 10 January 1945, Roll 71, M1642.

10. Cable, Donovan to Cheston, 23 January 1945, Roll 71, M1642.

11. Cable, Cheston to Donovan, 22 January 1945, Roll 71, M1642.

12. Memo, McHugh to Cheston, 26 January 1945, Box 2, Folder 1, McHugh Papers.

13. Letter, McHugh to Oscar Cox, 1 February 1945, Box 2, Folder 1, McHugh Papers.

14. Letter, McHugh to Donovan, 16 February 1945, Box 2, Folder 1, McHugh Papers.

15. Memo, McHugh to Oscar Cox, 8 March 1945, Box 2, Folder 1, McHugh Papers.

16. Letter, McHugh to Cox, 1 February 1945, Box 2, Folder 1, McHugh Papers.

17. Memo, Edwards to McHugh, 14 March 1945, Box 2, Folder 1, McHugh Papers.

18. Memo, Patterson to Knollenberg, 27 June 1945, Box 2, Folder 1, McHugh Papers.

19. Private letter from Shanghai, McHugh to "Darling," 14 August 1946, Box 2 (Military Intelligence Report Box), Folder 1, McHugh Papers.

20. Memo, Cheston to Heppner, 5 February 1945, Roll 132, M1642.

21. Memo, Heppner to Charles Cheston, 22 February 1945, Roll 132, M1642.

22. Cable, 109 to Heppner, 29 March 1945, Roll 132, M1642.

23. Telephone interview with Major Frank Mills, Fairfax, Virginia, 1992. Mills was Krause's operations officer and had extensive contact with Hu Zongnan.

24. Private letter, Krause to Betty MacDonald, now Betty McIntosh, 5 November 1946.
25. Ibid.
26. Krause letter to MacDonald, 6 November 1946.
27. "Father Lebbe's Subversive Activities Among the Work-Study Chinese Students in Europe" (Lei Mingyuan Pohuai Lu Ou Qingong Jianxue Yundong), *Selected Tianjin Culture and History Material* (Tianjin Wenshi Ziliao Xuanji), #15, May 1981, 147.
28. Qiao Jiacai, *Selected Writings*, 2: 177.
29. Ibid.
30. Ibid., 2: 178–179.
31. Ibid., 3: 179.
32. Ibid., 2: 179.
33. Ibid.
34. Ibid., 2: 180. Throughout the war, many of the BIS agents and Catholics, including some nuns, in Lebbe and Megan's organizations were killed by the Communists.
35. The Spaniel mission was also given the theater name Plymouth.
36. Report on activities of Spaniel mission, Coolidge to Heppner, 13 September 1945, Entry 148, Box 6, Folder 87 "Communists." The original target area was fifteen miles southwest of Kalgan; bad weather forced the change.
37. Ibid.
38. During much of the 1960s and 1970s, Geng was chief of the Department of Foreign Liaisons, the CCP intelligence organization. One of his comrades in that organization was Solomon Adler, the chief agent during World War II for the U.S. Treasury Department.
39. Report on activities of Spaniel mission, Coolidge to Heppner, 13 September 1945, Entry 148, Box 6, Folder 87 "Communists."
40. Ibid.
41. Ibid.
42. Ibid.
43. Cable, from Yenan to Chungking, COUSAOS to CGUSFCT, 11 June 1945, Entry 148, Box 6, Folder 87.
44. Minutes of meeting held at Ambassador Hurley's home, No. 2 Chialing village, 7:45 P.M. 30 August 1945, Box 87, Folder 87.6, Wedemeyer Papers, Hoover Institution. Also RG38, Miles Paper, Box 40, Folder "Chinese Communists."
45. Mao Zedong told Wedemeyer, "With reference to General Wedemeyer's letters and messages, I have not seen them" (ibid.). Colonel Ivan Yeaton, who replaced Peterkin as the head of the U.S. contingent in Yenan in July 1945, also made an investigation and confirmed that these were never delivered to Mao.
46. Ibid.
47. Cable, Heppner to Donovan's eyes alone, 20 April 1945, Entry 148, Box 11, Folder 161 "Yenan."
48. Directive for OSS, China theater, to operate YENSIG No. 4, 25 April 1945, Entry 154, Box 198, Folder 3369.
49. Cable, Bird to Heppner, subject: YENSIG plan #4, 28 April 1945, Entry 154, Box 198, Folder 3369.
50. Cable, Peterkin, Swensen, and Stelle to Heppner and Whitaker, 2 June 1945, Entry 148, Box 11, Folder 162, "Yensig."
51. Cable, Whitaker to Heppner, Entry 148, Box 11, Folder 162 "Yensig"
52. Paraphrased cable, Stelle to Wedemeyer for Dickey and Heppner, 3 June 1945, Entry 148, Box 11, Folder 162 "Yensig."
53. Memo, Porter to theater signal officer, 27 June 1945, Entry 154, Box 198, Folder 3369.
54. Letter, Krause to Betty MacDonald, 5 November 1946.
55. Quoted in ibid.
56. Memo, Captain J. W. Kruissink, adjutant officer, to HQ investigation boards, USF CT, subject: strength report of OSS taken from morning reports, 9 October 1945, RG 493,

records of Allied & U.S. Army commands in the China-Burma-India theater of operations (World War II), records of the China theater of operations, U.S. Army (CT), record of the general staff, G-5 (civil affairs) section, formerly classified report—special agencies in China, Section V, OSS, Box 61, Suitland Record Center, National Archives.

57. Report on OSS by investigation boards, RG 493, records of Allied & U.S. Army commands in the China-Burma-India theater of operations (World War II), records of the China theater of operations, U.S. Army (CT), record of the general staff, G-5 (civil affairs) section, formerly classified report—special agencies in China, Section V, OSS, Box 61, Suitland Record Center, National Archives.

58. OSS General Order #6, China theater, 1 August 1945, RG 493, records of Allied & U.S. Army commands in the China-Burma-India theater of operations (World War II), records of the China theater of operations, U.S. Army (CT), record of the general staff, G-5 (civil affairs) section, formerly classified report—special agencies in China, Section V, OSS, Box 61, Suitland Record Center, National Archives.

59. Manuscript, "History of SI Branch, Office of Strategic Services, China Theater," October 1945, Entry 154, Folder 3333.

60. Ibid.

61. Ibid.

62. Report by Lieutenant Colonel Robert Delaney, Office of Assistant Secretary of War, Strategic Service Unit, 23 March 1946, to commanding general, AAF, China theater, ATTN: military personnel officer, Entry 168, Box 16, Folder 225 "Death of Captain John Birch." In August, 1945, Delaney was the executive officer of OSS/China.

63. "History of SI Branch, Office of Strategic Service, China Theater," Entry 154, Folder 3333

64. Letter, Donovan to Wedemeyer, 10 August 1945, Entry 154, Box 192, Folder 3285, "OSS Wash/Donovan Trip, August 1945."

65. Letter, Donovan to Tai Li, 6 August 1945, Entry 148, Box 3, Folder 54.

66. Memo, David Shaw to Quentin Roosevelt, chief, SI, Chungking, subject: conversation with Mme. Sun Yat-sen and "friend," 7 August 1945, Entry 148, Box 6, Folder 87 "Communists."

67. Ibid.

68. Ibid.

69. Letter, Krause to Betty MacDonald, 6 November 1946.

70. Cable, Helliwell to Sargent, 5 August 1945, Entry 154, Box 192, Folder 3285, "OSS Wash/Donovan Trip, August 1945."

71. Cable, Kim Ku to Truman, via OSS Eagle project, relayed by Heppner to Davis for Wedemeyer, 17 August 1945, Entry 90, Box 1, Folder 11.

72. Smith, *Shadow Warriors,* 314.

73. Letter, Donovan to Wedemeyer, 10 August 1945, Entry 154, Box 192, Folder 3285 "OSS Wash/Donovan Trip, August 1945."

74. Letter, Krause to Betty MacDonald, 6 November 1946.

75. The official surrender announcement did not come until four days later.

Chapter 11. Surrender by Japan and Communist Hostility Toward OSS

1. Urgent cable, Heppner to Helliwell, 10 August 1945, Entry 154, Box 192, Folder 3285, "OSS Wash/Donovan Trip, August 1945."

2. Top secret cable, Heppner to Davis, 10 August 1945, Entry 90, Box 3, Folder 30, "Jap Surrender—in and out, Aug. 1945."

3. "Summary of Activities of Prisoner of War Humanitarian Teams," report to Wedemeyer, 9 October 1945, RG 493, records of Allied & U.S. Army commands in the China-Burma-India theater of operations (World War II), records of the China theater of operations,

U.S. Army (CT), record of the general staff, G-5 (civil affairs) section, formerly classified report—special agencies in China, Section V, OSS, Box 61, Suitland Record Center, National Archives.

4. Ibid.

5. Elizabeth P. MacDonald, *Undercover Girl* (New York: Macmillan, 1947), 231.

6. For a good description on this operation, see Major General John Singlaub's *Hazardous Duty: An American Soldier in the Twentieth Century* (New York: Summit, 1991), 83–101.

7. Charles Fenn, *Ho Chi-Minh,* 84.

8. Jean Sainteny, *Histoire d'une Paix Manquée,* (Paris: Amiot-Dumont, 1954), cited in Fenn, *Ho Chi-Minh,* 95

9. "Summary of Activities of Prisoner of War Humanitarian Teams."

10. Report, Davis to Heppner, 23 August 1945, Entry 168, Box 16, Folder 221.

11. Ibid.

12. Cable, Heppner to Donovan, 23 August 1945, Entry 168, Box 16, Folder 221.

13. Heppner to Davis, 23 August 1945, Entry 168, Box 16, Folder 221.

14. Cable, Heppner to Donovan, 23 August 1945, Entry 168, Box 16, Folder 221.

15. Priority cable, Donovan to Heppner, 24 August 1945, Entry 168, Box 16, Folder 221.

16. Cable, Heppner to Donovan, 26 August 1945, Entry 168, Box 16, Folder 221.

17. "Summary of Activities of Prisoner of War Humanitarian Teams."

18. After the war, Bird became a CIA operative, eventually married a Thai woman, and settled down in Bangkok. In 1959, in congressional testimony, Bird was publicly exposed: he had bribed a U.S. government official with $25,000 in order to gain a foreign aid construction contract in Laos (Smith, *Secret History,* 273).

The Chinese Communists have recently published material describing how Communist intelligence took advantage of Bird's love affairs with his secretary in Chungking and penetrated into OSS's operations in China. See Cao Jingyan, "Yan Baohang and the Secret Liaison Station of the Chungking Underground Party," in *Social Sciences of Changchun* (Changchun shehui kexue), rpt. in *Biographical Literature (Zhuanji wenxue),* 55, no. 6.

Heppner cabled Donovan on 26 August, "General Wedemeyer does not desire any harsh action taken against Bird. It is his feeling that he was guilty of bad judgment only, and that his actions exhibited great courage and ability. After a suitable time it is our plan to send him home and we want it clear that he is being sent home without any stigma attaching to him because of the Korea mission" (cable, Heppner to Donovan, 26 August 1945, Entry 168, Box 16, Folder 221).

19. Urgent cable, Thohill to Krause and Helliwell, 30 August 1945, Entry 154, Folder 3368

20. Report by War Department Office of Assistant Secretary of War, Strategic Service Unit, 23 March 1946, to commanding general, AAF, China Theater, ATTN: military personnel officer, Entry 168, Box 16, Folder 225 "Death of John Birch."

21. Welch, *The Life of John Birch: In the Story of One American Boy, the Ordeal of His Age* (Los Angeles: Western Islands Press, 1954).

22. For an example, see Michael Schaller, *The U.S. Crusade in China, 1938–1945,* 269–270.

23. The Soviet occupation of Port Arthur and Dairen continued until 1955.

24. OSS intelligence plan, Buzzard mission, June 1945, Entry 154, Box 201, Folder 3408.

25. Memo, Major Frank Mills to Krause, 23 June 1945, subject: special mission to Shantung area, Entry 154, Box 201, Folder 3408.

26. War Department report, 23 March 1946, "Death of John Birch."

27. Zhao Zhuoru, Liao Zhuozhi, "The Complete Evolution of Hao Pengju's Righteous Uprising" (Hao Pengju Qiyi Shimo); also Wu Junying, "What I Know About How Hao Pengju Was Executed" (Wo Suo Zhidao de Hao Pengju bei Chujue de Jingguo), in Cai Huilin,

An Feng, et al., ed., *The Noble Mission: Remembering Our Times of Fighting Within the Kuomintang Camp (Chonggao de Shiming—Yi Zhandou zai Guomindang Yinlei de suiyue)* [Beijing: Military Science Press, 1990], vol. 1, 383–407.

28. Both Chen and Rao paid a series of hasty secret visits to Hao at this time, promising that the CCP would respect Hao's military command over his troops after he crossed over to the CCP. Rao Shushi was formerly the organizer of the CCP underground network in New York, heavily pro-Soviet, and at the time was the political commissar of the CCP's Eastern China Military Zone. Rao was purged by Mao Zedong in 1955.

29. In late December 1945, Hao and his troops publicly went over to the Communists. Before long, however, the CCP decided to wrest Hao's military command and ordered him to leave his troops in Shandong and Jiangsu and to go to Yenan for "political studies." Hao felt cheated and returned to the KMT camp. On 6 February 1947, Hao Pengju was caught by the Communists, and General Chen Yi of the CCP personally presided over the public execution of Hao (Wu Junyin, "How Hao Pengju Was Executed," 394). Also see information on Hao Pengju in the intelligence report by the American acting military attaché (China), subject: who's who—Chinese personalities (Communist), number 322330, dated 28 October 1946.

30. Testimony of Tung Chin-sheng, a.k.a. Tung Fu Kuan, Entry 148, Box 16, Folder 225.

31. OSS investigation report, "Account of the Death of Captain John Birch," 14 September 1945, by John S. Thomson to Headquarters Central Command, OSS, Entry 148, Box 6, Folder 87.

32. Tung's testimony.

33. OSS investigation report.

34. Tung's testimony.

35. Ibid.

36. OSS investigation report and Tung's testimony.

37. OSS investigation report.

38. William Miller's report to General Wedemeyer, 1 September 1945, Entry 168, Box 16, Folder 225 "Death of Capt. John Birch"; also OSS investigation report.

39. OSS investigation report.

40. Report of judge advocate re the death of John Birch, 13 November 1945, Box 87, Folder 87.2, Wedemeyer Papers, Hoover Institution. Due to fierce American internal politics, archives related to Birch's death have become a center of controversy. Ironically, military records on the Birch incident were due to be declassified in 1972 because of a Freedom of Information Act request but were held up for a period so that their disclosure would not embarrass President Nixon on his trip to China.

41. Minutes of meeting held at Ambassador Hurley's home, 30 August 1945.

42. Ibid.

43. Report, Coolidge to Heppner, subject: analysis of Spaniel mission, 13 September 1945, Entry 148, Box 6, Folder 87 "Communists."

44. "History of SI Branch, Office of Strategic Services, China Theater," October 1945, Entry 154, Folder 3333.

45. Cable, Intelligence Division to Davis, 14 September 1945, Entry 148, Box 6, Folder 87 "Communists."

46. "History of SI Branch, Office of Strategic Services, China Theater."

47. Lohbeck, *Patrick J. Hurley,* 370.

48. President Roosevelt died while Hurley was in Tehran on his way to Moscow. Hurley met with Stalin on 15 April 1945 about protecting Chinese sovereignty. Stalin listened quietly to Hurley and said he agreed to America's policy in China completely. George Kennan, however, reported to the State Department that Stalin's assurance to Hurley was inconsequential because "it [is] understood that to the Russians words mean different things than they do to us" (Lohbeck, *Patrick J. Hurley,* 372–373).

49. Albert Wedemeyer, *Wedemeyer Reports!* 347.

50. Cable, Heppner to Krause, for information Magruder and Shepardson, 10 August 1945, Entry 90, Box 3, Folder 30, "Jap surrender—in and out, August 1945.

51. Ibid.

52. "Summary of Activities of Prisoners of War Humanitarian Teams."

53. MacDonald, *Undercover Girl*, 234.

54. Letter, Krause to Betty MacDonald, 6 November 1946.

55. These Catholic agents planted by OSS in Manchuria became a highly efficient and widespread network of intelligence. When Wedemeyer came back to China on an investigation tour for President Truman in 1947, both the Communist and Nationalist intelligence worked their best to concoct self-serving "intelligence reports." Wedemeyer eventually depended entirely upon this network of Catholic agents for objective intelligence reports.

56. Report, "Survey of the Mukden area situation as it has developed from August 16 to September 10 1945—Team Cardinal," by Major R. Lamar, Entry 148, Box 6, Folder 87," Communists."

57. Top secret cable, commanding general, USF CT, Chungking, to War Department, 5 October 1945, Entry 90, Box 3, Folder 36, "Mission to Mukden."

58. Cable, commanding general, USF CT, Chungking, to War Department, U.S. military mission Moscow, subject: order for expulsion of OSS group at Mukden, 7 October 1945, Entry 90, Box 3, Folder 36, "Mission to Mukden."

59. Top secret cable, commanding general, USF CT, Chungking, to War Department, 9 October 1945, Entry 90, Box 3, Folder 36, "Mission to Mukden."

60. Top secret cable, commanding general, USF CT, Chungking, to War Department, 5 October 1945, Entry 90, Box 3, Folder 36, "Mission to Mukden."

61. Top secret cable, Marshall to commanding general U.S. military mission to USSR, Moscow, Russia, and commanding general USF CT, Chungking, China, 5 October 1945, Entry 90, Box 3, Folder 36, "Mission to Mukden."

62. Stratemeyer to War Department and U.S. military mission in Moscow, 7 October 1945, Entry 90, Box 3, Folder 36, "Mission to Mukden."

63. Top secret cable, Stratemeyer to War Department, relayed to Maples in Moscow, 9 October 1945, Entry 90, Box 3, Folder 36, "Mission to Mukden."

64. Top secret cable, Maples to Marshall, 12 October 1945, Entry 90, Box 3, Folder 36, "Mission to Mukden."

65. Cable, War Department to CG USF CT, Shanghai, CG USMM to USSR, Moscow, Russia, 15 October 1945, Entry 90, Box 3, Folder 36, "Mission to Mukden."

Chapter 12. The Last Chapter

1. Troy, *Donovan and the CIA*, 284.

2. Ibid., 291.

3. Ibid., 292.

4. Park report, RG 263, CIA papers, Troy Files, Box 6, Folder 20, "OSS-Park's report," National Archives.

5. Ibid.

6. For a detailed discussion on this familiar story of doing away with Donovan and OSS in Washington, see Troy, *Donovan and the CIA*, and Brown, *Wild Bill Donovan*, 771–784.

7. Diary entry, 20 September 1945, Smith Papers, "Conferences with President Truman, 1945," in Troy, *Donovan and the CIA*, 302.

8. Troy, *Donovan and the CIA*, 303. Magruder was officially appointed the head of SSU by Secretary of War Robert P. Patterson on 27 September 1945 (memo to Magruder from Patterson, 27 September 1945, Entry 139, Box 216, Folder 2902).

9. Letter, Krause to Betty MacDonald, 6 November 1946.

10. Memo, Lovegren to Tai Li, 29 September 1945, Entry 148, Box 3, Folder 54.

11. Chen-main Wang, *A Daily Record of Marshall's Mediation in China (November 1945–January 1947)* (Taipei: Academia Historica, 1992), 31.

12. Yeaton, *Memoir*, 132.

13. Freta Utley lived in China for years. Formerly a member of the British Communist Party, Utley had married a Russian comrade who was arrested by Stalin during the Great Purge. Utley soon left the Communist Party in bitterness and became a strong supporter of Chiang Kai-shek and his anti-Soviet mission. While in Washington, she was recruited into OSS by C. V. Starr (Smith, *Secret History*, 267).

14. Yeaton, *Memoir*; quotations from 125–126, 132, 104, respectively.

15. Xiong Xianghui, *Zhou Enlai and My Twelve Years Underground (Dixia shi-er nian yu Zhou Enlai)* [Beijing: Press of the Party School of the CCP Central Committee, 1991], 46–56, 89.

After the Marshall mission failed in early 1947 and Marshall left China in anguish, Zhou Enlai instructed Xiong to come to the United States. In July 1947, Xiong Xianghui departed Shanghai. He first studied as a graduate student at the University of Michigan and then was transferred to a master's program at Case Western Reserve University in Ohio. After the Communist takeover, Xiong became Zhou Enlai's top aide in charge of intelligence, directly participating in negotiations with Henry Kissinger during the latter's secret visit to Beijing in 1971.

16. Qiao Jiacai, *Selected Writings*, 1: 421.

17. See files on this subject in RG 38, Box 39, National Archives.

18. Lovell, *Of Spies and Strategems*, 50.

19. Interview with Putzell, 23 May 1994, transcript.

20. "At General Marshall's request, General Wedemeyer has recommended to War Department that the China theater be inactivated 1st of May 1946 and that residual theater functions be transferred to military advisory group and other governmental agencies" (top secret cable, SHUAA to SSUAA, 26 February 1946, Entry 90, Box 3, Folder 34).

21. Letter, Colonel William W. Quinn to Lieutenant Colonel Amos D. Moscrip Jr., 1 May 1946, Roll 73, M1642. In early March, Wedemeyer's chief of staff had refused to grant clearance to SSU personnel then waiting to go to China until Marshall's reaction was obtained (top secret cable, from Shanghai, SHUAA to SSUAA, March 1946, Entry 90, Box 3, Folder 34).

22. Letter, Quinn to Moscrip.

23. Ibid.

24. Ibid.

25. "Plan for Continued SSU Operations After Theater Inactivation," to commanding general, SSU, War Department, Washington, D.C., 25 March 1946, Roll 73, M1642.

26. Memo, Yeaton to General Charles Willoughby, 25 March 1947, subject: report on Delaney, Appendix 26, Yeaton, *Memoir*.

27. Letter, Quinn to Moscrip.

28. "Revised Plan for Continued SSU Operations," to director, SSU, Washington, D.C., 20 April 1946, Roll 47, M1642.

29. Ibid.

30. Ibid.

31. A major portion of SSU/China reports have been declassified and are now available at the National Archives. These can be found in M1656, or Entry 153A, RG 226, entitled "SSU REPORTS." There are two other good sources at the National Archives on the Soviet-CCP intelligence operations in China at that time. One is the complete dossier of NKVD and other Soviet personalities in China compiled by U.S. naval attaché in China in November 1946 in RG 38, Entry ONI, Box 2. The other is the Murphy Collection in the CIA files, RG 263, National Archives.

32. Top secret cable, signed WORDAGE eyes only for Maddox from Wedemeyer, 10 May 1946, Roll 73, M1642.

33. Ibid.

34. In 1981, Zhang Zhiyi, a veteran Communist intelligence official in charge of the CCP's Shanghai bureau during World War II and then the number two man of the United Front Ministry of the CCP Central Committee (zhonggong zhongyang tongzhan bu), published a sensational long article in Beijing detailing the CCP Shanghai bureau's startling intelligence operations during World War II. In it, Zhang specifically mentioned Communist intelligence's penetration into Cox's unit in Shanghai after the war (Zhang Zhiyi, *In the Heart of the Enemy: What I Know About the Shanghai Bureau of the CCP Central Committee [Zai diren xinzang li—wo suo zhidao de zhonggong zhongyang shanghai ju]*, in *Documents of the Revolution's History [Geming shi ziliao]*, no. 5, November 1981, [Beijing: Press of the Culture and History Material Research Committee of the National Political Consultation Council, 1981]).

35. Cable, Delaney to Magruder, 19 June 1946, Entry 90, Box 3, Folder 34.

36. Cable, Delaney to Magruder, 17 June 1946, Entry 90, Box 3, Folder 34.

37. Cable, secret IVI, priority, eyes only, Gold 1065, from Nanking Liaison Group, Nanking, China, from General Marshall, to War Department to WARCOS, please pass to Wedemeyer info Carter eyes alone, 7 July 1946. Entry 90, Box 3, Folder 34.

38. Cable, Moscrip to SSU/Washington, 31 July 1946, Entry 90, Box 3, Folder 34.

39. Cable, Vandenberg to Moscrip for Marshall, 15 August 1946, Entry 90, Box 3, Folder 34.

40. Cable, Secret IVI, Priority, Commander, 7th Fleet to Chief of Naval Operations, 28 September 1946, Entry 90, Box 3, Folder 34.

41. For an excellent account of the early years of CIA field operations in China, see John Singlaub, *Hazardous Duty,* chapters 4, 5, and 6.

Epilogue

1. Memo, Donovan to Joint Psychological Warfare Committee, subject: response to J.P.W.C. 45/D., dated 24 October 1942, forwarded on 31 October 1942 and included as an enclosure to secret, J.P.W.C. 45/1, informational memorandum dated 2 November 1942, Entry 190, Roll 6, M1642.

2. The exact meaning of "psychological warfare" remained murky for a long time for Donovan's people. To combat ridicule and bafflement in Washington, particularly from the U.S. military high command, Donovan was forced to summon his scholars and lawyers to labor for six months in early 1942 to define the concept. The Joint Psychological Warfare Committee, filled with skeptical military brass, grudgingly accepted Donovan's definition on 7 September 1942. Psychological warfare, OSS stated, is "the coordination and use of all means, including moral and physical, by which the end is to be attained—other than those of recognized military operations, but including the psychological exploitation of the result of those recognized military actions—which tend to destroy the will of the enemy to achieve victory and to damage his political or economic capacity to do so; which tend to deprive the enemy of the support, assistance or sympathy of his allies or associates or of neutrals, or to prevent his acquisition of such support, assistance or sympathy; or which tend to create, maintain, or increase the will to victory of our own people and allies and to acquire, maintain, or increase the support, assistance and sympathy of neutrals" (*OSS War Report,* 99).

In September 1942, when Donovan asked Milton Miles to conduct psychological warfare in China on behalf of OSS, Miles sent a cable to Donovan asking for a definition. OSS subsequently sent a reply to Miles in Chungking, but the cable was garbled and indecipherable. Throughout the war, Miles never understood what "Psychological Warfare" truly meant and firmly believed that "OSS was just as ignorant about its meaning as he was." See Stratton, *Army-Navy Game,* 62.

3. Miles, *A Different Kind of War,* 587

4. For additional information on the haphazard way in which the COI was created by Roosevelt, see Troy, *Donovan and the CIA.*

5. There is little evidence from the voluminous COI/OSS intelligence reports in the FDR Library in Hyde Park that the president even read most of them.

6. Smith, *Secret History.*

7. Leahy, *I Was There,* 338.

8. McHugh, "Chiang Kai-shek and Stilwell," Box 11, Folder 9, McHugh Papers.

9. Fairbank, *China Watch,* 49–50.

10. Miles, *A Different Kind of War,* 117, 119, 129, etc.

11. Cable from Whitaker to Heppner, 15 May 1945, Entry 154, Box 196, Folder 3342.

12. Generally speaking, Miles and General Stilwell maintained a cordial if not enthusiastic friendship. This was exceptional considering Miles's close relationship with Tai Li and Stilwell's pungent anti-KMT temperament. Miles's name pops up only once in passing in Tuchman's acclaimed book, *Stilwell and the American Experience in China, 1911–1945.*

13. White, ed., *The Stilwell Papers;* Leahy, *I Was There,* 272.

14. This 170-page compilation of accusations was published under that title in 1952 by Devin-Adair, New York.

15. David McCullough, *Truman* (New York: Simon and Schuster, 1992), 743–744.

16. Taylor, *Awakening from History,* 346–347.

17. Miles, *A Different Kind of War,* 474–491; memo, John G.Coughlin to Donovan, "Tolstoy Mission," 18 September 1944, Entry 148, Box 3, Folder 58.

18. Memo, John Paton Davies to Ambassador Gauss, "Anglo-American Cooperations in East Asia," 15 November 1943, Entry 110, Box 52, Folder 16.

19. Cruickshank, *SOE in the Far East,* 160.

20. Ibid., 78

21. Ibid., 154–159

22. Tang Zong, *Diary: My Eight Years with Chiang Kai-shek,* 271, 295; also "Minutes of Meeting between Wedemeyer and Tai Li, 30 January 1945," Entry 139, Box 261, Folder 3852.

23. Miles, *A Different Kind of War,* 260.

24. Memo, John Hughes to Colonel G. Edward Buxton, 6 June 1944, Roll 91, A3041.

25. Memo, Langer to Donovan, 3 November 1943, Entry 110, Box 47, Folder 3.

26. See Troy, *Donovan and the CIA.*

27. RG 218, CCS 385.(2-8-42) Section 1, Part 7, National Archives.

28. Memo for Colonel Cecil J. Gridley from Magruder, RG 218, CCS 385.(2-8-42) Section 1, Part 7, National Archives.

29. Donovan's order to "Chiefs of OSS in the CBI and SEAC Theaters," 16 December 1943, Entry 148, Box 2, Folder 51.

30. General order, Number 37, 14 March 1944, "Organization and Duties of Principal Officers of OSS Theater Establishments," Entry 148, Box 2, Folder 51.

31. D. M. Hykes memo, "Summary of Proceedings at Dinner Party Given by General Tai Li on April 6," 7 April 1944, Entry 148, Box 17, Folder 244.

32. Miles, "The Navy Launched A Dragon," chapter 28, "Unit Nine, School of Intelligence and Counter-Espionage."

33. SI report on the CCP personalities, Entry 148, Box 11, Folder 161.

34. Cao Jingyan, "Yan Baohang and the Secret Liaison Station of the Chungking Underground Party," in *Social Sciences of Changchun,* rpt. in *Biographical Literature* 55, no. 6.

35. Ibid.; also Tian Yunchiao and Liu Yanru, "The Complete Story of the Crossover of KMT's Third Parachute Regiment" (Guomindang Sanbing Santuan Qiyi Shimo), *Selected Shanghai Culture and History Materials (Shanghai Wenshi Ziliao Xuanji),* no. 49, April 1985.

36. Zhang Zhiyi, *In the Heart of the Enemy,* in *Documents of the Revolution's History* no. 5, November 1981.

Bibliography

Main Archives

This book is largely based upon Record Group 226 (RG 226), the recently declassified records of the Office of Strategic Services, at the U.S. National Archives. RG 226 contains about six thousand cubic feet of OSS operations files. At the time this book was written, the OSS files were located at the Washington branch of the National Archives; they are now permanently kept at National Archives II in College Park, Maryland. All files quoted in this book are from RG 226 unless otherwise cited.

Various Chinese documents and publications are cited in full in notes.

Supplementary Archives

Norwood Allman Papers, Hoover Institution, Stanford, California.
David Barrett Papers, Hoover Institution, Stanford, California.
Oliver Caldwell Papers, Hoover Institution, Stanford, California.
Claire Chennault Papers, Hoover Institution, Stanford, California.
Lauchlin Currie Papers, Hoover Institution, Stanford, California.
James Donovan Papers, Hoover Institution, Stanford, California.
Paul Frillman Papers, Hoover Institution, Stanford, California.
Preston Goodfellow Papers, Hoover Institution, Stanford, California.
The James McHugh Papers, Cornell University, Ithaca, New York.
Milton Miles Papers, Hoover Institution, Stanford, California.
Wilbur Peterkin Papers, Hoover Institution, Stanford, California.
RG 38, papers of Vice Admiral Milton E. Miles, USN, Naval Group China, Entry NHC-75, National Archives, Washington, D.C.

RG 38, records of the chief of naval intelligence, foreign intelligence, the Far East Desk, National Archives, Washington, D.C.

RG 165, records of the operations division, the War Department, National Archives, Washington, D.C.

RG 218, records of the Joint Chiefs of Staff, the chairman's files, National Archives, Washington, D.C.

RG 263, CIA files, National Archives, Washington, D.C.

RG 493, records of American military mission to China (Magruder), AMMISCA files, National Archives, Suitland Records Center, Maryland.

RG 493, records of China-Burma-India theater of operations, U.S. Army (CBI), record of commanding general (Stilwell), personal messages files, National Archives, Suitland Records Center, Maryland.

RG 493, records of China theater of operations, U.S. Army, (Wedemeyer), record of general staff, G-5 (civil affairs) section, formerly classified reports—special agencies in China, National Archives, Suitland Records Center, Maryland.

Franklin Roosevelt Library, president's secretary's files (PSF), and the map room files, Hyde Park, New York.

Richard Harris Smith Papers, Hoover Institution, Stanford, California.

T. V. Soong Papers, Hoover Institution, Stanford, California.

Joseph Stilwell Papers, Hoover Institution, Stanford, California.

"United States Army, AMISCA File: The Magruder Mission to China, July 1941 through June 1942," microfilm, Government Documents Library, University of California at Berkeley.

U.S Naval Group China, historical collection, Naval War College, Newport, Rhode Island.

Albert Wedemeyer Papers, Hoover Institution, Stanford, California.

Ivan Yeaton Papers, Hoover Institution, Stanford, California.

Books and Manuscripts

Braun, Otto. *A Comintern Agent in China, 1932–1939.* Trans. Jeanne Moore. London: C. Hurst, 1982.

Brown, Anthony Cave. *Wild Bill Donovan: The Last Hero.* New York: Times Books, 1982.

Bureau of Intelligence, Defense Ministry. *The History of SACO (Zhong-Mei He Zuo Suo zhi).* Taipei: N.p., 1970.

Byron, John, and Robert Pack. *The Claws of the Dragon: Kang Sheng—Evil Genius Behind Mao and His Legacy of Terror in the People's Republic.* New York: Simon & Schuster, 1992.

Cai Huilin, An Feng, et al., eds. *The Noble Mission: Remembering Our Times of Fighting Within the Kuomintang Camp (Chonggao de Shiming—Yi Zhandou zai Guomindang Yinlei de suiyue).* 2 vols. Beijing: Military Science, 1990.

Caldwell, Oliver. *A Secret War.* Carbondale: Southern Illinois University Press, 1972.

CCP Yenan Headquarters. *1945 Project and Budget for Undermining and Bringing Over Puppet Forces (yijiusiwu nian dui weijun de zhengqu he pohuai gongzuo jihua yu yusuan).* Yenan, 1945.

Chen Hansheng. *My Life During Four Eras: A Memoir (Si Ge Shidai de wo)*. Beijing: China Culture and History, 1988.

Chennault, Claire. *Way of a Fighter*. New York: G. P. Putnam's Sons, 1949.

Chen Yung-fa. *The Shadow of Yenan*. Taipei: Institute of Modern History, Academia Sinica, 1990.

Corson, William R. *The Armies of Ignorance: The Rise of the American Intelligence Empire*. New York: Dial, 1977.

Cruickshank, Charles. *SOE in the Far East*. New York: Oxford University Press, 1983.

Darling, Arthur B. *The Central Intelligence Agency: An Instrument of Government, to 1950*. DCI Historical Series, HS 1.

Davies, John Paton, Jr. *Dragon by the Tail: American, British, Japanese, and Russian Encounters with China and One Another*. New York: Norton, 1972.

Documents of the Revolution's History (Geming shi ziliao). No. 5, November 1981. Beijing: Press of the Culture and History Material Research Committee of the National Political Consultation Council.

Fairbank, John King. *Chinabound: A Fifty-Year Memoir*. New York: Harper Colophon, 1982.

Faligot, Roger, and Remi Kauffer. *The Chinese Secret Service*. Trans. Christine Donougher. New York: William Morrow, 1989.

Fan Chengkang. *History of Concessions in China (Zhong Guo Zu Jie Shi)*. Shanghai: Shanghai Social Science Academy Press, 1991.

Fenn, Charles. *Ho Chi-Minh: A Biographical Introduction*. London: Studio Vista, 1973.

Garver, John W. "China's Wartime Diplomacy." In James C. Hsiung and Steven I. Levine, eds., *China's Bitter Victory: The War With Japan, 1937–1945*. New York: M. E. Sharpe, 1992.

Han Xinru. *History of New China Daily, 1938–1947*. Part 1. Beijing: China Prospect, 1987.

Jiang Yongjing. *Ho Chi-minh in China*. Taipei: Biographical Literature, 1972.

Kahn, David. *The Codebreakers: The Story of Secret Writing*. New York: Macmillan, 1967.

Katz, Barry. *Foreign Intelligence: Research and Analysis in the Office of Strategic Services, 1942–1945*. Cambridge: Harvard University Press, 1989.

King, Ernest, and Walter Muir Whitehill. *Fleet Admiral King: A Naval Record*. New York: Norton, 1952.

Langer, William. *In and Out of the Ivory Tower: The Autobiography Of William Langer*. New York: Academic, 1977.

Leahy, William. *I Was There*. London: Victor Gollancz, 1950.

LeFeber, Walter. *The American Age: United States Foreign Policy at Home and Abroad Since 1750*. New York: Norton, 1989.

Li Maosheng. *Biography of H. H. Kung (Kong Xiangxi Zhuan)*. Beijing: China Radio and Television Press, 1992.

Lin Yun Hui, et al. *Time of Triumph: History of China from 1949 to 1989 (Kaige Xingjin de Shiqi: yijiusijiu-yijiubajiu de Zhongguo)*. Zhengzhou: Henan People's Press, 1989.

Lohbeck, Don. *Patrick J. Hurley*. Chicago: Henry Regnery, 1956.

Lovell, Stanley. *Of Spies and Stratagems.* Englewood Cliffs, N.J.: Prentice-Hall, 1963.

MacDonald, Elizabeth P. *Undercover Girl.* New York: Macmillan, 1947.

Mao Zedong. *Selected Works of Mao Zedong.* Vol. 2. Beijing: People's Press, 1961.

McCullough, David. *Truman.* New York: Simon and Schuster, 1992.

Miles, Milton. *A Different Kind of War.* Garden City, N.Y.: Doubleday, 1967.

———. "The Navy Launched a Dragon." Unpublished manuscript. Naval War College, Newport, R.I.

Moon, Thomas, and Carl Eifler. *The Deadliest Colonel.* New York: Vantage, 1975.

Morison, Samuel Elioit. *History of United States Naval Operations in World War II.* Boston: Little Brown, 1947.

Mu Xin. *Comrade Chen Geng in Shanghai: His Fighting Experience While in the Special Service Section of the Central Committee (Chen Geng Tongzhi zai Shanghai—zai Zhongyang Teke de Douzheng Jingli).* Beijing: Cultural and Historical Materials Press, 1980.

Niu Jun. *From Yenan to the World.* Fuzhou: Fujian People's Press, 1992.

Qiao Jiacai. *Selected Writings of Qiao Jiacai.* 4 vols. Taipei: Chongwai, 1981.

Rittenberg, Sidney. *The Man Who Stayed Behind.* New York: Simon and Schuster, 1993.

Schaller, Michael. *The U.S. Crusade in China, 1938–1945.* New York: Columbia University Press, 1979.

Shen Meijuan. *Tai Li: A New Biography (Nie Hai Xiao Xiong—Dai Li Xin Zhuan).* Beijing: October Literature and Arts Press, 1992.

Shen Yuan. *Tai Li of Jiangshan County (Jiangshan Daili).* Beijing: China Culture and History Press, 1991.

Shi Wenqi. *Biography of Zhang Luping (Zhang Luping Zhuan).* Beijing: China Youth Press, 1985.

Shi Yufu. *A Brief History of Chinese Money and Finance.* Tianjin: Tianjin People's Press, 1984.

Shi Zhe. *Alongside the Great Men in History: Memoir of Shi Zhe (Zai Lishi Juren Shengbian: Shizhe Huiyi Lu).* Beijing: Central Documents Press, 1991.

Singlaub, John. *Hazardous Duty: An American Soldier in the Twentieth Century.* New York: Summit, 1991.

Smith, Bradley. *The Shadow Warriors: O.S.S. and the Origins of the C.I.A.* New York: Basic, 1983.

Smith, Richard Harris. *OSS: The Secret History of America's First Central Intelligence Agency.* Berkeley: University of California Press, 1972.

Spence, Jonathan. *To Change China: Western Advisors in China, 1620–1960.* New York: Penguin, 1969.

Stevenson, William. *The Man Called Intrepid.* New York: Harcourt Brace Jovanovich, 1976.

Stilwell, Joseph. *The Stilwell Papers.* Arranged by Theodore White. New York: Sloane, 1948. Rpt. New York: Da Capo, 1991.

Stratton, Roy. *The Army-Navy Game.* Falmouth, Mass.: Volta, 1977.

Tang Zong. *Diaries: My Eight Years as Chiang Kai-shek's Confidential Secretary (Zai Jiang Jieshi Shen Bian Ba Nian—Shicong Shi Gaoji Muliao Tangzong Riji, Gon An Bu Dang An Guab Mianzhu).* Ed. Archives of the Public Security Bureau. Beijing: Masses Press, 1991.

Taylor, Edmond. *Awakening from History*. Boston: Gambit, 1969.

Troy, Thomas. *Donovan and the CIA: A History of the Establishment of the Central Intelligence Agency*. Frederick, Md.: Alethia, University Publications of America, 1981.

Tuchman, Barbara. *Stilwell and the American Experience in China, 1911–1945*. New York: Bantam, 1971.

Wang Chen-main. *A Daily Record of Marshall's Mediation in China, November 1945–January 1947*. Taipei: Academia Historica, 1992.

Wang Ming. *The Chinese Communist Party in Its First Half Century and Traitor Mao Zedong*. Hong Kong: WanHai Language Press, 1980.

Wang Zhengyuan. *My Experience as Chiang Kai-shek's Operator for Twelve Years (Wei Jiang Jieshi jie dianhua shi-er nian jianwen)*. Nanjing: Jiangsu Culture and History Material Press, 1991.

Wedemeyer, Albert. *Wedemeyer Reports!* New York: Henry Holt, 1958.

West, William J. *Spymaster*. New York: Wynwood, 1990.

Xiong Xianghui. *Zhou Enlai and My Twelve Years Underground (Dixia shi-er nian yu Zhou Enlai)*. Beijing: Press of the Party School of the CCP Central Committee, 1991.

Yardley, Herbert. *The Chinese Black Chamber*. Boston: Houghton Mifflin, 1983.

Yeaton, Ivan. *Memoirs of Col. Ivan D. Yeaton, USA (RET), 1919–1953*. Stanford, Calif.: Hoover Institution on War, Revolution, and Peace, 1976.

Yeh Wen-hsin. *The Alienated Academy: Culture and Politics in Republican China, 1919–1937*. Cambridge: Harvard University Press, 1990.

Yun Yiqun. "T. V. Soong and H. H. Kung (Song Ziwen and Kong Xiangxi)." Wenshi Ziliao Xuanji, Shanghai, #2, 1980.

Zhong Kan. *A Critical Biography of Kang Sheng (Kang Sheng Ping Zhuan)*. Beijing: Red Flag, 1982.

Zhou Enlai. *Selected Works of Zhou Enlai*. Ed. Documents Compilation Committee of the Central Committee of the CCP. Beijing: People's Press, 1980.

Index